The Hidden Side of Things

(Volumes I & II)

C. W. Leadbeater

This publication is designed to provide authoritative and accurate information
in regard to the subject matter covered. It is sold on the understanding that the
Publisher is not engaged in rendering professional services.

British Library Cataloguing in Publication Data

A catalogue record for this book is available from the British Library

ISBN-13: 978-1-908388-49-0

Printed and bound in Great Britain by Lightning Souce UK Ltd., 6 Precedent
Drive, Rooksley, Milton Keynes MK13 8PR.

Cover Illustration: *Cupid's Hunting Fields*. Edward Burne-Jones (1880)

FOREWORD

This book has been in contemplation, and even in process of construction, for the last ten or twelve years, but only now has it been found possible to publish it. It has lost nothing by the delay, for a student of the occult never ceases to learn, and I know a good deal more in various ways now than I did twelve years ago, even though I see still more clearly than ever what an infinity of further knowledge stretches before us for our acquiring.

Much of what is written here has appeared in the form of articles in The Theosophist and elsewhere ; but all has been revised, and considerable additions have been made. I trust that it may help some brothers to realise the importance of that far larger part of life which is beyond our physical sight - to understand that, as the Lord Buddha Himself has taught us:
The unseen things are more.

C. W. Leadbeater

CONTENTS

FIRST SECTION INTRODUCTORY

CHAPTER I OCCULTISM

1.   The term ' occultism' is one which has been much misunderstood. In the mind of the ignorant it was, even recently, synonymous with magic, and its students were supposed to be practitioners of the black art, veiled in flowing robes of scarlet covered with cabalistic signs, sitting amidst uncanny surroundings with a black cat as a familiar, compounding unholy decoctions by the aid of satanic evocations.

2.   Even now, and among those whom education has raised above such superstition as this, there still remains a good deal of misapprehension. For them its derivation from the Latin word occultus ought to explain at once that it is the science of the hidden; but they often regard it contemptuously as nonsensical and unpractical, as connected with dreams and fortune-telling, with hysteria and necromancy, with the search for the elixir of life and the philosopher's stone. Students, who should know better, perpetually speak as though the hidden side of things were intentionally concealed, as though knowledge with regard to it ought to be in the hands of all men, but was being deliberately withheld by the caprice or selfishness of a few; whereas the fact is that nothing is or can be hidden from us except by our own limitations, and that for every man as he evolves the world grows wider and wider, because he is able to see more and more of its grandeur and its loveliness.

3.   As an objection against this statement may be cited the well-known fact that, at each of the great Initiations which mark the advance of the neophyte along the path of the higher progress, a definite new block of knowledge is given to him. That is quite true, but the knowledge can be given only because the recipient has evolved to the point at which he can grasp it. It is no more being withheld from ordinary humanity than the knowledge of conic sections is being withheld from the child who is still struggling with the multiplication-table. When that child reaches the level at which he can comprehend quadratic equations, the teacher is ready to explain to him the rules which govern them. In exactly the same way, when a man has qualified himself for the reception of the information given at a certain Initiation, he is forthwith initiated. But the only way to attain the capacity to imbibe that higher knowledge is to begin by trying to understand our present conditions, and to order our lives intelligently in view of the facts which we find.

4.   Occultism, then, is the study of the hidden side of nature; or rather, it is the study of the *whole* of nature, instead of only that small part of it which comes under the investigation of modern science. At the present stage of our development, by far

the greater part of nature is entirely unknown to the majority of mankind, because they have as yet unfolded only a minute proportion of the faculties which they possess. The ordinary man, therefore, is basing his philosophy (so far as he has any) upon entirely inadequate grounds; his actions are moulded more or less in accordance with the few laws of nature which he knows, and consequently both his theory of life and his daily practice are necessarily inaccurate. The occultist adopts a far more comprehensive view; he takes into account those forces of the higher worlds whose action is hidden from the materialist, and so he moulds his life in obedience to the entire code of Nature's laws, instead of only by occasional reference to a minute fragment of it.

5.　　It is difficult for the man who knows nothing of the occult to realise how great, how serious and how all-pervading are his own limitations. The only way in which we can adequately symbolise them is to suppose some form of consciousness still more limited than our own, and to think in what directions it would differ from ours. Suppose it were possible that a consciousness could exist capable of appreciating only solid matter - the liquid and gaseous forms of matter being to it as entirely non-existent as are the etheric and astral and mental forms to the ordinary man. We can readily see how for such a consciousness any adequate conception of the world in which we live would be impossible. Solid matter, which alone could be perceived by it, would constantly be found to be undergoing serious modifications, about which no rational theory could be formed.

6.　　For example, whenever a shower of rain took place, the solid matter of the earth would undergo change; it would in many cases become both softer and heavier when charged with moisture, but the reason of such a change would necessarily be wholly incomprehensible to the consciousness which we are supposing. The wind might lift clouds of sand and transfer them from one place to another; but such motion of solid matter would be entirely inexplicable to one who had no conception of the existence of the air. Without considering more examples of what is already so obvious, we see clearly how hopelessly inadequate would be such an idea of the world as would be attainable by this consciousness limited to solid matter. What we do not realise so readily, however, is that our present consciousness falls just as far short of that of the developed man as this supposed consciousness would fall short of that which we now possess.

7.　　Theosophical students are at least theoretically acquainted with the idea that to everything there is a hidden side; and they also know that in the great majority of cases this unseen side is of far greater importance than that which is visible to the physical eye.

8.　　To put the same idea from another point of view, the senses, by means of which we obtain all our information about external objects, are as yet imperfectly developed; therefore the information obtained is partial. What we see in the world about us is by no means all that there is to see, and a man who will take the trouble to cultivate his senses will find that, in proportion as he succeeds, life will become fuller and richer for him. For the lover of nature, of art, of music, a vast field of incredibly intensified and exalted pleasure lies close at hand, if he will fit himself to enter upon it. Above all, for the lover of his fellow-man there is the possibility of far more intimate comprehension and therefore far wider usefulness.

9.   We are only halfway up the ladder of evolution at present, and so our senses are only half-evolved. But it is possible for us to hurry up that ladder - possible, by hard work, to make our senses now what all men's senses will be in the distant future. The man who has succeeded in doing this is often called a seer or a clairvoyant.

10.   A fine word that - clairvoyant. It means `one who sees clearly'; but it has been horribly misused and degraded, so that people associate it with all sorts of trickery and imposture - with gypsies who for sixpence will tell a maid-servant what is the colour of the hair of the duke who is coming to marry her, or with establishments in Bond Street where for a guinea fee the veil of the future is supposed to be lifted for more aristocratic clients.

11.   All this is irregular and unscientific; in many cases it is mere charlatanry and bare-faced robbery. But not always; to foresee the future up to a certain point is a possibility; it can be done, and it has been done, scores of times; and some of these irregular practitioners unquestionably do at times possess flashes of higher vision, though usually they cannot depend upon having them when they want them.

12.   But behind all this vagueness there is a bed-rock of fact - something which can be approached rationally and studied scientifically. It is as the result of many years of such study and experiment that I state emphatically what I have written above - that it is possible for men to develop their senses until they can see much more of this wonderful and beautiful world in which we live than is ever suspected by the untrained average man, who lives contentedly in the midst of Cimmerean darkness and calls it light.

13.   Two thousand and five hundred years ago the greatest of Indian teachers, Gautama the BUDDHA, said to His disciples: ` Do not complain and cry and pray, but open your eyes and see. The truth is all about you, if you will only take the bandage from your eyes and look; and it is so wonderful, so beautiful, so far beyond anything that men have ever dreamt of or prayed for, and it is for ever and for ever.'

14.   He assuredly meant far more than this of which I am writing now, but this is a step on the way towards that glorious goal of perfect realisation. If it does not yet tell us quite all the truth, at any rate it gives us a good deal of it. It removes for us a host of common misconceptions, and clears up for us many points which are considered as mysteries or problems by those who are as yet uninstructed in this lore. It shows that all these things were mysteries and problems to us only because heretofore we saw so small a part of the facts, because we were looking at the various matters from below, and as isolated and unconnected fragments, instead of rising above them to a standpoint whence they are comprehensible as parts of a mighty whole. It settles in a moment many questions which have been much disputed - such, for example, as that of the continued existence of man after death. It explains many of the strange things which the Churches tell us; it dispels our ignorance and removes our fear of the unknown by supplying us with a rational and orderly scheme.

15.   Besides all this, it opens up a new world to us in regard to our every-day life - a new world which is yet a part of the old. It shows us that, as I began by saying, there is a hidden side to everything, and that our most ordinary actions often

produce results of which without this study, we should never have known. By it we understand the rationale of what is commonly called telepathy, for we see that just as there are waves of heat or light or electricity, so there are waves produced by thought, though they are in a finer type of matter than the others, and therefore not perceptible to our physical senses. By studying these vibrations, we see how thought acts, and we learn that it is a tremendous power for good or for ill - a power which we are all of us unconsciously wielding to some extent - which we can use a hundredfold more effectively when we comprehend its workings. Further investigation reveals to us the method of formation of what are called ` thought-forms,' and indicates how these can be usefully employed both for ourselves and for others in a dozen different ways.

16.   The occultist studies carefully all these unseen effects, and consequently knows much more fully than other men, the result of what he is doing. He has more information about life than others have, and he exercises his common-sense by modifying his life in accordance with what he knows. In many ways we live differently now from our forefathers in mediaeval times, because we know more than they did. We have discovered certain laws of hygiene; wise men live according to that knowledge, and therefore the average length of life is decidedly greater now than it was in the Middle Ages. There are still some who are foolish or ignorant, who either do not know the laws of health or are careless about keeping them; they think that because disease-germs are invisible to them, they are therefore of no importance; they do not believe in new ideas. Those are the people who suffer first when an epidemic disease arrives, or some unusual strain is put upon the community. They suffer unnecessarily, because they are behind the times. But they injure not only themselves by their neglect; the conditions caused by their ignorance or carelessness often bring infection into a district which might otherwise be free from it.

17.   The matter of which I am writing is precisely the same thing at a different level. The microscope revealed disease-germs; the intelligent man profited by the discovery, and rearranged his life, while the unintelligent man paid no attention, but went on as before. Clairvoyance reveals thought-force and many other previously unsuspected powers; once more the intelligent man profits by this discovery, and rearranges his life accordingly. Once more also the unintelligent man takes no heed of the new discoveries; once more he thinks that what he cannot see can have no importance for him; once more he continues to suffer quite unnecessarily, because he is behind the times.

18.   Not only does he often suffer positive pain, but he also misses so much of the pleasure of life. To painting, to music, to poetry, to literature, to religious ceremonies, to the beauties of nature there is always a hidden side - a fulness, a completeness beyond the mere physical; and the man who can see or sense this has at his command a wealth of enjoyment far beyond the comprehension of the man who passes through it all with unopened perceptions.

19.   The perceptions exist in every human being, though as yet undeveloped in most. To unfold them means generally a good deal of time and hard work, but it is exceedingly well worth while. Only let no man undertake the effort unless his motives

are absolutely pure and unselfish, for he who seeks wider faculty for any but the most exalted purposes will bring upon himself a curse and not a blessing.

20.　　　　But the man of affairs, who has no time to spare for a sustained effort to evolve nascent powers within himself, is not thereby debarred from sharing in some at least of the benefits derived from occult study, any more than the man who possesses no microscope is thereby prevented from living hygienically. The latter has not seen the disease-germs, but from the testimony of the specialist he knows that they exist, and he knows how to guard himself from them. Just in the same way a man who has as yet no dawning of clairvoyant vision may study the writings of those who have gained it, and in this way profit by the results of their labour. True, he cannot yet see all the glory and the beauty which are hidden from us by the imperfection of our senses; but he can readily learn how to avoid the unseen evil, and how to set in motion the unseen forces of good. So, long before he actually sees them, he can conclusively prove to himself their existence, just as the man who drives an electric motor proves to himself the existence of electricity, though he has never seen it and does not in the least know what it is.

21.　　　　We must try to understand as much as we can of the world in which we live. We must not fall behind in the march of evolution, we must not let ourselves be anachronisms, for lack of interest in these new discoveries, which yet are only the presentation from a new point of view of the most archaic wisdom. "Knowledge is power" in this case as in every other; in this case, as in every other, to secure the best results, the glorious trinity of power, wisdom and love must ever go hand in hand.

22.　　　　There is a difference, however, between theoretical acquaintance and actual realisation; and I have thought that it might help students somewhat towards the grasp of the realities to have a description of the unseen side of some of the simple transactions of every day life as they appear to clairvoyant vision - to one, let us say, who has developed within himself the power of perception through the astral, mental and causal bodies. Their appearance as seen by means of the intuitional vehicle is infinitely grander and more effective still, but so entirely inexpressible that it seems useless to say anything about it; for on that level all experience is within the man instead of without, and the glory and the beauty of it is no longer something which he watches with interest, but something which he feels in his inmost heart, because it is part of himself.

23.　　　　The object of this book is to give some hints as to the inner side of the world as a whole and of our daily life. We shall consider this latter in three divisions, which will resemble the conjugations of our youthful days in being passive, middle and active respectively - how we are influenced, how we influence ourselves, and how we influence others; and we shall conclude by observing a few of the results which must inevitably flow from a wider diffusion of this knowledge as to the realities of existence.

CHAPTER II THE WORLD AS A WHOLE

26.   A WIDER OUTLOOK

27.   When we look upon the world around us, we cannot hide from ourselves the existence of a vast amount of sorrow and suffering. True, much of it is obviously the fault of the sufferers, and might easily be avoided by the exercise of a little self-control and common-sense; but there is also much which is not immediately self-induced, but undoubtedly comes from without. It often seems as though evil triumphs, as though justice fails in the midst of the storm and stress of the roaring confusion of life, and because of this many despair of the ultimate result, and doubt whether there is in truth any plan of definite progress behind all this bewildering chaos.

28.   It is all a question of the point of view; the man who is himself in the thick of the fight cannot judge of the plan of the general or the progress of the conflict. To understand the battle as a whole, one must withdraw from the tumult and look down upon the field from above. In exactly the same way, to comprehend the plan of the battle of life we must withdraw ourselves from it for the time, and in thought look down upon it from above - from the point of view not of the body which perishes but of the soul which lives for ever. We must take into account not only the small part of life which our physical eyes can see, but the vast totality of which at present so much is invisible to us.

29.   Until that has been done we are in the position of a man looking from beneath at the under side of some huge piece of elaborate tapestry which is in process of being woven. The whole thing is to us but a confused medley of varied colour, of ragged hanging ends, without order or beauty, and we are unable to conceive what all this mad clatter of machinery can be doing; but when through our knowledge of the hidden side of nature we are able to look down from above, the pattern begins to unfold itself before our eyes, and the apparent chaos shows itself as orderly progress.

30.   A more forcible analogy may be obtained by contemplating in imagination the view of life which would present itself to some tiny microbe whirled down by a resistless flood, such as that which rushes through the gorge of Niagara. Boiling, foaming, swirling, the force of that stream is so tremendous that its centre is many feet higher than its sides. The microbe on the surface of such a torrent must be dashed hither and thither wildly amidst the foam, sometimes thrown high in air, sometimes whirled backwards in an eddy, unable to see the banks between which he is passing, having every sense occupied in the mad struggle to keep himself somehow above water. To him that strife and stress is all the world of which he knows; how can he tell whither the stream is going?

31.   But the man who stands on the bank, looking down on it all, can see that all this bewildering tumult is merely superficial, and that the one fact of real importance is the steady onward sweep of those millions of tons of water downwards towards the

sea. If we can furthermore suppose the microbe to have some idea of progress, and to identify it with forward motion, he might well be dismayed when he found himself hurled aside or borne backwards by an eddy; while the spectator could see that the apparent backward movement was but a delusion, since even the little eddies were all being swept onwards with the rest. It is no exaggeration to say that as is the knowledge of the microbe struggling in the stream to that of the man looking down upon it, so is the comprehension of life possessed by the man in the world to that of one who knows its hidden side.

32.   Best of all, though not so easy to follow because of the effort of imagination involved, is the parable offered to us by Mr. Hinton in his *Scientific Romances*. For purposes connected with his argument Mr. Hinton supposes the construction of a large vertical wooden frame, from top to bottom of which are tightly stretched a multitude of threads at all sorts of angles. If then a sheet of paper be inserted horizontally in the frame so that these threads pass through it, it is obvious that each thread will make a minute hole in the paper. If then the frame as a whole be moved slowly upwards, but the paper kept still, various effects will be produced. When a thread is perpendicular it will slip through its hole without difficulty, but when a thread is fixed at an angle it will cut a slit in the paper as the frame moves.

33.   Suppose instead of a sheet of paper we have a thin sheet of wax, and let the wax be sufficiently viscous to close up behind the moving thread. Then instead of a number of slits we shall have a number of moving holes, and to a sight which cannot see the threads that cause them, the movement of these holes will necessarily appear irregular and inexplicable. Some will approach one another, some will recede; various patterns and combinations will be formed and dissolve; all depending upon the arrangement of the invisible threads. Now, by a still more daring flight of fancy, think not of the holes but of the minute sections of thread for the moment filling them, and imagine those sections as conscious atoms. They think of themselves as separate entities, they find themselves moving without their own volition in what seems a maze of inextricable confusion, and this bewildering dance is life as they know it. Yet all this apparent complexity and aimless motion is in fact a delusion caused by the limitation of the consciousness of those atoms, for only *one* extremely simple movement is really taking place - the steady upward motion of the frame as a whole. But the atom can never comprehend that until it realises that it is not a separated fragment, but *part of a thread.*

34.   ` Which things are an allegory,' and a very beautiful one; for the threads are ourselves - our true selves, our souls - and the atoms represent us in this earthly life. So long as we confine our consciousness to the atom, and look on life only from this earthly standpoint, we can never understand what is happening in the world. But if we will raise our consciousness to the point of view of the soul, the thread of which the bodily life is only a minute part and a temporary expression, we shall then see that there is a splendid simplicity at the back of all the complexity, a unity behind all the diversity. The complexity and the diversity are illusions produced by our limitations; the simplicity and the unity are real.

35.   The world in which we live has a hidden side to it, for the conception of it in the mind of the ordinary man in the street is utterly imperfect along three quite distinct lines. First, it has an extension at its own level which he is at present quite incapable of appreciating; secondly, it has a higher side which is too refined for his undeveloped perceptions; thirdly, it has a meaning and a purpose of which he usually has not the faintest glimpse. To say that we do not see the whole of our world is to state the case far too feebly; what we see is an absolutely insignificant part of it, beautiful though that part may be. And just as the additional extension is infinite, compared to our idea of space, and cannot be expressed in its terms, so are the scope and the splendour of the whole infinitely greater than any conception that can possibly be formed of it here, and they cannot be expressed in any terms of that part of the world which we know.

36.   THE FOURTH DIMENSION

37.   The extension spoken of under the first head has often been called the fourth dimension. Many writers have scoffed at this and denied its existence, yet for all that it remains a fact that our physical world is in truth a world of many dimensions, and that every object in it has an extension, however minute, in a direction which is unthinkable to us at our present stage of mental evolution. When we develop astral senses we are brought so much more directly into contact with this extension, that our minds are more or less forced into recognition of it, and the more intelligent gradually grow to understand it; though there are those of less intellectual growth who, even after death and in the astral world, cling desperately to their accustomed limitations and adopt most extraordinary and irrational hypotheses to avoid admitting the existence of the higher life which they so greatly fear.

38.   Because the easiest way for most people to arrive at a realisation of the fourth dimension of space is to develop within themselves the power of astral sight, many persons have come to suppose that the fourth dimension is an exclusive appanage of the astral world. A little thought will show that this cannot be so. Fundamentally, there is only one kind of matter existing in the universe, although we call it physical, astral or mental according to the extent of its subdivision and the rapidity of its vibration. Consequently the dimensions of space - if they exist at all - exist independently of the matter which lies within them; and whether that space has three dimensions or four or more, all the matter within it exists subject to those conditions, whether we are able to appreciate them or not.

39.   It may perhaps help us a little in trying to understand this matter, if we realise that what we call space is a limitation of consciousness, and that there is a higher level at which a sufficiently developed consciousness is entirely free from this. We may invest this higher consciousness with the power of expression in any number of directions, and may then assume that each descent into a denser world of matter, imposes upon it an additional limitation, and shuts off the perception of one of these directions. We may suppose that by the time the consciousness has descended as far as the mental world only five of these directions remain to it; that when it descends or moves outward once more to the astral level it loses yet one more of its powers, and

so is limited to the conception of four dimensions; then the further descent or outward movement which brings it into the physical world cuts off from it the possibility of grasping even that fourth dimension, and so we find ourselves confined to the three with which we are familiar.

40.　　　Looking at it from this point of view, it is clear that the conditions of the universe have remained unaffected, though our power of appreciating them has changed; so that, although it is true that when our consciousness is functioning through astral matter we are able to appreciate a fourth dimension which normally is hidden from us while we work through the physical brain, we must not therefore make the mistake of thinking that the fourth dimension belongs to the astral world only and that physical matter exists somehow in a different kind of space from the astral or mental. Such a suggestion is shown to be unjustified by the fact that it is possible for a man using his physical brain to attain by means of practice the power of comprehending some of the four-dimensional forms.

41.　　　I do not wish here to take up fully the consideration of this fascinating subject; those who would follow it further should apply themselves to the works of Mr. C. H. Hinton - *Scientific Romances* and *The Fourth Dimension* - the former book for all the interesting possibilities connected with this study, and the latter for the means whereby the mind can realise the fourth dimension as a fact. For our present purposes it is necessary only to indicate that here is an aspect or extension of our world which, though utterly unknown to the vast majority of men, requires to be studied and to be taken into consideration by those who wish to understand the whole of life instead of only a tiny fragment of it.

42.　　　THE HIGHER WORLD

43.　　　There is a hidden side to our physical world in a second and higher sense which is well known to all students of Theosophy, for many lectures have been delivered and many books have been written in the endeavour to describe the astral and mental worlds - the unseen realm which interpenetrates that with which we are all familiar, and forms by far the most important part of it. A good deal of information about this higher aspect of our world has been given in the fifth and the sixth of the Theosophical manuals, and in my own book upon *The Other Side of Death*; so here I need do no more than make a short general statement for the benefit of any reader who has not yet met with those works.

44.　　　Modern physicists tell us that matter is interpenetrated by aether - a hypothetical substance which they endow with many apparently contradictory qualities. The occultist knows that there are many varieties of this finer interpenetrative matter, and that some of the qualities attributed to it by the scientific men belong not to it at all, but to the primordial substance of which it is the negation. I do not wish here to turn aside from the object of this book to give a lengthy disquisition upon the qualities of aether; those who wish to study this subject may be referred to the book upon *Occult Chemistry*, p. 93 . Here it must suffice to say that the true aether of space exists, just as scientific men have supposed, and possesses most of the curious contradictory qualities ascribed to it. It is not, however, of that aether itself, but of matter built up out of the bubbles in it, that the inner worlds of finer matter are built, of which we have spoken just now. That with which we are concerned at the moment is the fact that all the matter visible to us is interpenetrated not only by aether, but also by various kinds of finer matter, and that of this finer matter there are many degrees.

45. To the type which is nearest to the physical world, occult students have given the name astral matter; the kind next above that has been called mental, because out of its texture is built that mechanism of consciousness which is commonly called the mind in man; and there are other types finer still, with which for the moment we are not concerned. Every portion of space with which we have to do must be thought of as containing all these different kinds of matter. It is practically a scientific postulate that even in the densest forms of matter no two particles ever touch one another, but each floats alone in its field of aether, like a sun in space. Just in the same way each particle of the physical aether floats in a sea of astral matter, and each astral particle in turn floats in a mental ocean; so that all these additional worlds need no more space than does this fragment which we know, for in truth they are all parts of one and the same world.

46. Man has within himself matter of these finer grades, and by learning to focus his consciousness in it, instead of only in his physical brain, he may become cognisant of these inner and higher parts of the world, and acquire much knowledge of the deepest interest and value. The nature of this unseen world, its scenery, its inhabitants, its possibilities, are described in the works above mentioned. It is the existence of these higher realms of nature that makes occultism possible; and few indeed are the departments of life in which their influence has not to be considered. From the cradle to the grave we are in close relation with them during what we call our waking life; during sleep and after we are even more intimately connected with them, for our existence is then almost confined to them.

47. Perhaps the greatest of the many fundamental changes which are inevitable for the man who studies the facts of life is that which is produced in his attitude towards death. This matter has been fully treated elsewhere; here I need state only that the knowledge of the truth about death robs it of all its terror and much of its sorrow, and enables us to see it in its true proportion and to understand its place in the scheme of our evolution. It is perfectly possible to learn to know about all these things instead of accepting beliefs blindly at secondhand, as most people do; and knowledge means power, security and happiness.

48. THE PURPOSE OF LIFE

49. The third aspect of our world which is hidden from the majority is the plan and purpose of existence. Most men seem to muddle through life without any discernible object, except possibly the purely physical struggle to make money or attain power, because they vaguely think that these things will bring them happiness. They have no definite theory as to why they are here, nor any certainty as to the future that awaits them. They have not even realised that they are souls and not bodies, and

that as such their development is part of a mighty scheme of cosmic evolution.

50.　　　　When once this grandest of truths has dawned upon a man's horizon, there comes over him that change which occidental religion calls conversion - a fine word which has been sadly degraded by improper associations, for it has often been used to signify nothing more than a crisis of emotion hypnotically induced by the surging waves of excited feeling radiated by a half-maddened crowd. Its true meaning is exactly what its derivation implies, ` a turning together with' . Before it, the man, unaware of the stupendous current of evolution, has, under the delusion of selfishness, been fighting against it; but the moment that the magnificence of the Divine Plan bursts upon his astonished sight there is no other possibility for him but to throw all his energies into the effort to promote its fulfilment, to ` turn and go together with' that splendid stream of the love and the wisdom of God.

51.　　　　His one object then is to qualify himself to help the world, and all his thoughts and actions are directed towards that aim. He may forget for the moment under the stress of temptation, but the oblivion can be only temporary; and this is the meaning of the ecclesiastical dogma that the elect can never finally fail . Discrimination has come to him, the opening of the doors of the mind, to adopt the terms employed for this change in older faiths; he knows now what is real and what is unreal, what is worth gaining and what is valueless. He lives as an immortal soul who is a Spark of the Divine Fire, instead of as one of the beasts that perish - to use a biblical phrase which, however, is entirely incorrect, inasmuch as the beasts do *not* perish, except in the sense of their being reabsorbed into their group-soul.

52.　　　　Most truly for this man, an aspect of life has been displayed which erst was hidden from his eyes. It would even be truer to say that now for the first time he has really begun to live, while before he merely dragged out an inefficient existence.

SECOND SECTION - HOW WE ARE INFLUENCED

CHAPTER III BY PLANETS

57.   RADIATIONS

58.   The first fact which it is necessary for us to realise is that everything is radiating influence on its surroundings, and these surroundings are all the while returning the compliment by pouring influence upon it in return. Literally everything - sun, moon, stars, angels, men, animals, trees, rocks - *everything* is pouring out a ceaseless stream of vibrations, each of its own characteristic type; not in the physical world only, but in other and subtler worlds as well. Our physical senses can appreciate only a limited number of such radiations. We readily feel the heat poured forth by the sun or by a fire, but we are usually not conscious of the fact that we ourselves are constantly radiating heat; yet if we hold out a hand towards a radiometer the delicate instrument will respond to the heat imparted by that hand even at a distance of several feet, and will begin to revolve. We say that a rose has a scent and that a daisy has none; yet the daisy is throwing off particles just as much as the rose, only in the one case they happen to be perceptible to our senses, and in the other they are not.

59.   From early ages men have believed that the sun, the moon, the planets and the stars exercised a certain influence over human life. In the present day, most people are content to laugh at such a belief, without knowing anything about it; yet anyone who will take the trouble to make a careful and impartial study of astrology will discover much that cannot be lightly thrown aside. He will meet with plenty of errors, no doubt, some of them ridiculous enough; but he will also find a proportion of accurate results which is far too large to be reasonably ascribed to coincidence. His investigations will convince him that there is unquestionably some foundation for the claims of the astrologers, while at the same time he cannot but observe that their systems are as yet far from perfect.

60.   When we remember the enormous space that separates us from even the nearest of the planets, it is at once obvious that we must reject the idea that they can exercise upon us any physical action worth considering; and furthermore, if there were any such action, it would seem that its strength should depend less upon the position of the planet in the sky than upon its proximity to the earth - a factor which is not usually taken into account by astrologers. The more we contemplate the matter the less does it seem rational or possible to suppose that the planets can affect the earth or its inhabitants to any appreciable extent; yet the fact remains that a theory based upon

this apparent impossibility, often works out accurately. Perhaps the explanation may be found along the line that just as the movement of the hands of a clock shows the passage of time, though it does not cause it, so the motions of the planets indicate the prevalence of certain influences, but are in no way responsible for them. Let us see what light occult study throws upon this somewhat perplexing subject.

61.   THE DEITY OF THE SOLAR SYSTEM

62.   Occult students regard the entire solar system in all its vast complexity as a partial manifestation of one great living Being, and all its parts as expressing aspects of Him. Many names have been given to Him; in our Theosophical literature He has often been described under the Gnostic title of the Logos - the Word that was in the beginning with God, and was God; but now we usually speak of Him as the Solar Deity. All the physical constituents of the solar system - the sun with its wonderful corona, all the planets with their satellites, their oceans, their atmospheres and the various aethers surrounding them - all these are collectively His physical body, the expression of Him in the physical realm.

63.   In the same way, the collective astral worlds - not only the astral worlds belonging to each of the physical planets, but also the purely astral planets of all the chains of the system (such, for example, as planets B and F of our chain) - make up His astral body, and the collective worlds of the mental realm are His mental body - the vehicle through which He manifests Himself upon that particular level. Every atom of every world is a centre through which He is conscious, so that not only is it true that God is omnipresent, but also that whatever is is God.

64.   Thus we see that the old pantheistic conception was quite true, yet it is only a part of the truth, because while all nature in all its worlds is nothing but His garment, yet He Himself exists outside of and above all this in a stupendous life of which we can know nothing - a life among other Rulers of other systems. Just as all our lives are lived literally within Him and are in truth a part of His, so His life and that of the Solar Deities of countless other systems are a part of a still greater life of the Deity of the visible universe; and if there be in the depths of space/yet other universes invisible to us, all of their Deities in turn must in the same way form part of One Great Consciousness which includes the whole.

65.   DIFFERENT TYPES OF MATTER

66.   In these 'bodies' of the Solar Deity on their various levels there are certain different classes or types of matter, which are fairly equally distributed over the whole system. I am not speaking here of our usual division of the worlds and their subsections - a division which is made according to the density of the matter, so that in the physical world, for example, we have the solid, liquid, gaseous, etheric, super-etheric, sub-atomic and atomic conditions of matter - all of them physical, but differing in density. The types which I mean constitute a totally distinct series of cross-divisions, each of which contains matter in all its different conditions, so that if we denote the various types by numbers, we shall find solid, liquid and gaseous matter of the first type, solid,

liquid and gaseous matter of the second type, and so on all the way through.

67.   These types of matter are as thoroughly intermingled as are the constituents of our atmosphere. Conceive a room filled with air; any decided vibration communicated to the air, such as a sound, for example, would be perceptible in every part of the room. Suppose that it were possible to produce some kind of undulation which should affect the oxygen alone without disturbing the nitrogen, that undulation would still be felt in every part of the room. If we allow that, for a moment, the proportion of oxygen might be greater in one part of the room than another, then the oscillation, though perceptible everywhere, would be strongest in that part. Just as the air in a room is composed (principally) of oxygen and nitrogen, so is the matter of the solar system composed of these different types; and just as a wave (if there could be such a thing) which affected only the oxygen or only the nitrogen would nevertheless be felt in all parts of the room, so a movement or modification which affects only one of these types produces an effect throughout the entire solar system, though it may be stronger in one part than in another.

68.   This statement is true of all worlds, but for the sake of clearness, let us for the moment confine our thought to one world only. Perhaps the idea is easiest to follow with regard to the astral. It has often been explained that in the astral body of man, matter belonging to each of the astral sub-sections is to be found, and that the proportion between the denser and the finer kinds shows how far that body is capable of responding to coarse or refined desires, and so is to some extent an indication of the degree to which the man has evolved himself. Similarly in each astral body there is matter of each of these types, and in this case the proportion between them will show the disposition of the man - whether he is devotional or philosophic, artistic or scientific, pragmatic or mystic.

69.   THE LIVING CENTRES

70.   Now each of these types of matter in the astral body of the Solar Deity is to some extent a separate vehicle, and may be thought of as also the astral body of a subsidiary Deity or Minister, who is at the same time an aspect of the Deity of the system, a kind of ganglion or force-centre in Him. Indeed, if these types differ among themselves, it is because the matter composing them originally came forth through these different living Centres, and the matter of each type is still the special vehicle and expression of the subsidiary Deity through whom it came, so that the slightest thought, movement or alteration of any kind in Him, is instantly reflected in some way or other in all the matter of the corresponding type. Naturally each such type of matter has its own special affinities, and is capable of vibrating under influences which may probably evoke no response from the other types.

71.   Since every man has within himself matter of all these types, it is obvious that any modification in or action of any one of these great living Centres, must to some degree affect all beings in the system. The extent to which any particular person is so affected depends upon the proportion of the type of matter acted upon which he happens to have in his astral body. Consequently, we find different types of men as

of matter, and by reason of their constitution, by the very composition of their astral bodies, some of them are more susceptible to one influence, some to another.

72.   The types are seven, and astrologers have often given to them the names of certain of the planets. Each type is divided into seven sub-types, because each ' planet' may be either practically uninfluenced, or it may be affected predominantly by any one of the other six. In addition to the forty-nine definite sub-types thus obtained, there are any number of possible permutations and combinations of influences, often so complicated that it is no easy matter to follow them. Nevertheless, this gives us a certain system of classification, according to which we can arrange not only human beings, but also the animal, vegetable and mineral kingdoms, and the elemental essence which precedes them in evolution.

73.   Everything in the solar system belongs to one or other of these seven great streams, because it has come out through one or other of these great Force-Centres, to which therefore it belongs in essence, although it must inevitably be affected more or less by the others also. This gives each man, each animal, each plant, each mineral a certain fundamental characteristic which never changes - sometimes symbolised as his note, his colour or his ray.

74.   This characteristic is permanent not only through one chain-period, but through the whole planetary scheme, so that the life which manifests through elemental essence of type A will in the due course of its evolution ensoul successively minerals, plants, and animals of type A; and when its group-soul breaks up into units and receives the Third Outpouring, the human beings which are the result of its evolution will be men of type A and no other, and under normal conditions will continue so all through their development until they grow into Adepts of type A.

75.   In the earlier days of Theosophical study we were under the impression that this plan was carried out consistently to the very end, and that these Adepts rejoined the Solar Deity through the same subsidiary Deity or Minister through whom they originally came forth. Further research shows that this thought requires modification. We find that bands of egos of many different types join themselves together for a common object.

76.   For example, in the investigations connected primarily with the lives of Alcyone, it was found that certain bands of egos circled round the various Masters, and came closer and closer to Them as time went on. One by one, as they became fit for it, these egos reached the stage at which they were accepted as pupils or apprentices by one or other of the Masters. To become truly a pupil of a Master means entering into relations with Him whose intimacy is far beyond any tie of which we know on earth. It means a degree of union with Him which no words can fully express, although at the same time a pupil retains absolutely his own individuality and his own initiative.

77.   In this way, each Master becomes a centre of what may be truly described as a great organism, since his pupils are veritably members of Him. When we realise that He Himself is in just the same way a Member of some still greater Master we arrive at a conception of a mighty. organism which is in a very real sense one, although built up of thousands of perfectly distinct egos.

78.   Such an organism is the Heavenly Man who emerges as the result of

the evolution of each great root-race. In Him, as in an earthly man, are seven great centres, each of which is a mighty Adept; and the Manu and the Bodhisattva occupy in this great organism the place of the brain and the heart centres respectively. Round Them - and yet not *round* Them, but *in* Them and part of Them, although so fully and gloriously ourselves - shall we, Their servants, be; and this great figure in its totality represents the flower of that particular race, and includes all who have attained Adeptship through it. Each root-race is thus represented at its close by one of these Heavenly Men; and They, these splendid totalities, will, as Their next stage in evolution, become Ministers Themselves of some future Solar Deity. Yet each one of these contains within Himself men of all possible types, so that each of these future Ministers is in truth a representative not of one line but of all lines.

79.　　When looked at from a sufficiently high level the whole solar system is seen to consist of these great living Centres or Ministers, and the types of matter through which each is expressing Himself. Let me repeat here for the sake of clearness, what I wrote some time ago on this subject in *The Inner Life*, vol. i, page 217:

80.　　Each of these great living Centres has a sort of orderly periodic change or motion of his own, corresponding perhaps on some infinitely higher level to the regular beating of the human heart, or to the inspiration and expiration of the breath. Some of these periodic changes are more rapid than others, so that a complicated series of effects is produced; and it has been observed that the movements of the physical planets in their relation to one another furnish a clue to the operation of these influences at any given moment. Each of these Centres has His special location or major focus within the body of the sun, and a minor exterior focus which is always marked by the position of a planet.

81.　　The exact relation can hardly be made clear in our three-dimensional phraseology; but we may perhaps put it that each Centre has a field of influence practically co-extensive with a solar system; that if a section of this field could be taken it would be found to be elliptical; and that one of the foci of each ellipse would always be the sun, and the other would be the special planet ruled by that Minister. It is probable that, in the gradual condensation of the original glowing nebula from which the system was formed, the location of the planets was determined by the formation of vortices at these minor foci, they being auxiliary points of distribution of these influences - ganglia, as it were, in the solar system.

82.　　It must of course be understood that we are referring here not to the curious astrological theory which considers the sun himself as a planet, but to the real planets which revolve round him.

83.　　THEIR INFLUENCE

84.　　The influences belonging to these great types differ widely in quality, and one way in which this difference shows itself is in their action upon the living elemental essence both in man and around him. Be it ever remembered that this dominance is exerted in *all* worlds, not only in the astral, though we are just now confining ourselves to that for simplicity's sake. These mysterious agencies may have, and indeed must have, other and more important lines of action not at present known to us; but this at least forces itself upon the notice of the observer, that each Centre produces its own special effect upon the manifold varieties of elemental essence.

85.   One, for example, will be found greatly to stimulate the activity and the vitality of those kinds of essence which specially appertain to the Centre through which it comes, while apparently checking and controlling others; the sway of another type will be seen to be strong over a quite different set of essences which belong to its Centre, while apparently not affecting the previous set in the least. There are all sorts of combinations and permutations of these mystic powers, the action of one of them being in some cases greatly intensified and in others almost neutralised by the presence of another.

86.   Since this elemental essence is vividly active in the astral and mental bodies of man, it is clear that any unusual excitation of any of these classes of that essence - any sudden increase in its activity - must undoubtedly affect to some extent either his emotions or his mind, or both; and it is also obvious that these forces would work differently on different men, because of the varieties of essence entering into their composition.

87.   These influences neither exist nor are exercised for the sake of the man or with any reference to him, any more than the wind exists for the sake of the vessel which is helped or hindered by it; they are part of the play of cosmic forces of whose object we know nothing, though we may to some extent learn how to calculate upon them and to use them. Such energies in themselves are no more good nor evil than any other of the powers of nature: like electricity or any other great natural force they may be helpful or hurtful to us, according to the use that we make of them. Just as certain experiments are more likely to be successful if undertaken when the air is heavily charged with electricity, while certain others under such conditions will most probably fail, so an effort involving the use of the powers of our mental and emotional nature will more or less readily achieve its object according to the influences which predominate when it is made.

88.   LIBERTY OF ACTION

89.   It is of the utmost importance for us to understand that such pressure cannot dominate man's will in the slightest degree; all it can do is in some cases to make it easier or more difficult for that will to act along certain lines. In no case can a man be swept away by it into any course of action without his own consent, though he may evidently be helped or hindered by it in any effort that he chances to be making. The really strong man has little need to trouble himself as to the agencies which happen to be in the ascendant, but for men of weaker will it may sometimes be worth while to know at what moment this or that force can most advantageously be applied. These factors may be put aside as a negligible quantity by the man of iron determination or by the student of true occultism; but since most men still allow themselves to be the helpless sport of the forces of desire, and have not yet developed anything worth calling a will of their own, their feebleness permits these influences to assume an

importance in human life to which they have intrinsically no claim.

90.　　　For example, a certain variety of pressure may occasionally bring about a condition of affairs in which all forms of nervous excitement are considerably intensified, and there is consequently a general sense of irritability abroad. That condition cannot cause a quarrel between sensible people; but under such circumstances disputes arise far more readily than usual, even on the most trifling pretexts, and the large number of people who seem to be always on the verge of losing their tempers are likely to relinquish all control of themselves on even less than ordinary provocation. It may sometimes happen that such influences, playing on the smouldering discontent of ignorant jealousy, may fan it into an outburst of popular frenzy from which wide-spread disaster may ensue.

91.　　　Even in such a case as this we must guard ourselves against the fatal mistake of supposing the influence to be evil because man's passions turn it to evil effect. The force itself is simply a wave of activity sent forth from one of the Centres of the Deity, and is in itself of the nature of an intensification of certain vibrations - necessary perhaps to produce some far-reaching cosmic effect. The increased activity produced incidentally by its means in the astral body of a man offers him an opportunity of testing his power to manage his vehicles; and whether he succeeds or fails in this, it is still one of the lessons which help in his evolution. Karma may throw a man into certain surroundings or bring him under certain influences, but it can never force him to commit a crime, though it may so place him that it requires great determination on his part to avoid that crime. It is possible, therefore, for an astrologer to warn a man of the circumstances under which at a given time be will find himself, but any definite prophecy as to his action under those circumstances can only be based upon probabilities - though we may readily recognise how nearly such prophecies become certainties in the case of the ordinary will-less man. From the extraordinary mixture of success and failure which characterise modern astrological predictions, it seems fairly certain that the practitioners, of this art are not fully acquainted with all the necessary factors. In a case into which only those factors enter which are already fairly well understood, success is achieved; but in cases where unrecognised factors come into play we have naturally more or less complete failure as the result.

CHAPTER IV BY THE SUN

THE HEAT OF THE SUN

95.   Those who are interested in astronomy will find the occult side of that science one of the most fascinating studies within our reach. Obviously it would be at once too recondite and too technical for inclusion in such a book as this, which is concerned more immediately with such of the unseen phenomena as affect us practically in our daily life; but the connection of the sun with that life is so intimate that it is necessary that a few words should be said about him.

96.   The whole solar system is truly the garment of its Deity, but the sun is His veritable epiphany - the nearest that we can come in the physical realm to a manifestation of Him, the lens through which His power shines forth upon us.

97.   Regarded purely from the physical point of view, the sun is a vast mass of glowing matter at almost inconceivably high temperatures, and in a condition of electrification so intense as to be altogether beyond our experience. Astronomers, supposing his heat to be due merely to contraction, used to calculate how long he must have existed in the past, and how long it would be possible for him to maintain it in the future; and they found themselves unable to allow more than a few hundred thousand years either way, while the geologists on the other hand claim that on this earth alone we have evidence of processes extending over millions of years. The discovery of radium has upset the older theories, but even with its aid they have not yet risen to the simplicity of the real explanation of the difficulty.

98.   One can imagine some intelligent microbe living in or upon a human body and arguing about its temperature in precisely the same way. He might say that it must of course be a gradually cooling body, and he might calculate with exactitude that in so many hours or minutes it must reach a temperature that would render continued existence impossible for him. If he lived long enough, however, he would find that the human body did *not* cool, as according to his theories it should do, and no doubt this would seem to him very mysterious, unless and until he discovered that he was dealing not with a dying fire but with a living being, and that as long as the life remained the temperature would not sink. In exactly the same way if we realise that the sun is the physical manifestation of the Solar Deity, we shall see that the mighty life behind it will assuredly keep up its temperature, as long as may be necessary for the full evolution of the system.

99.   THE WILLOW-LEAVES

100.   A similar explanation offers us a solution of some of the other problems of solar physics. For example, the phenomena called from their shape the 'willow-leaves' or ' rice-grains,' of which the photosphere of the sun is practically composed, have often puzzled exoteric students by the apparently irreconcilable characteristics which they present. From their position they can be nothing else than masses of glowing gas at an exceedingly high temperature, and therefore of great tenuity; yet though they

must be far lighter than any terrestrial cloud, they never fail to maintain their peculiar shape, however wildly they may be tossed about in the very midst of storms of power so tremendous that they would instantly destroy the earth itself.

101.	When we realise that behind each of these strange objects there is a splendid Life - that each may be considered as the physical body of a great Angel - we comprehend that it is that Life which holds them together and gives them their wonderful stability. To apply to them the term physical body may perhaps mislead us, because for us the life in the physical seems of so much importance and occupies so prominent a position in the present stage of our evolution. Madame Blavatsky has told us that we cannot truly describe them as solar inhabitants, since the Solar Beings will hardly place themselves in telescopic focus, but that they are the reservoirs of solar vital energy, themselves partaking of the life which they pour forth.

102.	Let us say rather that the willow-leaves are manifestations upon the physical level maintained by the solar Angels for a special purpose, at the cost of a certain sacrifice or limitation of their activities on the higher levels which are their normal habitat. Remembering that it is through these willow-leaves that the light, heat and vitality of the sun come to us, we may readily see that the object of this sacrifice is to bring down to the physical level certain forces which would otherwise remain unmanifested, and that these great Angels are acting as channels, as reflectors, as specialisers of divine power - that they are in fact doing at cosmic levels and for a solar system what, if we are wise enough to use our privileges, we ourselves may do on a microscopical scale in our own little circle, as will be seen in a later chapter.

103.	VITALITY

104.	We all know the feeling of cheerfulness and well-being which sunlight brings to us, but only students of occultism are fully aware of the reasons for that sensation. Just as the sun floods his system with light and heat, so does he perpetually pour out into it another force as yet unsuspected by modern science - a force to which has been given the name ` vitality'. This is radiated on all levels, and manifests itself in each realm - physical, emotional, mental and the rest - but we are specially concerned for the moment with its appearance in the lowest, where it enters some of the physical atoms, immensely increases their activity, and makes them animated and glowing.

105.	We must not confuse this force with electricity, though it in some ways resembles it. The Deity sends forth from Himself three great forms of energy; there may be hundreds more of which we know nothing; but at least there are three. Each of them has its appropriate manifestation at every level which our students have yet reached; but for the moment let us think of them as they show themselves in the physical world. One of them exhibits itself as electricity, another as vitality, and the third as the serpent-fire, of which I have already written in *The Inner Life*.

106.	These three remain distinct, and none of them can at this level be converted into either of the others. They have no connection with any of the Three Great Outpourings; all of those are definite efforts made by the Solar Deity, while these seem rather to be results of His life - His qualities in manifestation without any visible effort. Electricity, while it is rushing through the atoms, deflects them and holds them in a certain way - this effect being in addition to and quite apart from the special rate of vibration which it also imparts to them.

107.   But the action of vitality differs in many ways from that of electricity, light or heat. Any of the variants of this latter force cause oscillation of the atom as a whole - an oscillation the size of which is enormous as compared with that of the atom; but this other force which we call vitality comes to the atom not from without, but from within.

108.   THE VITALITY GLOBULE

109.   The atom is itself nothing but the manifestation of a force; the Solar Deity wills a certain shape which we call an ultimate physical atom, and by that effort of His will some fourteen thousand million bubbles are held in that particular form. It is necessary to emphasise the fact that the cohesion of the bubbles in that form is entirely dependent upon that effort of will, so that if that were for a single instant withdrawn, the bubbles must fall apart again, and the whole physical realm would simply cease to exist in far less than the period of a flash of lightning. So true is it that the whole world is nothing but illusion, even from this point of view, to say nothing of the fact that the bubbles of which the atom is built are themselves only holes in koilon, the true aether of space.

110.   So it is the will-force of the Solar Deity continually exercised which holds the atom together as such; and when we try to examine the action of that force we see that it does not come into the atom from outside, but wells up within it - which means that it enters it from higher dimensions. The same is true with regard to this other force which we call vitality; it enters the atom from within, along with the force that holds that atom together, instead of acting upon it entirely from without, as do those other varieties of force which we call light, heat or electricity.

111.   When vitality wells up thus within the atom it endows it with an additional life, and gives it a power of attraction, so that it immediately draws round it six other atoms, which it arranges in a definite form, this making what has been called in *Occult Chemistry* a hyper-meta-proto-element. But this element differs from all others which have so far been observed, in that the force which creates it and holds it together comes from the second Aspect of the Solar Deity instead of from the third This vitality-globule is drawn upon page 45 of *Occult Chemistry*, where it stands first at the left hand of the top line in the diagram. It is the little group which makes the exceedingly brilliant bead upon the male or positive snake in the chemical element oxygen, and it is also the heart of the central globe in radium.

112.   These globules are conspicuous above all others which may be seen floating in the atmosphere, on account of their brilliance and extreme activity - the intensely vivid life which they show. These are probably the fiery lives so often mentioned by Madame Blavatsky, though she appears to employ that term in two senses. In *The Secret Doctrine*, vol. ii, 709, it seems to mean the globule as a whole, in vol. i, 283, it probably means the original additionally-vitalised atoms, each of which draws round itself six others.

113.   While the force that vivifies the globules is quite different from light, it

nevertheless appears to depend upon light for its power of manifestation. In brilliant sunshine this vitality is constantly welling up afresh, and the globules are generated with great rapidity and in incredible numbers; but in cloudy weather there is a great diminution in the number of globules formed, and during the night the operation appears to be entirely suspended. During the night, therefore, we may be said to be living upon the stock manufactured during the previous day, and though it appears practically impossible that it should ever be entirely exhausted, that stock evidently does run low when there is a long succession of cloudy days. The globule, once charged, remains as a sub-atomic element, and does not appear to be subject to any change or loss of force unless and until it is absorbed by some living creature.

114.   THE ABSORPTION OF VITALITY

115.   This vitality is absorbed by all living organisms, and a sufficient supply of it seems to be a necessity of their existence. In the case of men and the higher animals it is absorbed through the centre or vortex in the etheric double which corresponds with the spleen. It will be remembered that that centre has six petals, made by the undulatory movement of the forces which cause the vortex. But this undulatory movement is itself caused by the radiation of other forces from the centre of that vortex. Imaging the central point of the vortex as the hub of a wheel, we may think of these last-mentioned forces as represented by spokes radiating from it in straight lines. Then the vortical forces, sweeping round and round, pass alternately under and over these spokes as though they were weaving a kind of etheric basket-work, and in this way is obtained the appearance of six petals separated by depressions.

116.   When the unit of vitality is flashing about in the atmosphere, brilliant as it is, it is almost colourless, and may be compared to white light. But as soon as it is drawn into the vortex of the force-centre at the spleen it is decomposed and breaks up into streams of different colours, though it does not follow exactly our division of the spectrum. As its component atoms are whirled round the vortex, each of the six spokes seizes upon one of them, so that all the atoms charged with yellow rush along one, and all those charged with green along another, and so on, while the seventh disappears through the centre of the vortex - through the hub of the wheel, as it were. Those rays then rush off in different directions, each to do its special work in the vitalisation of the body. As I have said, however, the divisions are not exactly those which we ordinarily use in the solar spectrum, but rather resemble the arrangement of colours which we see on higher levels in the causal, mental and astral bodies.

117.   For example, what we call indigo is divided between the violet ray and the blue ray, so that we find only two divisions there instead of three; but on the other hand what we call red is divided into two - rose red and dark red. The six radiants are therefore violet, blue, green, yellow, orange, and dark red; while the seventh or rose red atom (more properly the first, since this is the original atom in which the force first appeared) passes down through the centre of the vortex. Vitality is thus clearly sevenfold in its constitution, but it rushes through the body in five main streams, as has been described in some of the Indian books,[1] ([1] "To them spoke the principal life: Be

not lost in delusion I even, fivefold dividing myself, uphold this body by my support." - *Prashnopanishad*. ii, 3. "From this proceed these seven flames." - *Ibid.*, iii, 5.) for after issuing from splenic centre the blue and the violet join into one ray, and so do the orange and the dark red.

(1) The violet-blue ray flashes upwards to the throat, where it seems to divide itself, the light blue remaining to course through and vivify the throat-centre, while the dark blue and violet pass on into the brain. The dark blue expends itself in the lower and central parts of the brain, while the violet floods the upper part and appears to give special vigour to the force-centre at the top of the head, diffusing itself chiefly through the nine hundred and sixty petals of the outer part of that centre.

(2) The yellow ray is directed to the heart, but after doing its work there, part of it also passes on to the brain and permeates it, directing itself principally to the twelve-petalled flower in the midst of the highest force-centre.

(3) The green ray floods the abdomen and, while centring especially in the solar plexus, evidently vivifies the liver, kidneys and intestines, and the digestive apparatus generally.

(4) The rose-coloured ray runs all over the body along the nerves, and is clearly the life of the nervous system. This is what is commonly described as vitality - the specialised vitality which one man may readily pour into another in whom it is deficient. If the nerves are not fully supplied with this rosy light they become sensitive and intensely irritable, so that the patient finds it almost impossible to remain in one position, and yet gains but little ease when he moves to another. The least noise or touch is agony to him, and he is in a condition of acute misery. The flooding of his nerves with specialised vitality by some healthy person brings instant relief, and a feeling of healing and peace descends upon him. A man in robust health usually absorbs and specialises so much more vitality than is actually needed by his own body that he is constantly radiating a torrent of rose-coloured atoms, and so unconsciously pours strength upon his weaker fellows without losing anything himself; or by an effort of his will he can gather together this superfluous energy and aim it intentionally at one whom he wishes to help.

118.   The physical body has a certain blind, instinctive consciousness of its own, corresponding in the physical world to the desire-elemental of the astral body; and this consciousness seeks always to protect it from danger, or to procure for it whatever may be necessary. This is entirely apart from the consciousness of the man himself, and it works equally well during the absence of the ego from the physical body during sleep. All our instinctive movements are due to it, and it is through its activity that the working of the sympathetic system is carried on ceaselessly without any thought or knowledge on our part.

119.   While we are what we call awake, this physical elemental is perpetually occupied in self-defence; he is in a condition of constant vigilance, and he keeps the nerves and muscles always tense. During the night or at any time when we sleep he lets the nerves and muscles relax, and devotes himself specially to the assimilation of vitality, and the recuperation of the physical body. He works at this most successfully during the early part of the night, because then there is plenty of vitality, whereas

immediately before the dawn the vitality which has been left behind by the sunlight is almost completely exhausted. This is the reason for the feeling of limpness and deadness associated with the small hours of the morning; this is also the reason why sick men so frequently die at that particular time. The same idea is embodied in the old proverb that "An hour's sleep before midnight is worth two after it." The work of this physical elemental accounts for the strong recuperative influence of sleep, which is often observable even when it is a mere momentary nap.

120.   This vitality is indeed the food of the etheric double, and is just as necessary to it as is sustenance to the grosser part of the physical body. Hence when the body is unable for any reason (as through sickness, fatigue or extreme old age) to prepare vitality for the nourishment of its cells, this physical elemental endeavours to draw in for his own use vitality which has already been prepared in the bodies of others; and thus it happens that we often find ourselves weak and exhausted after sitting for a while with a person who is depleted of vitality, because he has drawn away from us by suction the rose-coloured atoms before we were able to extract their energy.

121.   The vegetable kingdom also absorbs this vitality, but seems in most cases to use only a small part of it. Many trees draw from it almost exactly the same constituents as does the higher part of man's etheric body, the result being that when they have used what they require, the atoms which they reject are precisely those charged with the rose-coloured light which is needed for the cells of man's physical body. This is specially the case with such trees as the pine and the eucalyptus; and consequently the very neighbourhood of these trees gives health and strength to those who are suffering from lack of this part of the vital principle - those whom we call nervous people. They are nervous because the cells of their bodies are hungry, and the nervousness can only be allayed by feeding them; and often the readiest way to do that is thus to supply them from without with the special kind of vitality which they need.

122.   (5) The orange-red ray flows to the base of the spine and thence to the generative organs, with which one part of its functions is closely connected. This ray appears to include not only the orange and the darker reds, but also a certain amount of dark purple, as though the spectrum bent round in a circle and the colours began over again at a lower octave. In the normal man this ray energises the desires of the flesh, and also seems to enter the blood and keep up the heat of the body; but if a man persistently refuses to yield to his lower nature, this ray can by long and determined effort be deflected upwards to the brain, where all three of its constituents undergo a remarkable modification. The orange is raised into pure yellow, and produces a decided intensification of the powers of the intellect; the dark red becomes crimson, and greatly increases the power of unselfish affection; while the dark purple is transmuted into a lovely pale violet, and quickens the spiritual part of man's nature. The man who achieves this transmutation will find that sensual desires no longer trouble him, and when it becomes necessary for him to arouse the serpent-fire, he will be free from the most serious of the dangers of that process. When a man has finally completed this change, this orange-red ray passes straight into the centre at the base of the spine, and from that runs upwards along the hollow of the vertebral column, and so to the brain.

123.   VITALITY AND HEALTH

124.   The flow of vitality in these various currents regulates the health of the parts of the body with which they are concerned. If, for example, a person is suffering from a weak digestion, it manifests itself at once to any person possessing etheric sight, because either the flow and action of the green stream is sluggish or its amount is smaller in proportion than it should be. Where the yellow current is full and strong, it indicates, or more properly produces, strength and regularity in the action of the heart. Flowing round that centre, it also interpenetrates the blood which is driven through it, and is sent along with it all over the body. Yet there is enough of it left to extend into the brain also, and the power of high philosophical and metaphysical thought appears to depend to a great extent upon the volume and activity of this yellow stream, and the corresponding awakening of the twelve-petalled flower in the middle of the force-centre at the top of the head.

125.   Thought and emotion of a high spiritual type seem to depend largely upon the violet ray, whereas the power of ordinary thought is stimulated by the action of the blue mingled with part of the yellow. It has been observed that in some forms of idiocy the flow of vitality to the brain, both yellow and blue-violet, is almost entirely inhibited. Unusual activity or volume in the light blue which is apportioned to the throat-centre is accompanied by the health and strength of the physical organs in that part of the body. It gives, for example, strength and elasticity to the vocal chords, so that special brilliance and activity are noticeable in the case of a public speaker or a great singer. Weakness or disease in any part of the body is accompanied by a deficiency in the flow of vitality to that part.

126.   As the different streams of atoms do their work, the charge of vitality is withdrawn from them, precisely as an electrical charge might be. The atoms bearing the rose-coloured ray grow gradually paler as they are swept along the nerves, and are eventually thrown out from the body through the pores - making thus what was called in *Man Visible and Invisible* the health-aura. By the time that they leave the body most of them have lost the rose-coloured light, so that the general appearance of the emanation is bluish-white. That part of the yellow ray which is absorbed into the blood and carried round with it loses its distinctive colour in just the same way.

127.   The atoms, when thus emptied of their charge of vitality, either enter into some of the combinations which are constantly being made in the body, or pass out of it through the pores, or through the ordinary channels. The emptied atoms of the green ray, which is connected chiefly with digestive processes, seem to form part of the ordinary waste material of the body, and to pass out along with it, and that is also the fate of the atoms of the red-orange ray in the case of the ordinary man. The atoms belonging to the blue rays, which are used in connection with the throat-centre, generally leave the body in the exhalations of the breath; and those which compose the dark blue and violet rays usually pass out from the centre at the top of the head.

128.   When the student has learnt to deflect the orange-red rays so that they also move up through the spine, the empty atoms of both these and the violet-blue rays

pour out from the top of the head in a fiery cascade, which is frequently imaged as a flame in ancient statues of the BUDDHA and other great Saints. When empty of the vital force the atoms are once more precisely like any other atoms; the body absorbs such of them as it needs, so that they form part of the various combinations which are constantly being made, while others which are not required for such purposes are cast out through any channel that happens to be convenient.

129.   The flow of vitality into or through any centre, or even its intensification, must not be confused with the entirely different development of the centre which is brought about by the awakening of the serpent-fire at a later stage in man's evolution. We all of us draw in vitality and specialise it, but many of us do not utilise it to the full, because in various ways our lives are not as pure and healthy and reasonable as they should be. One who coarsens his body by the use of meat, alcohol or tobacco can never employ his vitality to the full in the same way as can a man of purer living. A particular individual of impure life may be, and often is stronger in the physical body than certain other men who are purer; that is a matter of their respective karma; but other things being equal, the man of pure life has an immense advantage.

130.   VITALITY NOT MAGNETISM

131.   The vitality coursing along the nerves must not be confused with what we usually call the magnetism of the man - his own nerve-fluid, generated within himself. It is this fluid which keeps up the constant circulation of etheric matter along the nerves, corresponding to the circulation of blood through the veins; and as oxygen is conveyed by the blood to all parts of the body, so vitality is conveyed along the nerves by this etheric current. The particles of the etheric part of man's body are constantly changing, just as are those of the denser part; along with the food which we eat and the air which we breathe we take in etheric matter, and this is assimilated by the etheric part of the body. Etheric matter is constantly being thrown off from the pores, just as is gaseous matter, so that when two persons are close together each necessarily absorbs much of the physical emanations of the other.

132.   When one person mesmerises another, the operator by an effort of will gathers together a great deal of this magnetism and throws it into the subject, pushing back his victim's nerve-fluid, and filling its place with his own. As the brain is the centre of this nervous circulation, this brings that part of the subject's body which is affected under the control of the manipulator's brain instead of the victim's, and so the latter feels what the mesmerist wishes him to feel. If the recipient's brain be emptied of his own magnetism and filled with that of the performer, the former can think and act only as the latter wills that he should think and act; he is for the time entirely dominated.

133.   Even when the magnetiser is trying to cure, and is pouring strength into the man, he inevitably gives along with the vitality much of his own emanations. It is obvious that any disease which the mesmeriser happens to have may readily he conveyed to the subject in this way; and another even more important consideration is that, though his health may be perfect from the medical point of view, there are mental and moral diseases

31

as well as physical, and that, as astral and mental matter are thrown into the subject by the mesmerist along with the physical current, these also are frequently transferred.

134. Vitality, like light and heat, is pouring forth from the sun continually, but obstacles frequently arise to prevent the full supply from reaching the earth. In the wintry and melancholy climes miscalled the temperate, it too often happens that for days together the sky is covered by a funeral pall of heavy cloud, and this affects vitality just as it does light; it does not altogether hinder its passage, but sensibly diminishes its amount. Therefore in dull and dark weather vitality runs low, and over all living creatures there comes an instinctive yearning for sunlight.

135. When vitalised atoms are thus more sparsely scattered, the man in rude health increases his power of absorption, depletes a larger area, and so keeps his strength at the normal level; but invalids and men of small nerve-force, who cannot do this, often suffer severely, and find themselves growing weaker and more irritable without knowing why. For similar reasons vitality is at a lower ebb in the winter than in the summer, for even if the short winter day be sunny, which is rare, we have still to face the long and dreary winter night, during which we must exist upon such vitality as the day has stored in our atmosphere. On the other hand the long summer day, when bright and cloudless, charges the atmosphere so thoroughly with vitality that its short night makes but little difference.

136. From the study of this question of vitality, the occultist cannot fail to recognise that, quite apart from temperature, sunlight is one of the most important factors in the attainment and preservation of perfect health - a factor for the absence of which nothing else can entirely compensate. Since this vitality is poured forth not only upon the physical world but upon all others as well, it is evident that, when in other respects satisfactory conditions are present, emotion, intellect and spirituality will be at their best under clear skies and with the inestimable aid of the sunlight.

137. All the colours of this order of vitality are etheric, yet it will be seen that their action presents certain correspondences with the signification attached to similar hues in the astral body. Clearly right thought and right feeling react upon the physical body, and increase its power to assimilate the vitality which is necessary for its well-being. It is reported that the Lord BUDDHA once said that the first step on the road to Nirvana is perfect physical health; and assuredly the way to attain that is to follow the Noble Eightfold Path which He has indicated. "Seek ye first the Kingdom of God and His righteousness, and all these things shall be added unto you" - yes, even physical health as well.

CHAPTER V BY NATURAL SURROUNDINGS

140.   THE WEATHER

141.   The vagaries of the weather are proverbial, and though observation and study of its phenomena enable us to venture upon certain limited predictions, the ultimate cause of most of the changes still escapes us, and will continue to do so until we realise that there are considerations to be taken into account besides the action of heat and cold, of radiation and condensation. The earth itself is living; this ball of matter is being used as a physical body by a vast entity - not an Adept or an angel, not a highly developed being at all, but rather something which may be imagined as a kind of gigantic nature-spirit, for whom the existence of our earth is one incarnation. His previous incarnation was naturally in the moon since that was the fourth planet of the last chain, and equally naturally his next incarnation will be in the fourth planet of the chain that will succeed ours when the evolution of our terrestrial chain is completed. Of his nature or the character of his evolution we can know but little, nor does it in any way concern us, for we are to him but as tiny microbes or parasites upon his body, and in all probability he is unaware even of our existence, for nothing that we can do can be on a scale large enough to affect him.

142.   For him the atmosphere surrounding the earth must be as a kind of aura, or perhaps rather corresponding to the film of etheric matter which projects ever so slightly beyond the outline of man's dense physical body; and just as any alteration or disturbance in the man affects this film of aether, so must any change of condition in this spirit of the earth affect the atmosphere. Some such changes must be periodic and regular, like the motions produced in us by breathing, by the action of the heart or by an even movement, such as walking; others must be irregular and occasional, as would be the changes produced in a man by a sudden start, or by an outburst of emotion.

143.   We know that violent emotion, astral in its origin though it be, produces chemical changes and variations of temperature in the human physical body; whatever corresponds to such emotion in the spirit of the earth may well cause chemical changes in *his* physical body also, and variations of temperature in its immediate surroundings. Now variations of temperature in the atmosphere mean wind; sudden and violent variations mean storm; and chemical changes beneath the surface of the earth not infrequently cause earthquakes and volcanic eruptions.

144.   No student of occultism will fall into the common error of regarding as evil such outbursts as storms or eruptions, because they sometimes destroy human life; for he will recognise that, whatever the immediate cause may be, all that happens is part of the working of the great immutable law of justice, and that He who doeth all things most certainly doeth all things well. This aspect of natural phenomena, however, will be considered in a later chapter.

145.   It cannot be questioned that men are much and variously affected by the weather. There is a general consensus of opinion that gloomy weather is depressing;

but this is mainly due to the fact that in the absence of sunlight there is, as has already been explained, a lack of vitality. Some people, however, take an actual delight in rain or snow or high wind. There is in these disturbances something which produces a distinct pleasurable sensation which quickens their vibrations and harmonises with the key-note of their nature. It is probable that this is not entirely or even chiefly due to the physical disturbance; it is rather that the subtle change in the aura of the spirit of the earth (which produces or coincides with this phenomenon) is one with which their spirits are in sympathy. A still more decided instance of this is the effect of a thunder-storm. There are many people in whom it produces a curious sense of overwhelming fear entirely out of proportion to any physical danger that it can be supposed to bring. In others, on the contrary, the electrical storm produces wild exultation. The influence of electricity on the physical nerves no doubt plays a part in producing these unusual sensations, but their true cause lies deeper than that.

146. The effect produced upon people by these various manifestations depends upon the preponderance in their temperament of certain types of elemental essence which, because of this sympathetic vibration, used to be called by mediaeval enquirers earthy, watery, airy or fiery. Exactly in the same way the effect of the various sections of our surroundings will be greater or less upon men according as they have more or less of one or other of these constituents in their composition. To the man who responds most readily to earth influences, the nature of the soil upon which his house is built is of primary importance, but it matters comparatively little to him whether it is or is not in the neighbourhood of water; whereas the man who responds most readily to the radiations of water would care little about the soil so long as he had the ocean or a lake within sight and within easy reach.

147. ROCKS

148. Influence is perpetually radiated upon us by all objects of nature, even by the very earth upon which we tread. Each type of rock or soil has its own special variety, and the differences between them are great, so that their effect is by no means to be neglected. In the production of this effect three factors bear their part - the life of the rock itself, the kind of elemental essence appropriate to its astral counterpart, and the kind of nature-spirits which it attracts. The life of the rock is simply the life of the Second Great Outpouring which has arrived at the stage of ensouling the mineral kingdom, and the elemental essence is a later wave of that same divine Life which is one chain-period behind the other, and has yet in its descent into matter reached only the astral world. The nature-spirit belong to a different evolution altogether, to which we shall refer in due course.

149. The point for us to bear in mind for the moment is that each kind of soil - granite or sandstone, chalk, clay or lava, has its definite influence upon those who live on it - an influence which never ceases. Night and day, summer and winter, year in and year out, this steady pressure is being exercised, and it has its part in the moulding of races and districts, types as well as individuals. All these matters are as yet but little comprehended by ordinary science, but there can be no doubt that in time to come

these effects will be thoroughly studied, and the doctors of the future will take them into account, and prescribe a change of soil as well as of air for their patients.

150.　　An entirely new and distinct set of agencies is brought into play wherever water exists, whether it be in the form of lake, river or sea - powerful in different ways in all of them truly, but most powerful and observable in the last. Here also the same three factors have to be considered - the life of the water itself, the elemental essence pervading it, and the type of nature-spirits associated with it.

151.　　TREES

152.　　Strong influences are radiated by the vegetable kingdom also, and the different kinds of plants and trees vary greatly in their effect. Those who have not specially studied the subject invariably under-rate the strength, capacity and intelligence shown in vegetable life. I have already written upon this in *The Christian Creed*, p. 51 (2nd edition), so I will not repeat myself here, but will rather draw attention to the fact that trees - especially old trees - have a strong and definite individuality, well worthy the name of a soul. This soul, though temporary, in the sense that it is not yet a reincarnating entity, is nevertheless possessed of considerable power and intelligence along its own lines.

153.　　It has decided likes and dislikes, and to clairvoyant sight it shows quite clearly by a vivid rosy flush an emphatic enjoyment of the sunlight and the rain, and distinct pleasure also in the presence of those whom it has learnt to like, or with whom it has sympathetic vibrations. Emerson appears to have realised this, for he is quoted in Hutton's *Reminiscences* as saying of his trees: "I am sure they miss me; they seem to droop when I go away, and I know they brighten and bloom when I go back to them, and shake hands with their lower branches."

154.　　An old forest tree is a high development of vegetable life, and when it is transferred from that kingdom it does not pass into the lowest form of animal life. In some cases its individuality is even sufficiently distinct to allow it to manifest itself temporarily outside its physical form, and when that is so, it often takes the human shape. Matters may be otherwise arranged in other solar systems for aught we know, but in ours the Deity has chosen the human form to enshrine the highest intelligence, to be carried on to the utmost perfection as His scheme develops: and because that is so, there is always a tendency among lower kinds of life to reach upwards towards that form, and in their primitive way to imagine themselves as possessing it.

155.　　Thus it happens that such creatures as gnomes or elves, whose bodies are of fluidic nature, of astral or etheric matter which is plastic under the influence of the will, habitually adopts some approximation to the appearance of humanity. Thus also when it is possible for the soul of a tree to externalise itself and become visible, it is almost always in human shape that it is seen. Doubtless these were the dryads of classical times; and the occasional appearance of such figures may account for the widely-spread custom of tree-worship. *Omne ignotum pro magnifico*; and if primitive man saw a huge, grave human form come forth from a tree, he was likely enough in his ignorance to set up an altar there and worship it, not in the least understanding that he himself stood far higher in evolution than it did, and that its very assumption of his image was an acknowledgment of that fact.

156. The occult side of the instinct of a plant is also exceedingly interesting; its one great object, like that of some human beings, is always to found a family and reproduce its species; and it has certainly a feeling of active enjoyment in its success, in the colour and beauty of its flowers and in their efficiency in attracting bees and other insects. Unquestionably plants feel admiration lavished upon them and delight in it; they are sensitive to human affection and they return it in their own way.

157. When all this is borne in mind, it will readily be understood that trees exercise much more influence over human beings than is commonly supposed, and that he who sets himself to cultivate sympathetic and friendly relations with *all* his neighbours, vegetable as well as animal and human, may both receive and give a great deal of which the average man knows nothing, and may thus make his life fuller, wider, more complete.

158. THE SEVEN TYPES

159. The classification of the vegetable kingdom adopted by the occultist follows the line of the seven great types mentioned in our previous chapter on planetary influences, and each of these is divided into seven sub-types. If we imagine ourselves trying to tabulate the vegetable kingdom, these divisions would naturally be perpendicular, nor horizontal. We should not have trees as one type, shrubs as another, ferns as a third, grasses or mosses as a fourth; rather we should find trees, shrubs, ferns, grasses, mosses of each of the seven types, so that along each line all the steps of the ascending scale are represented.

160. One might phrase it that when the Second Outpouring is ready to descend, seven great channels, each with its seven subdivisions, lie open for its choice; but the channel through which it passes gives it a certain colouring - a set of temperamental characteristics - which it never wholly loses, so that although in order to express itself it needs matter belonging to all the different types, it has always a preponderance of its own type, and always recognisably belongs to that type and no other, until after its evolution is over it returns as a glorified spiritual power to the Deity from whom it originally emerged as a mere undeveloped potentiality.

161. The vegetable kingdom is only one stage in this stupendous course, yet these different types are distinguishable in it, just as they are among animals or human beings, and each has its own special influence, which may be soothing or helpful to one man, distressing or irritating to another, and inert in the case of a third, according to *his* type and to his condition at the time. Training and practice are necessary to enable the student to assign the various plants and trees to their proper classes, but the distinction between the magnetism radiated by the oak and the pine, the palm tree and the banyan, the olive and the eucalyptus, the rose and the lily, the violet and the sunflower, cannot fail to be obvious to any sensitive person. Wide as the poles asunder is the dissimilarity between the ` feeling' of an English forest and a tropical jungle, or the bush of Australia or New Zealand.

162.   ANIMALS

163.   For thousand of years man has lived so cruelly that all wild creatures fear and avoid him, so the influence upon him of the animal kingdom is practically confined to that of the domestic animals. In our relations with these our influence over them is naturally far more potent than theirs over us, yet this latter is by no means to be ignored. A man who has really made friends with an animal is often much helped and strengthened by the affection lavished upon him. Being more advanced, a man is naturally capable of greater love than an animal is; but the animal's affection is usually more concentrated, and he is far more likely to throw the whole of his energy into it than a man is.

164.   The very fact of the man's higher development gives him a multiplicity of interests, among which his attention is divided; the animal often pours the entire strength of his nature into one channel, and so produces a most powerful effect. The man has a hundred other matters to think about, and the current of his love consequently cannot but be variable; when the dog or the cat develops a really great affection it fills the whole of his life, and he therefore keeps a steady stream of force always playing upon its object - a factor whose value is by no means to be ignored.

165.   Similarly the man who is so wicked as to provoke by cruelty the hatred and fear of domestic animals becomes by a righteous retribution the centre of converging forces of antipathy; for such conduct arouses deep indignation among nature-spirits and other astral and etheric entities, as well as among all right-minded men, whether living or dead.

166.   HUMAN BEINGS

167.   Since it is emphatically true that no man can afford to be disliked or feared by his cat or dog, it is clear that the same consideration applies with still greater force to the human beings who surround him. It is not easy to overestimate the importance to a man of winning the kindly regard of those with whom he is in constant association - to overrate the value to a schoolmaster of the attitude towards him of his pupils, to a merchant of the feeling of his clerks, to an officer of the devotion of his men; and this entirely apart from the obvious effects produced in the physical world. If a man holding any such position as one of these is able to arouse the enthusiastic affection of his subordinates, he becomes the focus upon which many streams of such forces are constantly converging. Not only does this greatly uplift and strengthen him, but it also enables him, if he understands something of the working of occult laws, to be of far greater use to those who feel the affection, and to do much more with them than would otherwise be possible.

168.   To obtain this result it is not in the least necessary that they should agree with him in opinion; with the particular effect with which we are at present concerned their mental attitude has no connection whatever; it is a matter of strong, kindly feeling. If the feeling should unfortunately be of an opposite kind - if the man is feared or despised - currents of antipathy are perpetually flowing towards him, which cause weakness and discord in the vibrations of his higher vehicles, and also cut him

off from the possibility of doing satisfactory and fruitful work with those under his charge.

169.   It is not only the force of the feeling sent out by the person; like attracts like in the astral world as well as the physical. There are always masses of vague thought floating about in the atmosphere, some of them good and some evil, but all alike ready to reinforce any decided thought of their own type. Also there are nature-spirits of low order, which enjoy the coarse vibrations of anger and hatred, and are therefore very willing to throw themselves into any current of such nature. By doing so they intensify the undulations, and add fresh life to them. All this tends to strengthen the effect produced by the converging streams of unfavourable thought and feeling.

170.   It has been said that a man is known by the company he keeps. It is also to a large extent true that he is *made* by it, for those with whom he constantly associates are all the while unconsciously influencing him and bringing him by degrees more and more into harmony with such undulations as they radiate. He who is much in the presence of a large-minded and unworldly man has a fine opportunity of himself becoming large-minded and unworldly, for a steady though imperceptible pressure in that direction is perpetually being exerted upon him, so that it is easier for him to grow in that way than in any other. For the same reason a man who spends his time loafing in a public-house with the idle and various is exceedingly likely to end by becoming idle and vicious himself. The study of the hidden side of things emphatically endorses the old proverb that evil communications corrupt good manners.

171.   This fact of the enormous influence of close association with a more advanced personality is well understood in the East, where it is recognised that the most important and effective part of the training of a disciple is that he shall live constantly in the presence of his teacher and bathe in his aura. The various vehicles of the teacher are all vibrating with a steady and powerful swing at rates both higher and more regular than any which the pupil can yet maintain, though he may sometimes reach them for a few moments; but the constant pressure of the stronger thought-waves of the teacher gradually raises those of the pupil into the same key. A person who has as yet but little musical ear finds it difficult to sing correct intervals alone, but if he joins with another stronger voice which is already perfectly trained, his task becomes easier - which may serve as a kind of rough analogy.

172.   The great point is that the dominant note of the teacher is always sounding, so that its action is affecting the pupil night and day without need of any special thought on the part of either of them. Growth and change must of course be ceaselessly taking place in the vehicles of the pupil, as in those of all other men; but the powerful undulations emanating from the teacher render it easy for this growth to take place in the right direction, and exceedingly difficult for it to go any other way, somewhat as the splints which surround a broken limb ensure that its growth shall be only in the right line, so as to avoid distortion.

173.   No ordinary man, acting automatically and without intention, will be able to exercise even a hundredth part of the carefully-directed influence of a spiritual teacher; but numbers may to some extent compensate for lack of individual power, so

that the ceaseless though unnoticed pressure exercised upon us by the opinions and feelings of our associates leads us frequently to absorb without knowing it many of their prejudices. It is distinctly undesirable that a man should remain always among one set of people and hear only one set of views. It is eminently necessary that he should know something of other sets, for only in that way can he learn to see good in all; only thoroughly understanding both sides of any case can he form an opinion that has any right to be called a real judgment. The prejudiced person is always and necessarily an ignorant person; and the only way in which his ignorance can be dispelled is by getting outside his own narrow little circle, and learning to look at things for himself and see what they really are - not what those who know nothing about them suppose them to be.

174.   TRAVEL ɔʃ ʜ(ʌʃ

175.   The extent to which our human surroundings influence us, is only realised when we change them for awhile, and the most effective method of doing this is to travel in a foreign country. But true travel is not to rush from one gigantic caravanserai to another, consorting all the time with one's own countrymen, and grumbling at every custom which differs from those of our particular Little Pedlington. It is rather to live for a time quietly in some foreign land, trying to get really to know its people and to understand them; to study a custom and see why it has arisen, and what good there is in it, instead of condemning it off-hand because it is not our own. The man who does this will soon come to recognise the characteristic traits of the various races - to comprehend such fundamental diversities as those between the English and the Irish, the Hindu and the American, the Breton and the Sicilian, and yet to realise that they are to be looked upon not as one better than another, but as the different colours that go to make up the rainbow, the different movements that are all necessary, as parts of the great oratorio of life.

176.   Each has its part to play in affording opportunity for the evolution of egos who need just its influence, who are lacking in just its characteristics. Each race has behind it a mighty angel, the Spirit of the Race, who under the direction of the Manu preserves its special qualities and guides it along the line destined for it. A new race is born when in the scheme of evolution a new type a temperament is needed; a race dies out when all the egos who can be benefited by it have passed through it. The influence of the Spirit of a Race thoroughly permeates the country or district over which his supervision extends, and is naturally a factor of the greatest importance to any visitor who is in the least sensitive.

177.   The ordinary tourist is too often imprisoned in the triple armour of aggressive race-prejudice; he is so full of conceit over the supposed excellencies of his own nation that he is incapable of seeing good in any other. The wiser traveller, who is willing to open his heart to the action of higher forces, may receive from this source much that is valuable, both of instruction and experience. But in order to do that, he must begin by putting himself in the right attitude; he must be ready to listen rather then to talk, to learn rather than to boast, to appreciate rather than to criticise, to

try to understand rather than rashly to condemn.

178.   To achieve such a result is the true object of travel, and we have a far better opportunity for this than was afforded to our forefathers. Methods of communication are so much improved that it is now possible for almost anyone to achieve quickly and cheaply journeys that would have been entirely impossible a century ago, except for the rich and leisured class. Along with these possibilities of intercommunication has come the wide dissemination of foreign news by means of the telegraph and the newspaper press, so that even those who do not actually leave their own country still know much more about others than was ever possible before. Without all these facilities there never could have been a Theosophical Society, or at least it could not have had its present character, nor could it have reached its present level of effectiveness.

179.   The first object of the Theosophical Society is the promotion of universal brotherhood, and nothing helps so much to induce brotherly feeling between nations as full and constant intercourse with one another. When people know one another only by hearsay, all sorts of absurd prejudices grow up, but when they come to know one another intimately, each finds that the other is after all a human being much like himself, with the same interests and objects, the same joys and sorrows.

180.   In the old days each nation lived to a large extent in a condition of selfish isolation, and if trouble of some sort fell upon one, it had usually no resources but its own upon which it could depend. Now the whole world is so closely drawn together that if there is a famine in India, help is sent from America; if an earthquake devastates one of the countries of Europe, subscriptions for the sufferers pour in at once from all the others. However far away as yet may be the perfect realisation of universal brotherhood, it is clear that we are at least drawing nearer to it; we have not yet learnt entirely to trust one another, but at least we are ready to help one another, and that is already a long step upon the roads towards becoming really one family.

181.   We know how often travel is recommended as a cure for many physical ills, especially for those which manifest themselves through the various forms of nervous derangement. Most of us find it to be fatiguing, yet also undeniably exhilarating, though we do not always realise that this is not only because of the change of air and of the ordinary physical impressions, but also because of the change of the etheric and astral influences which are connected with each place and district.

182.   Ocean, mountain, forest or waterfall - each has its own special type of life, astral and etheric as well as visible; and, therefore, its own special set of impressions and influences. Many of these unseen entities are pouring out vitality, and in any case, the vibrations which they radiate awaken unaccustomed portions of our etheric double, and of our astral and mental bodies, and the effect is like the exercise of muscles which are not ordinarily called into activity - somewhat tiring at the time, yet distinctly healthy and desirable in the long run.

183.   The town-dweller is accustomed to his surroundings, and usually does not realise the horror of them until he leaves them for a time. To dwell beside a busy main street is from the astral point of view like living on the brink of an open sewer - a river of fetid mud which is always throwing up splashes and noisome odours as it

rolls along. No man, however unimpressionable, can endure this indefinitely without deterioration, and an occasional change into the country is a necessity on the ground of moral as well as physical health. In travelling from the town into the country, too, we leave behind us to a great extent the stormy sea of warring human passion and labour, and such human thoughts as still remain to act upon us are usually of the less selfish and more elevated kind.

184.　　In the presence of one of nature's great wonders, such as the Falls of Niagara, almost everyone is for the time drawn out of himself, and out of the petty round of daily care and selfish desire, so that his thought is nobler and broader, and the thought-forms which he leaves behind him are correspondingly less disturbing and more helpful. These considerations once more make it evident that in order to obtain the full benefit of travel a man must pay attention to nature and allow it to act upon him. If he is wrapped up all the while in selfish and gloomy thoughts, crushed by financial trouble, or brooding over his own sickness and weakness, little benefit can be derived from the healing influences.

185.　　Another point is that certain places are permeated by certain special types of thought. The consideration of this matter belongs rather to another chapter, but we may introduce it so far as to mention that the frame of mind in which people habitually visit a certain place reacts strongly upon all the other visitors to it. Popular seaside resorts in England have about them an air of buoyancy and irresponsibility, a determined feeling of holiday life, of temporary freedom from business and of the resolution to make the most of it, from the influence of which it is difficult to escape. Thus the jaded and overworked man who spends his well-earned holiday in such a place, obtains quite a different result from that which would follow if he simply stayed quietly at home. To sit at home would probably be less fatiguing, but also much less stimulating.

186.　　To take a country walk is to travel in miniature, and in order to appreciate its healthful effect we must bear in mind what has been said of all the different vibrations issuing from various kinds of trees or plants, and even from different kinds of soil or rock. All these act as kind of massage upon the etheric, astral and mental bodies, and tend to relieve the strain which the worries of our common life persistently exert upon certain parts of these vehicles.

187.　　Glimpses of the truth on these points may sometimes be caught from the traditions of the peasantry. For example, there is a widely-spread belief that strength may be gained from sleeping under a pine-tree with the head to the north. For some cases this is suitable, and the rationale of it is that there are magnetic currents always flowing over the surface of the earth which are quite unknown to ordinary men. These by steady, gentle pressure gradually comb out the entanglements and strengthen the particles both of the astral body and of the etheric part of the physical, and thus bring them more into harmony and introduce rest and calm. The part played by the pine-tree is, first, that its radiations make the man sensitive to those magnetic currents, and bring him into a state in which it is possible for them to act upon him, and secondly, that (as has already been explained) it is constantly throwing off vitality in that special condition in which it is easiest for man to absorb it.

6/25

190.   AN EVOLUTION APART

191.   Another factor which exercises great influence under certain restrictions is the nature-spirit. We may regard the nature-spirits of the land as in a sense the original inhabitants of the country, driven away from some parts of it by the invasion of man, much as the wild animals have been. Just like wild animals, the nature-spirits avoid altogether the great cities and all places where men most do congregate, so that in those their effect is a negligible quantity. But in all quiet country places, among the woods and fields, upon the mountains or out at sea, nature-spirits are constantly present, and though they rarely show themselves, their influence is powerful and all-pervading, just as the scent of the violets fills the air though they are hidden modestly among the leaves.

192.   The nature-spirits constitute an evolution apart, quite distinct at this stage from that of humanity. We are familiar with the course taken by the Second Outpouring through the three elemental kingdoms, down to the mineral and upward through the vegetable and animal, to the attainment of individuality at the human level. We know that, after that individuality has been attained, the unfolding of humanity carries us gradually to the steps of the Path, and then onward and upward to Adeptship and to the glorious possibilities which lie beyond.

193.   This is our line of development, but we must not make the mistake of thinking of it as the only line. Even in this world of ours the divine life is pressing upwards through several streams, of which ours is but one, and numerically by no means the most important. It may help us to realise this if we remember that while humanity in its physical manifestation occupies only quite a small part of the surface of the earth, entities at a corresponding level on other lines of evolution not only crowd the earth far more thickly than man, but at the same time populate the enormous plains of the sea and the fields of the air.

194.   LINES OF EVOLUTION

195.   At this present stage we find these streams running parallel to one another, but for the time quite distinct. The nature-spirits, for example, neither have been nor ever will be members of a humanity such as ours, yet the indwelling life of the nature-spirit comes from the same Solar Deity as our own, and will return to Him just as ours will. The streams may be roughly considered as flowing side by side as far as the mineral level, but as soon as they turn to commence the upward arc of evolution, divergence begins to appear. This stage of immetalisation is naturally that at which life is most deeply immersed in physical matter but while some of the streams retain physical forms through several of the further stages of their development, making them, as they proceed, more and more an expression of the life within , there are other streams which at once begin to cast off the grosser, and for the rest of their unfolding

in this world use only bodies composed of etheric matter.

196.   One of these streams, for example, after finishing that stage of its evolvement in which it is part of the mineral monad, instead of passing into the vegetable kingdom takes for itself vehicles of etheric matter which inhabit the interior of the earth, living actually within the solid rock. It is difficult for many students to understand how it is possible for any kind of creature thus to inhabit the solid substance of the rock or the crust of the earth. Creatures possessing bodies of etheric matter find the substance of the rock no impediment to their motion or their vision. Indeed, for them physical matter in its solid state is their natural element and habitat - the only one to which they are accustomed and in which they feel at home. These vague lower lives in amorphous etheric vehicles are not readily comprehensible to us; but somehow they gradually evolve to a stage when, though still inhabiting the solid rock, they live close to the surface of the earth instead of in its depths, and the more developed of them are able occasionally to detach themselves from it for a short time.

197.   These creatures have sometimes been seen, and perhaps more frequently heard, in caves or mines, and they are often described in mediaeval literature as gnomes. The etheric matter of their bodies is not, under ordinary conditions, visible to physical eyes, so that when they are seen one of two things must take place; either they must materialise themselves by drawing round them a veil of physical matter, or else the spectator must experience an increase of sensitiveness which enables him to respond to the wave-lengths of the higher aethers, and to see what is not normally perceptible to him.

198.   The slight temporary exaltation of faculty necessary for this is not very uncommon nor difficult to achieve, and on the other hand materialisation is easy for creatures which are only just beyond the bounds of visibility; so that they would be seen far more frequently than they are, but for the rooted objection to the proximity of human beings which they share with all but the lowest types of nature-spirits. The next stage of their advancement brings them into the subdivision commonly called fairies - the type of nature-spirits which usually live upon the surface of the earth as we do, though still using only an etheric body; and after that they pass on through the air-spirits into the kingdom of the angels in a way which will be explained later.

199.   The life-wave which is at the mineral level is manifesting itself not only through the rocks which form the solid crust of the earth, but also through the waters of the ocean; and just as the former may pass through low etheric forms of life (at present unknown to man) in the interior of the earth, so the latter may pass through corresponding low etheric forms which have their dwelling in the depths of the sea. In this case also, the next stage or kingdom brings us into more definite though still etheric forms inhabiting the middle depths, and very rarely showing themselves at the surface. The third stage for them (corresponding to that of the fairies for the rock-spirits) is to join the enormous host of water-spirits which cover the vast plains of the ocean with their joyous life.

200.   Taking as they do bodies of etheric matter only, it will be seen that the entities following these lines of development miss altogether the vegetable and animal

kingdoms as well the human. There are, however, other types of nature-spirits which enter into both these kingdoms before they begin to diverge. In the ocean, for example, there is a stream of life which, after leaving the mineral level, touches the vegetable kingdom in the form of seaweeds, and then passes on, through the corals and the sponges and the huge cephalopods of the middle deeps, up into the great family of the fishes, and only after that joins the ranks of water-spirits.

201.   It will be seen that these retain the dense physical body as a vehicle up to a much higher level; and in the same way we notice that the fairies of the land are recruited not only from the ranks of the gnomes, but also from the less evolved strata of the animal kingdom, for we find a line of development which just touches the vegetable kingdom in the shape of minute fungoid growths, and then passes onward through bacteria and animalculae of various kinds, through the insects and reptiles up to the beautiful family of the birds, and only after many incarnations among these joins the still more joyous tribe of the fairies.

202.   Yet another stream diverges into etheric life at an intermediate point, for while it comes up through the vegetable kingdom in the shape of grasses and cereals, it turns aside thence into the animal kingdom and is conducted through the curious communities of the ants and bees, and then through a set of etheric creatures closely corresponding to the latter - those tiny humming-bird-like nature-spirits which are so continually seen hovering about flowers and plants, and play so large a part in the production of their manifold variations - their playfulness being often utilised in specialisation and in the helping of growth.

203.   It is necessary, however, to draw a careful distinction here, to avoid confusion. The little creatures that look after flowers may be divided into two great classes, though of course there are many varieties of each kind. The first class may properly be called elementals, for beautiful though they are, they are in reality only thought-forms, and therefore they are not really *living* creatures at all. Perhaps I should rather say that they are only temporarily living creatures, for though they are very active and busy during their little lives, they have no real evolving, reincarnating life in them, and when they have done their work, they just go to pieces and dissolve into the surrounding atmosphere, precisely as our own thought-forms do. They are the thought-forms of the Great Beings or angels who are in charge of the evolution of the vegetable kingdom.

204.   When one of these Great Ones has a new idea connected with one of the kinds of plants or flowers which are under his charge, he often creates a thought-form for the special purpose of carrying out that idea. It usually takes the form either of an etheric model of the flower itself or of a little creature which hangs round the plant or the flower all through the time that the buds are forming, and gradually builds them into the shape and colour of which the angel has thought. But as soon as the plant has fully grown, or the flower has opened, its work is over and its power is exhausted, and, as I have said, it just simply dissolves, because the will to do that piece of work was the only soul that it had.

205.   But there is quite another kind of little creature which is very frequently seen playing about with flowers, and this time it is a real nature-spirit. There are many

varieties of these also. One of the commonest forms is, as I have said, something very much like a tiny humming-bird, and it may often be seen buzzing round the flowers much in the same way as a humming-bird or a bee does. These beautiful little creatures will never become human, because they are not in the same line of evolution as we are. The life which is now animating them has come up through grasses and cereals, such as wheat and oats, when it was in the vegetable kingdom, and afterwards through ants and bees when it was in the animal kingdom. Now it has reached the level of these tiny nature-spirits, and its next stage will be to ensoul some of the beautiful fairies with etheric bodies who live upon the surface of the earth. Later on they will become salamanders or fire-spirits, and later still they will become sylphs, or air-spirits, having only astral bodies instead of etheric. Later still they will pass through the different stages of the great kingdom of the angels.

206.   OVERLAPPING

207.   In all cases of the transference of the life-wave from one kingdom to another great latitude is allowed for variation; there is a good deal of overlapping between the kingdoms. That is perhaps most clearly to be seen along our own line of evolution for we find that the life which has attained to the highest levels in the vegetable kingdom never passes into the lower part of the animal kingdom at all, but on the contrary joins it at a fairly advanced stage. Let me recall the example which I have already given; the life which has ensouled one of our great forest trees could never descend to animate a swarm of mosquitoes, nor even a family of rats or mice or such small deer; while these latter would be quite appropriate forms for that part of the life-wave which had left the vegetable kingdom at the level of the daisy or the dandelion.

208.   The ladder of evolution has to be climbed in all cases, but it seems as though the higher part of one kingdom lies to a large extent parallel with the lower part of that above it, so that it is possible for a transfer from one to the other to take place at different levels in different cases. That stream of life which enters the human kingdom avoids altogether the lowest stages of the animal kingdom; that is, the life which is presently to rise into humanity never manifests itself through the insects or the reptiles; in the past it did sometimes enter the animal kingdom at the level of the great antediluvian reptiles, but now it passes directly from the highest forms of the vegetable life into the mammalia. Similarly, when the most advanced domestic animal becomes individualised, he does not need to descend into the form of the absolutely primitive savage for his first human incarnation.

209.   The accompanying diagram shows some of these lines of development in a convenient tabular form, but it must not be considered as in any way exhaustive, as there are no doubt other lines which have not yet been observed, and there are certainly all kinds of variations and possibilities of crossing at different levels from one line to another; so that all we can do is to give a broad outline of the scheme.

210.   As will be seen from the diagram, at a later stage all the lines of evolution converge once more; at least to our dim sight there seems no distinction of glory among those Lofty Ones, though probably if we knew more we could make our table

more complete. At any rate we know that, much as humanity lies above the animal kingdom, so beyond and above humanity in its turn lies the great kingdom of the angels, and that to enter among the angels is one of the seven possibilities which the Adept finds opening before him. That same kingdom is also the next stage for the nature-spirit, but we have here another instance of the overlapping previously mentioned, for the Adept joins that kingdom at a high level, omitting altogether three of its stages, while the next step of progress for the highest type of nature-spirit is to become the lowest class of angel, thus beginning at the bottom of that particular ladder instead of stepping on to it half-way up.

211.   It is on joining the angel kingdom that the nature-spirit receives the divine Spark of the Third Outpouring, and thus attains individuality, just as the animal does when he passes into the human kingdom; and a further point of similarity is that just as the animal gains individualisation only through contact with humanity, so the nature-spirit gains it through contact with the angel - through becoming attached to him and working in order to please him, until at last he learns how to do angel's work himself.

212.   The more advanced nature-spirit is therefore not exactly an etheric or astral human being, for he is not yet an individual; yet he is much more than an etheric or astral animal, for his intellectual level is far higher than anything which we find in the animal kingdom, and is indeed quite equal along many lines to that of average humanity. On the other hand, some of the earlier varieties possess but a limited amount of intelligence, and seem to be about on an equality with the humming-birds or bees or butterflies which they so closely resemble. As we have seen from our diagram, this one name of nature-spirit covers a large segment of the arc of evolution, including stages corresponding to the whole of the vegetable and animal kingdoms, and to humanity up to almost the present level of our own race.

213.   Some of the lower types are not pleasing to the aesthetic sense; but that is true also of the lower kinds of reptiles and insects. There are undeveloped tribes whose tastes are coarse, and naturally their appearance corresponds to the stage of their evolution. The shapeless masses with huge red gaping mouths, which live upon the loathsome etheric emanations of blood and decaying flesh, are horrible both to the sight and to the feeling of any pure-minded person; so also are the rapacious red-brown crustacean creatures which hover over houses of ill-fame, and the savage octopus-like monsters which gloat over the orgies of the drunkard and revel in the fumes of alcohol. But even these harpies are not evil in themselves, though repulsive to man; and man would never come into contact with them unless he degraded himself to their level by becoming the slave of his lower passions.

214.   It is only nature-spirits of these and similar primitive and unpleasant kinds which voluntarily approach the average man. Others of the same sort, but a shade less material, enjoy the sensation of bathing in any specially coarse astral radiations, such as those produced by anger, avarice, cruelty, jealousy and hatred. People yielding themselves to such feelings can depend upon being constantly surrounded by these carrion crows of the astral world, who quiver in their ghastly glee as they jostle one another in eager anticipation of an outburst of passion, and in their blind, blundering way

do whatever they can to provoke or intensify it. It is difficult to believe that such horrors as these can belong to the same kingdom as the jocund spirits next to be described.

215.   FAIRIES

216.   The type best known to man is that of the fairies, the spirits who live normally upon the surface of the earth, though, since their bodies are of etheric matter, they can pass into the ground at will. Their forms are many and various, but most frequently human in shape and somewhat diminutive in size, usually with a grotesque exaggeration of some particular feature or limb. Etheric matter being plastic and readily moulded by the power of thought, they are able to assume almost any appearance at will, but they nevertheless have definite forms of their own, which they wear when they have no special object to serve by taking any other, and are therefore not exerting their will to produce a change of shape. They have also colours of their own, marking the difference between their tribes or species, just as the birds have differences of plumage.

217.   There are an immense number of subdivisions or races among them, and individuals of these sub-divisions vary in intelligence and disposition precisely as human beings do. Again like human beings, these divers races inhabit different countries, or sometimes different districts of the same country, and the members of one race have a general tendency to keep together, just as men of one nation do among ourselves. They are on the whole distributed much as are the other kingdoms of nature; like the birds, from whom some of them have been evolved, some varieties are peculiar to one country, others are common in one country and rare elsewhere, while others again are to be found almost anywhere. Again like the birds, it is broadly true that the most brilliantly coloured orders are to be found in tropical countries.

218.   NATIONAL TYPES

219.   The predominant types of the different parts of the world are usually clearly distinguishable and in a sense characteristic; or is it perhaps that their influence in the slow course of ages has moulded the men and animals and plants who lived near them, so that it is the nature-spirit who has set the fashion and the other kingdoms which have unconsciously followed it? For example, no contrast could well be more marked than that between the vivacious, rollicking, orange-and-purple or scarlet-and-gold mannikins who dance among the vineyards of Sicily and the almost wistful grey-and-green creatures who move so much more sedately amidst the oaks and the furze-covered heaths in Brittany, or the golden-brown "good people" who haunt the hill-sides of Scotland.

220.   In England the emerald-green variety is probably the commonest, and I have seen it also in the woods of France and Belgium, in far-away Massachusetts and on the banks of the Niagara River. The vast plains of the Dakotas are inhabited by a black-and-white kind which I have not seen elsewhere, and California rejoices in a lovely white-and-gold species which also appears to be unique.

221.   In Australia the most frequent type is a very distinctive creature of a wonderful

luminous skyblue colour; but there is a wide diversity between the etheric inhabitants of New South Wales or Victoria and those of tropical Northern Queensland. These latter approximate closely to those of the Dutch Indies. Java seems specially prolific in these graceful creatures, and the kinds most common there are two distinct types, both monochromatic - one indigo blue with faint metallic gleamings, and the other a study in all known shades of yellow - quaint, but wonderfully effective and attractive.

222.   A striking local variety is gaudily ringed with alternate bars of green and yellow, like a football jersey. This ringed type is possibly a race peculiar to that part of the world, for I saw red and yellow similarly arranged in the Malay Peninsula, and green and white on the other side of the Straits in Sumatra. That huge island also rejoices in the possession of a lovely pale heliotrope tribe which I have seen before only in the hills of Ceylon. Down in New Zealand their specialty is a deep blue shot with silver, while in the South Sea Islands one meets with a silvery-white variety which coruscates with all the colours of the rainbow, like a figure of mother-of-pearl.

223.   In India we find all sorts, from the delicate rose-and-pale-green, or paleblue-and-primrose of the hill country to the rich medley of gorgeously gleaming colours, almost barbaric in their intensity and profusion, which is characteristic of the plains. In some parts of that marvellous country I have seen the black-and-gold type which is more usually associated with the African desert, and also a species which resembles a statuette made out of a gleaming crimson metal, such as was the orichalcum of the Atlanteans.

224.   Somewhat akin to this last is a curious variety which looks as though cast out of bronze and burnished; it appears to make its home in the immediate neighbourhood of volcanic disturbances, since the only places in which it has been seen so far are the slopes of Vesuvius and Etna, the interior of Java, the Sandwich Islands, the Yellowstone Park in North America, and a certain part of the North Island of New Zealand. Several indications seem to point to the conclusion that this is a survival of a primitive type, and represents a sort of intermediate stage between the gnome and the fairy.

225.   In some cases, districts close together are found to be inhabited by quite different classes of nature-spirits; for example, as has already been mentioned, the emerald-green elves are common in Belgium, yet a hundred miles away in Holland hardly one of them is to be seen, and their place is taken by a sober-looking dark-purple species.

226.   ON A SACRED MOUNTAIN IN IRELAND

227.   A curious fact is that altitude above the sea-level seems to affect their distribution, those who belong to the mountains scarcely ever intermingling with those of the plains. I well remember, when climbing Slieve-namon, one of the traditionally sacred hills of Ireland, noticing the very definite lines of demarcation between the different types. The lower slopes, like the surrounding plains, were alive with the intensely active and mischievous little red-and-black race which swarms all over the south and west of Ireland, being especially attracted to the magnetic centres established nearly two thousand years ago by the magic-working priests of the old Milesian race to ensure and perpetuate their domination over the people by keeping them under the

48

influence of the great illusion. After half-an-hour's climbing, however, not one of these red-and-black gentry was to be seen, but instead the hillside was populous with the gentler blue-and-brown type which long ago owed special allegiance to the Tuatha-de-Danaan.

228.　　These also had their zone and their well-defined limits, and no nature-spirit of either type ever ventured to trespass upon the space round the summit, sacred to the great green angels who have watched there for more than two thousand years, guarding one of the centres of living force that link the past to the future of that mystic land of Erin. Taller far than the height of man, these giant forms, in colour like the first new leaves of spring, soft, luminous, shimmering, indescribable, look forth over the world with wondrous eyes that shine like stars, full of the peace of those who live in the eternal, waiting with the calm certainty of knowledge until the appointed time shall come. One realises very fully the power and importance of the hidden side of things when one beholds such a spectacle as that.

229.　　But indeed it is scarcely hidden, for the different influences are so strong and so distinct that anyone in the least sensitive cannot but be aware of them, and there is good reason for the local tradition that he who spends a night upon the summit of the mountain shall awaken in the morning either a poet or a madman. A poet, if he has proved capable of response to the exaltation of the whole being produced by the tremendous magnetism which has played upon him while he slept; a madman, if he was not strong enough to bear the strain.

230.　　FAIRY LIFE AND DEATH

231.　　The life-periods of the different subdivisions of nature-spirits vary greatly, some being quite short, others much longer than our human lifetime. The universal principle of reincarnation obtains in their existence also, though the conditions naturally make its working slightly different. They have no phenomena corresponding to what we mean by birth and growth; a fairy appears in his world full-sized, as an insect does. He lives his life, short or long, without any appearance of fatigue or need of rest, and without any perceptible signs of age as the years pass.

232.　　But at last there comes a time when his energy seems to have exhausted itself, when he becomes somewhat tired of life; and when that happens his body grows more and more diaphanous until he is left as an astral entity, to live for a time in that world among the air-spirits who represent the next stage of development for him. Through that astral life he fades back into his group-soul, in which he may have (if sufficiently advanced) a certain amount of conscious existence before the cyclic law acts upon the group-soul once more by arousing in it the desire for separation. When this happens, its pressure turns the stream of its energy outward once more, and that desire, acting upon the plastic astral and etheric matter, materialises a body of similar type, such as is suitable to be an expression of the development attained in that last life.

233.　　Birth and death, therefore, are much simpler for the nature-spirit than for us, and death is for him quite free from all thought of sorrow. Indeed, his whole life seems simpler - a joyous, irresponsible kind of existence, much such as a party of happy

49

children might lead among exceptionally favorable physical surroundings. There is no sex among nature-spirits, there is no disease, and there is no struggle for existence, so that they are exempt from the most fertile causes of human suffering. They have keen affections and are capable of forming close and lasting friendships, from which they derive profound and never-failing joy. Jealousy and anger are possible to them, but seem quickly to fade before the overwhelming delight in all the operations of nature which is their most prominent characteristic.

234.   THEIR PLEASURES

235.   They glory in the light and glow of the sunshine, but they dance with equal pleasure in the moonlight; they share and rejoice in the satisfaction of the thirsty earth and the flowers and the trees when they feel the level lances of the rain, but they play just as happily with the falling flakes of snow; they are content to float idly in the calm of a summer afternoon, yet they revel in the rushing of the wind. Not only do they admire, with an intensity that few of us can understand, the beauty of a flower or a tree, the delicacy of its colour or the grace of its form, but they take ardent interest and deep delight in all the processes of nature, in the flowing of sap, in the opening of buds, in the formation and falling of leaves. Naturally this characteristic is utilised by the Great Ones in charge of evolution, and nature-spirits are employed to assist in the blending of colours and the arrangement of variations. They pay much attention, too, to bird and insect life, to the hatching of the egg and to the opening of the chrysalis, and they watch with jocund eye the play of lambs and fawns, of leverets and squirrels.

236.   Another inestimable advantage that an etheric evolution possesses over one which touches the denser physical is that the necessity of eating is avoided. The body of the fairy absorbs such nourishment as it needs, without trouble and without stint, from the aether which of necessity always surrounds it; or rather, it is not, strictly speaking, that nourishment is absorbed, but rather that a change of particles is constantly taking place, those which have been drained of their vitality being cast out and others which are full of it being drawn in to replace them.

237.   Though they do not eat, nature-spirits obtain from the fragrance of flowers a pleasure analogous to that which men derive from the taste of food. The aroma is more to them than a mere question of smell or taste, for they bathe themselves in it so that it interpenetrates their bodies and reaches every particle simultaneously.

238.   What takes for them the place of a nervous system is far more delicate than ours, and sensitive to many vibrations which pass all unperceived by our grosser senses, and so they find what corresponds to a scent in many plants and minerals that have no scent for us.

239.   Their bodies have no more internal structure than a wreath of mist, so that they cannot be torn asunder or injured, and neither heat nor cold has any painful effect upon them. Indeed, there is one type whose members seem to enjoy above all things to bathe themselves in fire; they rush from all sides to any great conflagration and fly upward with the flames again and again in wild delight, just as a boy flies again and again down a toboggan-slide. These are the spirits of the fire, the salamanders of

mediaeval literature. Bodily pain can come to the nature-spirit only from an unpleasant or inharmonious emanation or vibration, but his power of rapid locomotion enables him easily to avoid these. So far as can be observed he is entirely free from the curse of fear, which plays so serious a part in the animal life which, along our line of evolution, corresponds to the level of the fairies.

240.   THE ROMANCES OF FAIRYLAND

241.   The fairy has an enviably fertile imagination, and it is a great part of his daily play with his fellows to construct for them by its means all kinds of impossible surroundings and romantic situations. He is like a child telling stories to his playmates, but with this advantage over the child that, since the playmates can see both etheric and lower astral matter, the forms built by his vivid thought are plainly visible to them as his tale proceeds.

242.   No doubt many of his narrations would to us seem childish and oddly limited in scope, because such intelligence as the elf possesses works in directions so different from our own, but to him they are intensely real and a source of never-ending delight. The fairy who develops unusual talent in fiction wins great affection and honour from the rest, and gathers round him a permanent audience or following. When some human being chances to catch a glimpse of such a group, he usually imports into his account of it preconceptions derived from his own conditions, and takes the leader for a fairy king or queen, according to the form which that leader may for the moment happen to prefer. In reality the realm of nature-spirits needs no kind of government except the general supervision which is exercised over it, probably unconsciously to all but its higher members, by the Devarajas and their subordinates.

243.   THEIR ATTITUDE TOWARDS MAN

244.   Most nature-spirits dislike and avoid mankind, and we cannot wonder at it. To them man appears a ravaging demon, destroying and spoiling wherever he goes. He wantonly kills, often with awful tortures, all the beautiful creatures that they love to watch; he cuts down the trees, he tramples the grass, he plucks the flowers and casts them carelessly aside to die; he replaces all the lovely wild life of nature with his hideous bricks and mortar, and the fragrance of the flowers with the mephitic vapours of his chemicals and the all-polluting smoke of his factories. Can we think it strange that the fairies should regard us with horror, and shrink away from us as we shrink from a poisonous reptile?

245.   Not only do we thus bring devastation to all that they hold most dear, but most of our habits and emanations are distasteful to them; we poison the sweet air for them (some of us) with loathsome fumes of alcohol and tobacco; our restless, ill-regulated desires and passions set up a constant rush of astral currents which disturbs and annoys them, and gives them the same feeling of disgust which we should have if a bucket of filthy water were emptied over us. For them to be near the average man is to live in a perpetual hurricane - a hurricane that has blown over a cesspool. They are not great angels, with the perfect knowledge that brings perfect patience; they are just

51

happy and on the whole well-disposed children - hardly even that, many of them, but more like exceptionally intelligent kittens; again, I say, can we wonder, when we thus habitually outrage their best and highest feelings, that they should dislike us, distrust us and avoid us?

246.　　　There are instances on record where, by some more than ordinarily unwarranted intrusion or annoyance on the part of man, they have been provoked into direct retaliation and have shown distinct malice. It speaks well for their kingdom as a whole that even under such unendurable provocation such cases are rare, and their more usual method of trying to repel an intruder is by playing tricks upon him, childish and mischievous often, but not seriously harmful. They take an impish delight in misleading or deceiving him, in causing him to lose his way across a moor, in keeping him walking round and round in a circle all night when he believes he is going straight on, or in making him think that he sees palaces and castles where no such structures really exist. Many a story illustrative of this curious characteristic of the fairies may be found among the village gossip of the peasantry in almost any lonely mountainous district.

247.　　GLAMOUR

248.　　　They are greatly assisted in their tricks by the wonderful power which they possess of casting a glamour over those who yield themselves to their influence, so that such victims for the time see and hear only what these fairies impress upon them, exactly as the mesmerised subject sees, hears, feels and believes whatever the magnetiser wishes. The nature-spirits, however, have not the mesmerist's power of dominating the human will, except in the case of quite unusually weak-minded people, or of those who allow themselves to fall into such a condition of helpless terror that their will is temporarily in abeyance.

249.　　　The fairies cannot go beyond deception of the senses, but of that they are undoubted masters, and cases are not wanting in which they cast their glamour over a considerable number of people at once. It is by invoking their aid in the exercise of this peculiar power that some of the most marvellous feats of the Indian jugglers are performed, such as the celebrated basket trick, or that other in which a rope is thrown up towards the sky and remains rigid without support while the juggler climbs up it and disappears. The entire audience is in fact hallucinated, and the people are made to imagine that they see and hear a whole series of events which have not really occurred at all.

250.　　　The power of glamour is simply that of making a clear, strong mental image, and then projecting that into the mind of another. To most men this would seem wellnigh impossible, because they have never made any such attempt in their lives, and have no notion how to set about it. The mind of the fairy has not the width or the range of the man's, but it is thoroughly well accustomed to this work of making images and impressing them on others, since it is one of the principal occupations of the creature's daily life.

251.　　　It is not remarkable that with such constant practice he should become expert at the business, and it is still further simplified for him when, as in the case of the

52

Indian tricks, exactly the same image has to be produced over and over again hundreds of times, until every detail shapes itself without effort as the result of unconscious habit. In trying to understand exactly how this is done, we must bear in mind that a mental image is a very real thing - a definite construction in mental matter, as has been explained in *Thought-Forms* (p.37); and we must also remember that the line of communication between the mind and the dense physical brain passes through the astral and etheric counterparts of that brain, and that the line may be tapped and an impression introduced at any of these points.

252.   Certain of the nature-spirits not infrequently exercise their talent for mimicry and mischief by appearing at spiritualistic séances held for physical phenomena. Anyone who has been in the habit of attending on such occasions will recollect instances of practical joking and silly though usually good-natured horse-play; these almost always indicate the presence of some of these impish creatures, though they are sometimes due to the arrival of dead men who were senseless enough during earth-life to consider such inanities amusing, and have not learnt wisdom since their death.

253.   INSTANCES OF FRIENDSHIP

254.   On the other hand there are instances in which some nature-spirits have made friends with individual human beings and offered them such assistance as lay in their power, as in the well known stories told of Scotch brownies or of the fire-lighting fairies of spiritualistic literature; and it is on record that on rare occasions certain favoured men have been admitted to witness elfin revels and share for a time the elfin life. It is said that wild animals will approach with confidence some Indian yogis, recognising them as friends to all living creatures; similarly elves will gather round one who has entered upon the Path of Holiness, finding his emanations less stormy and more agreeable than those of the man whose mind is still fixed upon worldly matters.

255.   Occasionally, fairies have been known to attach themselves to little children, and develop a strong attachment for them, especially for such as are dreamy and imaginative, since they are able to see and delight in the thought-forms with which such a child surrounds himself. There have even been cases in which such creatures took a fancy to some unusually attractive baby, and made an attempt to carry it away into their own haunts - their intention being to save it from what seems to them the horrible fate of growing up into the average human being! Vague traditions of such attempts account for part of the folk-lore stories about changelings, though there is also another reason for them to which we shall refer later.

256.   There have been times - more often in the past than in the present - when a certain class of these entities, roughly corresponding to humanity in size and appearance, made it a practice frequently to materialise, to make for themselves temporary but definite physical bodies, and by that means to enter into undesirable relations with such men and women as chose to put themselves in their way. From this fact, perhaps, come some of the stories of fauns and satyrs in the classical period; though those sometimes also refer to quite a different sub-human evolution.

257.   WATER-SPIRITS

258.   Abundant as are the fairies of the earth's surface almost anywhere away from the haunts of man, they are far outnumbered by the water-spirits - the fairies of the surface of the sea. There is just as much variety here as on land. The nature-spirits of the Pacific differ from those of the Atlantic, and those of the Mediterranean are quite distinct from either; the types that revel in the indescribably glorious blue of tropical oceans are far apart from those that dash through the foam of our cold grey northern seas. Dissimilar again are the spirits of the lake, the river and the waterfall, for they have many more points in common with the land fairies than have the nereids of the open sea.

259.   These, like their brothers of the land, are of all shapes, but perhaps most frequently imitate the human. Broadly speaking, they tend to take larger forms than the elves of the woods and the hills; the majority of the latter are diminutive, while the sea-spirit who copies man usually adopts his size as well as his shape. In order to avoid misunderstanding, it is necessary constantly to insist upon the protean character of all these forms; any of these creatures, whether of land or sea or air, can make himself temporarily larger or smaller at will, or can assume whatever shape he chooses.

260.   There is theoretically no restriction upon this power, but in practice it has its limits, though they are wide. A fairy who is naturally twelve inches in height can expand himself to the proportions of a man of six feet, but the effort would be a considerable strain, and could not be maintained for more than a few minutes. In order to take a form other than his own, he must be able to conceive it clearly, and he can hold the shape only while his mind is fixed upon it; as soon as his thought wanders he will at once begin to resume his natural appearance.

261.   Though etheric matter can readily be moulded by the power of thought, it naturally does not obey it as instantaneously as does astral matter; we might say that mental matter changes actually *with* the thought, and astral matter so quickly after it that the ordinary observer can scarcely note any difference; but with etheric matter one's vision can follow the growth or diminution without difficulty. A sylph, whose body is of astral matter, *flashes* from one shape into another; a fairy, who is etheric, swells or decreases quickly but *not* instantaneously.

262.   Few of the land-spirits are gigantic in size, while such stature seems quite common out at sea. The creatures of the land frequently weave from their fancies scraps of human clothing, and show themselves with quaint caps or baldrics or jerkins; but I have never seen any such appearance among the inhabitants of the sea. Nearly all these surface water-spirits seem to possess the power of raising themselves out of their proper element and floating in or flying through the air for a short distance; they delight in playing amidst the dashing foam or riding in upon the breakers. They are less pronounced in their avoidance of man than their brethren on land - perhaps because man has so much less opportunity of interfering with them. They do not descend to any great depth below the surface - never, at any rate, beyond the reach of light; so that there is always a considerable space between their realm and the domain of the far less

evolved creatures of the middle deeps

263.   FRESH-WATER FAIRIES

264.   Some very beautiful species inhabit inland waters where man has not yet rendered the conditions impossible for them. Naturally enough, the filth and the chemicals with which water is polluted near any large town are disgusting to them; but they have apparently no objection to the water-wheel in a quiet country nook, for they may sometimes be seen disporting themselves in a mill-race. They seem specially to delight in falling water, just as their brothers of the sea revel in the breaking of foam; for the pleasure which it gives them they will sometimes even dare a nearer approach than usual to the hated presence of man. At Niagara, for example, there are almost always some still to be seen in the summer, though they generally keep well out towards the centre of the Falls and the Rapids. Like birds of passage, in winter they abandon those northern waters, which are frozen over for many months, and seek a temporary home in more genial climes. A short frost they do not seem to mind; the mere cold has apparently little or no effect upon them, but they dislike the disturbance of their ordinary conditions. Some of those who commonly inhabit rivers transfer themselves to the sea when their streams freeze; to others salt water seems distasteful, and they prefer to migrate considerable distances rather than take refuge in the ocean.

265.   An interesting variety of the fairies of the water are the cloud-spirits - entities whose life is spent almost entirely among those "waters which be above the firmament". They should perhaps be classified as intermediate between the spirits of the water and those of the air; their bodies are of etheric matter, as are the former, but they are capable of remaining away from the water for comparatively long periods. Their forms are often huge and loosely knit; they seem near of kin to some of the fresh-water types, yet they are quite willing to dip for a time into the sea when the clouds which are their favourite habitat disappear. They dwell in the luminous silence of cloudland, and their favourite pastime is to mould their clouds into strange, fantastic shapes or to arrange them in the serried ranks which we call a mackerel sky.

266.   SYLPHS

267.   We come now to the consideration of the highest type in the kingdom of the nature-spirits - the stage at which the lines of development both of the land and sea creatures converge - the sylphs, or spirits of the air. These entities are definitely raised above all the other varieties of which we have been speaking, by the fact that they have shaken themselves free from the encumbrance of physical matter, the astral body being now their lowest vehicle. Their intelligence is much higher than that of the etheric species, and quite equal to that of the average man; but they have not yet attained a permanent reincarnating individuality. Just because they are so much more evolved, before breaking away from the group-soul they can understand much more about life than an animal can, and so it often happens that they know that they lack individuality and are intensely eager to gain it. That is the truth that lies at the back of all the widely-spread traditions of the yearning of the nature-spirit to obtain an immortal soul.

268.   The normal method for them to attain this is by association with and love for members of the next stage above them - the astral angels. A domestic animal, such as the dog or the cat, advances through the development of his intelligence and his affection which is the result of his close relationship with his master. Not only does his love for that master cause him to make determined efforts to understand him, but the vibrations of the master's mind-body, constantly playing upon his rudimentary mind, gradually awaken it into greater and greater activity; and in the same way his affection for him arouses an ever-deepening feeling in return. The man may or may not definitely set himself to teach the animal something; in any case, even without any direct effort, the intimate connection between them helps the evolvement of the lower. Eventually the development of such an animal rises to the level which will allow him to receive the Third Outpouring, and thus he becomes an individual, and breaks away from his group-soul.

269.   Now all this is also exactly what happens between the astral angel and the air-spirit, except that by them the scheme is usually carried out in a much more intelligent and effective manner. Not one man in a thousand thinks or knows anything about the real evolution of his dog or cat; still less does the animal comprehend the possibility that lies before him. But the angel clearly understands the plan of nature, and in many cases the nature-spirit also knows what he needs, and works intelligently towards its attainment. So each of these astral angels usually has several sylphs attached to him, frequently definitely learning from him and being trained by him, but at any rate basking in the play of his intellect and returning his affection. Very many of these angels are employed as agents by the Devarajas in their duty of the distributing of karma; and thus it comes that the air-spirits are often sub-agents in that work, and no doubt acquire much valuable knowledge while executing the tasks assigned to them.

270.   The Adept knows how to make use of the services of the nature-spirits when he requires them, and there are many pieces of business which he is able to entrust to them. In the issue of *Broad Views* for February, 1907, there appeared an admirable account of the ingenious manner in which a nature-spirit executed a commission given to him in this way.

271.   He was instructed to amuse an invalid who was suffering from an attack of influenza, and for five days he kept up an almost continuous entertainment of strange and interesting visions, his efforts being crowned with the most gratifying success, for the sufferer wrote that his ministrations "had the happy effect of turning what under ordinary circumstances would have been days of unutterable weariness and discomfort into a most wonderfully interesting experience".

272.   He showed a bewildering variety of pictures, moving masses of rock, seen not from the outside but from the inside, so that faces of creatures of various sorts appeared in them. He also exhibited mountains, forests and avenues, and sometimes great masses of architecture, portions of Corinthian columns, bits of statuary, and great arched roofs, often also the most wonderful flowers and palms, waving to and fro as if in a gentle breeze. Sometimes he seems to have taken the physical objects in the bedroom and woven them into a kind of magic transformation scene. One might

indeed surmise, from the curious nature of the entertainment offered, the particular type to which belonged the nature-spirit who was employed in this charitable work.

273.   The Oriental magician occasionally endeavours to obtain the assistance of the higher nature-spirits in his performances, but the enterprise is not without its dangers. He must adopt either invocation or evocation - that is, he must either attract their attention as a suppliant and make some kind of bargain with them, or he must try to set in motion influences which will compel their obedience - an attempt which, if it fails, will arouse a determined hostility that is exceedingly likely to result in his premature extinction, or at the least will put him in an extremely ridiculous and unpleasant position.

274.   Of these air-spirits, as of the lower fairies, there are many varieties, differing in power, in intelligence and in habits as well as in appearance. They are naturally less restricted to locality than the other kinds which we have described, though like the others they seem to recognise the limits of certain zones of elevation, some kinds always floating near the surface of the earth, while others scarcely ever approach it. As a general rule they share the common dislike to the neighbourhood of man and his restless desires, but there are occasions when they are willing to endure this for the sake of amusement or flattery.

275.   THEIR AMUSEMENT ~ view

276.   They extract immense entertainment sometimes out of the sport of ensouling thought-forms of various kinds. An author in writing a novel, for example, naturally makes strong thought-forms of all his characters, and moves them about his miniature stage like marionettes; but sometimes a party of jocund nature-spirits will seize upon his forms, and play out the drama upon a scheme improvised on the spur of the moment, so that the dismayed novelist feels that his puppets have somehow got out of hand and developed a will of their own.

277.   The love of mischief which is so marked a characteristic of some of the fairies persists to a certain extent among at least the lower types of the air-spirits, so that their impersonations are occasionally of a less innocent order. People whose evil karma has brought them under the domination of Calvinistic theology, but who have not yet the intelligence or the faith to cast aside its blasphemous doctrines, sometimes in their fear make awful thought-forms of the imaginary devil to which their superstition gives such a prominent role in the universe; and I regret to say that certain impish nature-spirits are quite unable to resist the temptation of masquerading in these terrible forms, and think it a great joke to flourish horns, to lash a forked tail, and to breathe out flames as they rush about. To anyone who understands the nature of these pantomime demons no harm is done; but now and then nervous children happen to be impressionable enough to catch a glimpse of such things, and if they have not been wisely taught, great terror is the result.

278.   It is only fair to the nature-spirit to remember that, as he himself is incapable of fear, he does not in the least understand the gravity of this result, and probably considers the child's fright as simulated, and as part of the game. We can

hardly blame the nature-spirit for the fact that we permit our children to be bound by the chains of a grovelling superstition, and neglect to impress upon them the grand fundamental fact that God is love and that perfect love casteth out all fear. If our air-spirit occasionally thus terrifies the ill-instructed living child, it must on the other hand be set to his credit that he constantly affords the keenest pleasure to thousands of children who are what we call ` dead,' for to play with them and to entertain them in a hundred different ways is one of his happiest occupations.

279.   The air-spirits have discovered the opportunity afforded to them by the spiritualistic séance, and some of them become habitual attendants, usually under some such name as Daisy or Sunflower. They are quite capable of giving a very interesting séance, for they naturally know a good deal about astral life and its possibilities. They will readily answer questions, truly enough as far as their knowledge goes, and with, at any rate, an appearance of profundity when the subject is somewhat beyond them. They can produce raps, tilts and lights without difficulty, and are quite prepared to deliver whatever messages they may see to be desired - not in the least meaning in this way harm or deceit, but naively rejoicing in their success in playing the part, and in the wealth of awe-stricken devotion and affection lavished upon them as "dear spirits" and "angel helpers". They learn to share the delight of the sitters, and feel themselves to be doing a good work in thus bringing comfort to the afflicted.

280.   Living astrally as they do, the fourth dimension is a commonplace fact of their existence, and this makes quite simple for them many little tricks which to us appear wonderful, such as the removal of articles from a locked box or the apport of flowers into a closed room. The desires and emotions of the sitters lie open before them, they quickly acquire facility in reading any but abstract thoughts, and the management of a materialisation is quite within their power when adequate material is provided. It will therefore be seen that without any exterior assistance they are competent to provide a varied and satisfactory evening's entertainment, and there is no doubt that they have often done so. I am not for a moment suggesting that nature-spirits are the only entities which operate at séances; the manifesting 'spirit' is often exactly what he claims to be, but it is also true that he is often nothing of the kind, and the average sitter has absolutely no means of distinguishing between the genuine article and the imitation.

281.   AN ABNORMAL DEVELOPMENT

282.   As has already been said, the normal line of advancement for the nature-spirit is to attain individuality by association with an angel, but there have been individuals who have departed from that rule. The intensity of affection felt by the sylph for the angel is the principal factor in the great change, and the abnormal cases are those in which that affection has been fixed upon a human being instead. This involves so complete a reversal of the common attitude of these beings towards humanity that its occurrence is naturally rare; but when it happens, and when the love is strong enough to lead to individualisation, it detaches the nature-spirit from his own line of evolution and brings him over into ours, so that the newly developed ego will incarnate not as an angel but as a man.

283.   Some tradition of this possibility lies at the back of all the stories in which a non-human spirit falls in love with a man, and yearns with a great longing to obtain an immortal soul in order to be able to spend eternity with him. Upon attaining his incarnation such a spirit usually makes a man of very curious type - affectionate and emotional but wayward, strangely primitive in certain ways, and utterly without any sense of responsibility.

284.   It has sometimes happened that a sylph who was thus strongly attracted to a man or a woman, but just fell short of the intensity of affection necessary to ensure individualisation, has made an effort to obtain a forcible entrance into human evolution by taking possession of the body of a dying baby just as its original owner left it. The child would seem to recover, to be snatched back from the very jaws of death, but would be likely to appear much changed in disposition, and probably peevish and irritable in consequence of the unaccustomed constraint of a dense physical body.

285.   If the sylph were able to adapt himself to the body, there would be nothing to prevent him from retaining it through a life of the ordinary length. If during that life he succeeded in developing affection sufficiently ardent to sever his connection with his group-soul he would thereafter reincarnate as a human being in the usual way; if not, he would fall back at its conclusion into his own line of evolution. It will be seen that in these facts we have the truth which underlies the widely disseminated tradition of changelings, which is found in all the countries of north-western Europe, in China, and also (it is said) among the natives of the Pacific slope of North America.

286.   THE ADVANTAGE OF STUDYING THEM

287.   The kingdom of the nature-spirits is a most interesting field of study, to which but little attention has been paid. Though they are often mentioned in occult literature, I am not aware that any attempt has yet been made to classify them in scientific fashion. This vast realm of nature still needs its Cuvier or its Linnaeus; but perhaps when we have plenty of trained investigators we may hope that one of them will take upon himself this role, and furnish us as his life's work with a complete and detailed natural history of these delightful creatures.

288.   It will be no waste of labour, no unworthy study. It is useful for us to understand these beings, not solely nor even chiefly because of the influence they exert upon us, but because the comprehension of a line of evolution so different from our own broadens our minds and helps us to recognise that the world does not exist for us alone, and that our point of view is neither the only one nor the most important. Foreign travel has the same effect in a minor degree, for it demonstrates to every unprejudiced man that races in every respect as good as his own may yet differ widely from it in a hundred ways. In the study of the nature-spirits we find the same idea carried much further; here is a kingdom radically dissimilar - without sex, free from fear, ignorant of what is meant by the struggle for existence - yet the eventual result of its unfoldment is in every respect equal to that attained by following our own line. To learn this may help us to see a little more of the many-sidedness of the Solar Deity, and so may teach us modesty and charity as well as liberality of thought.

CHAPTER VII   BY CENTRES OF MAGNETISM

291.   We all recognise to some extent that unusual surroundings may produce special effects; we speak of certain buildings or landscapes as gloomy and depressing; we understand that there is something saddening and repellent about a prison, something devotional about a church, and so on. Most people never trouble to think why this should be so, or if they do for a moment turn their attention to the matter, they dismiss it as an instance of the association of ideas.

292.   Probably it is that, but it is also much more than that, and if we examine into its rationale we shall find that it operates in many cases where we have never suspected its influence, and that a knowledge of it may be of practical use in everyday life. A study of the finer forces of nature will show us not only that every living being is radiating a complex set of definite influences upon those about him, but also that this is true to a lesser degree and in a simpler manner of inanimate objects.

293.   OUR GREAT CATHEDRALS

294.   We know that wood and iron and stone have their own respective characteristic radiations, but the point to be emphasised just now is that they are all capable of absorbing human influence, and then pouring it out again. What is the origin of that feeling of devotion, of reverential awe, which so permeates some of our great cathedrals that even the most hardened Cook's tourist cannot entirely escape it? It is due not only to the historical associations, not only to the remembrance of the fact that for centuries men have met here for praise and prayer, but far more to that fact itself, and to the conditions which it has produced in the substance of the fabric.

295.   To understand this we must first of all remember the circumstances under which those buildings were erected. A modern brick church, run up by contract in the shortest possible time, has indeed but little sanctity about it; but in mediaeval days faith was greater, and the influence of the outer world less prominent. In very truth men prayed as they built our great cathedrals, and laid every stone as though it had been an offering upon an altar. When this was the spirit of the work, every such stone became a veritable talisman charged with the reverence and devotion of the builder, and capable of radiating those same waves of sensation upon others, so as to stir in them similar feelings. The crowds who came afterwards to worship at the shrine not only felt these radiations, but themselves strengthened them in turn by the reaction of their own feelings.

296.   Still more is this true of the interior decorations of the church. Every touch of the brush in the colouring of a triptych, every stroke of the chisel in the sculpture of a statue, was a direct offering to God. Thus the completed work of art is surrounded by an atmosphere of reverence and love, and it distinctly sheds these qualities upon the worshippers. All of them, rich and poor alike, feel something of this effect, even

though many of them may be too ignorant to receive the added stimulus which its artistic excellence gives to those who are able to appreciate it and to perceive all that it means.

297.   The sunlight streaming through the splendid stained glass of those mediaeval windows brings with it a glory that is not all of the physical world, for the clever workmen who built up that marvellous mosaic did so for the love of God and the glory of His saints, and so each fragment of glass is a talisman also. Remembering always how the power conveyed into the statue or picture by the fervour of the original artist has been perpetually reinforced through the ages by the devotion of successive generations of worshippers, we come to understand the inner meaning of the great influence which undoubtedly does radiate from such objects as have been regarded as sacred for centuries.

298.   Such a devotional effect as is described in connection with a picture or a statue may be entirely apart from its value as a work of art. The bambino at the Ara Coeli at Rome is a supremely inartistic object, yet it has unquestionably considerable power in evoking devotional feeling among the masses that crowd to see it. If it were really a work of art, that fact would add but little to its influence over most of them, though of course it would in that case produce an additional and totally different effect upon another class of persons to whom now it does not in the least appeal.

299.   From these considerations it is evident that these various ecclesiastical properties, such as statues, pictures and other decorations, have a real value in the effect which they produce upon the worshippers, and the fact that they thus have a distinct power, which so many people can feel, probably accounts for the intense hatred felt for them by the savage fanatics who miscalled themselves puritans. They realised that the power which stood behind the Church worked to a great extent through these objects as its channels, and though their loathing for all higher influences was considerably tempered by fear, they yet felt that if they could break up these centres of magnetism, that would to a certain extent cut off the connection. And so in their revolt against all that was good and beautiful, they did all the harm that they could - almost as much perhaps as those earlier so-called Christians who, through sheer ignorance, ground up the most lovely Grecian statues to furnish lime to build their wretched hovels.

300.   In all these splendid mediaeval buildings the sentiment of devotion absolutely and literally exudes from the walls, because for centuries devotional thought-forms have been created in them by successive generations. In strong contrast to this is the atmosphere of criticism and disputation which may be felt by any sensitive person in the meeting-houses of some of the sects. In many a conventicle in Scotland and in Holland this feeling stands out with startling prominence, so as to give the impression that the great majority of the so-called worshippers have had no thought of worship or devotion at all, but only of the most sanctimonious self-righteousness, and of burning anxiety to discover some doctrinal flaw in the wearisome sermon of their unfortunate minister.

301.   An absolutely new church does not at first produce any of these effects; for in these days workmen build a church with the same lack of enthusiasm as a factory. As soon as the bishop consecrates it, a decided influence is set up as the

effect of that ceremony, but the consideration of that belongs to another chapter of our work. A few years of use will charge the walls very effectively, and a much shorter period than that will produce the result in a church where the sacrament is reserved, or where perpetual adoration is offered. The Roman Catholic or Ritualistic church soon becomes thoroughly affected, but the meeting-houses of some of the dissenting sects which do not make a special point of devotion, often produce for a long time an influence scarcely distinguishable from that which is to be felt in an ordinary lecture hall. A fine type of devotional influence is often to be found in the chapel of a convent or monastery, though again the type differs greatly according to the objects which the monks or the nuns set before themselves.

302.   TEMPLES

303.   I have been taking Christian fanes as an example, because they are those which are most familiar to me - which will also be most familiar to the majority of my readers; also perhaps because Christianity is the religion which has made a special point of devotion, and has, more than any other, arranged for the simultaneous expression of it in special buildings erected for that purpose. Among Hindus the Vaishnavite has a devotion quite as profound as that of any Christian, though unfortunately it is often tainted by expectation of favours to be given in return. But the Hindu has no idea of anything like combined worship. Though on great festivals enormous crowds attend the temples, each person makes his little prayer or goes through his little ceremony for himself, and so he misses the enormous additional effect which is produced by simultaneous action.

304.   Regarded solely from the point of view of charging the walls of the temple with devotional influence, this plan differs from the other in a way that we may perhaps understand by taking a physical illustration of a number of sailors pulling at a rope. We know that, when that is being done, a sort of chant is generally used in order to ensure that the men shall apply their strength at exactly the same moment; and in that way a much more effective pull is produced than would be achieved if each man put out exactly the same strength, but applied it just when he felt that he could, and without any relation to the work of the others.

305.   Nevertheless as the years roll by there comes to be a strong feeling in a Vaishnavite temple - as strong perhaps as that of the Christians, though quite different in kind. Different again in quite another way is the impression produced in the great temples dedicated to Shiva. In such a shrine as that at Madura, for example, an exceedingly powerful influence radiates from the holy of holies. It is surrounded by a strong feeling of reverential awe, almost of fear, and this so deeply tinges the devotion of the crowds who come to worship that the very aura of the place is changed by it.

306.   Completely different again is the impression which surrounds a Buddhist temple. Of fear we have there absolutely no trace whatever. We have perhaps less of direct devotion, for to a large extent devotion is replaced by gratitude. The prominent radiation is always one of joyfulness and love - an utter absence of anything dark or stern.

307.   Another complete contrast is represented by the Muhammadan mosque; devotion of a sort is present there also, but it is distinctly a militant devotion, and the particular impression that it gives one is that of a fiery determination. One feels that this population's comprehension of their creed may be limited, but there is no question whatever as to their dogged determination to hold by it.

308.   The Jewish synagogue again is like none of the others, but has a feeling which is quite distinct, and curiously dual - exceptionally materialistic on one side, and on the other full of a strong, pathetic longing for the return of vanished glories.

309.   SITES AND RELICS

310.   A partial recognition of another facet of the facts which we have been mentioning accounts for the choice of the site of many religious edifices. A church or a temple is frequently erected to commemorate the life and death of some saint, and in the first instance such a fane is built upon a spot which has some special connection with him. It may be the place where he died, the spot where he was born, or where some important event of his life occurred.

311.   The Church of the Nativity at Bethlehem and that of the Crucifixion at Jerusalem are instances of this, as is also the great Stupa at Buddhagaya where the Lord Gautama attained His Buddhahood, or the temple of the ` Bishanpad' where it is supposed that Vishnu left His foot-mark. All such shrines are erected not so much from an historical sense which wishes to indicate for the benefit of posterity the exact spot where an important event happened, as with the idea that that spot is especially blessed, especially charged with a magnetism which will remain through the ages, and will radiate upon and benefit those who bring themselves within the radius of its influence. Nor is this universal idea without adequate foundation.

312.   The spot at which the Lord BUDDHA gained the step which gives Him that august title is charged with a magnetism which causes it to glow forth like a sun for anyone who has clairvoyant vision. It is calculated to produce the strongest possible magnetic effect on anyone who is naturally sensitive to such influence, or who deliberately makes himself temporarily sensitive to such influence by putting himself in an attitude of heartfelt devotion.

313.   In a recent article on Buddhagaya in *The Lotus Journal* Alcyone wrote:

314.   When I sat quietly under the tree for awhile with Mrs. Besant, I was able to see the Lord BUDDHA, as He had looked when He sat there. Indeed, the record of His meditation is still so strong that it needs only a little clairvoyance to see Him even now. I had the advantage of having met Him in that life in 588 B.C., and become one of His followers, so that it was easier for me to see Him again in this present life. But I think almost anyone who is a little sensitive would see Him at Buddhagaya by staying quite quiet for a little time because the air is full of His influence, and even now there are always great Devas bathing in the magnetism, and guarding the place.

315.   Other churches, temples or dagobas are sanctified by the possession of relics of some Great One, and here again the connection of ideas is obvious. It is customary for those who are ignorant of these matters to ridicule the idea of paying reverence

to the fragment of bone which once belonged to a saint; but though reverence paid to the bone may be out of place, the influence radiating from that bone may nevertheless be quite a real thing, and well worthy of serious attention. That the trade in relics has led, all the world over, to fraud on the one hand and blind credulity on the other, is not a thing to be disputed; but that by no means alters the fact that a genuine relic may be a valuable thing. Whatever has been part of the physical body of a Great One, or even of the garments which have clothed that physical body, is impregnated with his personal magnetism. That means that it is charged with the powerful waves of thought and feeling which used to issue from him, just as an electrical battery may be charged.

316.   Such force as it possesses is intensified and perpetuated by the thought-waves poured upon it as the years roll by, by the faith and devotion of the crowds who visit the shrine. This when the relic is genuine; but most relics are not genuine. Even then, though they have no initial strength of their own, they acquire much influence as time goes on, so that even a false relic is by no means without effect. Therefore anyone putting himself into a receptive attitude, and coming into the immediate neighbourhood of a relic, will receive into himself its strong vibrations, and soon will be more or less attuned to them. Since those vibrations are unquestionably better and stronger than any which he is likely to generate on his own account, this is a good thing for him. For the time being it lifts him on to a higher level, it opens a higher world to him; and though the effect is only temporary, this cannot but be good for him - an event which will leave him, for the rest of his life, slightly better than if it had not occurred.

317.   This is the rationale of pilgrimages, and they are quite often really effective. In addition to whatever may have been the original magnetism contributed by the holy man or relic, as soon as the place of pilgrimage is established and numbers of people begin to visit it, another factor comes into play, of which we have already spoken in the case of churches and temples. The place begins to be charged with the devotional feeling of all these hosts of visitors, and what they leave behind reacts upon their successors. Thus the influence of one of these holy places usually does not decrease as time passes, for if the original force tends slightly to diminish, on the other hand it is constantly fed by new accessions of devotion. Indeed, the only case in which the power ever fades is that of a neglected shrine - as, for example, when a country is conquered by people of another religion, to whom the older shrines are as nothing. Even then the influence, if it has been originally sufficiently strong, persists almost without diminution for many centuries, and for this reason even ruins have often a powerful force connected with them.

318.   The Egyptian religion, for example, has been practised little since the Christian era, yet no sensitive person can stand amidst the ruins of one of its temples without being powerfully affected by the stream of its thought. In this particular instance another force comes into play; the Egyptian architecture was of a definite type, intentionally so erected for the purpose of producing a definite impression upon its worshippers, and perhaps no architecture has ever fulfilled its purpose more effectively.

319.   The shattered fragments which remain still produce that effect to no inconsiderable degree, even upon members of an alien race altogether out of touch with the type of the old Egyptian civilisation. For the student of comparative religion who happens to be sensitive, there can be no more interesting experience than this - to bathe in the magnetism of the older religions of the world, to feel their influence as their devotees felt it thousands of years ago, to compare the sensations of Thebes or Luxor with those of the Parthenon or of the beautiful Greek temples of Girgenti, or those of Stonehenge with the vast ruins of Yucatan.

320.   RUINS

321.   The religious life of the old world can best be sensed in this way through the agency of its temples; but it is equally possible in the same way to come into touch with the daily life of those vanished nations, by standing among the ruins of their palaces and their homes. This needs perhaps a keener clairvoyant sense than the other. The force which permeates the temple is powerful because it is to a considerable extent one-pointed - because all through the centuries people have come to it with one leading idea of prayer or devotion, and so the impression made has been comparatively powerful. In their homes, on the other hand, they have lived out their lives with all kinds of different ideas and warring interests, so that the impressions often cancel one another.

322.   Nevertheless there emerges, as years roll on, a sort of least common multiple of all their feelings, which is characteristic of them as a race, and this can be sensed by one who has the art of entirely suppressing those personal feelings of his own, which are so far nearer and more vivid to him, and listening earnestly to catch the faint echo of the life of those times so long ago. Such study often enables one to take a juster view of history; manners and customs which startle and horrify us, because they are so remote from our own, can in this way be contemplated from the point of view of those to whom they were familiar; and in seeing them thus, one often realises for the first time how entirely we have misconceived those men of the past.

323.   Some of us may remember how, in our childhood, ignorant though well-meaning relations endeavoured to excite our sympathy by stories of Christian martyrs who were thrown to the lions in the Colosseum at Rome, or reprobated with horror the callous brutality which could assemble thousands to enjoy the combats between gladiators. I am not prepared to defend the tastes and amusements of the ancient Roman citizen, yet I think that any sensitive person who will go to the Colosseum at Rome and (if he can for the moment escape from the tourist) sit down there quietly, and let his consciousness drift backwards in time until he can sense the real feeling of those enormous, wildly-excited audiences, will find that he has done them a gross injustice.

324.   First, he will realise that the throwing of Christians to the lions *because of their religious belief* is a pious falsehood of the unprincipled early Christians. He will find that the government of Rome was in religious matters distinctly more tolerant than most European governments at the present day; that no person was ever executed or persecuted on account of any religious opinion whatever, and that those so-called Christians who were put to death suffered not in the least because of their alleged

religion, but because of conspiracy against the State, or of crimes which we should all join in reprobating.

325.   He will find that the government allowed and even encouraged gladiatorial combats, but he will also find that only three classes of people took part in them. First, condemned criminals - men whose lives had been forfeited to the law of the time - were utilised to provide a spectacle for the people, a degrading spectacle certainly, but not in any way more so than many which receive popular approval at the present day. The malefactor was killed in the arena, fighting either against another malefactor or a wild beast; but he preferred to die fighting rather than at the hands of the law, and there was always just a possibility that if he fought well he might thereby contrive to earn the applause of the fickle population; and so save his life.

326.   The second class consisted of such prisoners of war as it was the fashion of the time to put to death; but in this case also these were people whose death was already decided upon, and this particular form of death utilised them for a certain form of popular entertainment, and also gave them a chance of saving their lives, at which they eagerly grasped. The third class were the professional gladiators, men like the prize-fighters of the present day, men who took up this horrible line of life for the sake of the popularity which it brought - accepting it with their eyes fully open to its danger.

327.   I am not for a moment suggesting that the gladiatorial show was a form of entertainment which could possibly be tolerated by a really enlightened people; but if we are to apply the same standard now, we shall have to admit that no enlightened nations have yet come into existence, for it was no worse than the mediaeval tournaments, than the cock-fighting and bear-baiting of a century ago, or than the bull-fight or prize-fight of the present day. Nor is there anything to choose between the brutality of its supporters and that of the people who go in vast crowds to see how many rats a dog can kill in a minute, or that of the noble sportsmen who (without the excuse of anything in the nature of a fair fight) go out to slaughter hundreds of inoffensive partridges.

328.   We are beginning to set a somewhat higher value on human life than they did in the days of ancient Rome; but even so I would point out that that change does not mark a difference between the ancient Roman race and its reincarnation in the English people, for our own race was equally callous about wholesale slaughter up to a century ago. The difference is not between us and the Romans, but between us and our very recent ancestors; for the crowds which in the days of our fathers went and jested at a public execution can hardly be said to have advanced much since the time when they crowded the benches of the Colosseum.

329.   It is true that the Roman Emperors attended those exhibitions, as the English Kings used to encourage the tournament, and as the Kings of Spain even now patronise the bull-fight; but in order to understand the varied motives which led them to do this we must make a thorough study of the politics of the time - a matter which is quite outside the scope of this book. Here it must suffice to say that the Roman citizens were a body of men in a very curious political position, and that the authorities considered it necessary to provide them with constant entertainments in

order to keep them in a good humour. Therefore they hit upon this method of utilising what they regarded as the necessary and customary execution of criminals and rebels, in order to provide for the proletariat a kind of entertainment which it enjoyed. A very brutal proletariat, you will say. One must certainly admit that they were not highly advanced, but at least they were far better than those much later specimens who took active part in the unspeakable horrors of the French Revolution, for these last felt an active delight in blood and cruelty, which were only unnoticed concomitants of the enjoyment in the case of the Roman.

330.   Anyone who, standing in the Colosseum, as I have said, will really allow himself to feel the true spirit of those crowds of long ago, will understand that what appealed to them was the excitement of the contest and the skill exhibited in it. Their brutality consisted not in the fact that they enjoyed bloodshed and suffering, but that in the excitement of watching the struggle they were able to ignore it - which after all is very much what we do when we eagerly follow in the columns of our newspapers the news from the seat of war in the present day. Level for level, case for case, we of the fifth sub-race have made a slight advance from the condition of the fourth sub-race of two thousand years ago; but that advance is much slighter than our self-satisfaction has persuaded us.

331.   Every country has its ruins, and in all alike the study of the older life is an interesting study. A good idea of the wonderfully varied activities and interests of the mediaeval monastic life in England may be obtained by visiting that queen of ruins, Fountains Abbey, just as by visiting the stones of Carnac (not in Egypt but in Morbihan) one may watch the midsummer rejoicings round the *tantad* or sacred fire of the ancient Bretons.

332.   There is perhaps less necessity to study the ruins of India, since daily life there has remained so unchanged throughout the ages that no clairvoyant faculty is required to picture it as it was thousands of years ago. None of the actual buildings of India go back to any period of appreciable difference, and in most cases the relics of the golden age of India under the great Atlantean monarchies are already deeply buried. If we turn to mediaeval times, the effect of environment and religion on practically the same people is curiously illustrated by the difference in feeling between any ancient city of the north of India and the ruins of Anuradhapura in Ceylon.

333.   MODERN CITIES

334.   Just as our ancestors of long ago lived their ordinary lives in what was to them the ordinary commonplace way, and never dreamed that in doing so they were impregnating the stones of their city walls with influences which would enable a psychometer thousands of years afterwards to study the inmost secrets of their existence, so we ourselves are impregnating *our* cities and leaving behind us a record which will shock the sensibilities of the more developed men of the future. In certain ways, which will readily suggest themselves, all great towns are much alike; but on the other hand, there are differences of local atmosphere, depending to some extent upon the average morality of the city, the type of religious views most largely held

in it, and its principal trades and manufactures. For all these reasons each city has a certain amount of individuality - and individuality which will attract some people and repel others, according to their disposition. Even those who are not specially sensitive can hardly fail to note the distinction between the feeling of Paris and that of London, between Edinburgh and Glasgow, or between Philadelphia and Chicago.

335.   There are some cities whose key-note is not of the present but of the past - whose life in earlier days was so much more forcible than it is now, that the present is dwarfed by its comparison. The cities on the Zuyder Zee in Holland are an instance of this; S. Albans in England is another. But the finest example which the world has to offer is the immortal city of Rome. Rome stands alone among the cities of the world in having three great and entirely separate interests for the psychic investigator. First, and much the strongest, is the impression left by the astonishing vitality and vigour of that Rome which was the centre of the world, the Rome of the Republic and the Caesars; then comes another strong and unique impression - that of mediaeval Rome, the ecclesiastical centre of the world: third and quite different from either, the modern Rome of to-day, the political centre of the somewhat loosely integrated Italian kingdom, and at the same time still an ecclesiastical centre of widespread influence, though shorn of its glory and power.

336.   I first went to Rome, I confess, with the expectation that the Rome of the mediaeval Popes, with the assistance of all the world-thought that must for so long have been centred upon it, and with the advantage also of being so much nearer to us in time, would have to a considerable extent blotted out the life of the Rome of the Caesars. I was startled to find that the actual facts are almost exactly the reverse of that. The conditions of Rome in the Middle Ages were sufficiently remarkable to have stamped an indelible character upon any other town in the world; but so enormously stronger was the amazingly vivid life of that earlier civilisation, that it still stands out, in spite of all the history that has been made there since, as the one ineffaceable and dominating characteristic of Rome.

337.   To the clairvoyant investigator, Rome is (and ever will be) first of all the Rome of the Caesars, and only secondarily the Rome of the Popes. The impression of ecclesiastical history is all there, recoverable to the minutest detail; a bewildering mass of devotion and intrigue, of insolent tyranny and real religious feeling; a history of terrible corruption and of world-wide power, but rarely used as well as it might have been. And yet, mighty as it is, it is dwarfed into absolute insignificance by the grander power that went before it. There was a robustness of faith in himself, a conviction of destiny, a resolute intention to live his life to the utmost, and a certainty of being able to do it, about the ancient Roman, which few nationalities of to-day can approach.

338.   PUBLIC BUILDINGS
339.   Not only has a city as a whole its general characteristics, but such of the buildings in it as are devoted to special purposes have always an aura characteristic of that purpose. The aura of a hospital, for example, is a curious mixture: a preponderance of suffering, weariness and pain, but also a good deal of pity for the suffering, and a

feeling of gratitude on the part of the patients for the kindly care which is taken of them.

340.　　　The neighbourhood of a prison is decidedly to be avoided when a man is selecting a residence, for from it radiate the most terrible gloom and despair and settled depression, mingled with impotent rage, grief and hatred. Few places have on the whole a more unpleasant aura around them; and even in the general darkness there are often spots blacker than the rest, cells of unusual horror round which an evil reputation hangs. For example, there are several cases on record in which the successive occupants of a certain cell in a prison have all tried to commit suicide, those who were unsuccessful explaining that the idea of suicide persistently arose in their minds, and was steadily pressed upon them from without, until they were gradually brought into a condition in which there seemed to be no alternative. There have been instances in which such a feeling was due to the direct persuasion of a dead man; but also and more frequently it is simply that the first suicide has charged the cell so thoroughly with thoughts and suggestions of this nature that the later occupants, being probably persons of no great strength or development of will, have found themselves practically unable to resist.

341.　　　More terrible still are the thoughts which still hang round some of the dreadful dungeons of mediaeval tyrannies, the *oubliettes* of Venice or the torture-dens of the Inquisition. Just in the same way the very walls of a gambling-house radiate grief, envy, despair and hatred, and those of the public-house, or house of ill-fame, absolutely reek with the coarsest forms of sensual and brutal desire.

342.　　CEMETERIES

343.　　　In such cases as those mentioned above, it is easy enough for all decent people to escape the pernicious influences simply by avoiding the place; but there are other instances in which people are placed in undesirable situations through the indulgence of natural good feeling. In countries which are not civilised enough to burn their dead, survivors constantly haunt the graves in which decaying physical bodies are laid; from a feeling of affectionate remembrance they gather often to pray and meditate there, and to lay wreaths of flowers upon the tombs. They do not understand that the radiations of sorrow, depression and helplessness which so frequently permeate the churchyard or cemetery make it an eminently undesirable place to visit. I have seen old people walking and sitting about in some of our more beautiful cemeteries, and nursemaids wheeling along young children in their perambulators to take their daily airing, neither of them probably having the least idea that they are subjecting themselves and their charges to influences which will most likely neutralise all the good of the exercise and the fresh air; and this quite apart from the possibility of unhealthy physical exhalations.

344.　　UNIVERSITIES AND SCHOOLS

345.　　　The ancient buildings of our great universities are surrounded with magnetism of a special type, which does much towards setting upon its graduates that peculiar seal which is so readily distinguishable, even though it is not easy to say in so many words exactly of what it consists. Men attending the university are of many and various types - reading men, hunting men, pious men, careless men; and sometimes one college of a university attracts only one of these classes. In that case its walls become permeated with those characteristics, and its atmosphere operates to keep up its reputation. But on the whole the university is surrounded with a pleasant feeling of work and comradeship, of association yet of independence, a feeling of respect for the traditions of the *Alma Mater* and the resolve to uphold them, which soon brings the new undergraduate into line with his fellows and imposes upon him the unmistakable university tone.

346.   Not unlike this is the influence exerted by the buildings of our great public schools. The impressionable boy who comes to one of these soon feels about him a sense of order and regularity and *esprit de corps*, which once gained can scarcely be forgotten. Something of the same sort, but perhaps even more pronounced, exists in the case of a battleship, especially if she is under a popular captain and has been some little time in commission. There also the new recruit very quickly finds his place, soon acquires the *esprit de corps*, soon learns to feel himself one of a family whose honour he is bound to uphold. Much of this is due to the example of his fellows and to the pressure of the officers; but the feeling, the atmosphere of the ship herself undoubtedly bears a share in it also.

347.   LIBRARIES, MUSEUMS AND GALLERIES

348.   The studious associations of a library are readily comprehensible, but those of museums and picture-galleries are much more varied, as might be expected. In both these latter cases the influence is principally from pictures or the objects shown, and consequently our discussion of it is part of a later chapter. As far as the influence of the actual buildings is concerned, apart from the objects exhibited in them, the result is a little unexpected, for a prominent feature is a quite overwhelming sense of fatigue and boredom. It is evident that the chief constituent in the minds of the majority of the visitors is the feeling that they know that they ought to admire or to be interested in this or that, whereas as a matter of fact they are quite unable to achieve the least real admiration or interest.

349.   THE STOCK-YARDS OF CHICAGO

350.   The awful emanations from the stock-yards in Chicago, and the effect they produce on those who are so unfortunate as to live anywhere near them, have often been mentioned in Theosophical literature. Mrs. Besant herself has described how on her first visit she felt the terrible pall of depression which they cause while she was yet in the train many miles from Chicago; and though other people, less sensitive than she, might not be able to detect it so readily, there can be no doubt that its influence lies heavily upon them whenever they draw near to the theatre of that awful iniquity. On that spot millions of creatures have been slaughtered and every one of them has added to its radiations its own feelings of rage and pain and fear and the sense of injustice; and out of it all has been

formed one of the blackest clouds of horror at present existing in the world.

351.   In this case the results of the influence are commonly known, and it is impossible for anyone to profess incredulity. The low level of morality and the exceeding brutality of the slaughterman are matters of notoriety. In many of the murders committed in that dreadful neighbourhood the doctors have been able to recognise a peculiar twist of the knife which is used only by slaughtermen, and the very children in the streets play no games but games of killing. When the world becomes really civilised men will look back with incredulous horror upon such scenes as these, and will ask how it could have been possible that people who in other respects seem to have had some gleams of humanity and common sense, could permit so appalling a blot upon their honour as is the very existence of this accursed thing in their midst.

352.   SPECIAL PLACES

353.   Any spot where some ceremony has been frequently repeated, especially if in connection with it a high ideal has been set up, is always charged with a decided influence. For example, the hamlet of Oberammergau, where for many years at set intervals the Passion Play has been reproduced, is full of thought-forms of the previous performances, which react powerfully upon those who are preparing themselves to take part in a modern representation. An extraordinary sense of reality and of the deepest earnestness is felt by all those who assist, and it reacts even upon the comparatively careless tourist, to whom the whole thing is simply an exhibition. In the same way the magnificent ideals of Wagner are prominent in the atmosphere of Bayreuth, and they make a performance there a totally different thing from one by identically the same players anywhere else.

354.   SACRED MOUNTAINS

355.   There are instances in which the influence attached to a special place is non-human. This is usually the case with the many sacred mountains of the world. I have described in a previous chapter the great angels who inhabit the summit of the mountain of Slieve-na-Mon in Ireland. It is their presence which makes the spot sacred, and they perpetuate the influence of the holier magic of the leaders of the Tuatha-de-Danaan, which they ordained to remain until the day of the future greatness of Ireland shall come, and its part in the mighty drama of empire shall be made clear.

356.   I have several times visited a sacred mountain of a different type - Adam's Peak in Ceylon. The remarkable thing about this peak is that it is held as a sacred spot by people of all the various religions of the Island. The Buddhists give to the temple on its summit the name of the shrine of the Sripada or holy footprint, and their story is that when the Lord BUDDHA visited Ceylon in His astral body (He was never there in the physical) He paid a visit to the tutelary genius of that mountain, who is called by the people Saman Deviyo. Just as He was about to depart, Saman Deviyo asked Him as a favour to leave on that spot some permanent memory of His visit, and the BUDDHA in response is alleged to have pressed His foot upon the solid rock, utilising some force which made upon it a definite imprint or indentation.

71

357.　　The story goes on to say that Saman Deviyo, in order that this holy footprint should never be defiled by the touch of man, and that the magnetism radiating from it should be preserved, covered it with a huge cone of rock, which makes the present summit of the mountain. On the top of this cone a hollow has been made which roughly resembles a huge foot, and it seems probable that some of the more ignorant worshippers believe that to be the actual mark made by the Lord BUDDHA; but all the monks who know emphatically deny that, and point to the fact that this is not only enormously too large to be a human footprint, but that it is also quite obviously artificial.

358.　　They explain that it is made there simply to indicate the exact spot under which the true footprint lies, and they point to the fact that there is unquestionably a crack running all round the rock at some distance below the summit. The idea of a sacred footprint on that summit seems to be common to the various religions, but while the Buddhists hold it to be that of the Lord BUDDHA, the Tamil inhabitants of the Island suppose it to be one of the numerous footprints of Vishnu, and the Christians and the Muhammadans attribute it to Adam - whence the name Adam's Peak.

359.　　But it is said that long before any of these religions had penetrated to the Island, long before the time of the Lord BUDDHA Himself, this peak was already sacred to Saman Deviyo, to whom the deepest reverence is still paid by the inhabitants - as indeed it well may be, since He belongs to one of the great orders of the angels who rank near to the highest among the Adepts. Although His work is of a nature entirely different from ours, He also obeys the Head of the Great Occult Hierarchy; He also is one of the Great White Brotherhood which exists only for the purpose of forwarding the evolution of the world.

360.　　The presence of so great a being naturally sheds a powerful influence over the mountain and its neighbourhood, and most of all over its summit, so that there is emphatically a reality behind to account for the joyous enthusiasm so freely manifested by the pilgrims. Here also, as at other shrines, we have in addition to this the effect of the feeling of devotion with which successive generations of pilgrims have impregnated the place, but though that cannot but be powerful, it is yet in this case completely overshadowed by the original and ever-present influence of the mighty entity who has done His work and kept His guard there for so many thousands of years.

361.　　SACRED RIVERS

362.　　There are sacred rivers also - the Ganges, for example. The idea is that some great person of old has magnetised the source of the river with such power that all the water that henceforth flows out from that source is in a true sense holy water, bearing with it his influence and his blessing. This is not an impossibility, though it would require either a great reserve of power in the beginning or some arrangement for a frequent repetition. The process is simple and comprehensible; the only difficulty is what may be called the size of the operation. But what would be beyond the power of the ordinary man might possibly be quite easy to some one at a much higher level.

CHAPTER VIII BY CEREMONIES

365.   In considering the influence exerted by our cathedrals and churches we have hitherto concerned ourselves with that which radiates from their walls. That is, however, only one small part of the effect that they are intended to produce upon the community - only incidental to the great plan of the Founder of the religion; and even that plan in turn is only part of a still mightier scheme. Let me try to explain.

366.   THE HIERARCHY

367.   Theosophical students are familiar with the fact that the direction of the evolution of the world is vested in the Hierarchy of Adepts, working under one great Leader, and that one of the departments of this government is devoted to the promotion and management of religion. The official in charge of that department is called in the East the Bodhisattva, and is known to us in the West as the Christ, though that is really the title of only one of His incarnations. The plan of the government is that during each world-period there shall be seven successive Christs - one for each root-race. Each of these in succession holds this office of Bodhisattva, and during His term of office He is in charge of all the religious thought of the world, not only of that of His own special root-race; and He may incarnate many times.

368.   To illustrate exactly what is meant, let us take the case of the previous holder of this office, whom we know as the Lord Gautama. He was technically the Bodhisattva of the Atlantean or fourth root-race, and in that He incarnated many times under different names through a period spreading over several hundreds of thousands of years; but though His special work thus lay with the fourth root-race, He was in charge of the religions of the whole world, and consequently He did not neglect the fifth root-race. In the earlier part of the history of each of its sub-races He appeared and founded a special religion. In the first sub-race He was the original Vyasa; the name which He bore in the second sub-race has not been preserved in history. In the third sub-race He was the original Zoroaster, the first of a long line who bore that name. For the great religion of Egypt He was Thoth - called by the Greeks Hermes Trismegistus, Hermes the Thrice-Greatest, and among the early Greeks of the fourth sub-race He was Orpheus the Bard, the founder of their mysteries.

369.   In each of such births He drew round Him a number of earnest disciples, naturally in many cases the same egos over again in new bodies, although He was steadily adding to their number. The fourth root-race has by no means finished its evolution, for the majority of the earth's inhabitants still belong to it - the vast hosts of Chinese, Tartars, Japanese, Malays and all the undeveloped peoples of the earth; but it has long passed its prime, the time when it was the dominant race of the world, and when all the most advanced egos were incarnated in it. When the glory had finally passed from it the Bodhisattva prepared for the culminating act of His work, which involves for Him the attainment of that very high level of Initiation which we call the

Buddha-hood and also the resigning of His office into the hands of His successor.

370.   The preparation required was to bring together into one country, and even to a great extent into part of that country, all the egos who had been His special followers in the different lives which lay behind Him. Then He Himself incarnated among them - or perhaps more probably one of His highest disciples incarnated among them and yielded up his body to the Bodhisattva when the appointed time drew near; and as soon as in that body He had taken the great Initiation and become the BUDDHA, He went forth to preach His Law. We must not attach to that word Law the ordinary English meaning, for it goes very much further than a mere set of commands. We must take it rather to signify His presentation of the Truth about humanity and its evolution, and His instructions, based upon that truth, as to how a man should act so as to co-operate in the scheme of that evolution.

371.   Preaching this Law He drew round Him all the hosts of His old disciples, and by the tremendous power and magnetism which belonged to Him as the BUDDHA He enabled large numbers of them to take that fourth step on the Path, to which is given the name of the Arhat. He spent the rest of His life on earth in preaching and consolidating this new faith, and when He passed away from physical life He definitely handed over His office of director of religion to His successor, whom we call the Lord Maitreya - the Great One who is honoured all through India under the name of Krishna and throughout the Christian world as Jesus the Christ. No Theosophical student will be confused by this last expression, for he knows that the Christ, who is the new Bodhisattva, took the body of the disciple Jesus, and held it for the last three years of its life in order to found the Christian religion. After its death He continued for some years to teach His more immediate disciples from the astral world, and from that time to this He has employed that disciple Jesus (now Himself a Master) to watch over and guide as far as may be the destinies of His Church.

372.   Immediately upon taking over the office, the Lord Maitreya availed Himself of the extraordinarily good conditions left behind Him by the BUDDHA to make several simultaneous attempts to promote the religious progress of the world. He not only descended into an almost immediate incarnation Himself, but He at the same time employed a number of those who had attained the Arhat level under the Lord BUDDHA, and were now ready to take rebirth at once. From this band of disciples came those whom we call Laotse and Confucius, who were sent to incarnate in China. From them also came Plato, and from among their followers Phidias and many another of the greatest of the Greeks.

373.   Within the same area of time came the great philosopher Pythagoras, who is now our Master K. H. He was not one of the immediate attendants of the Lord BUDDHA, as He had already attained the Arhat level and was needed for work elsewhere, but He travelled over to India to see Him and to receive His blessing. He also is upon the line of the Bodhisattva; and may be regarded as one of His foremost lieutenants.

374.   Simultaneously with all these efforts the Lord Maitreya Himself incarnated as Krishna, and led in India a very wonderful life, upon which is founded the devotional

aspect of the religion of that country, which shows us perhaps the most fervent examples of utter devotion to be seen anywhere in the world. This great incarnation must not be confounded with that of the Krishna described in the *Mahabharata*; the latter was a warrior and a statesman, and lived some two thousand five hundred years before the time of which we are speaking.

375.   Along with this came another great incarnation - not this time from the department of religion, but rather from one the departments of organisation - the great Shankaracharya, who travelled over India, founding the four chief monasteries and the Sannyasi order. Some confusion has been created by the fact that each of the long line of those who have since stood at the head of the monastic organisations has also taken the title of Shankaracharya, so that to speak of Shankaracharya is like speaking of the Pope without indicating which particular holder of the Papal Chair is intended. The great Founder to whom we have referred must not be confused with the better known holder of the office who some seven hundred years after Christ wrote a voluminous series of commentaries on the *Bhagavad-Gita* and some of the Upanishads.

376.   THE THREE PATHS

377.   These three great Teachers, who followed one another so quickly in India, furnished between them a fresh impulse along each of the three paths. The BUDDHA founded a religion giving minute directions for daily life, such as would be needed by those who should follow the path of action, while Shankaracharya provided the metaphysical teaching for those to whom the path is wisdom, and the Lord Maitreya (manifesting as Krishna) provided a supreme object of devotion for those to whom that is the most direct road to the truth. But Christianity must be considered as the first effort of the new Bodhisattva to build a religion which should go abroad into new countries, for His work as Krishna had been intended especially for India. For those who penetrate behind the external manifestation to the inner and mystical meaning, it will be significant that the ray or type to which belong the Lord BUDDHA, the Bodhisattva and our Master K. H. is in a special sense a manifestation of the second aspect of the Solar Deity - the second person of the Blessed Trinity.

378.   Religion has an objective side to it; it acts not only from within by stirring up the hearts and minds of its votaries, but also from without by arranging that uplifting and refining influences shall play constantly upon their various vehicles. The temple or the church is meant to be not merely a place of worship, but also a centre of magnetism, through which spiritual forces can be poured out upon the district surrounding it. People often forget that even the Great Ones must do their work subject to the laws of nature, and that it is for them an actual duty to economise their force as much as possible, and therefore to do whatever they have to do in the easiest possible manner.

379.   In this case, for example, if the object be to let spiritual force shine forth over a certain district, it would not be economical to pour it down indiscriminately everywhere, like rain, since that would require that the miracle of its materialisation to a lower level should be performed in millions of places simultaneously, once for

every drop, as it were, and each representing a mighty effort. Far simpler would it be to establish at certain points definite magnetic centres, where the machinery of such materialisation should be permanently set up, so that by pouring in only a little force from above it should instantly be spread abroad over a considerable area.

380. This had been achieved in earlier religions by the establishment of strongly magnetised centres, such as are offered by the image or by the lingam in a Hindu temple, by the altar of the sacred fire among the Parsis, or by the statue of the Lord BUDDHA among the Buddhists. As each worshipper comes before one of these symbols and pours himself out in devotion or gratitude, he not only draws down the answering force upon himself, but also causes a certain radiation upon those for some distance round him.

381. In founding the religion of Christianity the Bodhisattva tried a new experiment with the view of securing at least once daily a much more thorough and effective distribution of spiritual force. The fact that new experiments of this sort *may* be tried - that though the splendid system of the Hierarchy is unalterably founded upon the Rock of Ages, it yet permits so much of freedom to its Officials - is surely of deepest interest. It shows us that that organisation which is in all the world the most utterly conservative is yet at the same time amazingly liberal, and that the oldest form of government is also the most adaptable. It is only in reference to the august Head of the Hierarchy that we can use to the fullest extent those grand old words of a Collect of the Church of England: "In His service is perfect freedom."

382. Perhaps the most readily comprehensible way of explaining this new scheme will be to describe the way in which I myself was first enabled to see something of the details of its working. But first I must say a few words as to the present condition of the Christian Church.

383. As we see that Church now, it is but a poor representation of what its Founder meant it to be. Originally it had its higher mysteries, like all other faiths, and its three stages of purification, illumination and perfection, through which its children had to pass. With the expulsion as heretics of the great Gnostic doctors this aspect of the truth was lost to the Church, and the only idea which it now places before its members is the first of the three stages, and even that not understandingly. Origen, one of the greatest men that it has ever produced, described very clearly the two kinds of Christianity - the somatic or physical, and the spiritual - saying that the former is meant only to attract the ignorant masses, but that the latter is for those who know. In these days the Church has forgotten that true spiritual and higher side of her teaching, and has busied herself with pitiful attempts to explain that there is somehow or other a spiritual side to the lower teaching which is practically all that she has left.

384. CHRISTIAN MAGIC

385. Nevertheless, and in spite of all this, the old magic which was instituted by her Founder is still working and effective; so even in these days of her decadence she is still definitely under guidance and control. There is still a real and a vital power in the sacraments when truly performed - the power of the Solar Deity Himself - and it

comes through Him whom we call the Master Jesus, this being His special department.

386.   It was not He, but the Christ - the Lord Maitreya - who founded the religion, but nevertheless the special charge of Christianity has been given into the hands of Him who yielded His body for the work of the Founder. Belief in His personal interest in the Christian Church has almost died out in many branches of it; the members think of him as a Teacher who lived two thousand years ago rather than as an active power in the Church to-day. They have forgotten that He is still a living force, a real presence - truly with us always, even to the end of the world, as He has said. Not God in the idolatrous sense, yet the channel through which the Divine power has reached many millions - the official in charge of the devotional department of the work of the Christ.

387.   The Church has turned aside widely from the course originally marked out for it. It was meant to meet all types; now it meets only one, and that very imperfectly. The reconstruction of the links must come, and as intellectual activity is the sign of our time and of the latest sub-race, the intellectual revival which shows itself in the higher criticism has for its very purpose that of enabling religion to meet another type of mind. If only the priests and the teachers had the advantage of direct knowledge, they would be able to deal with and to help their people in this crisis - to guide their intellectual activity by means of their own knowledge of the truth, and to keep alive in the hearts of their flock the spirituality without which the intellectual effort can be but barren.

388.   Not only has the Church almost entirely forgotten the original doctrine taught by her Founder, but most of her priests have now little conception of the real meaning and power of the ceremonies which they have to perform. It is probable that the Christ foresaw that this would happen, for He has carefully arranged that the ceremonies should work even though neither celebrants nor people have any intelligent comprehension of their methods or their results. It would be difficult to explain the outline of His plan to the average Christian; to the Theosophist it ought to be more readily comprehensible, because he is already familiar with some of the general ideas involved in it.

389.   We who are students have often heard of the great reservoir of force which is constantly being filled by the Nirmanakayas in order that its contents may be utilised by members of the Adept Hierarchy and Their pupils for the helping of the evolution of mankind. The arrangement made by the Christ with regard to His religion was that a kind of special compartment of that reservoir should be reserved for its use, and that a certain set of officials should be empowered by the use of certain special ceremonies, certain words and signs of power, to draw upon it for the spiritual benefit of their people.

390.   The scheme adopted for passing on the power is what is called ordination, and thus we see at once the real meaning of the doctrine of the apostolic succession, about which there has been so much of argument. I myself held strongly to that doctrine while officiating as a priest of the Church; but when through the study of Theosophy I came to understand religion better and to take a far wider view of life, I began to doubt whether in reality the succession meant so much as we of the ritualistic

party had supposed. With still further study however, I was rejoiced to find that there was a real foundation for the doctrine, and that it meant even much more than our highest schools had ever taught.

391.　　THE MASS

392.　　My attention was first called to this by watching the effect produced by the celebration of the Mass in a Roman Catholic Church, in a little village in Sicily. Those who know that most beautiful of islands will understand that one does not meet with the Roman Catholic Church there in its most intellectual form, and neither the priest nor the people could be described as especially highly developed; yet the quite ordinary celebration of the Mass was a magnificent display of the application of occult force.

393.　　At the moment of consecration, the Host glowed with the most dazzling brightness; it became in fact a veritable sun to the eye of the clairvoyant, and as the priest lifted it above the heads of the people, I noticed that two distinct varieties of spiritual force poured forth from it, which might perhaps be taken as roughly corresponding to the light of the sun and the streamers of his corona. The first rayed out impartially in all directions upon all the people in the church; indeed, it penetrated the walls of the church as though they were not there, and influenced a considerable section of the surrounding country.

394.　　This force was of the nature of a strong stimulus and, its action was strongest of all in the intuitional world, though it was also exceedingly powerful in the three higher subdivisions of the mental world. Its activity was marked in the first, second and third subdivisions of the astral also, but this was a reflection of the mental, or perhaps an effect produced by sympathetic vibration. Its effect upon the people who came within the range of its influence was proportionate to their development. In a very few cases (where there was some slight intuitional development) it acted as a powerful stimulant, doubling or trebling for a time the amount of activity in those intuitional bodies and the radiance which they were capable of emitting. But forasmuch as in most people the intuitional matter was as yet almost entirely dormant, its chief effect was produced upon the causal bodies of the inhabitants.

395.　　Most of them, again, were awake and partially responsive only as far as the matter of the third subdivision of the mental world was concerned, and therefore they missed much of the advantage that they might have gained if the higher parts of their causal bodies had been in full activity. But at any rate, every ego within reach, without exception, received a distinct impetus and a distinct benefit from that act of consecration, little though he knew or recked of what was being done.

396.　　The astral vibrations also, though much fainter, produced a far-reaching effect, for at least the astral bodies, of the Sicilians are usually thoroughly well-developed so that it is not difficult to stir their emotions. Many people far away from the church, walking along the village street or pursuing their various avocations upon the lonely hill-sides, felt for a moment a thrill of affection or devotion, as this great wave of spiritual peace and strength passed over the country-side, though assuredly they never dreamt of connecting it with the Mass which was being celebrated in their little cathedral.

397.   It at once becomes evident that we are here in the presence of a grand and far-reaching scheme. Clearly, one of the great objects, perhaps the principal object, of the daily celebration of the Mass is that every one within reach of it shall receive at-least once each day one of these electric shocks which are so well calculated to promote any growth of which he is capable. Such an outpouring of force brings to each person whatever he has made himself capable of receiving; but even the quite undeveloped and ignorant cannot but be somewhat the better for the passing touch of a noble emotion, while for the few more advanced it means a spiritual uplifting the value of which it would be difficult to exaggerate.

398.   I said that there was a second effect, which I compared to the streamers of the sun's corona. The light which I have just described poured forth impartially upon all, the just and the unjust, the believers and the scoffers. But this second force was called into activity only in response to a strong feeling of devotion on the part of an individual. At the elevation of the Host all members of the congregation duly prostrated themselves - some apparently as a mere matter of habit, but some also with a strong upwelling of deep devotional feeling.

399.   The effect as seen by clairvoyant sight was most striking and profoundly impressive, for to each of these latter there darted from the uplifted Host a ray of fire, which set the higher part of the astral body of the recipient glowing with the most intense ecstasy. Through the astral body, by reason of its close relation with it, the intuitional vehicle was also strongly affected; and although in none of these peasants could it be said to be in any way awakened, its growth within its shell was unquestionably distinctly stimulated, and its capability of instinctively influencing the astral was enhanced. For while the awakened intuition can consciously mould and direct the astral, there is a great storehouse of force in even the most undeveloped intuitional vehicle, and this shines out upon and through the astral body, even though it be unconsciously and automatically.

400.   I was naturally intensely interested in this phenomenon, and I made a point of attending various functions at different churches in order to learn whether what I had seen on this occasion was invariable, or, if it varied, when and under what conditions. I found that at every celebration the same results were produced, and the two forces which I have tried to describe were always in evidence - the first apparently without any appreciable variation, but the display of the second depending upon the number of really devotional people who formed part of the congregation.

401.   The elevation of the Host immediately after its consecration was not the only occasion upon which this display of force took place. When the benediction was given with the Blessed Sacrament exactly the same thing happened. On several occasions I followed the procession of the Host through the streets, and every time that a halt was made at some half-ruined church and the benediction was given from its steps, precisely the same double phenomenon was produced. I observed that the reserved Host upon the altar of the church was all day long steadily pouring forth the

former of the two influences, though not so strongly as at the moment of elevation or benediction. One might say that the light glowed upon the altar without ceasing, but shone forth as a sun at those moments of special effort. The action of the second forces, the second ray of light, could also be evoked from the reserved Sacrament upon the altar, apparently at any time, though it seemed to me somewhat less vivid than the outpouring immediately after the consecration.

402.   Everything connected with the Host - the tabernacle, the monstrance, the altar itself, the priest's vestments, the insulating humeral veil, the chalice and paten - all were strongly charged with this tremendous magnetism, and all were radiating it forth, each in its degree.

403.   A third effect is that which is produced upon the communicant. He who receives into his body a part of that dazzling centre, from which flow the light and the fire, becomes himself for the time a similar centre, and radiates power in his turn. The tremendous waves of force which he has thus drawn into the closest possible association with himself cannot but seriously influence his higher bodies. For the time these waves raise his vibrations into harmony with themselves, thus producing a feeling of intense exaltation. This, however, is a considerable strain upon his various vehicles, which naturally tend gradually to fall back again to their normal rates. For a long time the indescribably vivid higher influence struggles against this tendency to slow down, but the dead weight of the comparatively enormous mass of the man's own ordinary undulations acts as a drag upon even its tremendous energy, and gradually brings it and themselves down to the common level. But undoubtedly every such experience draws the man just an infinitesimal fraction higher than he was before. He has been for a few moments or even for a few hours in direct contact with the forces of a world far higher than any that he himself can otherwise touch.

404.   Naturally, having watched all this, I then proceeded to make further investigations as to how far this outflowing of force was affected by the character, the knowledge or the intention of the priest. I may sum up briefly the results of the examination of a large number of cases in the form of two or three axioms, which will no doubt at first sight seem surprising to many of my readers.

405.   ORDINATION
406.   First, only those priests who have been lawfully ordained, and have the apostolic succession, can produce this effect at all. Other men, not being part of this definite organisation, cannot perform this feat, no matter how devoted or good or saintly they may be. Secondly, neither the character of the priest, nor his knowledge, nor ignorance as to what he is really doing, affects the result in any way whatever.

407.   If one thinks of it, neither of these statements ought to seem to us in any way astonishing, since it is obviously a question of being able to perform a certain action, and only those who have passed through a certain ceremony have received the gift of the ability to perform it. Just in the same way, in order to be able to speak to a certain set of people one must know their language, and a man who does not know that language cannot communicate with them, no matter how good and earnest and

devoted he may be. Also, his ability to communicate with them is not affected by his private character, but only by the one fact that he has, or has not, the power to speak to them which is conferred by a knowledge of their language. I do not for a moment say that these other considerations are without their due effect; I shall speak of that later, but what I do say is that no one can draw upon this particular reservoir unless he has received the power to do so which comes from a due appointment given according to the direction left by the Christ.

408.   I think that we can see a very good reason why precisely this arrangement has been made. Some plan was needed which should put a splendid outpouring of force within the reach of every one simultaneously in thousands of churches all over the world. I do not say that it might not be possible for a man of most exceptional power and holiness to call down through the strength of his devotion an amount of higher force commensurate with that obtained through the rites which I have described. But men of such exceptional power are always excessively rare, and it could never at any time of the world's history have been possible to find enough of them simultaneously to fill even one thousandth part of the places where they are needed. But here is a plan whose arrangement is to a certain extent mechanical; it is ordained that a certain act when duly performed shall be the recognised method of bringing down the force; and this can be done with comparatively little training by any one upon whom the power is conferred. A strong man is needed to pump up water, but any child can turn on a tap. It needs a strong man to make a door and to hang it in its place, but when it is once on its hinges any child can open it.

409.   Having myself been a priest of the Church of England, and knowing how keen are the disputes as to whether that Church really has the apostolic succession or not, I was naturally interested in discovering whether its priests possessed this power. I was much pleased to find that they did, and I suppose we may take that as definitely settling the much-disputed Parker question, and with it the whole controversy as to the authenticity of the Orders of the Church of England. I soon found by examination that ministers of what are commonly called dissenting sects did not possess this power, no matter how good and earnest they might be. Their goodness and earnestness produced plenty of other effects which I shall presently describe, but their efforts did not draw upon the particular reservoir to which I have referred.

410.   I was especially interested in the case of one such minister whom I knew personally to be a good and devout man, and also a well-read Theosophist. Here was a man who knew much more about the real meaning of the act of consecration than nine hundred and ninety-nine out of a thousand of the priests who constantly perform it; and yet I am bound to admit that his best effort did not produce this particular effect, while the others as unquestionably did. (Once more, of course he produced other things which they did not - of which more anon.) That at first somewhat surprised me, but I soon saw that it could not have been otherwise. Suppose, for example, that a certain sum of money is left by a rich Freemason for distribution among his poorer brethren, the law would never sanction the division of that money among any others than the Freemasons for whom it was intended; and the fact that other poor people

outside the Masonic body might be more devout or more deserving would not weigh with it in the slightest degree.

411.   Another point which interested me greatly was the endeavour to discover to what extent, if at all, the intention of the priest affected the result produced. In the Roman Church I found many priests who went through the ceremony somewhat mechanically, and as a matter of daily duty, without any decided thought on the subject; but whether from ingrained reverence or from long habit, they always seemed to recover themselves just before the moment of consecration and to perform that act with a definite intention.

412.   THE ANGLICAN CHURCH

413.   I turned then to what is called the Low Church division of the Anglican community to see what would happen with them, because I knew that many of them would reject altogether the name of priest, and though they might follow the rubric in performing the act of consecration, their intention in doing it would be exactly the same as that of ministers of various denominations outside the Church. Yet I found that the Low Churchman could and did produce the effect, and that the others outside did not. Hence I infer that the ` intention' which is always said to be required must be no more than the intention to do whatever the Church means, without reference to the private opinion of the particular priest as to what that meaning is. I have no doubt that many people will think that all this ought to be quite differently arranged, but I can only report faithfully what my investigations have shown me to be the fact.

414.   I must not for a moment be understood as saying that the devotion and earnestness, the knowledge and the good character of the officiant make no difference. They make a great difference; but they do not affect the power to draw from that particular reservoir. When the priest is earnest and devoted his whole feeling radiates out upon his people and calls forth similar feelings in such of them as are capable of expressing them. Also his devotion calls down its inevitable response, as shown in the illustration in *Thought-Forms*, and the down-pouring of force thus evoked benefits his congregation as well as himself; so that a priest who throws his heart and soul into the work which he does may be said to bring a double blessing upon his people, though the second class of influence can scarcely be considered as being of the same order of magnitude as the first. This second outpouring, which is drawn down by devotion itself, is of course to be found just as often outside the Church as within it.

415.   Another factor to be taken into account is the feeling of the congregation. If their feeling is devout and reverent it is of immense help to their teacher, and it enormously increases the amount of spiritual energy poured down as a response to devotion. The average intellectual level of the congregation is also a matter to be considered, for a man who is intelligent as well as pious has within him a devotion of a higher order than his more ignorant brother, and is therefore able to evoke a fuller response. On the other hand in many places of worship where much is made of the exercise of the intellectual faculties - where for example the sermon and not the service is thought of as the principal feature - there is scarcely any real devotion,

but instead of it a horrible spirit of criticism and of spiritual pride which effectually prevents the unfortunate audience from obtaining any good results at all from what they regard as their spiritual exercises.

416.   Devotional feeling or carelessness, belief or scepticism on the part of the congregation make no difference whatever to the downflow from on high when there is a priest in charge who has the requisite qualifications to draw from the appointed reservoir. But naturally these factors make a difference as to the number of rays sent out from the consecrated Host, and so to the general atmosphere of the Church.

417.   THE MUSIC

418.   Another very important factor in the effect produced is the music which is used in the course of the service. Those who have read *Thought-Forms* will remember the striking drawings that are there given of the enormous and splendid mental, astral and etheric erections which are built up by the influence of sound. The general action of sound is a question which I shall take up in another chapter, touching here only upon that side of it which belongs to the services of the Church.

419.   Here is another direction, unsuspected by the majority of those who participate in them, in which these services are capable of producing a wonderful and powerful effect. The devotion of the Church has always centred principally round the offering of the Mass as an act of the highest and purest adoration possible, and consequently the most exalted efforts of its greatest composers have been in connection with this service also. Here we may see one more example of the wisdom with which the arrangements were originally made, and of the crass ineptitude of those who have so blunderingly endeavoured to improve them.

420.   THE THOUGHT-FORMS

421.   Each of the great services of the Church (and more especially the celebration of the Eucharist) was originally designed to build up a mighty ordered form, expressing and surrounding a central idea - a form which would facilitate and direct the radiation of the influence upon the entire village which was grouped round the church. The idea of the service may be said to be a double one: to receive and distribute the great outpouring of spiritual force, and to gather up the devotion of the people, and offer it before the throne of God.

422.   In the case of the Mass as celebrated by the Roman or the Greek Church, the different parts of the service are grouped round the central act of consecration distinctly with a view to the symmetry of the great form produced, as well as to their direct effect upon the worshippers. The alterations made in the English Prayer Book in 1552 were evidently the work of people who were ignorant of this side of the question, for they altogether disturbed that symmetry - which is one reason why it is an eminently desirable thing for the Church of England that it should as speedily as possible so arrange its affairs as to obtain permission to use as an alternative the Mass of King Edward VI according to the Prayer Book of 1549.

423.   One of the most important effects of the Church Service, both upon

the immediate congregation and upon the surrounding district, has always been the creation of these beautiful and devotional thought-forms, through which the downpouring of life and strength from higher worlds can more readily take effect. These are better made and their efficiency enhanced when a considerable portion of those who take part in the service do so with intelligent comprehension, yet even when the devotion is ignorant the result is still beautiful and uplifting.

424.   Most of the sects, which unhappily broke away from the Church, entirely lost sight of this inner and more important side of public worship. The idea of the service offered to God almost disappeared, and its place was largely taken by the fanatical preaching of narrow theological dogmas which were always unimportant and frequently ridiculous. Readers have sometimes expressed surprise that those who write from the occult standpoint should seem so decidedly to favour the practices of the Church, rather than those of the various sects whose thought is in many ways more liberal. The reason is shown precisely in this consideration of the inner side of things on which we are now engaged.

425.   The occult student recognises most fully the value of the effort which made liberty of conscience and of thought possible; yet he cannot but see that those who cast aside the splendid old forms and services of the Church lost in that very act almost the whole of the occult side of their religion, and made of it essentially a selfish and limited thing - a question chiefly of "personal salvation" for the individual, instead of the grateful offering of worship to God, which is in itself the never-failing channel through which the Divine Love is poured forth upon all.

426.   The attainment of mental freedom was a necessary step in the process of human evolution; the clumsy and brutal manner in which it was obtained, and the foolishness of the excesses into which gross ignorance led its champions, are responsible for many of the deplorable results which we see at the present day. The same savage, senseless lust for wanton destruction that moved Cromwell's brutal soldiers to break priceless statues and irreplaceable stained glass, has deprived us also of the valuable effect produced in higher worlds by perpetual prayers for the dead, and by the practically universal devotion of the common people to the saints and angels. Then the great mass of the people was religious - even though ignorantly religious; now it is frankly and even boastfully irreligious. Perhaps this transitory stage is a necessary one, but it can hardly be considered in itself either beautiful or satisfactory.

427.   THE EFFECT OF DEVOTION

428.   No other service has an effect at all comparable to that of the celebration of the Mass, but the great musical forms may of course appear at any service where music is used. In all the other services (except indeed the Catholic Benediction of the Blessed Sacrament) the thought-forms developed and the general good which is done depend to a great extent upon the devotion of the people. Now devotion, whether individual or collective, varies much in quality. The devotion of the primitive savage, for example, is usually greatly mingled with fear, and the chief idea in his mind in connection with it is to appease a deity who might otherwise prove vindictive. But little better than this

84

is much of the devotion of men who consider themselves civilised, for it is a kind of unholy bargain - the offering to the Deity of a certain amount of devotion if He on His side will extend a certain amount of protection or assistance.

429.　　Such devotion, being entirely selfish and grasping in its nature, produces results only in the lower types of astral matter, and exceedingly unpleasant-looking results they are in many cases. The thought-forms which they create are often shaped like grappling-hooks, and their forces move always in closed curves, reacting only upon the man who sends them forth, and bringing back to him whatever small result they may be able to achieve. The true, pure, unselfish devotion is an outrush of feeling which never returns to the man who gave it forth, but constitutes itself in very truth a cosmic force producing widespread results in higher worlds.

430.　　Though the force itself never returns, the man who originates it becomes the centre of a downpour of divine energy which comes in response, and so in his act of devotion he has truly blessed himself, even though at the same time he has also blessed many others as well, and in addition to that has had the unequalled honour of contributing to the mighty reservoir of the Nirmanakaya. Anyone who possesses the book *Thought-Forms* may see in it an attempt to represent the splendid blue spire made by devotion of this type as it rushes upwards, and he will readily understand how it opens a way for a definite outpouring of the divine force of the Solar Deity.

431.　　He is pouring forth His wonderful vital energy on every level in every world, and naturally the outpouring belonging to a higher world is stronger and fuller and less restricted than that upon the world below. Normally, each wave of this great force acts in its own world alone, and cannot or does not move transversely from one world to another; but it is precisely by means of unselfish thought and feeling, whether it be of devotion or of affection, that a temporary channel is provided through which the force normally belonging to a higher world may descend to a lower, and may produce there results which, without it, could never have come to pass.

432.　　Every man who is truly unselfish frequently makes himself such a channel, though of course on a comparatively small scale; but the mighty act of devotion of a whole vast congregation, where it is really united, and utterly without thought of self, produces the same result on an enormously greater scale. Sometimes though rarely, this occult side of religious services may be seen in full activity, and no one who has even once had the privilege of seeing such a splendid manifestation as this can for a moment doubt the hidden side of a Church service is of an importance infinitely greater than anything purely physical.

433.　　Such an one would see the dazzling blue spiral or dome of the highest type of astral matter rushing upwards into the sky, far above the image of it in stone which sometimes crowns the physical edifice in which the worshippers are gathered; he would see the blinding glory which pours down through it and spreads out like a great flood of living light over all the surrounding region. Naturally, the diameter and the height of the spire of devotion determine the opening made for the descent of the higher life, while the force which expresses itself in the rate at which the devotional energy rushes upwards has its relation to the rate at which the corresponding downpouring can take place. The sight is indeed a wonderful one, and he who sees it can never doubt again that the unseen influences are more than the seen, nor can he fail to realise that the world which goes on its way heedless of the devotional man, or perhaps even scornful of him, owes to him all the time far more than it knows.

434.   The power of the ordained priest is a reality in other ceremonies than the celebration of the eucharist. The consecration of the water in the rite of baptism, or of the holy water which is to be distributed to the faithful or kept at the entrance of the church, pours into it a strong influence, which enables it in each case to perform the part assigned to it. The same is true of other consecrations and benedictions which come in the course of the regular work of the priest, though in many of these it seems that a somewhat larger proportion of the effect is produced by the direct magnetism of the priest himself, and the amount of that of course depends upon the energy and earnestness with which he performs his part of the ceremony.

435.   HOLY WATER

436.   We shall find it interesting to study the hidden side of some of these minor services of the Church, and the work done by her priests. Into the making of holy water, for example, the mesmeric element enters very strongly. The priest first takes clean water and clean salt, and then proceeds to demagnetise them, to remove from them any casual exterior influences with which they may have been permeated. Having done this very thoroughly, he then charges them with spiritual power, each separately and with many earnest repetitions, and then finally with further fervent adjurations he casts the salt into the water in the form of a cross, and the operation is finished.

437.   If this ceremony be properly and carefully performed the water becomes a highly effective talisman for the special purposes for which it is charged - that it shall drive away from the man who uses it all worldly and warring thought, and shall turn him in the direction of purity and devotion. The student of occultism will readily comprehend how this must be so, and when he sees with astral sight the discharge of the higher force which takes place when anyone uses or sprinkles this holy water, he will have no difficulty in realising that it must be a powerful factor in driving away undesirable thought and feeling, and quelling all irregular vibrations of the astral and mental bodies.

438.   In every case where the priest does his work the spiritual force flows through, but he may add greatly to it by the fervour of his own devotion, and the vividness with which he realises what he is doing.

439.   BAPTISM

440.   The sacrament of baptism, as originally administered, had a real and beautiful hidden side. In those older days the water was magnetised with a special view to the effect of its vibrations upon the higher vehicles, so that all the germs of good qualities in the unformed astral and mental bodies of the child might thereby receive a strong stimulus, while at the same time the germs of evil might be isolated

and deadened. The central idea no doubt was to take this early opportunity of fostering the growth of the good germs, in order that their development might precede that of the evil - in order that when at a later period the latter germs begin to bear their fruit, the good might already be so far evolved that the control of the evil would be a comparatively easy matter.

441.   This is one side of the baptismal ceremony; it has also another aspect, as typical of the Initiation towards which it is hoped that the young member of the Church will direct his steps as he grows up. It is a consecration and a setting apart of the new set of vehicles to the true expression of the soul within, and to the service of the Great White Brotherhood; yet is also has its occult side with regard to these new vehicles themselves, and when the ceremony is properly and intelligently performed there can be no doubt that its effect is a powerful one.

442.   UNION IS STRENGTH

443.   The economy and efficiency of the whole scheme of the Lord Maitreya depend upon the fact that much greater powers can easily be arranged for a small body of men, who are spiritually prepared to receive them, than could possibly be universally distributed without a waste of energy which could not be contemplated for a moment. In the Hindu scheme, for example, every man is a priest for his own household, and therefore we have to deal with millions of such priests of all possible varieties of temperament, and not in any way specially prepared. The scheme of the ordination of priests gives a certain greater power to a limited number, who have by that very ordination been specially set apart for the work.

444.   Carrying the same principle a little further, a set of still higher powers are given to a still smaller number - the bishops. They are made channels for the force which confers ordination, and for the much smaller manifestation of the same force which accompanies the rite of confirmation. The hidden side of these ceremonies is always one of great interest to the student of the realities of life. There are many cases now, unfortunately, where all these things are mere matters of form, and though that does not prevent their result, it does minimise it; but where the old forms are used as they were meant to be used, the unseen effect is out of all proportion to anything that is visible in the physical world.

445.   CONSECRATION

446.   To the bishop also is restricted the power of consecrating a church or a churchyard, and the occult side of this is a really pretty sight. It is interesting to watch the growth of the sort of fortification which the officiant builds as he marches round uttering the prescribed prayers and verses; to note the expulsion of any ordinary thought-forms which may happen to have been there, and the substitution for them of the orderly and devotional forms to which henceforth this building is supposed to be dedicated.

447. THE BELLS

448.   There are many minor consecrations which are of great interest - the blessing of bells, for example. The ringing of bells has a distinct part in the scheme of the Church,, which in these days seems but little understood. The modern theory appears to be that they are meant to call people together at the time when the service is about to be performed, and there is no doubt that in the Middle Ages, when there were no clocks or watches, they were put to precisely this use. From this restricted view of the intention of the bell has grown the idea that anything which makes a noise will serve the purpose, and in most towns of England Sunday morning is made into a purgatory by the simultaneous but discordant clanging of a number of unmusical lumps of metal.

449.   At intervals we recognise the true use of the bells, as when we employ them on great festivals or on occasions of public rejoicing; for a peal of musical bells, sounding harmonious notes, is the only thing which was contemplated by the original plan, and these were intended to have a double influence. Some remnant of this still remains, though but half understood, in the science of campanology, and those who know the delights of the proper performance of a trip-bob-major or a grandsire-bob-cator will perhaps be prepared to hear how singularly perfect and magnificent are the forms which are made by them.

450.   This then was one of the effects which the ordered ringing of the bells was intended to produce. It was to throw out a stream of musical forms repeated over and over again, in precisely the same way, and for precisely the same purpose, as the Christian monk repeats hundreds of *Ave Marias* or the northern Buddhist spends much of his life in reiterating the mystic syllables *Om Mani Padme Hum*, or many a Hindu makes a background to his life by reciting the name Sita Ram.

451.   A particular thought-form and its meaning were in this way impressed over and over again upon all the astral bodies within hearing. The blessing of the bells was intended to add an additional quality to these undulations, of whatever kind they may have been. The ringing of the bells in different order would naturally produce different forms; but whatever the forms may be, they are produced by the vibration of the same bells, and if these bells are, to begin with, strongly charged with a certain type of magnetism, every form made by them will bear with it something of that influence. It is as though the wind which wafts to us snatches of music should at the same time bear with it a subtle perfume. So the bishop who blesses the bells charges them with much the same intent as he would bless holy water - with the intention that, wherever this sound shall go, all evil thought and feeling shall be banished and harmony and devotion shall prevail - a real exercise of magic, and quite effective when the magician does his work properly.

452.   The sacring bell, which is rung inside the church, at the moment of the reciting of the *Tersanctus* or the elevation of the Host, has a different intention. In the huge cathedrals which mediaeval piety erected, it was impossible for all the worshippers to hear what the priest was saying in the recitation of the Mass, even before the present system of what is called "recitation in secret" was adopted. And

therefore the server, who is close to the altar and follows the movements of the priest, has it among his duties to announce in this way to the congregation when these critical points of the service are reached.

453.   The bell which is often rung in Hindu or Buddhist temples has yet another intention. The original thought here was a beautiful and altruistic one. When some one had just uttered an act of devotion or made an offering, there came down in reply to that a certain outpouring of spiritual force. This charged the bell among other objects, and the idea of the man who struck it was that by so doing he would spread abroad, as far as the sound of the bell could reach, the vibration of this higher influence while it was still fresh and strong. Now it is to be feared that the true signification has been so far forgotten that there are actually some who believe it necessary in order to attract the attention of their deity!

454.   INCENSE

455.   The same idea carried out in a different way shows itself to us in the blessing of the incense before it is burned. For the incense has always a dual significance. It ascends before God as a symbol of the prayers of the people; but also it spreads through the church as a symbol of the sweet savour of the blessing of God, and so once more the priest pours into it a holy influence with the idea that wherever its scent may penetrate, wherever the smallest particle of that which has been blessed may pass, it shall bear with it a feeling of peace and of purity, and shall chase away all inharmonious thoughts and sensations.

456.   Even apart from the blessing, its influence is good, for it is carefully compounded from gums the undulation-rate of which harmonises perfectly with spiritual and devotional vibrations, but is distinctly hostile to almost all others. The magnetisation may merely intensify its natural characteristics, or may add to it other special oscillations, but in any case its use in connection with religious ceremonies is always good. The scent of sandalwood has many of the same characteristics; and the scent of pure attar of roses, though utterly different in character, has also a good effect.

457.   Another point which is to a large extent new in the scheme prepared by its Founder for the Christian Church is the utilisation of the enormous force which exists in united synchronous action. In Hindu or Buddhist temples each man comes when he chooses, makes his little offering or utters his few words of prayer and praise, and then retires. Result follows each such effort in proportion to the energy of real feeling put into it, and in this way a fairly constant stream of tiny consequences is achieved; but we never get the massive effect produced by the simultaneous efforts of a congregation of hundreds or thousands of people, or the heart-stirring vibrations which accompany the singing of some well known processional hymn.

458.   By thus working together at a service we obtain four separate objects. (1) Whatever is the aim of the invocatory part of the service, a large number of people join in asking for it, and so send out a huge thought-form. (2) A correspondingly large amount of force flows in and stimulates the spiritual faculties of the people. (3) The simultaneous effort synchronises the undulations of their bodies, and so makes

them more receptive. (4) Their attention being directed to the same object, they work together and thus stimulate one another.

459. SERVICES FOR THE DEAD

460.   What I have said in the earlier part of this chapter will explain a feature which is often misunderstood by those who ridicule the Church - the offering of a Mass with a certain intention, or on behalf of a certain dead person. The idea is that that person shall benefit by the downpouring of force which comes on that particular occasion, and undoubtedly he does so benefit, for the strong thought about him cannot but attract his attention, and when he is in that way drawn to the church he takes part in the ceremony and enjoys a large share of its result. Even if he is still in a condition of unconsciousness, as sometime happens to the newly-dead, the exertion of the priest's will (or his earnest prayer, which is the same thing) directs the stream of force towards the person for whom it is intended. Such an effort is a perfectly legitimate act of invocatory magic; unfortunately an entirely illegitimate and evil element is often imported into the transaction by the exaction of a fee for the exercise of this occult power - a thing which is always inadmissible.

461. OTHER RELIGIONS

462.   I have been trying to expound something of the inner meaning of the ceremonies of the Christian Church - taking that, in the first place because it is with that that I am most familiar, and in the second place because it presents some interesting features which in their present form may be said to be new ideas imported into the scheme of things by our present Bodhisattva. I do not wish it to be supposed that I have expounded the Christian ceremonies because I regard that religion as in any way the best expression of universal truth; the fact that I, who am one of its priests, have publicly proclaimed myself a Buddhist, shows clearly that that is not my opinion.

463.   So far as its teaching goes, Christianity is probably more defective than any other of the great religions, with perhaps the doubtful exception of Muhammadanism; but that is not because of any neglect on the part of the original Founder to make His system a perfectly arranged exposition of the truth, but because most unfortunately the ignorant majority of the early Christians cast out from among themselves the great Gnostic Doctors, and thereby left themselves with a sadly mutilated doctrine. The Founder may perhaps have foreseen this failure, for He supplied His Church with a system of magic which would continue to work mechanically, even though His people should forget much of the early meaning of what He had taught them; and it is precisely the force which has lain behind this mechanical working which explains the remarkable hold so long maintained by a Church which intellectually has nothing to give to its followers.

464.   Those who profess other religions must not then suppose that I mean any disrespect to their faiths because I have chosen for exposition that with which I am most familiar. The general principles of the action of ceremonial magic which I have laid down are equally true for all religions, and each must apply them for himself.

465.   THE ORDERS OF CLERGY

466.   Perhaps I ought to explain, for the benefit of our Indian readers, that there are three orders among the Christian clergy - bishops, priests and deacons. When a man is first ordained he is admitted as a deacon, which means, practically, a kind of apprentice or assistant priest. He has not yet the power to consecrate the sacrament, to bless the people or to forgive their sins; he can, however, baptise children, but even a layman is permitted to do that in case of emergency. After a year in the diaconate he is eligible for ordination as a priest, and it is this second ordination which confers upon him the power to draw forth the force from the reservoir of which I have spoken. To him is then given the power to consecrate the Host and also various other objects, to bless the people in the name of the Christ, and to pronounce the forgiveness of their sins. In addition to all these powers, the bishop has that of ordaining other priests, and so carrying on the apostolic succession. He alone has the right to administer the rite of confirmation, and to consecrate a church, that is to say, to set it apart for the service of God. These three are the only orders which mean definite grades, separated from one another by ordinations which confer different powers . You may hear many titles applied to the Christian clergy, such as those of archbishop, archdeacon, dean or canon, but these are only the titles of offices, and involve differences of duty, but not of grade in the sense of spiritual power.

469.   SOUND, COLOUR AND FORM

470.   We have considered the influences radiating from the walls of our churches, and the effect of the ceremonies performed within them; it still remains for us to mention the hidden side of the music of their services.

471.   There are many people who realise that sound always generates colour - that every note which is played or sung has overtones which produce the effect of light when seen by an eye even slightly clairvoyant. Not every one, however, knows that sounds also build form just as thoughts do. Yet this is nevertheless the case. It was long ago shown that sound gives rise to form in the physical world by singing a certain note into a tube across the end of which was stretched a membrane upon which fine sand or lycopodium powder had been cast.

472.   In this way it was proved that each sound threw the sand into a certain definite shape, and that the same note always produced the same shape. It is not, however, with forms caused in this way that we are dealing just now, but with those built up in etheric, astral and mental matter, which persist and continue in vigorous action long after the sound itself has died away, so far as physical ears are concerned.

473.   RELIGIOUS MUSIC

474.   Let us take, for example, the hidden side of the performance of a piece of music - say the playing of a voluntary upon a church organ. This has its effect in the physical world upon those of the worshippers who have an ear for music - who have educated themselves to understand and to appreciate it. But many people who do not understand it and have no technical knowledge of the subject are yet conscious of a very decided effect which it produces upon them.

475.   The clairvoyant student is in no way surprised at this, for he sees that each piece of music as it is performed upon the organ builds up gradually an enormous edifice in etheric, astral and mental matter, extending away above the organ and far through the roof of the church like a kind of castellated mountain-range, all composed of glorious flashing colours coruscating and blazing in a most marvellous manner, like the aurora borealis in the arctic regions. The nature of this differs very much in the case of different composers. An overture by Wagner makes always a magnificent whole with splendid splashes of vivid colour, as though he built with mountains of flame for stones; one of Bach's fugues builds up a mighty ordered form, bold yet precise, rugged but symmetrical, with parallel rivulets of silver or gold or ruby running through it, marking the successive appearances of *motif*; one of Mendelssohn's *Lieder ohne Worte* makes a lovely airy erection - a sort of castle of filigree work in frosted silver.

476.   In the book called *Thought-Forms* will be found three illustrations in colour, in which we have endeavoured to depict the forms built by pieces of music by

Mendelssohn, Gounod and Wagner respectively, and I would refer the reader to these, for this is one of the cases in which it is quite impossible to imagine the appearance of the form without actually seeing it or some representation of it. It may some day be possible to issue a book containing studies of a number of such forms, for the purpose of careful examination and comparison. It is evident that the study of such sound forms would be a science in itself, and one of surpassing interest.

477.   These forms, created by the performers of the music, must not be confounded with the magnificent thought-form which the composer himself made as the expression of his own music in the higher worlds. This is a production worthy of the great mind from which it emanated, and often persists for many years - some times even over centuries, if the composer is so far understood and appreciated that his original conception is strengthened by the thoughts of his admirers. In the same manner, though with wide difference of type, magnificent erections are constructed in higher worlds by a great poet's idea of his epic, or a great writer's idea of the subject which he means to put before his readers - such, for example, as Wagner's immortal trilogy of *The Ring*, Dante's grand representation of purgatory and paradise, and Ruskin's conception of what art ought to be and of what he desired to make it.

478.   The forms made by the performance of the music persist for a considerable space of time, varying from one hour to three or four, and all the time they are sending out radiations which assuredly influence for good every soul within a radius of half a mile or more. Not that the soul necessarily knows it, nor that the influence is at all equal in all cases. The sensitive person is greatly uplifted, while the dull and preoccupied man is but little affected. Still, however unconsciously, each person must be a little the better for coming under such an influence. Naturally the undulations extend much farther than the distance named, but beyond that they grow rapidly weaker, and in a great city they are soon drowned in the rush of swirling currents which fill the astral world in such places. In the quiet country amidst the fields and the trees the edifice lasts proportionately much longer, and its influence has a wider area. Sometimes in such a case those who can, may see crowds of beautiful nature-spirits admiring the splendid forms built by the music, and bathing with delight in the waves of influence which they send forth. It is surely a beautiful thought that every organist who does his work well, and throws his whole soul into what he plays, is thus doing far more good than he knows, and helping many whom perhaps he never saw and never will know in this life.

479.   Another point which is interesting in this connection is the difference between the edifices built by the same music when rendered upon different instruments - as, for example, the difference in appearance of the form built by a certain piece when played upon a church organ and the same piece executed by an orchestra or by a violin quartet, or played on a piano. In these cases the form is identical if the music be equally well rendered, but the whole texture is different; and naturally, in the case of the violin quartet, the size of the form is far less, because the volume of sound is so much less. The form built by the piano is often somewhat larger than that of the violins, but is not so accurate in detail, and its proportions are less perfect. Again, a decided difference in texture is visible between the effect of a violin solo and the same solo played upon the flute.

480.   Surrounding and blending with these forms, although perfectly distinct from them, are the forms of thought and feeling produced by human beings under the influence of the music. The size and vividness of these depend upon the appreciativeness of the audience and the extent to which they are affected. Sometimes the form built by the sublime conception of a master of harmony stands alone in its beauty, unattended and unnoticed, because such mental faculties as the congregation may possess are entirely absorbed in millinery or the calculations of the money-market; while on the other hand the chain of simple forms built by the force of some well-known hymn may in some cases be almost hidden by great blue clouds of devotional feeling evoked from the hearts of the singers.

481.   Another factor which determines the appearance of the edifice constructed by a piece of music is the quality of the performance. The thought-form left hanging over a church after the performance of the Hallelujah Chorus infallibly and distinctly shows, for example, if the bass solo has been flat, or if any of the parts have been noticeably weaker than the others, as in either case there is an obvious failure in the symmetry and clearness of the form. Naturally there are types of music whose forms are anything but lovely, though even these have their interest as objects of study. The curious broken shapes which surround an academy for young ladies at the pupils' practising hour are at least remarkable and instructive, if not beautiful; and the chains thrown out in lasso-like loops and curves by the child who is industriously playing scales or arpeggios are by no means without their charm, when there are no broken or missing links.

482.   SINGING

483.   A song with a chorus constructs a form in which a number of beads are strung at equal distances upon a silver thread of melody, the size of the beads of course depending upon the strength of the chorus, just as the luminosity and beauty of the connecting thread depend upon the voice and expression of the solo singer, while the form into which the thread is plaited depends upon the character of the melody. Of great interest also are the variations in metallic texture produced by different qualities of voice - the contrast between the soprano and the tenor, the alto and the bass, and again the difference between a boy's voice and a woman's. Very beautiful also is the intertwining of these four threads (quite unlike in colour and in texture) in the singing of a glee or a part-song, or their ordered and yet constantly varied march side by side in the singing of a hymn.

484.   A processional hymn builds a series of rectangular forms drawn with mathematical precision, following one another in definite order like the links of some mighty chain - or still more (unpoetical though it sounds) like the carriages of some huge train belonging to the astral world. Very striking also is the difference in ecclesiastical music, between the broken though glittering fragments of the Anglican chant, and the splendid glowing uniformity of the Gregorian tone. Not unlike the latter is the effect produced by the monotonous chanting of Sanskrit verses by pandits in India.

485.   It may be asked here how far the feeling of the musician himself affects

the form which is built by his efforts. His feelings do not, strictly speaking, affect the musical structure at all. If the delicacy and brilliancy of his execution remain the same, it makes no difference to that musical form whether he himself feels happy or miserable, whether his musings are grave or gay. His emotions naturally produce vibrant forms in astral matter, just as do those of his audience, but these merely surround the great shape built by the music, and in no way interfere with it. His comprehension of the music, and the skill of his rendering of it, show themselves in the edifice which he constructs. A poor and merely mechanical performance erects a structure which, though it may be accurate in form, is deficient in colour and luminosity - a form which, as compared with the work of a real musician, gives a curios impression of being constructed of cheap materials. To obtain really grand results the performer must forget all about himself, must lose himself utterly in the music as only a genius may dare to do.

486.   MILITARY MUSIC

487.   The powerful and inspiring effect produced by military music is readily comprehensible to the clairvoyant who is able to see the long stream of rhythmically vibrating forms which is left behind by the band as it marches along at the head of the column. Not only does the regular beat of these undulations tend to strengthen those of the astral bodies of the soldiers, thus training them to move more strongly and in unison, but the very forms which are created themselves radiate strength and courage and material ardour, so that a body of men which before seemed to be hopelessly disorganised by fatigue, may in this way be pulled together again and endowed with a considerable accession of strength.

488.   It is instructive to watch the mechanism of this change. A man who is utterly exhausted has to a great extent lost the power of co-ordination; the central will can no longer hold together and govern as it should the different parts of the body; every physical cell is complaining - raising its own separate cry of pain and remonstrance; and the effect upon all the vehicles - etheric, astral and mental - is that a vast number of small separate vortices are set up, each quivering at its own rate, so that all the bodies are losing their cohesion and their power to do their work, to bear their part in the life of the man. Carried to its ultimate extreme this would mean death, but short of that it means utter disorganisation and the loss of the power to make the muscles obey the will. When upon the astral body in this condition there comes the impact of a succession of steady and powerful oscillations, that impact supplies for the time the place of the will-force which has so sorely slackened. The bodies are once more brought into synchronous vibration and are held so by the sweep of the music, thus giving the will-power an opportunity to recover itself and take again the command which it had so nearly abandoned.

489.   So marked and powerful are the waves sent forth by good military music that a sensation of positive pleasure is produced in those who move in obedience to them, just as effective dance-music arouses the desire for synchronous movement in all who hear it. The type of the instruments employed in military bands is also of a

nature which adds greatly to this effect, the strength and sharpness of the vibration being obviously of far greater importance for those purposes than its delicacy or its power to express the finer emotions.

490.   SOUNDS IN NATURE

491.   It is not only the ordered arrangement of sound which we call music which produces definite form. Every sound in nature has its effect, and in some cases these effects are of the most remarkable character. The majestic roll of a thunderstorm creates usually a vast flowing band of colour, while the deafening crash often calls into temporary existence an arrangement of irregular radiations from a centre suggestive of an exploded bomb; or sometimes a huge irregular sphere with great spikes projecting from it in all directions. The never-ceasing beating of the sea upon the land fringes all earth's coasts with an eternal canopy of wavy yet parallel lines of lovely changing colour, rising into tremendous mountain ranges when the sea is lashed by a storm. The rustling of the wind among the leaves of the forest covers it with a beautiful iridescent network, ever rising and falling with gentle wave-like movement, like the passing of the wind across a field of wheat.

492.   Sometimes this hovering cloud is pierced by curving lines and loops of light, representing the song of the birds, like fragments of a silver chain cast forth and ringing melodiously in the air. Of these there is an almost infinite variety, from the beautiful golden globes produced by the notes of the campanero, to the amorphous and coarsely-coloured mass which is the result of the scream of a parrot or of a macaw. The roar of the lion may be seen as well as heard by those whose eyes are opened; indeed, it is by no means impossible that some of the wild creatures possess this much of clairvoyance, and that the terrifying effect which is alleged to be produced by this sound may be largely owing to the radiations poured forth from the form to which it gives birth.

493.   IN DOMESTIC LIFE

494.   In more domestic life similar effects are observed; the purring cat surrounds himself with concentric rosy cloud-films which expand constantly outward until they dissipate, shedding an influence of drowsy contentment and well-being which tends to reproduce itself in the human beings about him. The barking dog, on the other hand, shoots forth well defined sharp-pointed projectiles which strike with a severe shock upon the astral bodies of those in his neighbourhood; and this is the reason of the extreme nervous irritation which this constantly repeated sound often produces in sensitive persons. The sharp, spiteful yap of the terrier discharges a series of forms not unlike the modern rifle bullet, which pierce the astral body in various directions, and seriously disturb its economy; while the deep bay of a bloodhound throws off beads like ostrich-eggs or footballs which are slower in motion and far less calculated to injure. Some of these canine missiles pierce like sword-thrusts, while some are duller and heavier, like the blows of a club, and they vary greatly in strength, but all alike are evil in their action upon the mental and astral bodies.

495.   The colour of these projectiles is usually some shade of red or brown,

varying with the emotion of the animal and the key in which his voice is pitched. It is instructive to contrast with these the blunt-ended, clumsy shapes produced by the lowing of a cow - forms which have often somewhat the appearance of logs of wood or fragments of a tree-trunk. A flock of sheep frequently surrounds itself with a many-pointed yet amorphous cloud of sound which is by no means unlike the physical dust-cloud which it raises as it moves along. The cooing of a pair of doves throws off a constant succession of graceful curved forms like the letter S reversed.

496.   The tones of the human voice also produce their results - results which often endure long after the sounds which made them have died away. An angry ejaculation throws itself forth like a scarlet spear, and many a woman surrounds herself with an intricate network of hard, brown-grey metallic lines by the stream of silly meaningless chatter which she ceaselessly babbles forth. Such a network permits the passage of vibration only at its own low level; it is an almost perfect barrier against the impact of any of the higher and more beautiful thoughts and feelings. A glimpse of the astral body of a garrulous person is thus a striking object-lesson to the student of occultism, and it teaches him the virtue of speaking only when it is necessary, or when he has something pleasant and useful to say.

497.   Another instructive comparison is that between the forms produced by different kinds of laughter. The happy laughter of a child bubbles forth in rosy curves, making a kind of scalloped balloon shape - an epicycloid of mirth. The ceaseless guffaw of the empty-minded causes an explosive effect in an irregular mass, usually brown or dirty green in colour - according to the pre-dominant tint of the aura from which it emanates. The sneering laugh throws out a shapeless projectile of a dull red colour, usually flecked with brownish-green and bristling with thorny-looking points. The constantly repeated cachinnations of the self-conscious create a very unpleasant result, surrounding them with what in appearance and colour resembles the surface of a pool of boiling mud. The nervous giggles of a school-girl often involve her in an unpleasant seaweed-like tangle of lines of brown and dull yellow, while the jolly-hearted, kindly laugh of genuine amusement usually billows out in rounded forms of gold and green. The consequences flowing from the bad habit of whistling are usually decidedly unpleasant. If it be soft and really musical it produces an effect not unlike that of a small flute, but sharper and more metallic: but the ordinary tuneless horror of the London street-boy sends out a series of small and piercing projectiles of dirty brown.

498.   NOISES

499.   An enormous number of artificial noises (most of them transcendently hideous) are constantly being produced all about us, for our so-called civilisation is surely the noisiest with which earth has yet ever been cursed. These also have their unseen side, though it is rarely one which is pleasant to contemplate. The strident screech of a railway engine makes a far more penetrating and powerful projectile than even the barking of a dog; indeed, it is surpassed in horror only by the scream of the steam siren which is sometimes employed to call together the hands at a factory, or by the report of heavy artillery at close quarters. The railway whistle blows forth

a veritable sword, with the added disintegrating power of a serious electrical shock, and its effect upon the astral body which is unfortunate enough to be within its reach is quite comparable to that of a sword-thrust upon the physical body. Fortunately for us, astral matter possesses many of the properties of a fluid, so that the wound heals after a few minutes have passed; but the effect of the shock upon the astral organism disappears by no means so readily.

500.	The flight through the landscape of a train which is not screaming is not wholly unbeautiful, for the heavy parallel lines which are drawn by the sound of its onward rush are as it were embroidered by the intermittent spheres or ovals caused by the puffing of the engine: so that a train seen in the distance crossing the landscape leaves behind it a temporary appearance of a strip of Brobdingnagian ribbon with a scalloped edging.

501.	The discharge of one of the great modern cannons is an explosion of sound just as surely as of gun-powder, and the tremendous radiation of impacts which it throws out to the radius of a mile or so is calculated to have a very serious effect upon astral currents and astral bodies. The rattle of rifle or pistol fire throws out a sheaf of small needles, which are also eminently undesirable in their effect.

502.	It is abundantly clear that all loud, sharp or sudden sounds should, as far as possible, be avoided by anyone who wishes to keep his astral and mental vehicles in good order. This is one among the many reasons which make the life of the busy city one to be avoided by the occult student, for its perpetual roar means the ceaseless beating of disintegrating vibrations upon each of his vehicles, and this is, of course, quite apart from the even more serious play of sordid passions and emotions which make dwelling in a main street like living beside an open sewer.

503.	No one who watches the effect of these repeated sound-forms upon the sensitive astral body can doubt that there must follow from them a serious permanent result which cannot fail to be to some extent communicated to the physical nerves. So serious and so certain is this, that I believe that if it were possible to obtain accurate statistics on such a point, we should find the length of life much shorter and the percentage of nervous breakdown and insanity appreciably higher among the inhabitants of a street paved with granite, than among those who have advantage of asphalt. The value and even the necessity of quiet is by no means sufficiently appreciated in our modern life. Specially do we ignore the disastrous effect upon the plastic astral and mental bodies of children of all this ceaseless, unnecessary noise; yet that is largely responsible for evils of many kinds and for weaknesses which show themselves with fatal effect in later life.

504.	There is a yet higher point of view from which all the sounds of nature blend themselves into one mighty tone - that which the Chinese authors have called the KUNG; and this also has its form - an inexpressible compound or synthesis of all forms, vast and changeful as the sea, and yet through it all upholding an average level, just as the sea does, all-penetrating yet all embracing, the note which represents our earth in the music of the spheres - the form which is our petal when the solar system is regarded from that plane where it is seen all spread out like a lotus.

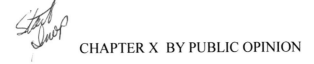

507.   RACE PREJUDICE

508.   When anything occurs to prevent us from doing or saying exactly what we should like to do, we are in the habit of congratulating ourselves that thought at least is free. But this is only another of the many popular delusions. For the average man thought is by no means free; on the contrary it is conditioned by a large number of powerful limitations. It is bound by the prejudices of the nation, the religion, the class to which he happens to belong, and it is only by a determined and long-continued effort that he can shake himself free from all these influences, and really think for himself.

509.   These restrictions operate on him in two ways; they modify his opinion about facts and about actions. Taking the former first, he sees nothing as it really is, but only as his fellow-countrymen, his co-religionists, or the members of his caste think it to be. When we come to know more of other races we shake off our preconceptions concerning them. But we have only to look back a century to the time of Napoleon, and we shall at once perceive that no Englishman then could possibly have formed an impartial opinion as to the character of that remarkable man. Public opinion in England had erected him into a kind of bogey; nothing was too terrible or too wicked to be believed of him, and indeed it is doubtful whether the common people really considered him as a human being at all.

510.   The prepossession against everything French was then so strong that to say that a man was a Frenchman was to believe him capable of any villainy; and one cannot but admit that those who had fresh in their minds the unspeakable crimes of the French Revolution had some justification for such an attitude. They were too near to the events to be able to see them in proportion; and because the offscourings of the streets of Paris had contrived to seize upon the government and to steep themselves in orgies of blood and crime, they thought that these represented the people of France. It is easy to see how far from the truth must have been the conception of the Frenchman in the mind of the average English peasant of that period.

511.   Among our higher classes the century which has passed since then has produced an entire revolution of feeling, and now we cordially admire our neighbours across the Channel, because now we know so much more of them. Yet even now it is not impossible that there may be remote country places in which something of that old and strongly established prejudice still survives. For the leading countries of the world are in reality as yet only partially civilised, and while everywhere the more cultured classes are prepared to receive foreigners politely, the same can hardly be said of the mill-hands or the colliers. And there are still parts of Europe where the Jew is hardly regarded as a human being.

512. POPULAR PREJUDICE

513.   It needs little argument to show that everywhere among the less cultured people prejudgments are still strong and utterly unreasonable; but we who think ourselves above them - even we need to be careful, lest unconsciously we allow them to influence us. To stand against a strong popular bias is no easy matter, and the student of occultism will at once see why this is so. The whole atmosphere is full of thought-forms and currents of thought, and these are ceaselessly acting and reacting upon every one of us. The tendency of any thought-form is to reproduce itself. It is charged with a certain rate of vibration, and its nature is to influence every mental and astral body with which it comes into contact in the direction of the same vibration.

514.   There are many matters about which opinion is reasonably equally divided, as (for example) the angle at which one should wear one's hat, or whether one should be a Liberal or a Conservative. Consequently the general average of thought on these matters is no stronger in one direction than in another; and about them and other such matters it may be said that thought is comparatively free. But there are other subjects upon which there is an overwhelming consensus of public opinion in one direction, and that amounts to so strong a pressure of a certain set of undulations connected with that subject upon the mental body, that unless a man is unusually strong and determined he will be swept into the general current. Even if he is strong enough to resist it, and is upon his guard against it, the pressure is still there, and its action is still continued, and if at any time he relaxes his vigilance for a moment, he may find himself unconsciously warped by it.

515.   I have explained in the second volume of *The Inner Life* that a man who allows himself to contract a prejudice of this kind on any subject causes a hardening of the matter of the mental body in the part of it through which the oscillations relating to that subject would naturally pass. This acts upon him in two ways; first, he is unable to see that subject as it really is, for the vibrations which would otherwise convey an impression of it come against this callosity of the mental body, and either they cannot penetrate it at all, or they are so distorted in their passage through it that they convey no real information. Secondly, the man cannot think truly with regard to that subject, because the very part of this mental body which he would use in such an effort is already so hardened as to be entirely inefficient, so that the only way to overcome the unfairness is to perform a surgical operation upon that wart in the mental body, and excise it altogether, and to keep for a long time a close watch upon it to see that it is not growing again. If that watch be not kept, the steady pressure of the thought-waves of thousands of other people will reproduce it, and it will be necessary to perform the operation all over again.

516. POLITICAL PREJUDICE

517.   In many parts of the country there is a vast amount of bitter political bias. The majority of the people in a district hold one view or the other (it matters little which), and they find it difficult to imagine that the members of the opposite party are ordinary human beings at all. They are so sure of their own point of view that

they appear to think that every one else must really hold it also, and that it is only out of malice prepense that their opponents are pretending to hold an entirely different view. Yet their own ideas are usually not arrived at by any process of thought or of weighing two lines of policy, but are hereditary, precisely as are most men's religious opinions. There is so much excitement and unpleasant feeling connected with politics in almost every country that the wisest course for the student of occultism is to have as little as possible to do with the whole matter. Not that, if he happens to reside in a country where he has a vote, he should refuse to use it, as many good people have done, because of the mass of corruption which sometimes surrounds political activity of the lower kind. If there is much that is evil in connection with such affairs, that is all the more reason why every good citizen should use the power that the system has vested in him (however foolish in itself that system may be) in favour of what seems to him the right and noble course.

518.   GOVERNMENT

519.   The occult theory of government, of the politics of the State, is preeminently the common-sense view. The management of a country is as much a matter of business as the management of a factory or a school. The country has many points of similarity to a great public school. It exists primarily for the benefit of its people, and the people are put there in order to learn. The head of the country makes whatever regulations he considers necessary to secure its efficiency, and there must be discipline and order and prompt obedience to those regulations, or there can be no progress. The king is the headmaster. His work is to exercise sleepless vigilance over the welfare of the school, to employ all methods in his power to make it the best of schools. Our business is not to criticise him, but to obey him, and loyally to give our heartiest co-operation in carrying out whatever he thinks best for the good of the country as a whole. The business of a government is to govern; the business of its people is to be good, loyal, law-abiding citizens so as to make that task of government easy.

520.   A king who thinks of or works for fancied private interests of his own, instead of acting only for his country, is obviously failing to do his work; but remember that any subject who in politics thinks of or works for supposed private interests of his own, and not for the good of the country as a whole, is also equally failing to do his duty as a good citizen. As to the outer form of a government, almost any form can be made to work satisfactorily if the people co-operate loyally and unselfishly, forgetting themselves as units and regarding the country as their unit; but no form of government, however excellent, can be successful and satisfactory if its people are selfish and refractory.

521.   RELIGIOUS PREJUDICE

522.   All that I have said of race prejudice is also true of religious prejudice, which is indeed in many ways even worse than the other. Few men choose their religion; most people are born into a religion, exactly as they are born into a race, and they have no valid reason for preferring it to any other form of faith; but because it

happens to be theirs, they arrogantly assume that it must be better than any other, and despise other people whose karma has led them into a slightly different environment. Precisely because this partiality is thus in the air, and because the ordinary man cannot see the pressure of public opinion, the unfairness steals in upon him unobserved and seems to him quite natural, and indistinguishable from an opinion which he has formed for himself on some reasonable grounds.

523.   It is necessary that we should constantly pull ourselves up, and examine our reasons for the opinions we hold. It is so fatally easy to go with the current and to accept other men's ready-made thoughts, instead of thinking for ourselves. "Almost every one does this, so why should not I?" That is the feeling of the average man, and yet if we would be just to all, as a student of occultism must be - if we seek to know the truth on all subjects, as a student of occultism should know it - then we must at all costs root out these prejudices, and keep a lynx-like watch against their return. We shall find ourselves in many ways differing from the majority, because the opinions of the majority are often unjust, ill-conceived, unreliable; but that after all we must expect, for we are setting before us a high ideal, which as yet does not appeal to that majority. If we think on all points as it thinks, and act in all ways as it acts, in what way have we raised ourselves above it, and how can we be drawing nearer to our goal?

524.   CLASS PREJUDICE
525.   More insidious still perhaps is the class or caste bias. It is so comforting to feel that we are somehow inherently and generically superior to everybody else - that no good feeling or good action can be expected from the other man, *because* he is a bloated aristocrat or a member of the proletariat, as the case may be. Here again, as with all the other misconceptions, the study of the hidden side of the matter shows us that what is needed is more knowledge and more charity. The occultist sees a prejudice to be a congestion of thought; what is necessary therefore is to stir up the thought, to get to know the people and try to comprehend them, and we shall soon find that fundamentally there is little difference between us and them.

526.   That there are classes of egos, that some are older and some are younger, and that some are consequently more ignorant than others, it is impossible to deny, for that is a fact in nature, as has been shown by our study of the order in which different divisions of mankind arrived from the moon-chain upon the earth-chain. But there is a common humanity which underlies all the classes, and to this we may always appeal with the certainty of obtaining some response.

527.   Those who feel sure that they belong to the higher class of egos must prove their nobility by great tolerance and charity towards the less fortunate younger members of the human race; *noblesse oblige*, and if they are the nobility they must act accordingly. A prejudice is usually so transparently foolish that when a man has freed himself from it he cannot believe that he ever really felt it, cannot understand how any of his fellow-creatures who have any pretence to reasoning powers can be subject to it. So there is a certain danger that he himself may become intolerant in turn - intolerant of intolerance. The occultist, however, who sees the mighty combined thought-form

and understands the almost irresistible power, and yet the curious insidiousness of its action, understands very well the difficulty of resisting it - the difficulty even of escaping sufficiently from its thraldom to realise that there is anything to resist.

528.   PUBLIC STANDARDS

529.   Fortunately this almost irresistible pressure of public opinion is not always wrong. In certain directions it is founded not upon the cumulative ignorance of the race, but on its cumulative knowledge - on the experience of generations that have gone before us. Public opinion is undoubtedly in the right when it condemns murder or robbery; and countries in which public opinion has not yet advanced so far as to express itself clearly on these points are universally admitted to be in the rearguard of civilisation. There are still in the world communities in which law and order are only beginning to exist, and violence is still the deciding factor in all disputes; but those countries are universally recognised as undesirable places of habitation and as lagging behind the progress of the world.

530.   There are other crimes besides robbery and murder which are universally condemned in all civilised countries, and in all these directions the pressure exerted by public opinion is a pressure in the right direction, tending to restrain those erratic spirits who might otherwise think only of their own desires and not at all of the welfare of the community.

531.   The occultist, seeing so much more of what is really happening, establishes for himself a far more exacting code of morals than does the ordinary man. Many things which the ordinary man would do, and constantly does do, without thinking twice about them, the occultist would not permit himself to do under any consideration, because he sees their effects in other worlds, which are hidden from the less developed man. This is a general rule, though here and there we meet with exceptions in which the occultist, who understands the case, will take steps which the ordinary man would fear to take. This is because his action is based upon knowledge, because he sees what he is doing, while the other man is acting only according to custom.

532.   The great laws of morality are universal, but temporary and local customs are often only ridiculous. There are still many people to whom it is a heinous crime to go for a walk on a Sunday or to play a game of cards. At such restrictions the occultist smiles, though he is careful not to hurt the feelings of those to whom such quaint and unnatural regulations seem matters of primary importance. In many cases, too, the superior knowledge gained by occult study enables him to see the real meaning of regulations which are misunderstood by others.

533.   CASTE PREJUDICE

534.   A good example of this is to be seen in regard to the caste regulations of India. These were established some ten thousand years ago by the Manu in charge of the fifth root-race, when He had moved down the main stock of that race from Central Asia to the plains of India. This was after the sub-races had been sent out to do their colonising work, and the remnant of the main stock of His race was but small

as compared to the teeming millions of Hindustan. Wave after wave of immigration had swept into the country, and mingled freely with the ruling race among its previous inhabitants, and He saw that, unless some definite command was given, the Aryan type, which had been established with so much trouble, would run great risk of being entirely lost. He therefore issued instructions that a certain division of His people should be made, and that the members of the three great types which He thus set apart should remain as they were, that they should not intermarry with one another or with the subject races.

535.   This was the only restriction that was laid upon them. Yet this very simple and harmless regulation has been expanded into a system of iron rigidity which at the present time interferes at every step and in every direction with the progress of India as a nation. The command not to intermarry has been distorted into an order to hold no fellowship with the members of another caste, not to eat with them, not to accept food from them. Not only that, but the great race divisions made by the Manu have been again divided and subdivided until we are now in the presence of not three castes but a great multitude of sub-castes, all looking down upon one another, all foreign to one another, all restricted from intermarrying or from eating together. And all this in spite of the fact, well-known to all, that within the written laws of Manu (though they contain much which the Manu himself certainly did not say) it is stated quite definitely that the man of higher caste *may* eat with one of the lowest caste whom he knows to be living in a rational and cleanly manner, and that in the *Mahabharata* caste is declared to depend not upon birth but upon character. For example,

536.   One's own ploughman, an old friend of the family, one's own cowherd, one's own servant, one's own barber, and whosoever else may come for refuge and offer service - from the hands of all such shudras may food be taken.

537.   (*Manusmriti, iv, 253.*)

538.   After doubt and debate, the Gods decided that the food-gift of the money-lending shudra who was generous of heart was equal in quality to the food-gift of the Shrotriya brahmana who knew all the Vedas, but was small of heart. But the Lord of all creatures came to them and said: Make ye not that equal which is unequal. The food-gift of that shudra is purified by the generous heart, while that of the Shrotriya brahmana is befouled wholly by the lack of goodwill.

539.   (*Manusmriti, iv, 224, 225*)

540.   Not birth, nor sacraments, nor study, nor ancestry, can decide whether a person is twice-born (and to which of the three types of the twice-born he belongs). Character and conduct only can decide.

541.   (*Mahabharata, Vanaparvan, cccxiii, 108*).

542.   Yet obvious as all this is, and well known as are the texts to which I have referred, there are yet thousands of otherwise intelligent people to whom the regulations made (not by religion but by custom only) are rules as strict as that of any savage with his taboo. All readily agree as to the absurdity of the taboo imposed in a savage tribe, whose members believe that to touch a certain body or to mention a certain name will bring down upon them the wrath of their deity. Yet all do not realise

that the extraordinary taboo which many otherwise sensible Christians erect round one of the days of the week is in every respect as utterly irrational. Nor do our Indian friends realise that they have erected a taboo, exactly similar and quite as unreasonable, about a whole race of their fellow men, whom they actually label as untouchable, and treat as though they were scarcely human beings at all. Each race or religion is ready enough to ridicule the superstitions of others, and yet fails to comprehend the fact that it has equally foolish superstitions itself.

543.   These very superstitions have done irreparable harm to the cause of religion, for naturally enough those who oppose the religious idea fasten upon these weak points and emphasise and exaggerate them out of all proportion, averring that religion is synonymous with superstition; whereas the truth is that there is a great body of truth which is common to all the religions, which is entirely unmarred by superstition, and of the greatest value to the world, as is clearly proved by Mrs. Besant's Universal Text Book of Religion and Morals. This body of teaching is the important part of every religion, and if the professors of all these faiths could be induced to recognise that and, - we will not say to abandon their private superstitions, but at least to recognise them as not binding upon any but themselves, there would be no difficulty whatever in arriving at a perfect agreement. Each person has an inalienable right to believe what he chooses, however foolish it may appear to others; but he can under no circumstances have any possible right to endeavour to force his particular delusion upon those others, or to persecute them in any way for declining to accept it. START

544.   THE DUTY OF FREEDOM

545.   It therefore becomes the duty of every student of occultism to examine carefully the religious belief of his country and his period, in order that he may decide for himself what of it is based upon reason and what is merely a superstitious accretion. Most men never make any such effort at discrimination, for they cannot shake themselves free from the influence of the great crowd of thought-forms which constitute public opinion; and because of those they never really see the truth at all, nor even know of its existence, being satisfied to accept instead of it this gigantic thought-form. For the occultist the first necessity is to attain a clear and unprejudiced view of everything - to see it as it is, and not as a number of other people suppose it to be.

546.   In order to secure this clearness of vision, unceasing vigilance is necessary. For the pressure of the great hovering thought-cloud upon us, is by no means relaxed because we have once detected and defied its influence. Its pressure is ever present, and quite unconsciously we shall find ourselves yielding to it in all sorts of minor matters, even though we keep ourselves clear from it with regard to the greater points. We were born under its pressure, just as we were born under the pressure of the atmosphere, and we are just as unconscious of one as of the other. As we have never seen anything except through its distorted medium, we find a great difficulty in learning to see clearly, and even in recognising the truth when we finally come face to face with it; but at least it will gradually help us in our search for truth to know of

this hidden side of public opinion, so that we may be on our guard against its constant and insidious pressure.

547.   BUSINESS METHODS

548.   For example, this public opinion is at a very low level with regard to what are called business methods.

549.   In these days of keen competition, things are done and methods are adopted in business that would have astonished our forefathers. Many of these actions and methods are perfectly legitimate, and mean nothing more than the application of shrewder thought and greater cleverness to the work which has to be done; but unquestionably the boundary of what is legitimate and honourable is not infrequently overstepped, and means are employed to which the honest merchant of an earlier age would never have descended.

550.   Indeed, there has come to be a sort of tacit understanding that business has a morality of its own, and that ordinary standards of integrity are not to be applied to it. A man at the head of a large mercantile house once said to me: "If I tried to do business according to the Golden Rule - ` Do unto others as ye would that they should do unto you' - I should simply starve; I should be bankrupt in a month. The form in which it runs in business matters is much nearer to that immortalised by David Harum: ` Do unto the other man as he would like to do unto you, and *do it first*. ' " And many others to whom this remark was quoted frankly agreed with him. Men who in all other respects are good and honest and honourable feel themselves bound in such matters to do as others do. "Business is business," they say, "and the moralist who objects does not know its conditions," and under this excuse they treat one another in business as they would never dream of treating a friend in private life, and make statements which they know to be false, even though outside of their trade they may be truthful men.

551.   All our virtues need widening out so that they will cover a greater area. At first man is frankly selfish, and takes care only of himself. Then he widens his circle of affection, and loves his family in addition to himself. Later on he extends a modified form of affection to his neighbours and his tribe, so that he will no longer rob them, though he is quite willing to join with them in robbing some other tribe or nation. Even thousands of years ago, if a dispute arose within a family the head of the family would act as arbitrator and settle it. We have now extended this as far as our neighbours or our fellow-citizens in the same State. If we have a dispute with any of them, a magistrate acts as an arbitrator, in the name of the law of the land. But we have not yet reached a sufficient state of civilisation to apply the same idea to national quarrels, though we are just beginning to talk about doing so, and one or two of the most advanced nations have already settled some difficulties in this way.

552.   In the same way the brothers of a family stand together; in dealing with one another they will not take advantage, or state what is untrue; but we have not yet reached the level on which they will be equally honest and open with those outside of the family, in what they call business. Perhaps if a man meets another in private life or at a friend's house, and enters into conversation with him, he would scorn to tell him

a falsehood; yet let the same man enter his shop or place of business, and his ideas of what is honourable or lawful for him at once undergo a sad deterioration.

553.   Undoubtedly, people who manage their affairs along the lines of sharp practice sometimes acquire large fortunes thereby; and those who regard life superficially, envy them for what they consider their success. But those who have accustomed themselves to look a little deeper into the underlying realities, recognise that it is not success at all - that in truth there has been no profit in such a transaction, but a very serious loss.

554.   If man is a soul in process of evolution towards perfection, temporarily stationed here on earth in order to learn certain lessons and to achieve a certain stage of his progress, it is obvious that the only thing that matters is to learn those lessons and to make that progress. If man be in truth, as many of us know he is, a soul that lives for ever, the true interest of the man is the interest of that soul, not of the body, which is nothing but its temporary vesture; and anything that hinders the progress of that soul is emphatically a bad thing for the man, no matter how advantageous it may appear for his body.

555.   The soul is acting through and advancing by means of his vehicles, and the physical body is only one of these, and that the lowest. Manifestly, therefore, before we are able to pronounce whether any course of action is really good or bad for us, we must know how it affects all of these vehicles, and not only one of them.

556.   Suppose that one man overreaches another in some transaction, and boasts blatantly of his success and the profit which it has brought him. The student of the inner side of nature will tell him that there has been in reality no gain, but a heavy loss instead. The trickster chinks his money in his hand, and in his shortsightedness triumphantly cries: "See, here is the best of proof; here are the golden sovereigns that I have won; how can you say that I have not gained?"

557.   The occultist will reply that the gold may do him a little good or a little harm, according to the way in which he uses it; but that a consideration of far greater importance is the effect of the transaction upon higher levels. Let us put aside altogether, for the moment, the injury done to the victim of the fraud - though, since humanity is truly a vast brotherhood, that is a factor by no means to be ignored; but let us restrict ourselves now exclusively to the selfish aspect of the action, and see what harm the dishonest merchant has done to himself.

558.   THE RESULTS OF DECEIT

559.   Two facts stand out prominently to clairvoyant sight. First, the deceiver has had to think out his scheme of imposture; he has made a mental effort, and the result of that effort is a thought-form. Because the thought which gave it birth was guileful and ill-intentioned, that thought-form is one which cramps and sears the mental body, hindering its growth and intensifying its lower vibrations - a disaster in itself far more than counter-balancing anything whatever that could possibly happen in the physical world. But that is not all.

560.   Secondly, this duplicity has set up a habit in the mental body. It is

represented therein by a certain type of vibration, and since this vibration has been set strongly in motion, it has created a tendency towards its own repetition. Next time the man's thoughts turn towards any commercial transaction, it will be a little easier than before for him to adopt some knavish plan, a little more difficult than before for him to be manly, open and honest. So that this one act of double-dealing may have produced results in the mental body which it will take years of patient striving to eliminate.

561.   Clearly, therefore, even from the most selfish point of view, the speculation has been a bad one; the loss enormously outweighs the gain. This is a certainty - a matter not of sentiment or imagination, but of fact; and it is only because so many are still blind to the wider life, that all men do not at once see this. But even those of us whose sight is not yet open to higher worlds, should be capable of bringing logic and common sense to bear upon what our seers tell us - sufficiently at least to comprehend that these things must be so, and to take timely warning, to realise that a transaction may appear to be profitable in one direction and yet be a ruinous loss in another, and that all the factors must be taken into account before the question of profit or loss is decided.

562.   It is clear that a student of the occult who has to engage in business must needs watch closely what are called business methods, lest the pressure of public opinion on this matter should lead him to perform or to condone actions not perfectly straightforward or consistent with true brotherhood.

563.   PREJUDICE AGAINST PERSONS

564.   This applies also in the case of public opinion about a particular person. There is an old proverb which says: "Give a dog a bad name and you may as well hang him at once." The truth which it expresses in so homely a manner is a real one, for if the community has a bad opinion of any given person, however utterly unfounded that opinion may be, the thought-form of it exists in the atmosphere of the place, and any stranger who comes will be likely to be influenced by it. The newcomer, knowing nothing of the victim of evil report, is unlikely to begin his acquaintance with him by charging him with specific crimes; but he may find himself predisposed to think ill of him, without being able to account for it, and may have a tendency to place a sinister interpretation upon the simplest of his actions. If we are trying to follow the truth we must be on our guard against these influences also; we must learn to judge for ourselves in such cases and not to accept a ready-made public judgment, which is just as truly a superstition as though it were connected with religious subjects.

565.   THE INFLUENCE OF FRIENDS

566.   An influence which often bears a very large part in a man's life is that of his friends. This is recognised in a popular proverb which says that a man may be known by his friends. I take that to mean that the man usually chooses his friends from men of a certain type or a certain class, and that that in turn means that he finds himself in sympathy with the ideas of that type or that class, and so is likely to reproduce them himself; but it also means much more than this. When a man is with a friend whom he

loves, he is in the most receptive attitude. He throws himself open to the influence of his friend, and whatever characteristics are strongly developed in that friend will tend to produce themselves in him also.

567.   Even in the physical world the belief of a friend commends itself to us merely because it is belief. It comes to us with a recommendation which assures for it our most favourable consideration. The hidden side of this is in truth merely an extension of the idea to a higher level. We open ourselves out towards our friends, and in doing so put ourselves in a condition of sympathetic vibration with them. We receive and enfold their thought-waves; whatever is definite in them cannot but impress itself upon our higher bodies, and these undulations come to us enwrapped in those of affection; an appeal is made to our feelings, and therefore to a certain extent our judgment is for the time less alert. On the one side, this may imply a certain danger that an influence may be accepted without sufficient consideration; on the other hand, it has its advantage in securing for that opinion a thoroughly sympathetic reception and examination. The path of wisdom will be to receive every new opinion as sympathetically as though it came from our best friend, and yet to scrutinise it as carefully as though it had reached us from a hostile source.

568.   POPULAR SUPERSTITIONS

569.   It must be remembered that superstition is by no means confined to religious matters. Most travelled Englishmen are aware that in certain parts of the Continent there exists a very decided superstition against the admission of fresh air into a room or a railway carriage, even though science teaches us that fresh air is a necessity of life. We know without a shadow of doubt, from scientific teaching, that sunlight destroys many disease germs, and vitalises the atmosphere; so it is impossible to question that it ought to be admitted to our houses as freely as possible, more especially in those unfortunate countries where we see so little of it. Yet instead of accepting this blessing and exulting in it, many a housewife makes determined efforts to shut it out when it appears, because of a superstition connected with the colours of curtains and carpets. It is not to be denied that sunlight causes certain colours to fade, but the curious lack of proportion of the ignorant mind is shown in the fact that faded colours are regarded as of greater importance than the physical health and cleanliness which the admission of the sunlight brings. Civilisation is gradually spreading, but there are still many towns and villages in which the superstitious following of the customs of our unscientific forefathers prevents the adoption of modern methods of sanitation.

570.   Even among people who think themselves advanced, curious little fragments of primeval superstition still survive. There are still many among us who will not commence a new undertaking on a Friday, nor form one of a party of thirteen. There are many who regard certain days of the week or of the month as fortunate for them and others as unfortunate, and allow their lives to be governed accordingly. I am not prepared to deny that a larger number of instances than could reasonably be accounted for by coincidence can be adduced to show that certain numbers are always connected in some way with the destiny of certain persons or families. I do not

yet fully understand all that is involved in this, but it would be silly to deny the fact because we have not immediately at hand an adequate explanation of it. Those who are interested in pursuing this question further will find some of the instances to which I am referring in the appendix to Baring Gould's *Curious Myths of the Middle Ages*.

571.　　　I do not doubt the existence of what are commonly called planetary influences, for I have already explained the hidden side of them; but I say that, while these influences may make it easier or more difficult to do a certain thing on a certain day, there is nothing whatever in any of them, or all of them combined, that can prevent a man of determined will from ordering his life precisely as he thinks best. As has been said, the wise man rules his stars, the fool obeys them. To let oneself become a slave to such influences is to make a superstition of them.

572.　　THE FEAR OF GOSSIP

573.　　　Perhaps the greatest and most disastrous of all the taboos that we erect for ourselves is the fear of what our neighbours will say. There are many men and women who appear to live only in order that they may be talked about; at least that is what one must infer from the way in which they bring everything to this as to a touchstone. The one and only criterion which they apply with regard to any course of action is the impression which it will make upon their neighbours. They never ask themselves: "Is it right or wrong for me to do this?" but: "What will Mrs. Jones say if I do this?"

574.　　　This is perhaps the most terrible form of slavery under which a human being can suffer, and yet to obtain freedom from it, it is only necessary to assert it. What other people say can make to us only such difference as we ourselves choose to allow it to make. We have but to realise within ourselves that it does not in the least matter what anybody says, and at once we are perfectly free. This is a lesson which the occultist must learn at an early stage of his progress. He lives upon a higher level, and he can allow himself to be influenced only by higher considerations. He takes into account the hidden side of things of which most people know nothing; and, basing his judgment upon that, he decides for himself what is right and what is wrong, and (having decided) he troubles himself no more as to what other people say of him than we trouble ourselves as to the flies that circle round our heads. It never matters in the least to us what anyone else says, but it matters much to us what we ourselves say.

575.　　A BETTER ASPECT

576.　　　Happily this mighty power of thought can be used for good as well as for evil, and, in some ways, the pressure of public opinion is occasionally on the side of truth and righteousness. Public opinion, after all, represents the opinion of the majority, and therefore the pressure which it exercises is all to the good when it is applied to those who are below the level of the majority. It is indeed only the existence of this mass of opinion which renders social and civilised life possible; otherwise we should be at the mercy of the strongest and the most unscrupulous among us. But the student of occultism is trying to raise himself to a level much above the majority, and for that purpose it is necessary that he should learn to think for himself, and not to accept ready-made opinions without examining them. This much at least may be said - that, if public opinion does not yet exact a very high level of conduct, at least the public ideal is a high one, and it never fails to respond to the noble and the heroic when that is put before it. Class feeling and *esprit de corps* do harm when they lead men to despise others; but they do good when they establish a standard below which the man feels that he cannot fall.

577.　　In England we have a way of attributing our morals to our religion, whereas the truth seems to be that there is little real connection between them. It must be admitted that large numbers of the cultured classes in almost any European country have no real effective belief in religion at all. Perhaps to a certain extent they take a few general dogmas for granted, because they have never really thought about them or weighed them in their minds, but it would be an error to suppose that religious considerations direct their actions or bear any large part in their life.

578.　　They are, however, greatly influenced, and influenced always for good, by another body of ideas which is equally intangible - the sense of honour. The gentleman in every race has a code of honour of his own; there are certain things which he must not do, which he cannot do because he is a gentleman. To do any of those things would lower him in his own estimation, would destroy his feeling of self-respect; but in fact he has never even the temptation to do them, because he regards them as impossible for him. To tell an untruth, to do a mean or dishonourable action, to be disrespectful to a lady; these and such as these, he will tell you, are things which are *not done* in his rank of life. The pressure of such class feeling as this is all to the good, and is by all means to be encouraged. The same thing is to be found in a minor degree in the tradition of our great schools or colleges, and many a boy who has been strongly tempted to escape from some difficulty by an act of dishonour has said to himself: "I cannot do that, for the sake of the old school; it shall never be said that one of its members descended to such an action." So there is a good side as well as a bad one to this matter of public opinion, and our business is to use always the great virtue of discrimination, so that we may separate the desirable from the undesirable.

579.　　Another point worth remembering is that this great, clumsy, stupid force of public opinion can itself be slowly and gradually moulded and influenced. We ourselves are members of the public, and under the universal law our views must to some extent affect others. The wonderful change, which during the last thirty years has come over modern thought in connection with the subjects which we study, is largely due to the persistent work of our Society. Through all those years we have steadily continued to speak, to write, and above all to think sanely and rationally about these questions. In doing so we have been pouring out vibrations, and their effect is plainly visible in a great modification of the thought of our day. Only those men who are fully ready can be brought as far as Theosophy, but thousands more may be brought half-way - into New Thought, into Spiritualism, into liberal Christianity. In this case, as in every other, to know the law is to be able to wield its forces.

582.   A FUNERAL

583.   So far we have been considering chiefly the influences which, whether emanating from nature or from humanity around us, are steadily exercising upon us a fairly constant pressure, of which we are usually ignorant precisely because it is constant. It will now be well to mention the hidden side of such occurrences as come only occasionally into our lives, as, for example, when we attend a funeral, when we undergo a surgical operation, when we attend a lecture, a political meeting, or a spiritualistic séance, when there is a religious revival in our neighbourhood, when a great national festival is celebrated, or when there is a war, an earthquake, an eruption or some great calamity in the world.

584.   First, then, how is a man affected by the hidden side of a funeral? I do not mean how is a man affected by his own funeral, though that also is a question of interest, for it affects some people to an extraordinary extent. No person of philosophical temperament would trouble himself as to what was done with his body, which is after all only a wornout garment; but there are many people in the world who are not philosophical, and to them it is sometimes a matter of great moment.

585.   All classical history assures us that the ancient Greek, when he died, was exceedingly anxious that his body should receive what he considered decent sepulture - mainly because he laboured under the illusion that unless this was done he would not be free to pursue the even tenor of his way after death. Most of the ghost stories of ancient Greece related to people who came back to arrange for the due disposal of their bodies.

586.   The poorer classes among the modern Irish seem to share this extraordinary anxiety about the disposal of their bodies, for on several occasions I have come across Irish women whose one thought after death was not in the least for the welfare or progress of their souls, but that the number of carriages following their funeral procession should not fall below a certain number, or that the coffin provided for the body should not be in any respect inferior to that which Mrs. So-and-So had had a few weeks before.

587.   This, however, is a mere digression, and what we have to consider is the effect of a funeral upon the survivors, and not upon the dead man (who , nevertheless, is usually present, and regards the proceedings from various points of view, according to his temperament).

588.   A funeral is distinctly a function to be avoided by the occultist; but sometimes he may find himself in circumstances where his refusal to attend might be misconstrued by ignorant and uncomprehending relations. In such a case he should exert his will, and put himself into a determined and positive attitude, so that he may on no account be affected by the influences around him, and at the same time be in a position powerfully to affect others.

589.   He should think first of the dead man (who will most likely be present) with strong, friendly interest and affection, and with a determined will for his peace and advancement. He should adopt also a positive attitude of mind in his thought towards the mourners, endeavouring strongly to impress upon them that they must not grieve, because the man whom they mourn as dead is in reality, still living, and their grief will hinder him in his new condition. He must try mentally to hold them firmly in hand, and to prevent them from relaxing into hysterics and helplessness.

590.   The modern funeral is far from ideal. It seems to be an established convention that there must be some kind of ceremony connected with the disposal of the discarded clothing of the liberated ego; but surely something better might be devised than what is usually done at present. The funeral in the village church is not without a certain amount of appropriateness - even a certain consolation; the mourners are in a building which has for them holy and elevating associations of all sorts, and the service appointed by the Church of England is beautiful, though here and there one would like to infuse into it a note of more enthusiastic certainty.

591.   But for the service performed in a cemetery chapel there is nothing whatever to be said. The place is never used for any other purpose than a funeral, and its whole atmosphere is pervaded with hopeless grief. Everything is usually as bare and as gloomy as possible; the very walls reek of the charnel-house. We must remember that, for one person who understands the truth about death and takes an intelligently hopeful view of it, there are hundreds who have nothing but the most irrational and gruesome ideas. Such a place as that, therefore, is filled with the blackest despair and the most poignant mental suffering; and it is consequently of all places the most undesirable into which to take those who have experienced what seems to them to be a bereavement.

592.   THE DISPOSAL OF THE DEAD BODY

593.   No one who has the faintest glimpse of the hidden side of things can approve of our present barbarous method of disposing of the bodies of the dead. Even on the physical earth there is no single point in its favour, and there are many weighty considerations against it. From the sentimental point of view alone, it is impossible to understand how any person can reconcile himself to the idea that the cast-off garment of one whom he loves should be left to a slow and loathsome decay under conditions from which imagination shrinks with horror; and when to this we add the dreadful danger of disease to the living from the unspeakable pollution of air and of water, we begin to understand that our funeral customs are one of the many indications that our boasted civilisation is, after all only a veneer.

594.   Still more decidedly is this impression confirmed when we gain an insight into that side of these matters which is as yet unknown to the majority. We become aware then what kind of entity it is that is attracted by the process of slow putrefaction, and we see that in this way also terrible, unnecessary harm is being done to the survivors.

595.   For the dead man, if he is wise, it matters little what becomes of the worn-

out garment; but it should be remembered that all dead men are not necessarily wise, and that for some of them (who know no better) this abominable custom of ours makes possible a serious mistake, which under proper conditions could not be committed.

596.   The average man, in his ordinary thinking, is not in the habit of separating himself into body and soul as definitely as does the student of occultism. True, the dead man has finally left his physical vehicle, and it is practically impossible for him again to take possession of it; but he is intimately acquainted with it, and its rates of vibration are familiar and sympathetic to him. Under all normal and clean and proper conditions he has done with it entirely; but there are those who, having had no ideas, no conceptions of any sort beyond the physical during life, become crazy with fear when they find themselves altogether cut adrift from it. Such men sometimes make frantic efforts to return into some sort of touch with physical life. Most do not succeed; but when any of them do succeed to some limited extent, it can be only by means of their own physical bodies.

597.   Such *Rapport* as they still retain with the decaying vestures sometimes enables them to draw from them the basis of an imperfect and unnatural half-materialisation - not nearly enough to bring them back into touch with the physical world, but yet sufficient to tear them for the time from healthy astral life. Such people make for themselves for awhile - fortunately only for awhile - a dim, grey world of horror in which they see physical happenings as in a glass darkly - as through a world of mist in which they wander, lost and helpless.

598.   They cannot get back entirely into the dense bodies; a man who did would become a vampire. But they do get hold of the etheric matter of their discarded vehicles, and drag it about with them, and this is the cause of all their suffering; and until they can get rid of this entanglement, until they can plunge through the grayness and get into the light, there can be no rest for them. There are unpleasant forms of black magic, too, known in oriental countries and to those who have studied the methods of the Voodoo or the Obeah, which depend for their success upon the decaying physical body; though this is happily not a consideration of practical importance to those who live among communities unversed in such evil lore.

599.   But at least this is clear - that all possibilities of evil, both for the dead and for the living, are avoided by the rational disposal of the discarded vesture of flesh. When we return to the custom of cremation, practised by the Hindus, the Greeks and the Romans, we reduce the physical vehicle as rapidly as possible to its constituent elements in a manner which is at once clean, decent, and wholly satisfactory to the aesthetic sentiment as well as to the rational view of the man of sense.

600.   Some people have feared the possibility that, especially in the cases of sudden death, the dead man might feel the flame - might be in some way not yet fully separated from his body, and so might suffer when that body was burned. Even if the death be sudden, so long as it is death, the astral and etheric matter have been completely separated from the denser physical, and it would be quite impossible that the dead man could under any circumstances feel what was done to the physical body.

I mean that he could not really feel it, because the connection through which he feels is definitely broken; what is perhaps possible is that, seeing the cremation, he might have a certain fear lest he should feel it - the idea that he ought to be feeling it, as it were; and so imagination might come into play to some extent.

601.   I have never seen such a case in connection with cremation; but I remember hearing on good authority of a young man whose teeth were all drawn after his death by a dishonest undertaker, in order that they might be sold as artificial teeth. The young man appeared to his father with blood flowing from his mouth, exclaiming in great indignation that they had tortured him by drawing his teeth. The body was exhumed, and it was found that his story was correct. In this case, if the man was really dead, it is quite impossible that he could have felt any pain; but he became aware of what was being done, and was very angry about it; and no doubt he may have thought of himself as really injured, because during life the idea of tooth-drawing had been associated with great pain.

602.   The difference which the knowledge of the hidden side of things makes in the consideration of the whole subject of death is very aptly shown by two of the figures reproduced in the book on *Thought-Forms* - those which illustrate the thought-images created by two men standing side by side at a funeral. There it is seen that the man who had lived in the ordinary blank ignorance with regard to death, had no thought in connection with it but selfish fear and depression; whereas the man who understood the facts was entirely free from any suggestion of those feelings, for the only sentiments evoked in him were those of sympathy and affection for the mourners, and of devotion and high aspiration.

603.   Indeed, knowledge of the hidden side of life entirely changes a man's attitude towards death, for it shows him instantly that instead of being the end of all things, as is often ignorantly supposed, it is simply the passage from this stage of life to another which is freer and pleasanter than the physical, and that consequently it is to be desired rather than to be feared. He sees at once how utterly a delusion is the theory that those who cast aside their physical bodies are lost to us, for he knows that they remain near us just as before, and that all that we have lost is the power to see them. To the consciousness of the man who possesses even astral sight, the so-called dead are just as definitely present as the so-called living, and since he sees how readily they are affected by the vibrations which we send out to them, he understands how harmful is the attitude of mourning and grief so often unfortunately adopted by the friends who still retain their physical bodies.

604.   A knowledge of the hidden side of life by no means teaches us to forget our dead, but it makes us exceedingly careful as to how we think of them; it warns us that we must adopt a resolutely unselfish attitude, that we must forget all about ourselves, and the pain of the apparent separation, and think of them neither with grief nor with longing, but always with strong affectionate wishes for their happiness and their progress.

605.   The clairvoyant sees exactly in what manner such wishes affect them, and at once perceives the truth which underlies the teaching of the Catholic Church with regard to the advisability of prayers for the dead. By these both the living and the dead

are helped; for the former, instead of being thrown back upon his grief with a hopeless feeling that now he can do nothing, since there is a great gulf between himself and his loved one, is encouraged to turn his affectionate thought into definite action which promotes the happiness and advancement of him who has passed from his sight in the physical world. Of all this and much more I have written fully in the book called *The Other Side Of Death*, so here I will only thus far touch upon the subject, and refer to that volume any who wish for more detailed information.

606.   A SURGICAL OPERATION

607.   In these days of the triumph of surgery, it not infrequently happens that a man has to submit himself to an operation. There is less of a hidden side to this than to many other events, because the use of anaesthetics drives the man away from his physical body altogether. But in that very absence much that is of interest to him takes place, and it is well to endeavour to note and remember as far as may be what occurs. This is a difficult thing to do; more difficult than the bringing through of the memory from the astral world, because what is driven out by the anaesthetic is the etheric part of the physical man, and as the etheric double is only a portion of the physical body, and in no sense a perfect vehicle in itself, a man cannot usually bring through a clear memory.

608.   I remember a case of this nature which I was asked by the victim to attend. He was much interested in the occult side of the affair, and anxious to remember all that he could. He was placed upon the operating table, and the anaesthetic was administered. Almost immediately the man sprang out in his astral body, recognised me, and started down the room towards me with an expression of vivid delight upon his face, evidently overjoyed at finding himself fully conscious in the astral world. But in a moment came pouring forth from the physical body a great cloud of etheric matter which was forced out by the anaesthetic. This cloud immediately wrapped itself round him, and I could see the intelligence fade out of his face until it became a mere mask.

609.   When I was permitted to see him again two days afterwards, his memory of what had happened tallied exactly with that I had seen. He remembered the rush out of his body; he recollected clearly seeing me at the other end of the room, and feeling greatly delighted that everything seemed so real. Then he started down the room towards me, but somehow he never arrived, and knew nothing more until he came back into the body an hour later when the whole operation was over. I felt on that occasion what an advantage the possession of clairvoyance would have been to the two doctors engaged. They gave the patient too much of the anaesthetic, and came within an ace of finally driving out the whole of his etheric double, instead of only part of it as they intended. As my clairvoyant companion forcibly remarked, they left hardly enough of it to cover half-a-crown, and the consequence was that the patient came perilously near to death, and they had to pump oxygen into his lungs for ten minutes in order to bring him back to life at all.

610.   A few years ago a visit to the dentist frequently meant a minor operation, in which the patient passed through a somewhat similar but much shorter experience,

owing to the administration of nitrous oxide, and many curious phenomena have shown themselves in connection with that. An example in point will be found in my book on *Dreams* (page 38). In these days of local anaesthetics the dentist is usually able to do his work without the administration of gas, and consequently the experiences connected with his operation are of a less occult nature.

611.   A LECTURE

612.   We have in a previous chapter considered the consequences which attend upon the action of going to church; let us now consider the inner side of attending a lecture, a political meeting, a spiritualistic séance, or a religious revival.

613.   Of these forms of excitement the lecture is usually the mildest, though even that to some extent depends upon its subject. There is generally much less uniformity about the audience at a lecture than about a congregation in a church. There are often many and rather decisive points of likeness between those who adopt the same religious belief, whereas the people who are interested in a lecture upon some particular subject may come from many different folds, and be of all sorts of quite different types. Still, for the time being there is a link between them, the link of interest in a particular subject: and therefore, however different their minds may be, the same portion of the mind is for the moment being brought into activity in all of them, and that creates a certain superficial harmony.

614.   Since the Theosophical student frequently has to deliver lectures as well as to endure them, it is perhaps well not entirely to neglect that side of the subject, but to note that, if the lecturer wishes to act effectively upon the mind-bodies of his audience, he must first of all have a clearly defined idea expressing itself through his own mind-body. As he thinks earnestly of the different parts of his subject and tries to put them before his people, he is making a series of thought-forms - unusually strong thought-forms because of the effort.

615.   He has a fine opportunity, because his audience is necessarily to a great extent in a receptive condition. They have taken the trouble to come in order to hear about this particular subject, and therefore we must suppose that they are in a condition of readiness to hear. If under these favourable conditions he fails to make them understand him, it must be because his own thought upon the subject is not sufficiently clearcut. A clumsy and indefinite thought-form makes but a slight impression, and even that with much difficulty. A clearly-cut one forces the mental bodies in the audience to try to reproduce it. Their reflections of it will almost invariably be less definite and less satisfactory than it is, but still, if its edges are sharp enough, they will convey the idea to some extent; but if that from which they have to copy is itself blurred, it is eminently probable that the reproductions will prove entirely unrecognisable.

616.   Sometimes the lecturer receives unexpected assistance. The fact that he is engaged in thinking strongly of one particular subject attracts the attention of disembodied entities who happen to be interested in that subject, and the audience often includes a greater number of people in astral than in physical bodies. Many of

117

music, technician

these come simply to hear, as do their brothers in the physical world, but sometimes it happens that one of those who are attracted knows more about the subject than the lecturer. In that case he sometimes assists by suggestions or illustrations. These may come to the lecturer in various ways. If he is clairvoyant he may see his assistant, and the new ideas or illustrations will be materialised in subtler matter before him. If he is not clairvoyant, it will probably be necessary for the helper to impress the ideas upon his brain, and in such a case he may well suppose them to be his own. Sometimes the assistant is not disembodied, or rather only temporarily disembodied; for this is one of the pieces of work frequently taken in hand by the invisible helpers.

617.　　　In some cases the ego of the lecturer manifests himself in some curious exterior way. For example, I have heard the greatest orator now living say that, while she is speaking one sentence of a lecture, she habitually sees the next sentence actually materialise in the air before her, in three different forms, from which she consciously selects that one which she thinks the best. This must be the work of the ego, though it is a little difficult to see why he takes that method of communication, since after all it is he who is delivering the lecture through the physical organs. At first blush it seems that it would be as easy for him - or perhaps even easier - to select a form himself, and impress only that one upon lower matter; and even then it might as well come directly to the brain as be materialised in the air before it.

618.　　　Returning from the lecturer to his audience, we may note that it is possible for his hearers to give him great assistance in his work. Older members of a branch have sometimes been heard to say that they did not feel it necessary to go down to the lodge meeting on a certain occasion, as the lecture was about a subject with which they were already thoroughly acquainted. Apart from the large assumption involved in the statement that one can ever be *fully* acquainted with any Theosophical teaching, it is not accurate to say that a man's presence is useless because he knows the subject. Exactly the opposite remark would have much more truth in it; because he knows the subject thoroughly he also can make strong and clear thought-forms of the different illustrations required, and in that way he can greatly assist the lecturer in impressing on the audience what he wishes to convey to them.

619.　　　The greater the number of people present at a lecture who thoroughly understand its subject, the easier will it be for all those to whom it is new to obtain a clear conception of it. The lecturer, therefore, is distinctly helped by the presence of those who can fully comprehend him. He also may be much helped or hindered by the general attitude of his audience. In the main that is usually friendly, since the majority of people who come to a lecture come because they are interested in the subject and wish to learn something about it. Sometimes, however, one or two appear whose main desire is to criticise, and their presence is anything but helpful.

620.　　　A POLITICAL MEETING

621.　　　This latter effect is much more in evidence at a political meeting, for there it seems to be the rule that, while some people go for the purpose of supporting the speaker, others go merely for the purpose of challenging and interrupting him.

Consequently the feelings to be experienced, and the thought-forms to be seen, at political meetings are not easy to predict beforehand. But one often sees cases in which forms composed entirely or principally of the thoughts of the adherents of one party make huge waves of enthusiasm, which rush over the audience, surround the speaker and work him up into a corresponding condition of enthusiasm.

622.   Many years ago I remember attending a meeting of this description, and being much struck by the effect produced by getting all the people to join together in singing. Some great gun of the party was to speak, and consequently the huge hall was crowded to suffocation a couple of hours before the advertised time; but the organisers of the meeting were wise in their generation, and they employed that time most efficiently by working up that vast heterogeneous crowd into a condition of loyal enthusiasm. All sorts of patriotic songs followed one another in quick succession, and though few really knew the tunes, and still fewer the words, there was at least no lack of enthusiastic good feeling. The two hours of waiting passed like an entertainment, and I think most people were surprised to find how quickly time had fled.

623.   The occult side of the average political meeting, however, is far from attractive, for from the astral world it not unfrequently bears a strong general resemblance to an exceedingly violent thunderstorm. There is often much warring feeling, and even a good deal of personal enmity. On the whole we have usually a preponderance of a sort of rough and perhaps rather coarse, good-humoured jollity, often pierced, however, by spears of anxious feeling from the promoters. Unless duty actually calls one to such gatherings it is generally better to avoid them, for on such occasions there is always a clash of astral currents that cannot but induce great fatigue in anyone who is in the least sensitive.

624.   CROWDS

625.   It is also desirable to avoid as far as possible the mixing of magnetism which comes from too close contact with a promiscuous crowd. Not that we must assume for a moment that the persons composing the crowd are necessarily lower or worse than ourselves. It would be most undesirable that the student should become self-conscious, self-conceited or self-righteous. It is probably true that the aims and objects of the majority of people in any crowd, taken at random, are of more worldly type than those of the Theosophical student; but it would be both wrong and foolish to despise the people on that account. The point to bear in mind is, not that we are better than they, but that there is a difference in the rates of vibration, and that consequently to be in constant contact with others causes disturbance in the various vehicles, which it is better to avoid.

626.   Nevertheless, when duty renders it necessary or desirable that the student should enter a crowd, there are at his disposal various means by which he can protect himself. The most usual is the making of a shell, either etheric, astral or mental; but the best protection of all is a radiant goodwill and purity. I shall presently devote a chapter to the consideration of this question of protection.

627. A SÉANCE

628. Of all forms of meeting one of the most interesting from the occult point of view is the spiritualistic séance, though of this there are so many different types that hardly anything can be said which would apply equally to all of them - except perhaps that one almost invariable characteristic is an atmosphere of joyousness and hopefulness. The circles to which outsiders are often introduced, those of which we hear and of which we may occasionally read in the newspapers - these are after all the few, and behind them, forming the real block of spiritualism, are two other variants of which we hear very little.

629. There is the ordinary séance, quite among the poor, with a medium probably of the stout washer-woman type, where no sensational phenomena take place, where the spirits are frequently ungrammatical. Thousands of such séances are being held all over the world, and there is a strong family likeness between them. To a visitor their proceedings would appear profoundly uninteresting. Usually the medium gives a kind of fourth-rate ethical address - or perhaps it is really given *through* the medium - but in any case it usually faithfully reproduces all her favourite errors in grammar and in pronounciation. Then as a general rule a few words are said specially to each of the persons present, often taking the form of a description of their surroundings or of the spirits which are supposed to be hovering about them. Such descriptions are usually vague and uncertain to the last degree, but now and again striking identifications are made - far too many to be explicable on any theory of mere coincidence. And however dull all this may seem to the outsider, it does undoubtedly carry peace and conviction to the members of the circle, and gives them a real living knowledge and certainty with regard to the continued existence of man after death, which puts to shame the faith of the fashionable churches.

630. The hidden side of a séance such as this has often something pathetic about it. Behind the medium there is usually what is called a spirit-guide - a dead person, sometimes of the medium's own class in life, sometimes of a decidedly higher type - a dead person who has by much patient effort learned how to influence with a reasonable amount of certainty the clumsy organism of the medium, which, however unsuitable it may be in most other respects, at least possesses the invaluable faculty that it *can* be influenced and that communications can in some way or other be got through. The patience with which this entity deals with the poor souls that come to him from both sides of the veil is admirable; for he has to try to bring into harmony not only the tearful inconsequence of scores of sorrowing relations on this side, but also the feverish and clamorous excitement of a crowd who are trying to rush into manifestation from the other. With his class and in his way such an entity does a great deal of good, and his life of unnoticed toil in some obscure district adds more to the sum total of human happiness than many far more showy efforts which receive greater credit in the eyes of the public. Even such a séance as this, when examined with astral sight, is seen to be a centre of a kind of vortex. the departed rushing in from all directions, desiring either themselves to manifest or to watch the manifestation.

631. There is another variety of séance of which few know anything - the private family circle to which no outsider is ever admitted. This is infinitely the most satisfactory side of spiritualism, for through it many thousands of families communicate

day by day with friends or relations who have passed from the physical world, and in this way not only learn a number of interesting facts but are kept constantly in touch with spiritual subjects and at a high level of thought with regard to them. Most commonly the central figure at these private séances is some departed member of the family, and the communications ordinarily are affectionate little sermonettes of a devotional character, often somewhat rhapsodical.

632.   Occasionally, however, where the departed relation happens to be a man of original thought or of a scientific turn of mind, a great volume of definite information is gradually gathered together. There are far more of these private revelations in existence than is generally suspected, for hardly one in a hundred of those who receive them is prepared to face an exposure to public ridicule of what to him is above all things a holy thing, in the hope of so improbable a result as the conversion of some sceptical stranger.

633.   At such séances as these, remarkable phenomena are not infrequent, and materialisations of the most startling kind are sometimes part of the daily programme. Often the so-called dead are just as much part of the daily life of the family as the living, as was the case, for example, with the phenomena which took place at the house of Mr. Morel Theobald, at Haslemere. The séances described by Mr. Robert Dale Owen are largely of this character, and they represent the highest possible kind of spiritualism, though in the very nature of the case it is hardly ever available to the ordinary enquirer.

634.   The hidden side of such séances as these is truly magnificent, for they form points of habitual contact between the astral and physical worlds - vortices again, but this time only of the higher and nobler varieties of astral life. The thought-forms surrounding them are of the religious or the scientific type according to the nature of the manifestations, but they are always good thought-forms, calculated to raise the mental or spiritual level of the district in which they are to be found.

635.   Putting aside these two large classes, we have next the smaller group of public séances which to most outsiders represent the whole of spiritualism. All sorts of people are admitted to these, usually, on payment of a small sum of money, and the entities who appear on the astral side are just as curious a conglomerate as those who attend on the physical. Here also there is almost always a spirit-guide in charge. The highest astral types are not to be found among the habitués of such séances as these, but there is usually a sprinkling of dead people who have devoted themselves to the idea of being useful to those still on the physical earth, by the exhibition of phenomena and the giving of various small tests.

636.   The aura of such a séance is usually on the whole somewhat unpleasant, for it attracts a great deal of attention in the astral world as well as in the physical, and consequently round every one of them is always a clamorous crowd of the most undesirable entities, who are restrained only by force from pushing in and seizing upon the medium. Among the dangers attending these séances is the possibility that one of these desperate creatures may seize upon any sensitive sitter and obsess him; worse still, that he may follow him home, and seize upon his wife or daughter. There

have been many such cases, and usually it is almost impossible to get rid of an entity which has thus obsessed the body of a living human being.

637.　　　The hidden side of such a séance is generally a confused network of cross-currents, some good and some bad, but none very good and some very bad. The clairvoyant attending such a séance may obtain a certain amount of instruction from watching the various methods by which the phenomena are produced, which are sometimes exceedingly ingenious. He will be astonished at the cleverness of the personations, and at the amazing facility with which those who know nothing of this side of life can be deceived.

638.　　A RELIGIOUS REVIVAL

639.　　　From the point of view of the student of the inner worlds, one of the most remarkable phenomena of our day is what is called a religious revival. A religious revival, as seen from the physical world, usually means a gathering of people of the lower classes whose feelings are inflamed by highly emotional and often lurid appeals from some fanatical exponent of the gospel of a particular sect. Day after day these meetings take place, and they are often accompanied by the most extraordinary phenomena of nervous excitement.

640.　　　People work themselves up into some sort of hysterical condition in which they feel themselves to be saved, as they call it - to have escaped forever from the bondage of the ordinary life of the world, and to have become members of a spiritual community whose aims are of the highest description. Often they are moved to confess in public what they consider to have been their misdeeds, and they are apt to do this with a wealth of emotion and repentance entirely out of proportion to anything that they have to confess. The wave of nervous excitement spreads like an infectious disease, and usually it lasts for some weeks, though often towards the end of that time symptoms of universal exhaustion appear and the whole thing somewhat shamefacedly dies down into commonplace life again.

641.　　　In a small percentage of the cases the spiritual elevation appears to be maintained, and the victims continue to live a life at a distinctly higher level than that which had been theirs previously; but by far the greater number of the cases relapse either suddenly and dramatically, or by slow and gradual stages, into much the same kind of life as they had led before the excitement came. Statistics show that the culmination of this emotional excitement is accompanied by great sexual disturbance, and that the number of illegitimate unions of all sorts is temporarily greatly increased. There are certain sects which take as part of their regular system a much modified form of this excitement, and consider it necessary for their junior members to pass through a crisis which is sometimes described as "being convinced of sin," and in other cases simply as "getting religion".

642.　　　Such a revival as this is seen in its most extravagant form among the negroes of America, among whom it reaches a level of frenzy not commonly attained by the white races. The negroes find it necessary to relieve their feelings by dances and leaps and contortions of the wildest kind, and these are often carried on for hours together, accompanied by yells and groans of a truly alarming character.

643. That this sort of thing should take place in the twentieth century, and among people who think themselves civilised is surely a most remarkable phenomenon, and one deserving careful consideration from a student of the inner side of things. For one who possesses astral vision such an outburst is a wonderful but unpleasant sight. The missioner or revivalist preacher who first commences such a movement is usually animated by the highest motives. He becomes impressed with the overflowing love of God, or with the wickedness of a particular section of the community, and he feels that the spirit moves him to proclaim the one and to rebuke the other. He works himself up into a condition of tremendous emotional excitement, and sets his astral body swinging far beyond the degree of safety.

644. For a man may yield himself to emotion up to a certain point, and yet recover himself, just as a ship may roll to a certain extent and yet swing back again to her normal position; but just as the ship capsizes if she rolls beyond that point of safety, so if the man lets his astral body entirely escape from control, he dies, or becomes insane or is obsessed. Such an obsession need not necessarily be what we should call an evil one, though the truth is that all obsession is evil; but I mean that we need not credit the obsessing entity with anything but good intentions, though he usually takes advantage of such an opportunity more for the sake of the excitement and the feeling which he himself gets out of it than from any altruistic motive.

645. In many cases, however, the obsessing entity is a departed preacher of the same religion, style and type as the man obsessed, and thus we have temporarily two souls working through one body. The double force thus gained is poured out recklessly upon any audience that can be gathered together. The tremendous swinging energy of these hysterical excesses is contagious, and since such revivals are usually set on foot among people whose emotions are not under the control of a strongly developed intellect, the preacher soon finds others who can be reduced by sympathetic vibration to a condition as unbalanced as his own.

646. Every one who swings over the safety point adds to the strength of these exaggerated vibrations, and soon an astral disturbance is set up of the nature of a gigantic whirlpool. Towards this, from all sides pour astral entities whose one desire is for sensation - no longer merely or even chiefly human beings, but all kinds of nature-spirits who delight in and bathe in the vibrations of wild excitement just as children play in the surf. It is they who supply and constantly reinforce the energy which is expended with such terrible recklessness. It is they who try to keep up the level of the excitement, so long as they can find any human beings who can be dragged into the vortex and induced to give them the pleasurable sensations which they desire.

647. The emotion, remember, is emphatically not of a high type, for it is intensely personal. It is always motived by an exalted egoism, the desire to save one's own soul; so that the dominant idea is a selfish one. That defines the kind of matter which is set in motion in these tremendous swirlings, and that again limits the nature-spirits who enjoy it to such types as find themselves in tune with that kind of matter. These are naturally by no means the highest types; they are usually creatures without much

intelligence or comprehension, understanding nothing about their human victims; and quite unable to save them from the consequences of their mad excitement, even if they could be supposed to care to do so.

648.   This then is the hidden side of such a movement; this is what the clairvoyant sees when he watches one of these most astonishing meetings. He sees a number of human beings who are taken out of themselves, whose higher vehicles are for the time being no longer their own, but are being used to supply this torrent of energy. All these people are pouring out their emotions in order to make a vast astral whirlpool into which these great nature-spirits throw themselves with intense delight, plunging and flying through it again and again in wild abandonment of utter pleasure. For they can abandon themselves to pleasure with a thoroughness of which the heavier human being knows nothing. Their whole life for the time is one wild paroxysm, and this feeling reacts upon the human beings who unconsciously minister to their pleasures, and gives them also a sensation of intense exultation.

649.   Here we see the explanation of the passional side of these extraordinary displays. All that the nature-spirits desire is intense emotion of one kind or other on the part of their human slaves. It is nothing to them whether that emotion be religious or sexual; probably they do not even know the difference. Certainly they cannot know whether either is helpful or harmful to the evolution of the human beings concerned. The whole thing is a wild, mad orgie of non-human entities, precisely the same thing as the mediaeval witches' sabbath, but provoked in this case by an emotion which many consider as belonging to the good side instead of to the evil side of life. But to these nature-spirits all that makes no difference. They know nothing of good or evil; what they enjoy is the tremendous excitement which they can gain only by swaying masses of human beings simultaneously into a condition imminently dangerous to the sanity of their victims. No one man alone could reach so dangerous a level of excitement. There must be a great number reacting upon and, as it were, encouraging and strengthening one another. Indeed, I should advise the student not to attend revival meetings, because, unless he is in good health and well poised, there is definite danger that even he may be swept off his feet.

650.   I wish it to be distinctly understood that in what I have written I am in no way denying the great fact that what is called "sudden conversion" does sometimes take place, and that the man to whom it happens is ever after the better for it. The word ` conversion' is a noble one, if we can only dissociate it from such undignified surroundings as those that I have been describing. It means "to turn along with," and its implication is that the man, who has hitherto been working along his own selfish road, realises for the first time the mighty truth that God has a plan for man, and that it is within his power to adapt himself intelligently to this plan and fulfil the part in it which is destined for him. When he realises this, he turns round and "goes together with" the divine Will, instead of ignorantly working against it; and after he has once done this, although he may become what the Christians call a backslider, although his vehicles may run away with him, and carry him into all sorts of excesses, he can never again sin without feeling remorse - without knowing that he has fallen, and regretting the fall.

651.   This knowledge of the great facts of life is called in the East "the acquirement of discrimination" or sometimes "the opening of the doors of the mind". Usually it is a gradual process, or at least one which comes as the result of continual thought or reasoning. Sometimes, however, the final conviction is borne in upon the man in an instant, and that is a case of what is called "sudden conversion". If the man to whom that instantaneous flash of conviction comes has previously reasoned the thing out with himself (perhaps in other lives) and has almost persuaded himself, so that he needs merely a final touch of illumination to make him quite certain - then the effect of such a conversion is permanent. Not that, even then, the man may not frequently fall back, but he will always recover from such falls, and will on the whole make steady progress.

652.   As has been described, the emotional effect of a great revival meeting is very powerful. Not only will it give the little additional touch which is needed for the ' conversion' of a man who is nearly ready for that process, but it will sometimes seize upon a man who is as yet by no means ready, and it may be powerful enough to swing him over the dividing line, and make him profess himself for the moment (and quite honestly) as heartily converted as the other. But the permanent effect is by no means the same. In this latter case, the man is not really ready; there is a vast amount of force still uncontrolled in the lower part of his nature, and although that was for the time dominated by the forces present at the revival meeting, when that is over, it reasserts itself, and the man inevitably falls back again into his former courses. We must not blame him for that; the strength which is needed for the permanent control of the lower nature grows very slowly, and it would be unreasonable to expect that it can ever be developed in a moment of enthusiasm. The cases in which it appears to be so developed are simply those in which the force has been secretly gathering itself for a long time previously.

653.   Therefore I say again that I do not for a moment deny the occasional reality of sudden conversions; I do not deny that a certain amount of good must follow from all the devotional enthusiasm which is thrown into a religious revival. But I also say that every word that I have written above as to the general effect of such gatherings, and the part taken in them by non-human entities, is absolutely true; and for that reason I cannot but think that such excitement should be avoided by the student of occultism.

654.   In the rare cases where a vast crowd is moved by a dominant idea which is wholly unselfish, quite a different order of entities comes into play - the astral angels, who have an active delight in good. Under such guidance as theirs, the excessive temporary vibration is safe and even helpful, for these beings understand humanity and know how to bring it back again safely into its ordinary condition.

655.   Some years ago, I happened to see a remarkable instance of this which I will presently describe, but I must first say a few words as to the virtue which caused the outburst. For the whole difference is in the motive: in the case previously described it was fundamentally selfish, but in this it was unselfish; in that it was the hope of personal salvation, in this it was loyalty and patriotism.

125

656.   A WAVE OF PATRIOTISM

657.   Patriotism is a virtue upon which in these days it is very necessary to insist. But we must be sure of what we mean by the term. It is not prejudice, nor is it ill-mannered boasting. There are those who can see no good in any country but their own, who are constantly vaunting with offensive swagger what they consider its superlative excellencies, and disparaging all others. These are not patriots, but mere braggarts: they exhibit not the strength of their loyalty, but the depth of their ignorance.

658.   True patriotism is the very antithesis of all this; it recognises that each country has its advantages and its disadvantages, that each nation has its excellencies, but also always its deficiencies, since no political or social scheme is yet perfect, and there is a good deal of human nature everywhere. Nevertheless it also sees that just as man owes consideration to the parents who have tended him and to the family of which he finds himself a part, so does he also owe something to the country into which he is born, for that birth is not a matter of chance but of karma. He is put there because these are the surroundings that he has deserved, and they are also those best suited to help onward his evolution. He is put there not to receive only, but to give; for man learns best by service. Thus he should be prepared when called upon to work for his country; he should acquiesce cheerfully in such measures as may be necessary for the general good, even though they may bring loss to him individually; he should forget for his country's sake his private interests and desires, and when the opportunity arises he should give himself unsparingly to her service.

659.   I am aware that, among students of what is called advanced thought, there are those who sneer at patriotism as a virtue which is half a vice - as an evidence of a low stage of development. But that is a mistaken view: as well might one rail at family affection for exactly the same reasons. Truly both love for family and love for country are more limited than universal love, but they are nevertheless stages on the way to it. If primitive man thinks only for himself, it is an advance for him to extend his love to that wider self which we call the family, and to learn to feel and to think for his nation is but a further step on the same road. Later still he will learn to think and to feel for humanity as a whole, and then he will come to see that the animal and the plant are our brothers, even though they may be younger brothers, and that all life is the divine Life, and so the love which was once confined to himself, to his family, to his clan, to his nation, has become wide as the shoreless sea of the divine Love.

660.   But a very necessary stage on the way to this goal is that patriotism which leads a man to forego his own ease and comfort, to put aside his private opportunities of gain, nay, to sacrifice his very life, in order to serve his country. Naturally also he personifies his country in the person of her ruler, and so is developed the other virtue of loyalty, and his character is thereby greatly elevated and purified. That individual kings have in the past often been unworthy of this high feeling is a sad fact, but it does not interfere with the other fact of the benefit which accrues to those in whom such feeling is evoked. When it fortunately happens that the sovereign is all that a ruler should be, we have a collocation of circumstances in which loyalty can work with its greatest effect, and splendid results may be achieved both for the King and his people.

661.   A remarkable instance of this was seen in the enthusiasm evoked by the celebration of the Diamond Jubilee of the late Queen Victoria. For those who could see it, the inner side of the proceedings of that day was a spectacle never to be forgotten.

662.   It happened that on that occasion I had, through the kindness of a friend, a seat at one of the office-windows in the City on the route of the great procession. Even from the physical point of view, the decorations had transformed the gloomy London streets. The whole of the fronts of the tall houses on both sides of the dingy street were covered with a sort of scaffolding which formed temporary balconies to each of the windows, and all these were closely packed with men, women and children, so that the grim house-fronts were like cliffs lined with faces, rising tier above tier, and the procession wound its way at the foot, as along a gorge whose sides were built of human bodies.

663.   Mostly the people were business men with their wives and families, and country friends; and these latter introduced an element of gaiety and curiosity to which those stern, dark City streets are unaccustomed, for as a rule the people gave themselves up to the enjoyment of the occasion, and to the criticising of their neighbours' toilets. The City men themselves were in the majority of cases unable to shake off their anxieties, and were to be seen still surrounded by thought-forms of prices and percentages. Occasionally, a privileged carriage would dash by, or a regiment of soldiers on its way to take part in the pageant; but those rarely claimed more than a moment's attention from these business men, who collapsed almost immediately into their calculations again. Even when at last the great procession itself appeared, their interest in it was but half-hearted, and they saw it against a background of stocks and shares and financial anxiety.

664.   Now and again some specially popular visitor received a little ovation, but on the whole the astral appearance of that huge crowd differed little at that period from that of other similar gatherings. The delight of the children at so unusual a holiday showed itself in many a flash and coruscation of colour, while their fathers' thoughts frequently offered the unfavourable contrast of dark and leaden patches, blots upon the variegated brilliancy of the scene, for they were but little affected by the waves of excitement which were beginning to leap across from side to side of the street. But the vibration of feeling grew stronger and stronger, and when the splendour of that marvellous pageant culminated in the approach of the Queen herself, a startling change took place, for all the thousands of little local flashes and vortices of colour disappeared utterly, overwhelmed in the tremendous cataract of mingled blue and rose and violet, which was pouring, like a veritable Niagara down both sides of that living valley of faces.

665.   Literally the only comparison possible for it was that smooth, resistless rush which is so impressive as one looks up from below at the greatest waterfall of the world, but here it was combined with a wealth of indescribably glorious colour, far beyond any conception on the physical plane. No words can give any idea of the effect of that tremendous outburst of simultaneous enthusiasm, that coruscating cascade of love and loyalty and veneration, all converging upon the carriage in which the Royal

Lady sat, unrestrainedly weeping in sympathy with the overflowing emotion of her subjects. Yes, and her subjects wept also - wept for pure joy and depth of feeling - and those hard-headed business men forgot their calculations and their anxieties, forgot themselves and their sordid financial considerations utterly for the time, and were transported into a higher world, lifted clear out of themselves, up to a plane of thought and feeling which many of them had not touched since early days of innocent childhood.

666.   An unique experience, not easily to be had in prosaic times like these, but a most salutary one, which could not but leave a beneficial impression upon everyone who passed through it. That strong soul-shaking was transient, no doubt, yet every heart had, for the moment, been stirred to its profoundest depths by noble, unselfish emotion, and every heart was the better for it.

667.   A similar and even more splendid exhibition of unselfish emotion has taken place recently at the Coronation of His Majesty King George V. I had not myself the privilege of seeing that in the physical body; but an account from those clairvoyants who did see it shows that it must have surpassed even that other demonstration.

668.   WAR

669.   Another occasional event - happily very occasional and growing rarer and rarer - which profoundly stirs the hearts of the people, is war. Now I suppose that few at the present day would venture to deny that war is an absurd and atrocious anachronism. If we pause for a moment to think, we all know perfectly well that the result of a battle does not in the least decide the original question at issue. It may show which army has the cleverest general or the greatest weight of artillery; it certainly does *not* show which side is in the right in the quarrel, if there be any right. So far as individuals are concerned, all except the very lowest classes have passed beyond the stage of attempting to decide personal disputes by ordeal of battle; when our convictions as to a boundary line differ pronouncedly from our neighbour's, we no longer assemble our servants and try to argue the matter with rifles or bludgeons, but we refer the case instead to a tribunal in whose impartiality we both have reasonable confidence.

670.   As nations, however, we are not yet at the level of evolution which we have reached as individuals; we are willing (some of us) to submit comparatively unimportant matters of dispute to arbitration, but there is as yet no court in which the races of the world have sufficient trust to accept its decision in a question vital to their existence. So the irrational appeal to brute force still remains as a possibility hovering ever in the background of national life like a menacing thundercloud.

671.   Poets have sung of the glories of war, but the legions of the Red Cross, who go forth not to hurt but to help, who come upon the battle-field after the rifle and the cannon have done their work - these can tell us something of the true meaning of war, and of all the ghastly horrors involved in the gallant defence or the successful charge. War may still be sometimes a necessity - the lesser of two evils; but it is so only because our boasted civilisation is still lamentably deficient. Yet, horrible and

senseless though it be, it is capable in a certain way of utilisation; it has its part to play at an early stage of evolution.

672.   Unquestionably the egos incarnated in the Zulu hordes, that did not hesitate to march to certain death at the command of Chaka or Cetewayo, acquired in that way qualities of obedience, self-control and self-sacrifice, which will be valuable to them in later births amid surroundings where they can be put to more rational use; and it is to the Zulu level of development that war properly belongs. The same lessons, however, are needed by many who obtain birth in higher races than the Zulu; and without abating one jot of our horror of the ghastly cruelty and senselessness of war, we may yet admit that such devotion to the abstract idea of patriotism, as will lead a man to be ready to die for it, means a distinct advance upon the normal attitude of the class from which our common soldiers are chiefly drawn. Those who are closely acquainted with our agricultural population cannot have failed also to observe the difference which military or naval training makes in the young man - how, from being slow of speech and comprehension, he becomes alert, dexterous, resourceful and self-respecting. Unfortunately he sometimes picks up other and less desirable habits at the same time, but at least he is less bovine and more human.

673.   There is, however, no reason why an excellent system of physical training should not be universally adopted even when peace reigns supreme, so that we might gain all the benefit which is at present derived by those who are trained in the army and navy, without the sinful and ridiculous waste of life and money in actual warfare. A step in this direction is already being taken by the admirable organisation called the Boy Scouts, and it is fervently to be hoped that this may spread over the whole world, so that its benefits may be shared by all.

674.   Terrible and wicked though it be, war, when it does occur (that is, when it cannot longer be prevented), is always utilised and turned to at least some sort of compensatory good by the Authorities who stand behind. It is sometimes employed also as an alternative to something still worse, or a smaller war is permitted in order to avoid a more disastrous one.

675.   I have been told that if the war which England recently waged in South Africa had not taken place, a colossal and terrible European war would have been inevitable, which would have involved far more widespread destruction. It is also certain that that war was utilised to bind more closely together the different parts of the British Empire, so that in standing side by side upon the battle-field, men might learn to become more brotherly and to understand one another better. Indeed, that is an effect which has often followed upon war, that the factions within a country have agreed to forget their differences in the face of the common enemy. The attack of Italy upon Tripoli may or may not be in the abstract justifiable; but no one who has lived in the country can doubt that it has had its value in bringing the somewhat heterogeneous population of Italy into a closer unity than ever before - into a realisation of its solidarity as a nation.

676.   The hidden side of the actual fighting is perhaps less remarkable than might be expected. The sound-forms produced by the discharge of artillery and by the

ceaseless rattling of the rifles are naturally of a striking nature, but as far as the astral world is concerned, a surging mass of confusion is the principal characteristic in the neighbourhood of the battle-field.

677. There is inevitably a certain amount of fear coming from those who are new to the ghastly work; but there is usually comparatively little of actual hatred. The pain and grief of the wounded are terrible enough, yet even then there is in most cases little of hatred or personality. There is generally a strong sense of order, obedience, determination, coming perhaps principally from the officers and the older soldiers. But unless the spectator senses the thought-forms of the generals, it is difficult to get any coherent idea of the scene as a whole.

678. Many invisible helpers are brought together during a battle, to receive the dead and extend to them any assistance of which they may be in need. But, taking it as a whole, there is far more feeling excited about war in the minds of countrymen and relations than in those of the soldiers themselves who actually take part in it.

679. CATASTROPHES

680. Sometimes great catastrophes other than war overtake the world. Two hundred thousand people perished suddenly in an earthquake at Messina; what is the occult side of such a happening as that? The inner sight helps us to look more understandingly on such events as this, and while we pity the sufferers no less, we yet avoid the feeling of overwhelming horror and dismay which paralyses many at the thought of such an occurrence. Let us think calmly, analytically, what really happened in that case. Two hundred thousand people were suddenly released from the burden of the flesh. Surely we have no need to pity *them*. We cannot speak of them as sufferers, for they have been lifted suddenly and painlessly into a higher and happier life, and in such a catastrophe as this there is really less of suffering than in connection with many isolated cases of death.

681. The suffering caused by sudden death is never to the dead man, but to the relations who, not understanding the facts of death, suppose themselves to have lost him. But precisely in a great catastrophe of this nature, few are left to mourn for the others, since the families within a certain area are almost all destroyed. The direct relations in most cases die together, and those who are left to mourn are more distant relations settled in far-away districts.

682. Some there were beyond doubt who suffered terribly - men who were wounded and left for days awaiting succour; others who were shut in beneath heaps of ruins and suffocated or starved to death. Towards these indeed our keenest sympathy may well go forth. Yet remember that they can have been at most but few, a smaller number than those who die of starvation every week in our capital city of London, for starvation is not merely absolute lack of food for a certain number of days. A man who has insufficient food, or bad food containing insufficient nourishment, for a period of years, is starving to death quite as surely as the man who for a few days has no food at all, and there is far more prolonged suffering in the former case than in the latter.

683. But again, it may be said, in the earthquake there was a vast amount

of suffering, because many people were rendered homeless, and because they were bereft of their ordinary supplies of food. That again is true, and to those also our heartiest sympathy must be extended. Indeed, we know that the whole world did so extend it, and from the occult view by far the most important effect of that earthquake was the great wave of sympathy and pity which came rolling in upon the place from every part of the habitable globe to which the news had been carried.

684.   It is not death which we should regard as an evil fate; our Theosophical knowledge has at least taught us that. It is never the dead whom we should pity, but the living who still suffer under all the cramping restrictions of this strange physical plane. For those whose consciousness knows no other world, it seems terrible to have to quit this; a man whose sight ranges over the higher worlds knows, with a vivid certainty that nothing can shake, that, if one is to consider happiness alone, the happiest moment for every man is that in which he escapes from this world into the wider and more real life above.

685.   Granted that our life here is a necessity, that we have development to make which can be made only under these hard conditions; it is for that reason that our physical life is necessary, and so we come forth into it as a man goes forth from his home to some unpleasant task which nevertheless he knows must be done. Pity by all means the poor fellow who is exiled from that higher life, but do not waste your sorrow upon those who have gone home again to the glory, the beauty and the rest.

686.   Seen from the physical world everything is distorted, because we see only so tiny a part of it, and then with strange stupidity insist upon taking that for the whole. Occultism teaches us a finer proportion, and brings our life into perspective for us, and so, while we lack nothing of sympathy for all who suffer, we yet learn that those who most need our sympathy are not those upon whom the undiscerning world showers it most freely.

687.   All worlds alike are part of the great Solar Deity; in Him "we live and move and have our being," and since we cannot fall away from His presence nor escape His guiding hand, what matters all the rest?

CHAPTER XII BY UNSEEN BEINGS

690.   SENSITIVE PEOPLE

691.   The occasional events to which we have hitherto referred have been such as might come into the life of almost anyone. There is another class of occasional events which usually come only to a certain type of people; but upon those people they exercise an influence so great that it cannot readily be measured - great enough often to alter the whole current of a life. There are those among us who are more sensitive than the majority of men, who dream dreams and see visions; and to these people their visions are the most important fact of life. Naturally also, such people are attracted to the study of occultism, so that the proportion of them among our readers is likely to be far greater than in the world which cares for none of these things. To these visions also there is a hidden side, one which it is of great importance to study.

692.   Visions are of many kinds - some trivial and unimportant, others profoundly interesting and productive of far-reaching effects to those who experience them. In some cases their genesis is obvious; in others curious and unexpected associations play their part, and a number of quite separate causes may combine to produce what seems to be a single story.

693.   As I have written several books upon the conditions of the astral world, it not unfrequently happens that persons who have had psychic experiences or visions which they have not fully comprehended, send me accounts of them and ask me whether my experience along these lines suggests any explanation. Such letters are not always easy to answer - not that there is usually any difficulty in formulating a hypothesis which will fit the facts, but because there are too many such hypotheses. Almost every experience described might equally easily have been produced in any one of half-a-dozen ways, and without undertaking a special and detailed investigation, it is often impossible to say which of these methods was employed in a particular case. Naturally, but few of the hundreds of cases submitted are of sufficient general interest to warrant such expenditure of time and force; but occasionally one is encountered which is specially characteristic - so good an example of its type that an analysis of it might conceivably be of use to many others to whom similar experiences have come.

694.   A REMARKABLE CASE

695.   Such an one came to me recently from a lady - an account of a long and complicated vision or series of visions, coupled with impressive experiences, which had left behind them a permanent result. In order to understand what had really happened a certain amount of investigation was necessary, in course of which it became evident that several distinct factors had come into play to produce the curious effects described. Each of these factors had to be followed up separately and traced to its source, and I think that students can hardly fail to be interested in an examination of the way in which these independent and disconnected causes worked to bring forth

a somewhat startling whole.

696.   I give here an epitome of the story as sent to me, using in many cases the exact words of the narrator, but condensing as much as I can without losing the spirit and style of the original. It should be premised that the lady had become dissatisfied with the religious doctrines of her childhood, and had commenced the study of comparative religion, reading several Theosophical books - among others *The Secret Doctrine*. She was very earnestly desirous to know the truth and to make whatever progress might be possible for her. In the course of her reading she came across Swami Vivekananda's book on *Raja Yoga*, and practised the breathing exercises therein recommended. The result was that she rapidly developed a certain kind of clairvoyance and began to write automatically. For some five days she indulged her astral controls, writing all day long whatever they wished.

697.   It seems that she was strongly opposed to the idea of capital punishment, and had felt great sympathy and pity for a murderer who had recently been executed in her neighbourhood. Among other entities this dead murderer came and communicated, and brought with him other men of the same stamp. She made the most earnest efforts to help these people, trying in every way to give them hope and comfort and to teach them as much of Theosophy as she knew. She soon found, however, that the murderer dominated and obsessed her, and that she was unable to eject him. Her case became rapidly worse, and her life and reason hung in the balance. For a long time no suggestion, no effort, mitigated her sufferings, though she prayed continually with all the power of her soul.

698.   At last one day she became conscious of the presence of another being who brought her relief. He told her that the prayer of her spirit had been recognised, that he had been appointed as her ` guide,' and that because of her spiritual development and the power which she had shown in prayer, she was considered especially hopeful and was about to be the recipient of most unusual favours. In fact, he said so much about her remarkable position and the recognition which she had gained, that she asked wonderingly:

699.   "Who then am I?"

700.   "You are Buddha," was the startling reply.

701.   "And who are *you*? " she asked.

702.   "I am the Christ," he answered, "and I will now take charge of you."

703.   Our correspondent here showed her commonsense and her great superiority over the majority of those who receive such communications by absolutely refusing to believe these astonishing statements, but she nevertheless accepted the guidance (and the teaching upon other points) of the entity who made these astounding claims.

704.   He then told her that she was to pass through an initiation, and that if she succeeded she would be admitted to the "council of heaven," which had been called together to decide whether the world should now be destroyed, or whether yet another effort for its salvation should be made. He urged her to hasten to qualify herself to attend this meeting while the fate of the world still hung in the balance, so that she might give her voice in favour of salvation. Her attitude of mind was rather curious;

she certainly did not accept these extravagant claims, but still she half-believed that there was some great work to be done, and she was willing to continue the experiment and submit herself to the guidance of the entity who had saved her from obsession.

705.   As a preliminary to the initiation she was directed to have a bed put into a room where she could lock the door, to lie down upon it and make herself comfortable. The guide then instructed her to breathe the yoga breath as taught by Vivekananda. He told her that her previous efforts had raised the serpent-fire to the solar plexus, and that now she must raise it to the brain - a process in which he would help and direct her.

706.   She describes the sensations which followed as exactly resembling the travail of a woman in labour, except that the pain was along the spine, and it seemed that the birth was to take place in the brain. Many times her sufferings were so excruciating that she grew desperate and was about to abandon the struggle, but the guide seemed most anxious and always implored her not to yield, but to carry through the ordeal to the end. He hovered over her like an attendant physician or nurse, encouraging, directing, helping, doing everything that he could to assist the birth. At last she prevailed, and she asserts that the birth appeared to her just as definite and real a thing as that of one of her own children. When it had taken place the guide was greatly relieved, and exclaimed: "Thank God it is over."

707.   This extraordinary experience was, however, only the prelude to a long series of marvellous visions, lasting altogether through twelve days of our physical time. These visions were partly of a directly personal character, and partly of the nature of general instruction - often incoherent and indescribable, yet always interesting and impressive. The personal part consisted of her relation with the so-called "council of heaven" and the result of her dealings with it, and also included some curious symbolical visions in which persons well known to her in physical life seemed to play the part of the world which she was trying to save and of the arch-enemy Satan, a fallen angel who resisted her. She pertinently remarks that this was all the more strange since for many years she had quite outgrown any belief in a personal devil or in the necessity of what is ordinarily called 'salvation'.

708.   The general instruction was broadly Theosophical in its character, and referred chiefly to the stages of creation and the evolution of the various root-races. She describes the first stage of this as follows:

709.   "I then beheld a wonderful vision. At first, in the midst of darkness, I saw a vast Darkness which seemed to brood and brood for ages. Then a slight movement began, as if it might be the faintest *dream* in this great darkness. Little by little the movement increased, until at last a definite *thought* seemed to evolve. Little by little constantly changing forms appeared. All was chaos. Even the forms were in the midst of chaos, and the travail of the Universe was terrible. All was one. It seemed as if the effort to evolve order and to make of so many forms a unit, demonstrated beyond doubt that all was made by One Great Being, and that the pain and responsibility were felt by Him alone. This continued for a long time, with another expression of birth-giving, with enlarging results and unchanging solemnity.

710.   "I do not know when I first began to see *souls*. It must have been early

in the wonderful exhibition; for I remember very distinctly how thickly they lay everywhere in the midst of chaos, and in the midst of forms. In the continual vibration of this marvellous evolution these souls were swallowed up in forms, which forms again changed to souls. These souls were egg-shaped and of all sizes, from tiny ones to larger ones, but none so large as I saw later in a wonderful sequel.

711.   "After a time the panorama of marvels changed and the world assumed a shape familiar to my mode of thought. Symbol upon symbol passed, including all history and mythology. Thousands of pictures passed in review, as if revealing the whole of Cosmos and of history. I can recall but few now, but one will serve as an illustration.

712.   "I saw a cow of immense proportions - almost as large as one of our mountains. A ladder was placed against her, and a man crept slowly and laboriously up the ladder, round by round. He represented Humanity. When at last he reached her back, he stretched forward and grasped both her horns. Humanity claimed the products and bounty of the earth for all, not for a few only. My guide called the cow ` The cow of Demeter' . My reading of the classics had taught me that Demeter represented the earth."

713.   It was apparently at this stage that she was introduced to the "council of heaven". She found it to consist of a small number of colossal figures seated in a semicircle. The members seemed impatient with the world and determined that it should be destroyed, but she begged most earnestly that another chance should be given to humanity, saying that she had lived and died many times for the world, and was quite ready to devote herself once more to its service. Her guide told her afterwards that she had no idea in the physical world how eloquent she had been in her pleadings on that occasion. There seems to have been some difference of opinion in the council, but eventually the majority yielded to her prayer, and promised to send help to her and to her guide in order that they might work for the world. (An examination into the truth lying behind this remarkable vision of the "council of heaven" was one of the most interesting features of the investigation, of which I shall write later.) After this the semi-theosophical visions were resumed. Once more I quote the words of her letter:

714.   "That night other visions succeeded, but the story of symbology changed. I saw a valley in which lay the human race, and over it hovered a swarm of beings clad in white, but the whiteness radiated no light. Humanity was dark and shadowed. I rushed to awaken them, but at my approach the white-clad figures rushed into strong, determined and powerful groups to prevent my accomplishing my purpose. I recognised that they were deceiving spirits, self-appointed teachers and preachers of the earth, and that they resolutely beat down and held down the dazed and shadowed humanity. But even as I looked I saw here and there an awakening soul among the human multitude. As this soul awoke it grew luminous as with a light from within, and at the same time it arose from its prone position and began to move about over the sleeping world, trying to arouse others. I seemed to stand on a distant mountain, but could distinctly see whenever a soul began to awaken and to shine, and before the vision passed, many of these radiant lights seemed to burst out here and there, and

even a golden light of sun-rays began to gild the tops of the surrounding mountains, and the whiterobed figures fled as this golden radiance increased. They, however, continued to exercise themselves in strenuous endeavours to counteract and oppose my efforts to help the world or to live my life.

715.   "All night the visions continued, but those towards morning were vague. My guide awoke me and told me to get up and get a cup of coffee and to gather myself together, as I was so much in the spirit as to be about to depart from the body altogether. When I had obeyed I found myself dazed. All the time in which I was endeavouring to make a fire and to prepare the cup of coffee, my guide was present and I was conscious of a most wonderful condition. Angels seemed to surround me and to sing hymns of thanksgiving. It was Thanksgiving morning, and the former inclemency of the weather had given place to balminess. I opened the door and turned my face to the south-west. I felt myself surrounded by supernal Beings, and sang with them a wonderful hymn of praise and thanksgiving. It resembled the Assumption of the Virgin-mother, the immaculate conception, the birth and presence of the wonderful Child at once. A peculiarly refreshing but unfamiliar odour permeated the atmosphere. My guide said that the angels were burning frankincense. Later in the day my guide again told me to go to bed.

716.   "The vision was most wonderful. Again I beheld Creation, but this time it was different. I saw the races in the aggregate. As the races appeared and vanished, my guide said solemnly: ` And the evening and the morning were the first day,' ` And the evening and the morning were the second day,' etc. Somehow, though I cannot now explain it, although I felt that I understood it at the time, the fifth race was born in the fourth day, and seemed to be of special importance. To that birth my special attention was called, as the full-fledged fifth-race man lay stretched on the hands of a great Being, and was held out to me to observe. In this vision I saw that, up to the fifth race, mankind was all sorts. Some were large and some were small. Chaos prevailed, and there was little order anywhere in the human universe. But after the birth of the fifth race man I saw that all had become equal and all worked in perfect harmony. I saw also, at this time, that the race took solid form, like a phalanx - the form, however, being circular - and that a band was slipped around the whole mass, passing from man to man, and that no man could get outside of that binding band. The passing of the race was marked by the whole human race being suddenly transformed into the soul form - egg-shaped.

717.   "In the sixth race the development was very marked indeed. The individuals were equal, but much larger than in the fifth race. The tendency of the whole race was much more upward, and the movement had become greatly accelerated. At some time towards the close of the fifth or the beginning of the sixth - I cannot accurately recall just when - I saw sunlight again gilding the peaks. The race emerged from shadow into sunlight, and the onward and upward tendency became swifter and swifter. Then, the hour having once more struck, the eggs lay together just as do the eggs in a nest, but their number was countless.

718.   "My guide left me here. He said he could not go on with me, that I must

go on alone and interpret for myself the meaning of my visions. He warned me to be careful not to give up my life; for upon my going through successfully and not giving up my life would depend my success and the salvation of the world, for which all this that we had seen had been done. In other words, I believed myself to be passing through a terrible ordeal for the salvation of the world.

719.   "As I beheld the development of the seventh race I seemed to go to unimaginable altitudes indeed. The band that I first saw binding the fifth race was strongly encompassing the sixth and seventh races. It became unbreakable. And as I looked into the faces of the men of the seventh race, I saw that gradually they shone more and more brightly with an inner light. Their radiance no longer came from without, but each was shining, living, dazzling light.

720.   "My body was now very weary, and when evening came I begged for rest. But this was not given. I was put through many trials. Many were terrible, and it required the utmost exertion of my powers to enable me to endure. What was the nature of this I do not know. I know only that I promised to deliver God's message under any and all conditions, no matter what they might be, if He should require it. But the trials were awful. At one time I refused the visions, though they were becoming more and more beautiful. They then ceased, and I seemed to find myself in the power of Satan. (All these orthodox terms I personally had long disclaimed but they became real again in the visions.)

721.   "For a time I believed that as a punishment for my perverseness, or rather as a result of this mistake, I had lost all. The awful crisis had passed. The world was lost as a result of my failure; and now it seemed to be not only this world, but the Universe. How I prayed and struggled then! Before all could be restored I promised not only to give up my life but the lives of my children and even the very *life of my soul*, if need be for the salvation of the world.

722.   "I cannot linger here. Towards morning a wonderful breath came into my body, going up and down the spine as if there were absolutely no physical obstruction in my body, and as it breathed or flowed through me, it sang a wonderful, divine anthem, and ended in a marvellous union, in which I felt myself fully united with God. That was a condition it were folly to attempt to describe.

723.   "During this time I beheld a new series of visions - all of glory. There were no forms that I can recall, but glory after glory of *colour*, each brighter and grander than the last. At last it was a wonderful violet, and as it shone upon me in unspeakable glory, I was told that I might go on and see God if I would. I asked if from there I might return, and was told that if I went on I could not return. I then said once more, as I had done in a hundred other trials: ` I must live to save the world.' And as I said that and refused to go on, the sun rose in the world, where I was then conscious, and I looked up at my beautiful vision, thinking how dull the sun was, and then gradually the vision faded.

724.   "Just when, I cannot say, but about this time, I was laid on a cross during the night, placed in a sepulchre, and believed my body was dead. My physical heart, as I thought, was arrested, and the pain which I endured was excruciating. But the

bliss of my soul in the higher visions was as great as was the pain in the body in the sacrificial trials.

725.   "After this, I must desist from any effort at description. I really cannot tell the strange things that befell me, nor are they clear in my memory. One of the ideas was that I was put through preparation for the work I was to do; another, I seemed to hear, and be a part of, involution as well as evolution. Perhaps it represented the experiences of the soul preparing for incarnation.

726.   "When at last I came out of it all, I found my sorrow-stricken family around my bed. They had thought that I was dying. From the beginning of my abnormal condition to the final close had been twelve days, and for five days and nights I had not slept. On the last day, I had believed myself that after all I was not to live longer in this world, and when I awoke to full and normal consciousness, the voice that I had heard so mysteriously gradually faded away, as did the visions, and neither have appeared to me since.

727.   "But since then, I have been conscious of a new spiritual life, and in meditation I reach a blissful condition, and I feel sure that some wonderful thing has happened to me."

728.   THE VISION INVESTIGATED

729.   It must be understood that the extracts given above are only a small part of the visions described by our correspondent, but I think that I have given a fair sample of them, and have not omitted any point of special interest.

730.   Anyone who is accustomed to analyse psychic phenomena will at once see that there are in the account several features which differentiate it from the average. Many visions, even though quite elaborate and detailed, and intensely realistic to the seer, prove on examination to be entirely self-created. I mean that a man first thinks out a subject himself along certain lines, thereby creating a series of thought-forms; and then he proceeds to pass out of his body in sleep or trance, sees his own thought-forms without recognising them as his, and supposes them to be actualities instead of imperfect reflections. Thus he is strongly confirmed in his particular belief or superstition, whatever it happens to be, because he himself has seen it in a vision which he is sure to regard as celestial. Such a man is of course perfectly honest in his conviction, and even perfectly right in saying that he has seen certain things; the weak point is that he has not the training which would enable him to distinguish the nature of what he has seen. In the case now before us, however, there are various little touches, which are extremely unlikely to have been the thoughts of the seer, and there is considerable evidence that a mind differing much from hers must have been responsible for a great deal of what was seen.

731.   As our correspondent was anxious to understand the genesis of her visions, and as their history gave promise of somewhat unusual features, it seemed worth while to make a definite investigation into the matter.

732.   A *rapport* was therefore obtained with the lady, and it was further found

necessary to examine the astral and mental records connected with her, and thus ascertain what had really happened to her. It was soon obvious that many distinct factors entered into the matter, and it was only by patiently disentangling the threads and following each one up to its origin that all the causes could be clearly seen. To put the case briefly:

733. The lady, as hundreds of other people have done, had got herself into serious trouble by an unwise use of breathing exercises. Her desperate efforts to escape from the result of these exercises attracted the attention of a dead man who was strong enough to be of some use to her. But this man had objects of his own to gain - objects not consciously selfish, but belonging to a curious personal delusion of his - and as he helped her, he realised that he had here what might be a powerful instrument for the furtherance of his plans. He promptly modified his scheme, gave her a prominent part in it, and pushed her on into experiences which without him she would probably not have had for several incarnations yet.

734. Much of what resulted was evidently not at all what he had expected, though he tried bravely to turn it all to account. Eventually he dropped her, partly because he was alarmed at the turn which matters were taking, and partly because he began to see that he could not use her quite as he had hoped. The outcome of the whole adventure, so far as our correspondent is concerned, has been good, but this is a piece of good fortune for which she cannot be too thankful, since the risks were enormous, and by any ordinary calculations there was scarcely the barest possibility that she would escape with her life and with reason unimpaired from such an experience.

735. In order to comprehend all that occurred, we must first try to understand what manner of man was this ` guide,' and how he came to be what he was. During physical life he had been a small farmer, a kindly but ignorant man, fanatically religious in a narrow protestant way. His only literature was the Christian Bible, over which he pored during the long winter evenings until his whole life became saturated with his conception of its teachings. Needless to say, his conceptions were usually misconceptions, often so grossly material as to be ludicrous, yet the man was so thoroughly in earnest that it was impossible to laugh at him.

736. He lived in a thinly populated part of the country, and as he found his few neighbours out of sympathy with his religious views, he became more and more a recluse as years rolled by, living frugally on the produce of a small part of his farm, and devoting himself with increasing ardour to the study of his one book. This constant brooding over one idea brought him eventually into a condition of religious monomania, in which he came to believe himself the chosen saviour of the world, the Christ who was destined to offer to it once more the opportunity of salvation which two thousand years ago it had received only very partially. A prominent feature in his scheme was the rescue from its false belief of the vast mass of non-Christian humanity, and his idea was that this should be done not along ordinary missionary lines but through the influence of its own great leaders. It was this part of his programme which induced him to take so keen an interest in our correspondent, as we shall see later.

737. While still fully possessed by these religious delusions, the worthy farmer

died. Naturally enough, his astral life was simply a continuation of the physical, raised as it were to a higher power. He soon found himself amidst the crude thought-forms of the golden Jerusalem, a special corner of which he seems to have modelled for himself to suit his idiosyncrasies. The result of his efforts to visualise the descriptions given in the Apocalypse were sometimes really ingenious and original. I noticed specially his image of the four and twenty elders bowing perpetually in adoration before the throne, and casting at the feet of the deity their golden crowns, which immediately rose from the ground and fluttered back automatically on to their heads, only to be cast down again. His "sea of glass mingled with fire" was not altogether successful, and looked rather like some unusually weird product of a volcanic eruption. His image of the All-Father was quite conventional - a stern-looking old man with a long white beard. In the earlier part of his physical life he had evidently had a thought-image of the Christ - the usual impossible combination of a crucifix and a lamb bearing a flag; but during the later period, when he was persuaded that he himself was the Christ, this figure had not been strengthened, and it was consequently inconspicuous and inactive.

738.   It is among these thought-forms of his that we have to seek for the "council of heaven" which plays a part in our correspondent's vision, and the constitution of that council proved to be both interesting and instructive. The idea seems originally to have been that the council was a sort of selection of about ten of the more important biblical characters (Elijah, Moses, Peter, etc.) represented by colossal figures seated in a semicircle on uncomfortable-looking high-backed golden chairs, which, though supposed to be celestial thrones, were manifestly derived from an imperfect recollection of the sedilia in some Gothic cathedral. The deity himself presided over their deliberations.

739.   Originally the members of this council had obviously been nothing but thought-forms; but at the time when our enquiries brought us into contact with them, several of them had been seized and ensouled by living entities, and this ensoulment introduced some new and interesting factors. Two of these entities were dead men, both of them religious people, each working from his own point of view. One of them was a man of German extraction, who during earth-life had been a shoe-maker - a simple and uninstructed man not altogether unlike the former. He too had studied the Bible diligently; he too was a dreamer of vague, mystical dreams; he too felt that he had a special revelation or interpretation to offer to the world - something far more rational than the farmer's. He had come to feel that the essential truth of Christianity lay in the mystical union of Christ and his heavenly bride, the Church. To him the Christ was far less the historical personality of the Gospels than the living spirit of the Church, and the task of the true Christian was to awaken within himself the Christ-spirit. The message which humanity needed, he thought, was that every man could and should become a Christ - a message which seemed to him so clear and simple that it needed only to be delivered to command instant attention, and thus to save the world from sin and lift it at once into the light of truth. He had begun preaching to this effect while still on the physical earth, but had died before he had done much towards the conversion of humanity.

740.   Arriving in the astral world, he was still as eager as ever to spread his views, and having met the farmer he struck up a friendship with him. They had much in common, and each felt that the other might be helpful to him in the prosecution of his scheme. The shoemaker did not recognise the farmer as the sole Christ, but he did apply his theory to him, and consider him as a person in whom the Christ-spirit was exceptionally developed. The farmer understood only vaguely the shoe-maker's central idea, but he realised that he had found some one who was willing to co-operate in saving the world. Each regarded the other as somewhat eccentric, but still each with a simple cunning thought that he could make use of the other for his own purposes.

741.   Between them they had conceived this curious idea of a "council of heaven" of which they were both members; or possibly they may have found a thought-form of this kind made by some one else, and may simply have adopted it and joined themselves to it. The thought-forms as viewed by trained vision were clumsy and imperfect, though no doubt quite satisfactory to their makers. Moses, for example, was seriously incomplete. He sat, stiff and rigid, as though glued to his uncomfortable golden throne, but in reality he was only a face and front projecting from the chair, and had never been properly finished off behind. In this respect be resembled many of the thought-forms found in the Summerland, where it is not infrequent to see mothers fondling children which are defective in exactly the same way. The creators of such forms are always completely happy with them and never perceive their imperfections, for though there is no life in such dolls except the thought which is put into them, that thought will always respond to its generator and do exactly what it is expected to do. Peter was another very inefficient person on this council - quite insignificant-looking; but at least he carried a large bunch of keys, the jingling of which was his principle contribution to the deliberations.

742.   While the majority of this council was of the type just described, the thought-forms of the deity, of S. Paul (the image chosen for occupation by the shoemaker) and of the prophet Elijah were much more definite and original. The latter indeed quite surprised us by his activity, and on examination it was found that he, too, was being occupied (for at least used as a kind of mouthpiece) by another dead man, a Welshman, who at some early period in his earth-life had gone through the experience called ` conversion,' and had later on emigrated to America, where he had lived for some years and eventually died. During his physical life he had always been seeking religious experiences of the emotional type; for instance, he had attended some of the negro revival meetings, and had there witnessed and taken part in the celebrated "Jerusalem jump." Intermingled with his religion were curious socialistic proclivities, and his dream was of a golden millennium which was half irrational, emotional Chiristianity and half materialistic Socialism.

743.   He had grasped rather more than the others the relation between the physical and astral worlds, and the possibilities of the latter, and he understood that before he could hope to influence the physical world he must somehow or other get into touch with it. He was not thinking of reincarnation, for he had never heard of such an idea; but he knew that he had passed from the physical world into the astral,

and therefore he thought there must be some way of passing back again. His attention was much occupied with this problem, and when he became aware that the farmer had found a medium through whom he could come to some extent into touch with the physical world, he decided to make use of both in any way that he could. This seemed a possible first step in the direction of gaining his ends, and it occurred to him to enter the thought-form of Elijah in the "council of heaven" as a means of presently introducing himself on such a footing as would at once ensure respect from the others. I do not think he was in any way self-seeking or self-conceited in doing this; it was to him simply a means to an end, providentially put in his way.

744.   But now ensued an unexpected result. Masquerading thus as Elijah, he tried to bear himself as he thought the prophet would have done, and to impart an Old-Testament flavour to his impersonation. This reacted upon his ordinary astral life; he began to live all the while in the character, and by degrees to wonder whether he was not really Elijah! He is literally in process of transforming himself, and will assuredly soon be a confirmed monomaniac. At the time of our investigation he still knew that he was a Welshman who occasionally impersonated Elijah; but I feel certain that in the near future he will pass beyond that stage, and will be as sure that he is really Elijah as the farmer is that he is the Christ.

745.   Meantime he had not yet introduced himself as the Welshman to the other human members of the council, but flattered himself that as Elijah he was inspiring great respect and in fact directing their decisions. We have, therefore, the astonishing spectacle of a council whose only effective members were three dead men, each one of whom thought that he was manipulating the others for the furtherance of his own objects; and yet none of those objects was selfish, and all the men concerned were religious, well-meaning and honest in intention. Only in the astral world would such an extraordinary combination be possible; yet the most astounding and the most characteristic fact still remains to be told.

746.   It has been already mentioned that the All-Father himself was supposed to preside over the meetings of the council. He was of course a thought-form like all the rest, but he occasionally manifested a spasmodic and inappropriate activity which showed the presence of some exterior force, different in quality from the others. Careful investigation showed that just as the form of Elijah was ensouled by the Welshman, so was this form of the deity ensouled by - a frolicsome nature-spirit!

747.   I have already described some of the characteristics of this delightful kingdom of Nature. It may be remembered what a keen pleasure some of such creatures take in theatrical performances among themselves, in any sort of masquerade (most especially if thereby they can gain the triumph of deceiving or frightening a member of the superior human evolution), and also how they enjoy telling some enthralling tale to their fellows. Bearing this in mind, we shall at once see that, from the point of view of a tricksy nature-spirit, here was an absolutely unique opportunity. He could (and did) play a joke on the most colossal scale conceivable upon three human beings, and we may readily imagine what a soul-satisfying story he had to tell afterwards to his admiring fellows. Needless to say, he had not the faintest idea of irreverence ; he

would probably be no more capable of such a conception than a fly would; to him the whole thing was nothing but an unequalled opportunity for a really gorgeous hoax, and he did his very best with it.

748.   Of course he could neither understand nor join in the deliberations, so for the most part he preserved a cryptic silence which was very effective. He had somehow acquired a small number of biblical phrases appropriate to his part, and he emptied these out upon the council at intervals as a parrot might, apparently having no conception of their meaning. "Thus saith the Lord"; "Amen, so be it"; "I am the Lord thy God; thou shalt have none other Gods but me"; "I will smite the earth with a curse" - these were some of the gems of his collection, the specimens of his unconscious eloquence. Now and again the joke became too much for him, or perhaps the restraint was irksome, and he abandoned the thought-form for a few moments in order to relieve his overstrained feelings by wild dancing and outbursts of laughter, somewhere out of sight of his council. When this happened it was most interesting to see how the thought-form collapsed from alertness to stolidity, and the unfortunate human members of the council immediately supposed that something had occurred to provoke that divine wrath which is always so prominent a part of this type of religion.

749.   This, then, was the reality behind the awe-inspiring "council of heaven" before which our correspondent pleaded so earnestly. It will be understood that only the dead men could really contribute to whatever discussion may have taken place; the other members of the council could not originate anything, though they may have had enough vitality to give a formal assent to a proposition.

750.   To understand the part played in the vision by the Theosophical thought-forms we must glance at the history and mental condition of our correspondent. Falling away from a rather materialistic form of Christianity, she became practically an atheist. Then she lost a beloved child; and in such a nature these various experiences naturally produced deep emotions, each of which had its part in the moulding of her temperament. At this period she came into contact with Theosophy, and commenced its study with no less formidable a book than *The Secret Doctrine*. Undaunted by its difficulties she applied herself to it diligently and strove to grasp its teaching, to make mental pictures of what is described in the Stanzas of Dzyan. Certain of its ideas had a special attraction for her. The thought of initiation with its mysterious and dangerous ordeals was one of them; another was the succession of the races, coupled with the great question as to who shall and who shall not pass the final test and reach in safety the further shore. All this was inevitably to some extent coloured by earlier Christian conceptions about "conversion" and 'salvation,' even though at the same time the splendid horizons of the great oriental religions opened before her.

751.   Thus it came about that she surrounded herself with a great mass of strong thought-forms of a more or less Theosophical character, and by the very fact of doing so unconsciously set in motion certain occult laws. In the higher worlds, like attracts like, and her thought-forms soon drew to themselves others of similar nature. Some hundreds of miles from where she lived there was an earnest Theosophical Lodge, which among other activities maintained a *Secret Doctrine* class. A vast

mass of thought-forms and speculations had been thrown off by this class, and our correspondent was soon in touch with this astral storehouse. How the first contact was made I did not observe. Perhaps when travelling in the astral body our correspondent may have been attracted by the presentations of subject in which she was so deeply interested; or on the other hand some member of the class may have astrally noticed her thoughts and tried to add to them; or it may have been simply that sympathetic vibrations attracted one another, as they invariably do, without human interference. However that may have been, the fact remains that she was surrounded by an enormous body of thought-forms of a particular type, she herself being at the very same time precisely in the condition to be most deeply affected by them.

752.   At this period she began to practise breathing exercises, and by that means laid herself open to astral influences. Her keen sympathy with suffering caused her to seek the dead murderer, or perhaps brought him to her, and the automatic writing and the obsession followed in the natural course of events. The murderer put forth all his power to maintain the advantage which he had gained, and she struggled desperately to protect and free herself, making herself for the time quite a conspicuous object in the astral world by the vehemence of her efforts and the amount of energy which she put forth.

753.   As the farmer wandered about, the affray attracted his attention, and in his character as the Christ he felt it his duty to interfere and expel the murderer. He had never before encountered so brilliant an astral body, nor had he seen such impressive surrounding as those of the person whom he had rescued - a mass of forms at once so unusual in type (connected as it was with cosmic processes considered from the oriental point of view) and at the same time so far larger in quantity than any one person normally carries with him. Here were the forms of oriental Gods, of the founders of religions, of Masters, Adepts, Angels, and all sorts of magnificent but unfamiliar conceptions. If we remember that the farmer could not know that these were only thought-forms, but must inevitably have taken them as actual living beings, we shall see that it is small wonder that with his ignorance on all such matters and his constant expectation of celestial assistance in his appointed work, he should feel that he had been specially guided by providence to help one who could help him in return - a person of importance in the oriental world commensurate with that which he arrogated to himself for the occident. At once he seized his opportunity; he proclaimed himself as the appointed guide and proceeded to take charge of the lady's further development.

754.   A curious fact noticed here was that, though he posed as guide, he was largely influenced by the thoughts of our correspondent, and in many cases simply gave her back those thoughts in other language. He knew nothing of the serpent fire, but he thought of it as some form of divine afflatus; he saw that some process of awakening was being performed by its aid: and he did his best to help and encourage this. Their joint efforts succeeded in arousing what may be called the upper layers of that mysterious force, though fortunately for the lady, from ignorance as to what is really needed for full achievement, they were not able to stir it to its depths, otherwise her body would surely have been destroyed. Further, they evidently did not know

through what centres it must be sent in order to bring continuous consciousness, and so they missed their aim. But the description given of the sufferings endured is accurate as far as it goes, and some of the expressions used are strikingly suggestive. How dangerous their experiments were may be seen from the lady's account of these sufferings, and from her family's testimony as to the condition in which she had been. The whole story gives a most impressive warning against the risk of attempting premature development along such lines.

755.	It is useless to criticise in detail what may be called the Theosophical part of the vision; wonderful, uplifting, awe-inspiring as it no doubt was to the seer, it after all represents not the actual occurrences of evolution, but the combination and synthesis of a number of thought-images. Parts of the symbology are interesting and illuminative, while others obviously require modification. Certain features, such as the chanting of the angels, are clearly due to the influence of the Christian stream of thought in the mind of the guide. He watched the unfolding of the vision along with our correspondent, but being ignorant of oriental teaching he understood but little of it. For example, he seems to have confused the successive races with the various tribes of Israel, and tried to fit in what he saw with the story of the sealing of the 144,000.

756.	It is in the monomania of the guide that we must seek for the cause of the weighty feeling of responsibility which overshadowed the whole vision, the conviction that upon our correspondent's success depended the salvation of the world. This sort of naïve self-conceit or megalomania is one of the commonest characteristics of communications from the astral plane. It seems to be one of the most ordinary illusions of a dead man that, if he can only get some lady to act as a medium for him, he can revolutionise the entire thought of the planet by a simple statement of a few self-evident facts. But in this case there was rather more than the usual excuse for the attitude adopted. The poor farmer was deeply impressed with the thought that unless the world accepted him this time it would lose its final chance of salvation, and he propounded this theory one day to the deity in council at a moment when the nature-spirit happened to be in charge. It is little likely that the nature-spirit had any clear conception of the purport of the question, but at least he understood that his assent was being asked to some proposition or other, so he gave it in his most pompous manner; and this naturally enough confirmed the farmer in his delusion, and made it the one dominating thought of his life. Apart from his influence no such impression would ever have come into the mind of the lady, whose view of her own position and powers was much saner and more modest.

757.	The personification of the world and the devil in human forms is also due to the thought of the guide, for the lady herself knew much better than to believe in the exploded superstition of a personal Satan. This seems to have come at a period of the experience when she was much exhausted, and therefore more fully under the domination of the guide's mind, and less able to exercise her own natural power of discrimination. The nervous tension attendant upon the conditions through which she passed must have been indescribable; indeed, it brought her perilously near to the possibility of physical hallucination. She writes of certain acts of reverence made to her on the physical earth by animals, but investigation does not confirm this, showing the actions of the animals to have been quite normal and dictated by their ordinary instinct, though the lady in her overstrained condition gave them a different interpretation.

758.   The special interest of the case to those who examined it was the manner in which a number of independent and quite ordinary astral factors combined to produce a dramatic and imposing whole. The ruling force was the will of the guide, and the strength of his extraordinary delusion; yet this would have been ineffective, or at least would have worked quite differently, but for the action of our correspondent in rashly laying herself open to astral influence. *The Secret Doctrine* class and its thought-forms, the other dead men on the council, the sportive nature-spirit - all these played their part, and if any one of them had been absent the picture would have been less complete, or the plot must have worked itself out on other lines.

759.   It seems to me that the story has its value as showing the astonishing fertility and abundance of the resources of the astral world, and the imperative necessity of that full knowledge which is only to be gained by thorough occult training. All through it we see really good and well-intentioned people deceiving themselves quite pitiably for want of this knowledge - putting themselves often into such positions that one cannot wonder that they were deluded. One must presume that it was needful for them to learn in the hard school of experience, and it is also well to remember that no trial of this nature ever comes to any one without an adequate opportunity of preparation. No one who had studied the Bible as closely as the guide had done could have failed to remark the warnings therein contained as to possible deception by false Christs and lying prophets, and even in the book of Svami Vivekananda there is to be found an earnest adjuration against the premature or promiscuous use of his instructions. Unfortunately people never will take these cautions to themselves, but invariably apply them to their neighbours or opponents.

760.   Yet it should be noticed that for our correspondent the outcome was good. The forms seen were largely illusory, but the high emotions awakened, the awe and the rapture - all these produced permanent results which cannot but have in them much of good. The boundless enthusiasm for spiritual things, the unselfish desire to help even at the cost of any sacrifice - these are in themselves mighty forces, and when generated they evoke a response from worlds far higher than any which are actually reached by the consciousness in the vision itself. The feeling is genuine, however imperfectly conceived may be that which occasions it; and so while we congratulate our correspondent on having come safely through perils more tremendous than she can readily realise, we may be permitted to hope that the peace and uplifting which she gained through them may prove a permanent heritage. The deep sense of union with the divine which brought with it such bliss was unquestionably a true touch of the lower fringe of the intuitional world, and to have attained this is no doubt worth all the suffering through which the patient passed. But the student knows that all that (and much more) could have been obtained without the pain and without the awful risk, by the investment of the same amount of energy in the more ordinary methods

which have approved themselves to the wisdom of the ages. To force one's way into unknown realms without the guidance of one who really knows, is to court disaster; and it is a danger to which none need expose himself, for the old paths are always open, and the old saying still remains true: "When the pupil is ready the Master appears."

761.　　IN WRITING A BOOK

762.　　Many of us are constantly being influenced by unseen entities in a great many ways of which we have not the slightest idea. We have spoken of pride of race and caste. This often exists in an even more intense form as pride of family, and in that case not infrequently it is largely due to the influence of our ancestors. I have known several cases in which a man contrived to keep himself for a long time in the astral world in order that he might hover over his descendants and try to induce them to keep up the pride of their race. The late Queen Elizabeth, for example, had so intense a love for her country that it is only quite recently that she has lapsed into the heaven-world, having spent the whole intervening time in endeavouring, and until recently almost entirely without success, to impress her successors with her ideas of what ought to be done for England. Hers is perhaps an extreme case, but in several other royal families the continuity of tradition which has been maintained has been in the same way largely due to constant pressure, intentionally exercised, by older members of the family, from the astral world.

763.　　It is by no means uncommon for fathers and mothers who have set their hearts upon some particular alliance for their sons or daughters to endeavour even after death to bring about the fulfilment of their wishes. In rarer cases they have been able to show themselves as apparitions in order to emphasise their commands. More often they exercise an insidious because unsuspected influence, by constantly keeping their thought upon the matter before the mind of the person whom they wish to influence - a steady pressure which the ordinary man is likely to take for his own sub-conscious desire.

764.　　Cases in which the dead have constituted themselves guardian angels to the living are exceedingly numerous, and in this way mothers often protect their sons, and deceased husbands their widows, for many years. Sometimes such influence is not of a protective character, but is exercised in order that the dead man may find a means of expressing some ideas which he is anxious to put before the world. The person upon whom the impression is made is sometimes conscious of it, and sometimes entirely unconscious. A certain distinguished novelist has told me that the wonderful plots of his stories invariably come to him as though by a kind of inspiration, that he writes them without knowing beforehand how they will work out - that in fact, as he puts it, they are actually written through him. Far more often than we think, authors and musical composers are influenced in this way, so that many books credited to the living are really the work of the dead.

765.　　In some cases the dead man desires to announce his authorship, so that books confessedly written by the dead are becoming quite a feature of modern literature; or perhaps a better way to express it would be that many of us are gradually coming to recognise that there is no such thing as death in the old, bad sense of the word, and that though a man who has laid aside his physical body may find a certain difficulty in writing a book with his own hand, he is quite as capable of dictating one as any living author. Sometimes such books are moral or metaphysical treatises, but sometimes also they are novels, and in this latter shape they undoubtedly do good, for they reach many who are quite unlikely to encounter a more serious essay on occult matters, and would be still less likely to take the trouble to read it if they did encounter it.

766.   A good specimen of this class (and it is a class which is becoming more numerous year by year) is *The Strange Story of Ahrinziman* - a book which was brought to my notice some years ago. Let me take it as an example and explain what it is and how it came to be written. I know that the first impulse of those who are dozing in the comfortable haze which surrounds the average intelligence and cushions it against the real facts of life, will naturally, be to proclaim that the whole thing must be nonsense, on the crude theory that when a man is dead he is dead, and it is therefore quite impossible that he should dictate anything; and even those who know better than that may be tempted to suspect that to assign the authorship to a man out of the body is nothing but a novel form of advertisement - a trick of the trade, as it were. So perhaps I had better begin by saying that I have trustworthy assurance that this book is at least a genuine dictation from the astral world, though naturally that by no means guarantees that it is in all other respects what it claims to be.

767.   People who are unacquainted with the conditions of life among those whom we are in the habit of miscalling "the dead," seem to find it impossible to realise how natural in all respects that life is, or to understand that human nature may and does exhibit all its varied aspects just as quaintly on the other side of the grave as on this. The dead man has not necessarily been canonised, nor has he suddenly become grave and reverend; he is exactly the same man as before, just as susceptible to the influence of vanity or jealousy, just as capable of making mistakes.

768.   An astral author may employ the same literary machinery as a physical author, and may cast his tale into any form that pleases him. When we find Mr. Rider Haggard writing in the first person under the name of Allan Quartermain of Ludwig Horace Holly, we do not necessarily assume that he is relating personal experiences of his own, nor even that Quartermain or Holly had a historical existence. In exactly the same way we must realise that when a dead man dictates in the first person *The Story of Ahrinziman,* he may be trying to give us a more or less modified autobiography, or he may simply be casting an allegory or a problem-novel into an attractive and striking form; and this suggestion must no more be considered a reflection upon the *bona fides* of the dead author than was the previous sentence a reflection upon that of Mr. Haggard.

769.   Be this as it may, Ahrinziman tells us a good story - a story which is thoroughly oriental in its setting. He describes himself as the illegitimate son of a Persian king. His mother, a Greek vestal virgin captured in some Persian foray, is murdered by the rightful queen in a fit of jealousy, and to avoid further unpleasant expression of this same consuming jealousy, the child is brought up by a peasant among

the mountains in a distant corner of the empire. The boy is by nature clairvoyant to a certain extent, able to see the nature-spirits which surround him, and also his dead mother. Presently he comes into contact with some priests, learns much from them, and is eventually taken into the temple and becomes a medium for them. Discontent seizes him, and he absconds and joins a band of robbers in the mountains, but after a few years abandons them in turn. He then meets with a practitioner of the darker magic, and attaches himself to him as a pupil; but the master dies in the performance of one of his enchantments, and the student is saved from sharing his fate only by the interference of his dead mother.

770.   During further wanderings he meets the prince, who is in reality his step-brother (the son of the queen who murdered his mother), and is enabled by his clairvoyant power to cure him of an obsession. This prince in due course comes to the throne and raises our hero to a position of honour, knowing nothing, however, of the real relationship between them. By this time Ahrinziman is married, unfortunately to an entirely unworthy woman who never really appreciates him, and is false to him without hesitation when she finds that she has attracted the favourable regards of the king. Through his partial clairvoyance Ahrinziman becomes aware of this, and in his jealous rage causes the death of the king by astral means. He himself succeeds to the throne (having declared his parentage), but after a short reign is slain by another claimant.

771.   The rest of the book is devoted to a description of his experiences in the astral world. He is represented as, at first, filled with jealousy and hatred, and consequently mating with all sorts of horrible entities in order through them to achieve revenge; but gradually the good within him asserts itself, and he begins to try to aid instead of to injure, and so through a long and toilsome upward progress he at last attains to perfect bliss.

772.   How far is it possible that all this can be true? May we take it wholly or partly as the autobiography which it professes to be, or must we regard it as a romance? Certainly of much of it we may say: "*Se non è vero, è ben trovato.*" As to the physical part of the story, we have but meagre records of what took place in Persia in the fifth century before the Christian era, but as far as it goes, our fragmentary history of that period seems to fit in fairly accurately with what Ahrinziman writes. The interest of the student of the hidden side of nature will naturally be centred chiefly on the astral experiences, for the sake of which mainly the book is put forth, and he will desire to know how far these can be confirmed from the point of view of such occult knowledge as has reached our western world.

773.   Those who have studied most deeply will be the first to admit that in this splendid science of the soul we are as yet but picking up pebbles on the shore of the great ocean of knowledge, that our fullest information is as yet far from exhaustive, and that the marvellous variety and adaptability of astral conditions are so great that it would be rash to say that anything is impossible. Still, certain broad rules are well established, and some of these seem to be violated by Ahrinziman's story, if we are to take it literally, though all falls readily into place if we allow for certain limitations

upon his part. If the whole thing is simply a parable, well and good; but it is interesting to see how Ahrinziman may be perfectly honest in his narration, even though some points in it are contrary to accepted facts.

774.   The first great question is whether a stay of anything like such a period as two thousand three hundred years in the astral world is at all possible, since we know that twenty or thirty years is a fair average for ordinary persons. It is true that a man of unusual will-power may greatly prolong his astral life by intensifying his passions and desires, and throwing all his strength into the lower rather than the higher side of himself; and this is exactly what Ahrinziman represents himself to have done. I have read of a case in Germany where an erring priest was earth-bound for four hundred years, and I have myself known one where ambition and a determined will detained a person in astral life for three hundred; but such instances are infrequent, and none of them even approach the vista of centuries claimed by Ahrinziman. It is clear, too, that he does not consider himself by any means as a special case, for he speaks of many friends and contemporaries as still with him, some in advance of him in progress, and some behind him. If, therefore, we are to accept his story as genuine, it becomes more probable if we regard it rather as an attempt to describe conditions through which he passed during the first century after his death than as indicating anything at present existing.

775.   Though eager for occult knowledge, he did not show much attraction towards spirituality, except in childhood; his actions were chiefly the result of ambition, passion and revenge, and he died by violence in the prime of life. Considering all these factors, we should expect a protracted and stormy astral existence, the earlier part of which would probably be extremely unpleasant; we should expect also that gradually the passions would wear themselves out, that the better side of his nature would assert itself, and that opportunities would be offered for progress.

776.   All this is what Ahrinziman describes, but he surrounds it with a wealth of allegory that may easily be misunderstood, and he spreads over two thousand three hundred years what may well have occupied forty or fifty. We must not forget that in the astral world none of our ordinary methods of time-measurement are available, and that if, even in physical life, a few hours of suffering or anxiety seem to us almost interminable, this characteristic is exaggerated a hundredfold in an existence of which feelings and passions are the very essence. While it is scarcely conceivable that Ahrinziman can really have spent two thousand years in the astral world, it is easy to believe that his sojourn there *seemed* to him an eternity.

777.   Still the fact remains that, if he is to be credited as to the physical part of his life, about that length of time has passed since his assassination; what then has he been doing during all these years? I have no personal acquaintance with him, and no right to make impertinent enquiries, but a case somewhat parallel to his which I recently investigated may suggest to us a possible explanation.

778.   I was consulted by a lady who stated that her "spirit guide" was a priest of ancient Egypt; and as the advice which he gave was good, and his teaching accurate, it seemed worth while to inquire into his reasons for making so extraordinary a claim,

as it appeared scarcely likely that so dignified and upright a man would stoop to the common and petty device of impersonation. On meeting him I saw at once that he had unquestionably been initiated up to a certain level into the Mysteries according to the Egyptian Rite, and naturally I wondered how it could be that he was still active in the astral world. Upon examination I found that since his life as an Egyptian priest he had had another incarnation, which he had spent wearily and unsatisfactorily within the walls of a monastery, devoting it apparently to the working out of some accumulations of karma; but after his death certain circumstances (it *seemed* a mere accident) brought him into touch with the thought-current of his old Egyptian surroundings.

779.   Instantly the memory of that previous life flashed into his consciousness (I think it had always been hovering upon the threshold, and he had always been hungering, though he did not know for what), and it was so much more vivid and real than the dull monastic round, that the latter became to him a mere evil dream. He soon forgot it altogether, or regarded it as nothing more than a wearisome part of his astral punishment, and so he was really quite honest in his statement that he *was* that Egyptian priest - the powerful personality with which he had identified himself up to the close of his last life in the heaven-world, just before his descent into the comparatively recent incarnation in which he became a monk. I do not assert that Ahrinziman's case is similar, but it is at least possible that it may be.

780.   Naturally Ahrinziman writes as a man of his day, and uses the terminology to which he is accustomed, much of which sounds odd in our ears to-day, especially as he constantly confounds his symbols with material facts. Of course it is not actually true, as he supposes, that men are divided into three great groups, having at their heads angels bearing respectively white, red, and golden stars, any more than it is actually true that Phoebus drives his chariot daily across the sky from east to west, or that the Sun God is newly born at Christmas when the days begin to grow longer. But it *is* true that some ancient religions adopted a system of symbology closely allied to that which this book puts forth, and that a man passing into astral life with his mind filled with such preconceived ideas might go on for a long time interpreting everything in accordance with them, and ignoring facts which they did not cover.

781.   It is true also that mighty spirits exist whose method of evolution is so entirely different from our own, that *for us* it would be evil; but with them we do not normally come into contact, nor is it of them that Ahrinziman speaks, for he himself admits that his angels of light and darkness are after all human beings who have lived their life on earth. He describes vividly the stupendous thought-edifices reared by man's passions, though he often fails to distinguish the temporary thought-images from the more permanent realities of the world. He gives us a horrible description of a kind of astral battle in which the plain is strewn with the *disjecta membra* of the combatants - a gruesome detail which could not really occur, as will at once be manifest to anyone who comprehends the fluidic nature of the astral body.

782.   Indeed, if his remarks are really to be taken as representing the ancient Persian knowledge with regard to things astral, we are compelled to recognise that that presentation was less definitely scientific, as well as less comprehensive, than that

which is put before students of the occult at the present day. For example, Ahrinziman does not seem to have any clear grasp of the great central fact of reincarnation, or perhaps regards it as an occasional possibility, instead of recognising it as the appointed means of evolution for humanity.

783.　　His use of terms is somewhat perplexing until one becomes accustomed to it, for it is fairly evident that he gives the name of "spiritual body" to what we now call the astral vehicle, and that his "astral body" is nothing more than the etheric double - as may be seen when he describes the latter as slightly larger than the physical, and as capable of being influenced by powerful acids; remarks which are true of the etheric double, but would be inaccurate if they referred to what is now termed the astral body. He has also a confusing habit of speaking of unpleasant astral conditions as below the earth-plane, and pleasant ones as above it, though he describes them both as less material than our earth. He has probably been misled by the fact that the denser astral matter does interpenetrate our physical globe, and that those who are confined to the least desirable subdivision may often find themselves actually within the crust of the earth. In addition to this there is, no doubt, a world lower than the physical - one with which normal humanity has happily no connection; but it is more, and not less, material than the world which we think we know.

784.　　Quite frequently he describes something in language which at once convinces the student that he has unquestionably seen that of which he writes; and then he proceeds to disappoint us by accounting for it in an involved and unscientific manner, or by treating poetic symbols as though they were material facts. Once or twice he shows his conceptions to be tainted by the twin-soul theory - a line of thought to be sedulously avoided by all who wish to make any real advance in occult study.

785.　　He is in error when he speaks of mediumship as a necessity for spiritual evolution - though perhaps this is once more merely a question of terminology, as he may be using the word in the sense of psychic sensitiveness. He is, however, clearly wrong when he says that it is impossible for a man, still possessing a physical body fully to comprehend or to control astral forces and beings, or to have perfect spiritual sight. What he no doubt means, or at least ought to mean, is that a man who is still *confined* to his physical body cannot possess these higher powers, for he has not realised that a man may learn during life how to leave his physical body as completely as at death, and may yet return to it when he wishes. Also he shows ignorance of the Oriental teaching when he stigmatises it as selfish, and opines that by it "the eager hunger of the starving many for light is left unsatisfied". On the whole, however, his teaching is commendably free from sectarianism.

786.　　Though the student of occultism thus finds himself compelled to differ from Ahrinziman on certain points, I hasten to add that there are many upon which we must all most thoroughly agree with him. To take at random a few of the many gems which may be found, his criticisms on war and conquest, and on the history of religions, are admirable. We are all with him when he writes:

787.　　I hold that truth and error, good and evil, are to be found everywhere and in all religions and amongst all peoples; and no matter how pure the original doctrines of any form of faith may be, it is impossible to prevent the ambitions and the lusts, the greed and the cruelty of the undeveloped human soul from perverting the purity of the teachings and turning them to the basest purposes and overlaying them with the grossest errors . . . The absurd ordinances, the horrible sacrifices, the revolting practices, the grotesque beliefs, the fantastic theories, that had crept into the teaching of this religion, were all excrescences fastened one by one upon the simple purity of the teaching of its founder.

788.   His terminology is perhaps not the best possible, yet there is much truth in his thought that all evil is a perversion of some good quality, into which it will one day be transmuted. Many of his ideas as to spiritual development are also greatly to be commended. The dangers of mediumship and hypnotism could hardly be better expressed than in this solemn warning:

789.   Let no one ever resign the sovereignty of himself, his mind or body, into the hands of another, be he priest or layman. For a man's freedom is his divine prerogative, and he who yields it to another is more abject than the lowest slave.

790.   Again it is explained in one of the notes:

791.   A perfect trance should be the conscious flight of the soul into a superior condition, from which it ought to return strengthened and refreshed and capable of wider thoughts and nobler and freer actions, and a stronger and more perfect possession of its own individuality. To apply the word ` trance' to those exhibitions of semi-conscious mental aberration of persons whose sensitiveness lays them open to the mesmeric control of either incarnate or excarnate minds, is to propagate an error which ought long ago to have been exploded. With the spread of mediumistic development, all and every variety and degree of sub-conscious conditions have come to be classed as ` trances,' yet they bear no more resemblance to the true trance of the developed mystic of the older occult faiths than does the sleep which is produced by the use of powerful narcotic drugs resemble that of healthy, tired nature. The hypnotically-induced trance is as pernicious to the soul as would be the habitual use of narcotics to the body. Whether the magnetiser be in the flesh or out of it, the results are the same; an habitual use of magnetism to induce sleep or ` trance' is an evil.

792.   He describes accurately how the lower dead crowd to séances, and how the so-called guides are by no means always strong enough to keep off evil influences. Clearly also does he warn us how readily the ideas of the earthly enquirers mingle with the revelations of the magnetised medium, so that by such a method of investigation a man usually receives such information or counsel as he desires or expects. He understands that asceticism as such is useless and often harmful, and that the physical body must be in perfect health and power if visions are to be reliable. He realises, too, something of the difficulties of the way:

793.   Few, very few, who possess the needful clearness of sight ever learn how to use it successfully; still fewer have the indomitable will and the unquenchable thirst for knowledge which will carry them through all the dangers and trials and disappointments, and the infinite toil and labour involved in these studies.

794.   He has all history on his side when he tells us that those who develop the

highest degrees of power will do well entirely to withdraw themselves from active life in the physical world, and his strange congeries of characters is gradually brought to understand that only through unselfishness is real progress possible.

795.   Again and again little touches of knowledge leap to the eyes of the student, showing that things have been rightly seen, even though the expression may be confused for want of more definite classification of the facts. Ahrinziman understands the making of talismans and potions; he sees how a single action or thought of revenge opens the door to evil influences which may cling to its author for years to come; he describes how the presence of the dead causes the living to think of them, even though not sufficiently developed to perceive them.

796.   In writing of astral life, he gives us a fine description of the wicked queen surrounded after death by evil thoughts and memories, which to her were as actual events; and a grimly realistic touch is the account of the slave who spends his time in crawling ever backwards and forwards through the secret passage in the making of which he was murdered. He tells us of the dead who have a confused impression that they are still in their earthly bodies, and of those others who, having realised their separation, try to use the earthly bodies of living men as mediums for the gratification of their passion. He comprehends, too, how men who stand side by side, as far as space is concerned, may yet be absolutely unconscious of one another; he knows the glorious truth that no evil can be eternal, that however far from the Path the erring soul may wander, at long, long last it also will find its homeward way.

797.   He ends with a hope which we all may echo - that, as the barriers of ignorance which so long have divided nation from nation are gradually wearing thinner before the radiating force of knowledge, and the light of brotherhood is beginning faintly to shine through, so the same wider knowledge and clearer insight may, by degrees, set at naught the imaginary barrier which we have misnamed death, showing us that there is in truth no separation after all, since whether at the moment we happen to have physical bodies, or not, we are all members of the same great fraternity, all moving towards the same goal, all enveloped in the sunlight of the same Eternal Love.

CHAPTER XIII OUR ATTITUDE TOWARDS THESE INFLUENCES

801.   PROTECTIVE SHELLS

802.   We have considered specimens of the various kinds of influences which are coming in upon us from all sides, and we find that among such influences are many which are disturbing and undesirable; so a question naturally arises as to how we can best avoid or neutralise these. It is an easy matter to form round oneself when necessary a sort of temporary suit of armour of higher matter - what is commonly called by students a protective shell. But is this the best way to meet the difficulty? An authority on the subject once remarked that, as far as self-protection is concerned, the best thing to do with a shell is not to form it in the first place, and if one has formed it, to break it up as speedily as possible! There is certainly a good deal of truth in these words, for in the majority of cases (at least among all but the most elementary students) all that can be achieved by the formation of a shell round oneself can also be done more effectively and with less danger in other ways, as we shall see later. Exact knowledge as to the formation of shells of various kinds is sometimes useful; but, like most other knowledge, it may be abused, so before directing one's energies along these lines it is desirable to know exactly what one wishes to do and how it is to be achieved.

803.   The first great principle to bear in mind is that a shell should be used far more frequently for the protection of others than for oneself. The Invisible Helpers, for example, frequently find it desirable to make such a defence for some of those whom they are trying to save from evil influences of various sorts. But the average enquirer has more often in mind the idea of protecting himself against various outer influences, and he usually asks how he may form a shell for that purpose. There are occasions in which such action is allowable, and we may perhaps group these under three heads corresponding to the etheric, the astral and the mental vehicles.

804.   In all cases alike these shells are constructed by the power of the will, but before exercising that power it is well to know of what kind of matter the shell is to be built and what it is desired to keep out. The directions usually given are that the student should think of his aura as surrounding him in ovoid form, should concentrate strongly upon the outer surface of that aura, and should then exert his will to harden it so that it may become impervious to any influences from without. These directions are good, and a fairly strong shell can be made in that way; but the effort will be at the same time much less laborious and much more effective if the man understands exactly what he is doing and why, and so can send forth the energy of his will in the right direction only, instead of flooding the whole neighbourhood with a stream of ill-directed force. Let us then consider the three varieties somewhat in detail, and see for what purpose each is appropriate.

805. THE ETHERIC SHELL

Thinking such thoughts enhances the problem.
Maintain forceful, cheerful + relaxed attitude

806.   We will take first that which is intended to protect the physical body (including the etheric double) from various dangers to which it may be liable. The more common uses of such a shell are three - to protect a sensitive man when in a crowd, to shield the physical body at night when the man leaves it in sleep, and to prevent the danger of physical infection on some occasion when the student has in the course of his duty to subject himself to it. In all these cases it is obvious that the shell must be of etheric matter and of etheric matter only, if it is to be effective for its purpose, although it may sometimes be desirable to create other shells in other worlds simultaneously to afford protection from other classes of dangers.

807.   The object of a shell in a crowd is usually twofold. In a mixed multitude of ordinary people there will almost certainly be a great deal of physical magnetism of a kind distasteful to the student and even prejudicial to him, and part of his object in shelling himself is to defend himself against that. It is also probable that in any large crowd there may be a certain number of those unfortunate persons who, being themselves in some way physically weak, are constantly drawing large amounts of vitality from others. Such absorption often takes place entirely without the knowledge of the person temporarily benefited by it, so that he may be regarded as a kind of unconscious etheric kleptomaniac.

808.   One who has thus the misfortune to be an unconscious vampire may be compared to a gigantic sponge, always ready to absorb any amount of specialised vitality which it can obtain. If he confines himself to seizing upon the bluish-white radiations, which every normal person throws out, he will do no harm, for the matter of which these are composed has already been received and dealt with by the person from whose aura it is taken. But usually this is not all that he takes, for on the approach of the vampire this outpouring is greatly stimulated by his drawing force, so that not only the already-utilised bluish-white fluid is lost, but by intense suction the whole circulation of the vitality through the body of the victim is so hastened that the rose-coloured matter is drawn out with the refuse through all the pores of the body, and the unfortunate original owner has not time to assimilate it; so that a capable vampire can drain a person of the whole of his strength in a visit of a few minutes.

809.   Such an unconscious vampire is assuredly always an object of pity; yet it would be a great mistake if, because of that pity, any victim voluntarily allowed himself to be depleted, with the idea that he was thereby serving and helping one in sore need. The vampire invariably wastes the substance which he thus nefariously acquires. It rushes through him and is dissipated again without proper assimilation, so that his ever-present thirst is never satiated, and to endeavour by abundant self-sacrifice to fill him up is exactly, to use an expressive Indian proverb, like pouring water into a bag with a hole in it.

810.   The only thing that can really be done to help a confirmed unconscious vampire is to supply the vitality for which he craves in strictly limited quantities, while endeavouring, by mesmeric action, to restore the elasticity of the etheric double, so that the perpetual suction and corresponding leakage shall no longer take place. Such

a leakage invariably flows through every pore of the body on account of this lack of etheric elasticity - not through a sort of tear or wound in the etheric body, as some students have supposed; indeed, the idea of anything in the nature of a permanent tear or wound is incompatible with the conditions of etheric matter and the constitution of the etheric double.

811.   A strong shell is one way of guarding oneself against such vampirism, and there are many people for whom at present it may be the only way open.

812.   In the case of normal and healthy people there is usually no trouble with the physical body which is left behind when the man himself moves away in sleep or in trance, for in the improbable event of any sort of attack being made upon it the body would instantly recall the wandering soul, so that the whole man would be at hand to defend himself if necessary. The physical body has a consciousness of its own, quite apart from that of the man who inhabits it - a vague consciousness truly, but still capable of knowing when its vehicle is in danger, and of instinctively taking whatever steps are in its power to protect it. I have myself seen that consciousness manifest itself when the owner of the body had been driven out of it by a dentist's administration of laughing gas - manifest itself in a vague outcry and an inefficient attempt at protesting action when the tooth was extracted, though the man himself afterwards reported that he had been absolutely unconscious of the operation.

813.   As the physical body always remains intimately attached by sympathetic vibration to the astral, even when the latter is far away from it, any disturbance which threatens the physical is almost sure to be communicated instantly to the ego, who promptly returns to investigate.

814.   There are, however, abnormal and unfortunate people who are subject to the attacks of certain entities who desire to seize upon and obsess their bodies, and such people sometimes find it necessary to take strong measures to retain possession of their personal property. Or again, perhaps circumstances may compel the student to sleep in exceedingly undesirable surroundings - as, for example, in a railway carriage in close physical contact with people of the vampirising type or of coarse and forbidding emanations. In either of these cases a strong etheric shell might be the best way of meeting the difficulty, though the student has the alternative of making a strong thought-form animated with the purpose of guarding the body. Such a thought-form may be made even more effective and vivid if a nature-spirit of appropriate type can be induced to enter into it and take a delight in carrying out its object.

815.   The idea of protection from infection is sufficiently obvious to need no special comment. Such infection can enter only by means of physical germs of some sort, and against these a dense wall of etheric matter is a sure protection. It must never be forgotten, however, that a shell which keeps *out* matter of a certain type must also keep it *in* ; so that in guarding ourselves against germs which may bring contagion we are also keeping in close contact with the physical body a great mass of its own emanations, many of which are distinctly poisonous in character.

816.   In the cases above mentioned the shell to be made is of etheric matter only, and the man who wishes to make it must recollect that his etheric body is by no means

coterminous with the astral or mental. Both of the latter adopt the shape and size of that ovoid section of the causal body, which alone of its characteristics can manifest in the lower worlds. The etheric body, however, is of the shape of the physical, and projects slightly from its surface in all directions - perhaps a quarter of an inch or so. If, therefore, the plan of densifying the periphery of the aura is to be adopted, the man, who tries the experiment must recollect where that periphery lies, and direct his will-power accordingly.

817.   He has, however, the alternative of making an ovoid shell of etheric matter drawn from the surrounding atmosphere. That course is in many ways preferable, but demands a far greater exertion of the will and a much more definite knowledge of the way in which physical matter is moulded by it. Such a shell as has been described, though invisible to ordinary sight, is purely in the physical world, and therefore guards its creator only against definitely physical emanations. It does not in the least affect the entrance of wandering thoughts or of astral vibrations tending to produce passions and emotions of various kinds.

818.   Some sensitive people find it impossible to come near those suffering from any weakness or disease without immediately reproducing in their own physical bodies the symptoms of the sufferers. In such cases an etheric shell may be useful, as without it the sensitive man is largely precluded by this abnormal keenness of sympathy from assisting such people.

819.   Again, for those whose business makes it necessary for them to live and move in the midst of the horrible din of our modern civilisation such a shell may sometimes prove useful, as giving the tired and harassed nerves at least something of an opportunity for recovery, by protecting them for a while from the otherwise incessant hammering of all the multiplex vibrations which constitute modern life.

820.   SHIELDS

821.   In some cases what is called for is not a shell surrounding the whole body, but simply a small local shield to guard oneself against some special temporary contact. All sensitive people are aware that the western custom of shaking hands often brings with it positive torment, lasting not infrequently for some hours after the moment of contact. Often to go out of one's way to avoid shaking hands may cause offence, or may give an impression of pride or of an assumption of superiority. The difficulty may usually be obviated by making an effort of the will which covers the right hand with a strong temporary shield of etheric matter, so that the sensitive may endure the unpleasant contact without allowing a single particle charged with undesirable magnetism to enter his body.

822.   Of the same nature as this, though requiring for their successful manipulation a far greater knowledge of practical magic, are the shells which are sometimes used as a protection against fire. I have myself had such a shell of etheric matter made over the palm of my hand at a spiritualistic séance - made so effectively that, although it was too thin to be observable by the senses, it yet enabled me to hold in my hand for several minutes a glowing coal, from which, while I held it, I was able to light a piece

of paper. A still more extended application of the same idea is the much larger shield spread over the glowing ashes, or over the feet of the participants, in the fire-walking experiment which has been so often described.

823. A WARNING

824.   Students wishing for some reason to guard their physical bodies during sleep may be warned not to repeat the mistake made some time ago by a worthy friend who took a great deal of trouble to surround himself with a specially impenetrable shell on a certain occasion, but made it of astral instead of etheric matter, and consequently took it away with him when he left his physical body! Naturally the result was that his physical body was left entirely unprotected, while he himself floated about all night enclosed in triple armour, absolutely incapable of sending out a single vibration to help anybody, or of being helped or beneficially influenced by any loving thoughts which may have been directed towards him by teachers or friends.

825. THE ASTRAL SHELL

826.   The objects aimed at in making an astral shell are naturally of an entirely different type, since they must be connected only with passions and emotions. Most of them also fall under three heads. A shell may be formed round the astral body, first, to keep out emotional vibrations intentionally directed by others at the student, such as those of anger, envy or hatred; secondly, to keep out casual vibrations of low type (such as those evoking sensuality) which are not intentionally directed at the student, but are to be found floating in the surrounding atmosphere, and impinge upon him as it were by accident in the course of ordinary life; thirdly, a student may find it useful to surround his astral body with a special shell during the time which he devotes to meditation, if he has been troubled with the intrusion of thoughts of a low type, which bring with them astral matter and are calculated to provoke undesirable emotion.

827.   In any or all of these cases the effort of the will should be directed to the surface of the astral body - not to that counterpart of denser astral matter which is exactly the shape and size of the physical vehicle, but the egg of surrounding aura, as depicted in the illustrations in *Man Visible and Invisible*. In this, and in all other cases of forming shell, a clear mental picture must be made, and the whole of the person's will-power must be concentrated for at least some minutes upon the definite effort to create the necessary shape. It must also be remembered that such densifications are to a certain extent unnatural; that is to say, they are an arrangement of matter which is not that, normally contemplated in the scheme of things, and consequently there is a constant tendency in the vehicle concerned to resume its normal condition, which, of course, means a constant tendency to disintegration in the shell. The effort of will, therefore, must make a definite impression, sufficient to resist for at least some hours this gentle but persistent effort at disintegration, otherwise the shell will gradually become pervious and ragged, and so fail to fulfil its object. A shell which is required for any length of time should be frequently renewed, as without that process it will soon collapse.

828.   In connection with the astral body we must bear in mind the same consideration to which I referred in the case of the etheric body - that if a shell will keep out vibrations it will also keep them in. The student who makes an astral shell round himself should therefore be careful to build it only of the material of the lower sub-divisions of the astral, as it is exclusively this matter which responds to the low and undesirable vibrations connected with sensuality, malice, hatred, envy and all other such ignoble passions. The finer emotions, on the contrary, always express themselves through the matter of the higher subdivision. It is unnecessary that any matter of this kind should be used in a shell. Indeed, the effects if such matter were used would be eminently unsatisfactory, as, first, a man would keep away from himself any currents of friendly feeling which might be sent to him, and secondly, he would render himself for the time incapable of sending out similar currents of affectionate feeling to others.

829.   It may be asked how it is possible for the ordinary man or even for the younger student to know what kind of astral matter he is employing in the making of his shell. The answer is that that is after all no more difficult than the conception of making a shell at all. If he is to make the shell of astral matter he must first think of the limits of his aura, and then proceed to densify the matter at all those points. The process may therefore be described as an intelligent use of the imagination; and this imagination may just as well be directed with a little more trouble to the conception that the astral body consists of seven degrees of matter, differing in density. The will should be directed to sorting out these, selecting only the material of (let us say) the three lower sub-planes, and forming the shell exclusively of that; and though the student may be unable to see clairvoyantly the result of his effort, he need not doubt that it will produce its effect, and that no types of matter but those of which he thinks will be directly influenced by the currents which he is enabled to send forth.

830.   THE MENTAL SHELL

831.   The shell made round the mental body differs from that in the astral world in that the object is no longer to prevent undesirable emotion, but undesirable thought. Once more, there are three principal occasions on which such a shell may be useful: first, in meditation; secondly, when sleep is approaching; thirdly, under special conditions where without its help lower thoughts would be likely to obtrude themselves.

832.   The office of the mental shell in meditation is to exclude the mass of lower thought which is perpetually playing about in the atmosphere. No shell can prevent wandering thoughts from arising within the man's own mind; but most of our thought-wandering is caused by the impact from without of casual floating thoughts which have been left about by other people, and the intrusion of these at least can be prevented by a shell. But here again it is advisable that only the lower mental matter should be employed in the making of such a shell, as otherwise helpful thought might be kept out, or the man's own thought might be hampered as he poured it forth towards the Master.

833.   Many people find themselves troubled with streams of wandering thought

when they are trying to fall asleep; a mental shell will deliver them from such of these thoughts as come from without. Such a shell need only be temporary, since all that is required is peace for an interval sufficient to allow the man to fall asleep. The man will carry away with him this shell of mental matter when he leaves his physical body, but its work will then be accomplished, since the whole object of making it is to permit him to leave that body. The stream of idle thoughts or mental worry will probably reassert itself when the shell breaks up, but as the man will then be away from his physical brain this will not interfere with the repose of the body. So long as he is in his physical body the mental action will affect the particles of the brain and produce there such activity as may easily make it impossible for the man to quit the physical vehicle; but when once he is away from the latter, the same worry or wandering thought will not bring him back to it.

834.   The third case to which reference has been made is less simple. It occurs not infrequently that certain groups of thought, some wholly desirable, and some equally undesirable, are closely linked together. To take the first example which comes: it is well known that deep devotion and a certain form of sensuality are frequently almost inextricably mingled. A man who finds himself troubled by this unpleasant conjunction may reap the benefit of the devotion without suffering from the ill effects of the sensuality, by surrounding his mental body with a rigid shell so far as its lower subdivisions are concerned, for in this way he will effectually shut out the lower influences while still allowing the higher to play upon him unhindered. This is but one example of a phenomenon of which there are many varieties in the mental world.

835.   THE BEST USE OF A SHELL

836.   When a shell has to be made, the method which I have indicated above is probably the easiest by which to make it, but there still remains a further consideration - the question as to whether on the whole the shell is an undesirable thing. It has its uses - indeed it is eminently necessary as applied to other people. The Invisible Helper frequently finds it invaluable when he is trying to relieve some poor harassed soul who has not as yet the strength to protect himself, either against definite and intentional attacks from without, or against the ever-present swirl of the wearisome wandering thought. But to think of using a shell for oneself is to a certain extent a confession of weakness or of defect, for there seems little doubt that, if we were all that we ought to be, we should need no protection of this nature.

837.   A BEAUTIFUL STORY

838.   A beautiful little story from the traditions of the Christian Church illustrates this very happily. It is recorded that somewhere in the desert at the back of Alexandria there was once a monastery whose abbot possessed the power of clairvoyance. Among his monks there were two young men who had an especial reputation for purity and holiness - qualities which ought to be common to all monks, but sometimes are not. One day when they were singing in the choir it occurred to the abbot to turn his clairvoyant faculty upon these two young men, in the endeavour to discover how they

contrived to preserve this especial purity amidst the temptations of daily life. So he looked at the first young man and saw that he had surrounded himself with a shell as of glittering crystal, and that when the tempting demons (impure thought-forms we should call them) came rushing at him, they struck against this shell, and fell back without injuring him, so that he remained inside his shell, calm and cold and pure. Then the abbot looked at the second young monk, and he saw that he had built no shell round himself, but that his heart was so full of the love of God that it was perpetually radiating from him in all directions in the shape of torrents of love for his fellow men, so that when the tempting demons sprang at him with fell intent they were all washed away in that mighty outpouring stream, and so he also remained pure and undefiled. And it is recorded that the abbot said that the second monk was nearer to the kingdom of heaven than the first.

839. THE BETTER WAY

840. It may be that many of us have not yet reached the level of this second young monk; but at least the story sets before us a higher ideal than that of mere self-protection, and we may learn something of a lesson from him. We must, however, carefully guard ourselves against the feeling of superiority or separateness. We must avoid the danger of thinking too much about the self. We must keep ourselves constantly in a condition of outpouring; we must be active, not passive. When we meet a person our attitude surely should be not: "How can I guard myself against you?" but rather: "What can I do for you?" It is this latter attitude which calls into play the higher forces, because it reflects the attitude of the Solar Deity. It is when we give that we become fit to receive, that we are channels of the mighty force of the Deity Himself.

841. We need not even think too much about personal progress. It is possible to be so exclusively occupied with the idea: "How can I get on?" as to forget the even more important question: "What can I do to help?" And there are some good brothers, even among the best that we have, who are so perpetually examining themselves as to their progress as to remind one forcibly of those children who, when special plots of garden-ground are given to them, are constantly pulling up their plants to see how the roots are growing. This over-anxiety is a real danger; I know many who, while doing the most beautiful altruistic actions, can yet never feel quite sure that their intentions are truly unselfish, since they always doubt whether it is not perhaps a selfish desire to avoid the discomfort caused by seeing pain in others which moves them to action!

842. Such brothers should remember that self-examination may degenerate into morbid introspection, and that the main object is that they should point themselves in the right direction and then simply go ahead and do the best they can - that, to quote our Christian story, they should first fill their hearts with the love of God and then (without spending all their time in weighing that love, to see whether it is increasing or diminishing) should turn their whole attention to the practical expression of it in love of their fellow men. Not only is such outpouring of love a better defence than any number of shells, but it is also an investment producing stupendous results. For the man who thinks nothing of result is precisely he who is producing the greatest of all results.

843.   We have read of the splendid self-sacrifice of the Nirmanakayas, who, having won the right to untold ages of rest in bliss unspeakable, yet have chosen to remain within touch of earth, in order that they may spend their time in the generation of incalculable streams of spiritual force, which are poured into a mighty reservoir, to be spent in helping on the evolution of their less developed fellows. The great Hierarchy of Adepts is entrusted with the dispensing of this force for the good of the "great orphan" humanity, and it is upon this that They (and even Their pupils, under Their direction) draw when necessity arises.

844.   Needless to say, nothing that we can do, can come within measurable distance of the marvellous achievement of the Nirmanakaya; yet it is in the power of every one of us to add some tiny drops at least to the contents of that mighty reservoir, for whenever we pour out from ourselves love or devotion which is utterly without thought of self, we produce results which lie far beyond our ken.

845.   All affection or devotion, however noble, which has in it the least thought of self (as in the case of one who desires the return of his affection, or a reward of protection or salvation for his devotion - one who thinks not: "How much I love so-and-so!" but: "I wonder how much so-and-so loves *me*") - all such affection or devotion sends its force in closed curves which return upon those who generated it, and the karma which such force makes binds a man and brings him back to birth, that he may receive the result of it, just as surely as if the karma were evil.

846.   But when self has been absolutely forgotten, when such thought has neither part nor lot in the stream which is outpoured, when the curve is no longer closed but open, then the karma does *not* bind the man nor bring him back to earth. Yet the effect is produced - an effect far transcending any imagination of ours, for that open curve reaches up to the Solar Deity Himself, and it is from Him that the response comes; and though that response inevitably brings as its result something of advancement to the man whose love and devotion have called it into existence, yet it also at the same time pours spiritual force into the great reservoir of the Adepts. So it comes to pass that every thought, which has no slightest taint of self in it, is a thought which directly helps the world, and thus the outpouring of love is a better defence than the strongest of shells, and the man who is filled with the powers of that Divine Love needs no protection, because he lives within the heart of God Himself.

THIRD SECTION HOW WE INFLUENCE OURSELVES

CHAPTER XIV BY OUR HABITS

851.   FOOD

852.   A saying is attributed to the Christ to the effect that not what is put into the mouth but what comes out of the mouth really defiles a man. Whether He ever made that remark or not, there can be no possible question that a man may be most decidedly defiled by what he puts into his mouth.

853.   The food which we eat is taken into the body and we actually make it part of ourselves, so it is clearly evident that the magnetism with which it is charged is a matter of great moment to us. Both its physical and its magnetic purity are important, yet some people neglect one and some the other. In India, for example, great weight is attached to magnetic purity, and a man will not eat food which has been subjected to the magnetism of some one of lower caste. On the other hand he is much less careful than we are in the West as to the physical cleanliness of the preparations, forgetting that nothing which is physically dirty can ever be magnetically pure. We are usually particular as to the physical cleanliness, but we never think of the question of magnetic purity.

854.   The fact which most seriously affects the magnetism of food is that it is touched so much by the hands of the cook in the course of its preparation. Now the special magnetism of a person flows out most strongly through the hands, and consequently food which is touched by the hands cannot but be highly charged with that magnetism. This is specially true in the case of pastry and bread, which are kneaded by hand in countries which are too backward to have learnt the use of machinery for these purposes. All food made in that way would be absolutely unfit to be eaten at all, were it not for the fact that fortunately the action of fire in the baking or the cooking removes the traces of most kinds of physical magnetism. Still it is eminently desirable that the cook should touch the food as little as possible, and so ladles and spoons, which can readily be demagnetised, should always be used in cooking and serving everything; and they should be kept rigorously clean.

855.   In order to prevent any avoidable mixture of magnetism many an occult student insists upon always using his own private cup and spoon. Madame Blavatsky strongly advised this, and said that when it could not be done the cup and the spoon that were used should be demagnetised before each meal. The ordinary man pays no attention whatever to matters such as these, but the student of occultism who is trying to enter upon the Path must be more careful. It is possible to demagnetise food by a

firm effort of the will, and with a little practice a mere wave of the hand coupled with a strong thought will do the thing almost instantaneously. But it must be remembered that demagnetisation removes neither physical dirt nor its astral counterpart, though it may take away other astral influence; and therefore every precaution must be taken to see that cleanliness is perfect in all culinary arrangements.

856.   Food also absorbs the magnetism of those who are in close proximity to us when we are eating. It is for that reason that in India a man prefers to eat alone, and must not be seen eating by one of lower caste. The mixture which arises from eating in public amidst a crowd of strangers, as in a restaurant, is always undesirable, and should be avoided as much as possible. The magnetism of one's own family is usually more sympathetic, and at any rate one is accustomed to it, so that it is much less likely to be harmful than the sudden introduction of a combination of entirely strange vibrations, many of which are most likely quite out of harmony with our own.

857.   There are, however, always two kinds of magnetism in every article of food - the internal and the external - the former belonging to its own character, the latter impressed upon it from without. The magnetism of the merchant who sells it and of the cook are both of the latter kind, and can therefore be removed by the action of the fire; but the magnetism which is inherent in it is not at all affected by that action. No amount of cooking of dead flesh, for example, can take away from it its inherently objectionable character, nor all the feelings of pain and horror and hatred with which it is saturated. No person who can see that magnetism and the vibrations which it sets up can possibly eat meat.

858.   INTOXICATING LIQUORS

859.   Indeed, many of the pernicious habits of life of the ignorant would become instantly impossible for them if they could see the hidden side of their selfish indulgences. Even the undeveloped specimens of humanity who cluster round the bar of a public-house would surely shrink back with terror, if they could see the class of entities by which they are surrounded - the lowest and most brutal types of a rudimentary evolution, a bloated, livid fungus growth of indescribable horror; and far worse even than they, because they are degraded from something that should be so much better, are the ghastly crowds of dead drunkards - drink-sodden dregs of humanity, who have drowned the divine image in depths of direful debauchery and now cluster round their successors, urging them on to wilder carousals with hideous leers and mocking laughter, yet with a loathly lust awful to behold.

860.   All this is entirely apart from the unquestionable deterioration which is brought about in both astral and mental bodies by the indulgence in intoxicating liquors. The man who is eagerly seeking for excuses for the gratification of ignoble cravings, frequently asserts that food and drink, belonging as they do purely to the physical world, can have but little effect upon a man's inner development. This statement is obviously not in accordance with common sense, for the physical matter in man is in exceedingly close touch with the astral and mental - so much so, that each is to a great extent a counterpart of the other, and coarseness and grossness in the

physical body imply a similar condition in the higher vehicles.

861.		There are many types and degrees of density of astral matter, so that it is possible for one man to have an astral body built of exceedingly coarse and gross particles, while another may have one which is much more delicate and refined. As the astral body is the vehicle of the emotions and passions, it follows that a man whose astral body is of the ruder type will be chiefly amenable to the lower and rougher varieties of passion and emotion; whereas a man who has a finer astral body will find that its particles most readily vibrate in response to higher and more refined emotions and aspirations. Thus a man who is building for himself a gross and impure physical body is building for himself at the same time coarse and unclean astral and mental bodies as well. This effect is visible at once to the eye of the trained clairvoyant, and he will readily distinguish between a man who feeds his physical vehicle with pure food and another who contaminates it by intoxicating drink or decaying flesh.

862.		There can be no question that it is the duty of every man to develop all his vehicles as far as possible in order to make them perfect instruments for the use of the soul, which in itself is being trained to be a fit instrument in the hands of the Solar Deity, and a perfect channel for the divine love. The first step towards this is that the man himself should learn thoroughly to control the lower bodies, so that there shall be in them no thought or feeling except those he approves.

863.		All these vehicles, therefore, must be in the highest possible condition of efficiency; they must be pure and clean and free from taint; and it is obvious that this can never be, so long as the man puts into the physical body undesirable constituents. Even the physical vehicle and its sense perceptions can never be at their best unless the food is pure, and the same thing is true to a much greater extent with regard to the higher bodies. Their senses also cannot be clear if impure or coarse matter is drawn into them; anything of this nature clogs and dulls them, so that it becomes far more difficult for the soul to use them. Indulgence in alcohol or carnivorous diet is absolutely fatal to anything like real development, and those who adopt these habits are putting serious and utterly unnecessary difficulties in their own way.

864.		Nor is the effect during physical life the only point which is to be borne in mind in connection with this matter. If, through introducing impure particles into his physical body, the man builds himself an unseemly and unclean astral body, we must not forget that it is in this degraded vehicle that he will have to spend the first part of his life after death. Just as, here in the physical world, his coarseness draws into association with him all sorts of undesirable entities who, like parasites, make his vehicles their home, and find a ready response within him to their lower passions, so also will he suffer acutely from similar companionship after death, and from the working out in astral life of the conditions which he has here set in motion.

865.		FLESH-EATING

866.		All this applies not only to indulgence in intoxicating liquor, but also to the prevalent practice of feeding upon corpses. This habit also, like the other, produces a consistent effect; this also, like the other, draws round its votaries all kinds of undesirable entities - horrible gaping red mouths, such as those that gather round the shambles to absorb the aroma of blood. It is indeed strange and pitiable to a clairvoyant to see a lady, thinking herself dainty and refined (*truly* refined and dainty she cannot be, or she would not be there) surrounded by an incongruous nightmare of such strange forms in a butcher's shop, where she goes to examine the corpses left by the grim, ceaseless slaughter on the battle-field between man's bestial, tigerish lust for blood and the divine Life incarnated in the animal kingdom. Little she realises that there will come a time when those who by their support make possible this ghastly blot on the record of humanity, this daily hecatomb of savage, useless murder of the forms through which the Deity is patiently trying to manifest, will find themselves face to face with His ineffable Majesty, and hear from the Voice that called the worlds into existence the appalling truth: "Inasmuch as you have done this unto one of the least of these My little ones, you have done it unto Me."

867.   Surely it is time, with all our boasted advance, that this foul stain upon our so-called civilisation should be removed. Even if it were only for selfish reasons, for the sake of our own interests, this should be so. Remember that every one of these murdered creatures is a definite entity - not a permanent reincarnating individual, but still an entity that has its life in the astral world. Remember that every one of these remains there for a considerable time, to pour out a feeling of indignation and horror at all the injustice and torment which have been inflicted; and perhaps in that way it may be possible faintly to realise something of the terrible atmosphere which hangs over a slaughter-house and a butcher's shop, and how it all reacts at many points upon the human race.

868.   Most of all, these horrors react upon those who are least able to resist them - upon the children, who are more delicate and sensitive than the hardened adult; and so for them there are constant feelings of causeless terror in the air - terror of the dark, or of being alone for a few moments. All the time there are playing about us tremendous forces of awful strength, which only the occult student can understand. The whole creation is so closely interrelated that we cannot do horrible murder in this way upon our younger brothers without feeling the effect upon our own innocent children.

869.   The pitiable thing about it is that a lady is actually *able* to enter a butcher's shop - that because of the indulgence of her forefathers in this shocking form of food, her various vehicles have become so coarsened that she can stand amidst those bleeding carcasses without being overcome by loathing and repulsion, and can be in the midst of the most ghastly astral abominations without being in the slightest degree conscious of it. If we take into such a place any person who has never corrupted himself with such carrion, there is no doubt that he will shrink in disgust from the loathsome, bleeding masses of physical flesh, and will also feel stifled by the actively and militantly-evil astral entities which swarm there. Yet here we have the sad spectacle of a lady who ought, by her very birthright, to be delicate and sensitive, whose physical and astral fibre is so coarsened that she neither observes the visible nor senses the invisible horrors which surround her.

870.   The pity of it is, too, that all the vast amount of evil which people bring upon themselves by these pernicious habits might so easily be avoided. No man needs either flesh or alcohol. It has been demonstrated over and again that he is better without them. This is a case in which actually all the arguments are on one side and there is nothing whatever to be said on the other, except the man's assertion: "I will do these horrible things, because I like them."

871.   With regard to flesh-eating, for example, it cannot be questioned that: (1) the right kind of vegetables contain more nutriment than an equal amount of dead flesh; (2) many serious diseases come from this loathsome habit of devouring dead bodies; (3) man is not naturally made to be carnivorous and therefore this abominable food is not suited to him; (4) men are stronger and better on a vegetable diet; (5) the eating of dead bodies leads to indulgence in drink and increases animal passions in man; (6) the vegetable diet is in every way cheaper as well as better than flesh; (7) many more men can be supported by a certain number of acres of land which are devoted to the growing of wheat than by the same amount of land which is laid out in pasture; (8) in the former case healthy work upon the land can be found for many more men than in the latter; (9) men who eat flesh are responsible for the sin and degradation caused in the slaughter-men; (10) carnivorous diet is fatal to real development, and produces the most undesirable results on both astral and mental bodies; (11) man's duty towards the animal kingdom is not to slaughter it recklessly, but to assist in its evolution.

872.   These are not points about which there can be any question; the fullest evidence in support of each of them will be found in my book, *Some Glimpses of Occultism*. No man needs these things, and to take them is just a matter of selfish indulgence. Most men commit this act in ignorance of the harm that it is doing; but remember, to continue to commit it when the truth is known is a crime. Widely spread as they are, these are nothing but evil habits, and with a little effort they can be laid aside like any other habit.

873.   SMOKING

874.   Another custom, also pernicious and equally widely spread, is that of smoking. In this, as in so many other cases, a man at once resents any suggestions that he should give up his bad habits, and says: "Why should I not do as I like in these matters?" With regard to flesh-diet the answer to this is perfectly clear, for that is a practice which not only seriously injures the man who adopts it, but also involves terrible crime and cruelty in the provision of the food. In the case of alcohol also a clear answer can be given, quite apart from the effect upon the drinker himself, for by buying this noxious fluid he is encouraging a pernicious trade, helping to create a demand for a liquor which tempts thousands of his fellow-creatures to excess and lures them to their own destruction. No man who buys alcohol for drinking purposes can escape his share in the responsibility of that.

875.   It may be said that with regard to smoking the position is somewhat different, since no cruelty is necessary in obtaining tobacco, nor are lives destroyed by it as by alcohol. This is true, and if the smoker can entirely shut himself away from any

contact with his fellow-men, and if he has no desire to make anything in the nature of occult progress, his argument may, so, far, hold good. If, not being actually a hermit, he has sometimes at least to come into touch with his fellowmen, he can have no possible right to make himself a nuisance to them. There are many people who, being deeply steeped in the same pollution themselves, have no objection to the nauseating odour of tobacco; but all who have kept themselves pure from this thing know how strong is the disgust which its coarse and fetid emanations inevitably arouse. Yet the smoker cares little for that. As I have said elsewhere, this is the only thing that a gentleman will deliberately do when he knows it to be offensive to others; but the hold which this noxious habit gains upon its slaves appears to be so great that they are utterly incapable of resisting it, and all their gentlemanly instincts are forgotten in this mad and hateful selfishness.

876.   Anything which can produce such an effect as that upon a man's character is a thing that all wise men will avoid. The impurity of it is so great and so penetrating that the man who habitually uses it is absolutely soaked in it, and is most offensive to the sense of smell of the purer person. For this purely physical reason no one who comes into contact with his fellows should indulge in this most objectionable practice, and, if he does, he thereby brands himself as one who thinks only of his own selfish enjoyment and is willing in taking it to inflict much suffering upon his fellow-creatures. And all this is quite apart from the deadening effect which it produces, and from the various diseases - smoker's throat, smoker's heart, cancer in the mouth, indigestion and others - which it brings in its train. For nicotine, as is well known, is a deadly poison, and the effect of even small quantities of it can never be good.

877.   Why should any man adopt a custom which produces all these unpleasant results? To this there is absolutely no answer except that he has taught himself to like it; for it cannot be pretended that it is in any way necessary or useful. I believe it to be quite true that in certain circumstances it soothes the nerves; that is part of its deadening effect as a poison, but that result can be equally well achieved by other and far less objectionable means. It is always evil for a man to adopt a habit to which he becomes a slave - evil for himself, I mean; it is doubly evil when that habit brings with it the bad karma of inflicting constant annoyance upon others.

878.   No child by nature likes the loathsome taste of this evil weed but, because others older than himself indulge in it, he struggles painfully through the natural nausea which it causes him at first - the protest of his healthy young body against the introduction of this polluting matter - and so gradually he forces himself to endure it, and eventually becomes a slave to it, like his elders. It stunts his growth; it leads him into bad company; but what of that? He has asserted his dawning manhood by proving himself capable of a ` manly' vice. I know that parents frequently advise their children not to smoke; perhaps if they set them the example of abstention, their sage counsels would produce a greater effect. This is another habit with evil results which could so easily be avoided - all that is needed being simply not to do it.

879.   The impurity produced by this obscene practice is not only physical. It may be taken as an axiom that physical filth of any sort always implies astral filth as well,

for the counterpart of that which is impure cannot itself be pure. Just as the physical nerve-vibrations are deadened by the poison, so are both astral and mental undulations. For occult progress a man needs to have his vehicles as finely strung as possible, so that they may be ready at any moment to respond in sympathy to any kind of vibration. Therefore he does not want to have his thought-waves deadened and his astral body weighed down with foul and poisonous particles. Many who call themselves students still cling to this unpleasant habit, and try to find all sorts of weak excuses to cover the fact that they have not the strength to break away from its tyranny; but facts remain facts, for all that, and no one who can see the effects on the higher vehicles of this disastrous custom can avoid the realisation that it does serious harm.

880.   Its effect in the astral world after death is a remarkable one. The man has so filled his astral body with poison that it has stiffened under its influence, and has become unable to work properly or to move freely. For a long period the man is as though he were paralysed - able to speak, yet debarred from movement, and almost entirely cut off from all higher influences. In process of time he emerges from this unpleasant predicament, when the part of his astral body which is affected by this poison has gradually worn away.

881.   DRUGS

882.   The taking of opium or cocaine, though happily less common, is equally disastrous, for from the occult point of view it is entirely ruinous and fatal to progress. These drugs are sometimes a necessity in order to relieve great pain; but they should be taken as sparingly as possible, and on no account be allowed to degenerate into a habit. One who knows how to do it, however, can remove the evil effect of the opium from the astral and mental bodies after it has done its work upon the physical.

883.   Nearly all drugs produce a deleterious effect upon the higher vehicles, and they are therefore to be avoided as much as possible. There are definite cases in which they are clearly required, when they are really specifics for certain diseases; but these are few, and in far the greater number of cases nature herself will work a rapid cure if the surroundings are pure and healthy.

884.   With regard to the treatment of the body, prevention emphatically better than cure, and those who live rationally will rarely need the services of a doctor. Under all circumstances animal serums and products in any way connected with or obtained by means of vivisection should be absolutely avoided. It should be remembered that tea and coffee contain as their essence drugs called respectively theine and caffeine, which are poisonous, so that an excess of these beverages is a bad thing, especially for growing children; indeed, I incline to the opinion that, while in moderation they do no serious harm, those who find themselves able to avoid them are all the better for it.

885.   CLEANLINESS

886.   Doctors are usually agreed as to the necessity for physical cleanliness, but the requirements of occultism are far more stringent than theirs. The waste matter which is constantly being thrown off by the body in the shape of imperceptible perspiration is rejected because it is poisonous and decaying refuse, and the astral

and mental counterparts of its particles are of the most undesirable character. Dirt is often more objectionable in the higher worlds than in the physical, and, just as in the physical world, it is not only foul and poisonous in itself but it also inevitably breeds dangerous microbes, so in these higher worlds it attracts low-class nature-spirits of a kind distinctly prejudicial to man. Yet many people habitually carry a coating of filth about with them, and so ensure for themselves the possession of an unpleasant retinue of astral and etheric creatures.

887.   The thorough daily bath, therefore, is even more an occult than a hygienic necessity, and purity of mind and feeling cannot exist without purity of body also. The physical emanations of dirt are unpleasant, but those in the astral and mental worlds are much more than merely unpleasant; they are deleterious to the last degree, and dangerous not only to the man himself, but to others. It is through the pores of the body that the magnetism of the person rushes out, bearing with it what remains of the vital force. If therefore these pores are clogged with filth, the magnetism is poisoned on its way out, and will produce a pernicious effect upon all those around.

888.   We must remember that we are constantly interchanging the particles of our bodies with those about us, and that our bodies therefore are not wholly our own; we cannot do just as we like with them, because of the fact that they thus constantly influence those of our brothers, the children of our common Father. A comprehension of the most rudimentary idea of brotherhood shows us that it is an absolute duty to others to keep our bodies healthy, pure and clean. If the person be perfectly clean, his emanations will carry health and strength, and so when we make ourselves purer we are helping others also.

889.   OCCULT HYGIENE

890.   This radiation is strongest of all from the ends of the fingers and toes, so that even more than usual care should constantly be lavished upon the strictest cleanliness in the case of these channels of influence. A careless person who allows filth to accumulate under his finger-nails is all the time pouring forth from the ends of his fingers what in the astral world exactly corresponds to a torrent of peculiarly noisome sewage in the physical - an effect which makes his neighbourhood exceedingly unpleasant to any sensitive person, and causes him to do harm in many cases where, but for that, he might be doing good.

891.   For a similar reason special care of the feet is desirable. They should never be encased in boots too tight for them, and thick, heavy walking boots should never be worn an instant longer than is absolutely necessary, but should be replaced by something soft, loose and easy. Indeed it is far better that whenever possible the feet should be left uncovered altogether, or when that is considered impossible, that a light sandal should be used without stockings or socks. This plan could hardly be adopted out-of-doors amidst the horrible filth of our large towns, but it surely ought to be possible in country houses and at the seaside. It could be done indoors everywhere, and would be healthier and more comfortable physically, as well as correct from the occult point of view. But while we are all such slaves of fashion that any man who lived and dressed rationally would probably be regarded as insane, I suppose that it is

hopeless to expect people to have sufficient strength of mind to do what is obviously best for them.

892.   From the point of view of occult hygiene great care should be taken also with regard to the head, which should be left uncovered whenever possible, and never allowed to get hot. A hat is an utterly unnecessary article of clothing, and people would be much better in every way without it; but here again probably the foolishness of fashion will, as usual, stand in the way of common sense. The folly of wearing a hat becomes immediately obvious when we remember that even in the coldest weather we habitually leave the face entirely uncovered, even though there is usually but little hair on it, whereas we are careful to put a considerable and most insanitary weight upon the upper part of the head, which nature has already abundantly covered with hair! Think, too, how much money might be saved by discarding all unnecessary and positively harmful articles of dress - hats, boots, stockings, collars, cuffs, corsets.

893.   But people never use their own brains with regard to such matters; they think only of what some one else is doing, and they never realise that their boasted liberty is the merest sham, since they do not feel themselves free to follow the plainest dictates of their reason, even with regard to a matter which is so clearly their own private business as the clothing that they shall wear. Future and more enlightened generations will look back with wonder and pity upon the dreary monotony of ugliness to which this senseless thraldom condemns us.

894.   Another of the objectionable customs of our modern civilisation is that of hair-cutting. It is outrageous that we should be expected to submit to have our heads pawed about for a quarter of an hour or so by a person who is not usually of the higher classes, who generally smells offensively of tobacco or onions or pomatum, who breathes in our faces and worries us with a stream of inane chatter - and in any case has been promiscuously pawing the heads of a score of others of His Majesty's lieges without any intermediate process of purification. Considering the fact that the head is precisely the part of the human body where unpleasant alien magnetism will produce the greatest effect, and that it is through the hands that magnetism flows most easily, one sees at once what a peculiarly unscientific abomination this is. I do not suggest that every man should let his hair grow to its full length; that is a matter entirely for his private taste; but I do say that the person who cuts it should be his wife or his mother, his brother or his sister, or at least somebody of the same family or in close friendship, whose magnetism is likely to be on the whole harmonious and reasonably pure. It may be that until we all have had a certain amount of practice, the hair would not be quite so well cut as by the professional person; but we should be far more than compensated by freedom from headache, from unpleasant smells and from foreign influences.

895.   PHYSICAL EXISTENCE

896.   In order that its reaction upon higher vehicles should be satisfactory, it is necessary that the physical body should be regularly exercised. This, which doctors tell us is so desirable from the point of view of physical health, is still more desirable from the point of view of health in other worlds. Not only do unused muscles deteriorate

and become feeble, but their condition produces a congestion of magnetism, a check to its proper and healthy flow; and that means a weak spot in the etheric double, through which a hostile influence can easily penetrate. A man who keeps his physical body thoroughly well exercised also keeps his etheric body in good order, which means in the first place that he is far less liable to the penetration of unpleasant physical germs, such as those of infection, for example. And in the second, because of the reaction of this upon the astral and mental bodies, thoughts of depression or of animal passion will find it almost impossible to seize upon him. Therefore we see that due and regular physical exercise has great importance from the occult standpoint; indeed we may say that all such practices as have been found by experiment to promote the health of the physical body are also found to react favourably upon the higher vehicles.

897.   READING AND STUDY

898.   There is an occult side to ever act of daily life, and it often happens that if we know this occult side we can perform these daily actions more perfectly or more usefully. Take, for example, the case of reading. Broadly speaking, we read for two purposes, for study and for amusement. If one watches with clairvoyant vision a person who is reading for the purpose of study, one is often surprised to see how little the real meaning of what is written penetrates into the mind of the reader. In a book that is carefully written, in order that it may be studied, each sentence or paragraph usually contains a clear statement of a certain definite idea. That idea expresses itself as a thought-form, the shape or size of which varies according to the subject. But whether it is small or large, whether it is simple or complicated, it is at least clear and definite of its kind. It is usually surrounded with various subsidiary forms, which are the expressions of corollaries or necessary deductions from the statement. Now an exact duplicate of this, which is the author's thought-form, should build itself up in the reader's mind, perhaps immediately, perhaps only by degrees. Whether the forms indicating corollaries also appear; depends upon the nature of the student's mind - whether he is or is not quick to see in a moment all that follows from a certain statement.

899.   As a general rule, with a good student the image of the central idea will reproduce itself fairly accurately at once, and the surrounding images will come into being one by one as the students revolves the central idea in his mind. But unfortunately with many people even the central idea is by no means properly represented. Less developed mentally, they cannot make a clear reflection at all, and they create a sort of amorphous, incorrect mass instead of a geometrical form. Others manufacture something, which is indeed recognisable as the same form, but with blunted edges and angles, or with one part of it entirely out of proportion to the rest - a badly drawn representation, in fact.

900.   Others succeed in making a kind of skeleton of it, which means that they have grasped the outline of the idea, but are as yet quite unable to make it living to themselves, or to fill in any of its detail. Others - perhaps the most numerous class - touch one side of the idea and not the other, and so build only half the form. Others

seize one point in it and neglect all the rest, and so generate a figure which may be accurate as far as it goes, but is not recognisable as a copy of that given in the book. Yet these people will all assert that they have studied the book in question, though if they were asked to reproduce its contains from memory, the resulting essays would have little in common.

901.   This means in the first place a lack of attention. These people presumably read the words, but the ideas expressed by those words do not effect a lodgment in their minds. Often it is easy for the clairvoyant to see the reason for this, for if he watches the mental body of the student he sees it to be occupied with half a dozen subjects simultaneously. Household cares, business worries, thoughts of some recent pleasure or expectations of an approaching one, a feeling of weariness and repulsion at having to study and a longing for the time when the half-hour of study shall be over; all such feelings as these are seething in the man's brain, and occupying between them nine-tenths of the matter of his mental body, while the poor remaining tenth is making a despairing effort to get hold of the thought-form which he is supposed to be assimilating from the book. Under these circumstances, naturally enough, it is hopeless to expect any real benefit, and it would probably, on the whole, be better for such a man of he did not attempt to study at all.

902.   From the examination of this hidden side of study, then, certain definite rules emerge which it would be well for the intending student to follow. First, he must begin by emptying his mind of all other thoughts and must see to it that they are not permitted to return until his time of study is over. He must free his mind from all cares and perplexities, and then he must concentrate it wholly on the matter in hand. He should read through his paragraph slowly and carefully, and then pause to see whether the image is clear in his mind. Then he should read the passage over again with equal care, and see whether any additional features have been added to his mental image; and he should repeat this until he feels that he has a thorough grasp of the subject, and that no new idea upon it will immediately suggest itself. When that is done he may usefully see whether he can pick out any of the corollaries, whether he can surround his central thought-form with planets depending on it.

903.   All this while, a mass of other thoughts will have been clamouring for admission; but if our student is worthy of the name he will sternly refuse them and keep his mind fixed exclusively on the question in hand. The original thought-form which I have described represents the author's conception as he wrote, and it is always possible by earnest study to get thus into touch with the mind of the author. Often through his thought-form he himself may be reached, and additional information may be obtained or light may be gained on difficult points. Usually the student, unless highly developed, cannot come into *conscious* touch with the author, so as actually to interchange ideas with him; any new thought will probably appear to the student as his own, because it always comes into his physical brain from above, just as much when it is suggested from outside as when it originates in his own mental body; but that matters little so long as he gets a clear conception of his object.

904. SYSTEM AND THOROUGHNESS

905.   All this the occult student does as a matter of course, and he does it daily with the most exemplary regularity, for he recognises its importance, first because he knows the necessity of systematic work or training, and secondly because one of the duties most strongly impressed upon him is that of thoroughness. His motto must be: "Whatsoever thy hand findeth to do, do it with thy might." He knows that whatever he does he ought to do better than the man of the world does it, that nothing will suffice but the best that is possible to him, and that he must try ceaselessly to attain perfection in all his work, developing all his vehicles to the utmost, in order that he nay gain that perfection.

906. NOVEL AND NEWSPAPER-READING

907.   Even when we read for amusement it is still eminently desirable that we should form a habit of concentration upon what is read. After much study or hard mental labour of any kind, it is often a great relief to turn to a good novel, and there is no harm whatever in doing so, so long as moderation is observed. The person who gives up his whole life to novel-reading is yielding to mental dissipation, and if he continues to treat his mind in that way he will probably soon find that it is of little use to him as an instrument for serious study. But, as I have said, occasional novel-reading for relief is harmless and even beneficial.

908.   Even then it is well not to read carelessly, but to try to form a clear conception of each character, to make the people live and move before one. When the author wrote his story he made such a series of thought-forms. Many other readers since have come into touch with them and strengthened them, (though some prefer to construct a fresh set of their own), and it is frequently possible to see with the mind the author's original set, and so to follow his story exactly as he meant it.

909.   Of some well-known stories there are many renderings in the mental and astral worlds. Of the biblical stories, for example, each nation has usually its special presentation, and generally with the characters all dressed in its particular national garb. Children have vivid and capable imaginations, so books much read by them are sure to be well represented in the world of thought-forms; we find many excellent and life-like portraits of such people as Sherlock Holmes, Captain Kettle, John Silver, or Dr. Nikola.

910.   On the whole, however, the thought-forms evoked from the novels of to-day are by no means so clear as those which our forefathers made of Robinson Crusoe or of the characters in Shakespeare's plays. That comes largely from the fact that we rarely give more than half our attention to anything, even to a good story, and that in turn is the consequence of the curious literary conditions of our modern life. In the older days, if a man read at all, he read earnestly and fixed his mind upon what he was doing. If he took up any subject, he read serious books upon that subject. In these days a large number of people dependent for almost all the information they possess upon newspapers and magazines. The magazine or newspaper article conveys in a handy form for easy assimilation a certain amount of superficial information upon its

subject, whatever that may be; it gives enough to enable a man to talk lightly about the matter at a dinner-table, but not enough to tax his intellect or to give him a sense of mental effort. It is an age of information by snippets, and the ultimate expression of its spirit is shown by the enormous circulation of such papers as *Tit-Bits* and *Answers*. The mind which gains its information in this way has no real grasp of any subject - no solid foundation; and because it has accustomed itself to feeding upon highly-spiced fragments it finds itself incapable of digesting a more satisfying meal.

911.   An unpleasant feature of the newspaper press of the present day is the great prominence given to murders and divorce cases, and the wealth of sickening detail about them which is put before the public, day after day. This is bad enough from any point of view, but when, we add to ordinary considerations those which are shown to us by the study of the hidden side of all these things, we are fairly appalled. The result of this prurient publicity is that all over the country great masses of vivid and most objectionable thought-forms are constantly being generated; people picture the horrible details of the murder, or gloat libidinously over suggestive facts or remarks connected with the divorce case, and the resulting thought-forms in the first case are of a terrifying character to any nervous person who can be influenced by them, and in the second case constitute a distinct temptation towards evil thought and action for those who have in them germs of sensuality. This is no mere supposition as to what must occur - it is a definite chronicle of what constantly *does* occur. No clairvoyant can avoid noticing the great increase in unpleasant thought-forms during the progress of any of these sensational cases.

912.   On the other hand, it is only fair to remember that the curious fragmentary literature of to-day reaches a multitude of people who in the old days did not read at all. A man who is at heart and by disposition a reality serious student still studies just as of old. A certain number of people who in the older days might have studied seriously, are now diverted from doing so by the facility with which they can obtain superficial information in small doses; but a much greater number of people who would never under any circumstances have taken up serious study are now beguiled into acquiring at least a certain amount of information by the ease with which it can be done. Many a man buys a magazine on a railway-journey, for the purpose of reading the stories in it; finishing them before the journey is over, he fills up his time by imbibing the other contents of his periodical, and in that way learns many things which he did not know before, and may even have his attention attracted to some subject which appeals to him - in which presently he will learn to take serious interest.

913.   So these curious basketfuls of miscellaneous information may be said to do good as well as harm, for though the taste for desultory reading and bad jokes may not in itself be a great gain to the errand-boy or the shop assistant, it is nevertheless for him the beginning of literature, and it occupies a certain amount of his time which might easily be worse spent in public-houses or in doubtful company. In days before the school-board, the place of the cheap magazine was largely taken by the spoken story, and it is to be feared that many of the stories told by young men when they were alone together were often of a nature that would certainly not be admitted into our weekly

papers. So we must not altogether despise these things, though the serious student does well to avoid them, just because they fill the mental body with a mass of little unconnected thought-forms like pebbles, instead of building up in it an orderly edifice.

914.   SPEECH

915.   It is emphatically necessary to remember that speech must be absolutely true. Accuracy in speech is a quality rarely shown in these days, and careless exaggeration is painfully common. Many people are habitually so loose in their statements that they lose all sense of the meaning of words; they constantly say ` awfully' when they mean ` very,' or describe something as ` killing' when they are trying to convey the idea that it is mildly amusing. The occultist must not be led away by custom in this matter, but must be meticulously exact in all that he says. There are people who consider it allowable to tell a falsehood by way of what they call a joke, in order to deceive another and then to laugh at his credulity - a credulity which is surely in no way blameworthy, since the victim has simply given the narrator credit for being enough of a gentleman to speak the truth! I need hardly say that such falsehood is absolutely unpermissible. There can never under any circumstances be anything amusing in telling a lie or deceiving anyone, and the word or the action is just as definitely a wicked thing when spoken or done for that purpose as for any other.

916.   The wise man will never argue. Each man has a certain amount of force, and is responsible for using it to the best possible advantage. One of the most foolish ways in which to fritter it away is to waste it in argument. People sometimes come to me and want to argue about Theosophy. I invariably decline. I tell them that I have certain information that I can give, certain testimony that I can offer as to what I have myself seen and experienced. If this testimony is of value to them, they are more than welcome to it, and I am glad to give it to them, as indeed I have done over and over again in this and in other books; but I have not time to argue the matter with people who do not believe me. They have the full right to their own opinion, and are at perfect liberty to believe or disbelieve as they choose. I have no quarrel with those who cannot accept my testimony; but I have also no time to waste over them, for that time may be far better occupied with those who are prepared to accept such message as I have to give.

917.   Whistler is credited with having once remarked in the course of a conversation on art: "I am not arguing with you; I am telling you the facts." It seems to me that that is the wisest position for the Theosophical student. We have studied certain things; so far as we have gone we know them to be true, and we are willing to explain them; if people are not yet prepared to accept them, that is exclusively their affair, and we wish them good speed in whatever line of investigation they wish to take. Argument leads constantly to heated feelings and to a sense of hostility - both things by all means to be avoided. When it is necessary to discuss any subject in all its bearings, in order to decide upon a course of action, let it be done always gently and temperately, and let each man state his own case kindly and deliberately, and listen with all politeness and deference to the opinions of others.

918.   MEDITATION

919.   Just as a man who wishes to be strong finds it advisable to use definite, prescribed exercises to develop his physical body, so the student of occultism uses definite and prescribed exercises to develop his astral and mental vehicles. This is best done by meditation. Of this there are many kinds, and each teacher enjoins that which he thinks most suitable. All the religions recommend it, and its desirability has been recognised by every school of philosophy. This is not the place to suggest any particular system; those who belong to the Theosophical Society know that within it there is a school for such practices, and those who wish for further information are referred to it.

920.   All systems alike set before themselves certain objects, which are not difficult to comprehend. They all direct that a man should spend a certain time each day in thinking steadily and exclusively of holy things, and their objects in doing so are: first, to ensure that at least once each day a man shall think of such things, that his thoughts shall at least once in twenty-four hours be taken away from the petty round of daily life, from its frivolities and its troubles; secondly, to accustom the man to think of such matters, so that after a time they may be present always at the back of his mind, as a kind of background to his daily life - something to which his mind returns with pleasure when it is released from the immediate demands of his business; thirdly, as I began by saying, as a kind of astral and mental gymnastics, to preserve these higher bodies in health, and to keep the stream of divine life flowing through them (and for these purposes it should be remembered that the *regularity* of the exercises is of the first importance); fourthly, because this is the way, even though it be only the first halting step upon the way, which leads to higher development and wider knowledge, the gate of the road which through many a struggle and many an effort leads to the attainment of clairvoyance, and eventually into the higher life beyond this world altogether.

921.   Although the man in his daily meditation may see but little progress, and it may seem to him that his efforts are altogether unsatisfactory and without result, a clairvoyant watching him will see exactly how the astral and mental bodies are slowly coming out of chaos into order, slowly expanding and gradually learning to respond to higher and higher vibrations. He can see, though the experimenter cannot, how each effort is gradually thinning the veil that divides him from that other world of direct knowledge. He can see how the man's thought-forms grow day by day more definite, so that the life poured into them from above becomes fuller and fuller, and reacts more and more strongly upon their originator, even though that originator may be entirely unconscious of it; and so, speaking from his knowledge of the hidden side of things, the clairvoyant advises all aspirants to meditate, to meditate regularly, and to continue their meditation with the certain conviction that (quite irrespective of their own feelings) they are producing results, and steadily drawing nearer and nearer to their goal.

922.   Old Dr. Watts is alleged to have perpetrated a hymn which said that "Satan finds some mischief still for idle hands to do". He probably referred exclusively to

the physical world; but the wise man knows that that is true at any rate with regard to the mind. The time when an evil thought springs up in the mind is the time when it is lying fallow and unoccupied. Therefore the surest way to avoid temptation is to keep steadily at work, and since even the most indefatigable of mortals cannot work always, it is well that for those dangerous moments of leisure he should have a safeguard in the shape of a definite subject upon which his mind always instinctively falls back when not otherwise occupied. Most men have some such background, but often its nature is trivial or even undesirable. There are men who have impure thoughts at the back of their minds all the time, and others have jealousy or hatred. Many mothers are thinking all the time of their children, and the man in love usually has a portrait of his charmer always on view, often indeed occupying the foreground as well as the background of his mind.

923.   When a man has attained to the dignity of having the right sort of background to his life, he is in a position of far greater security. For some natures religion provides such a background; but these natures are rare. For most men only the study of the great truths of nature can provide it - only that knowledge of the scheme of things which in these modern days we call Theosophy. When that great plan is once grasped, the mind and the higher emotions are both engaged on it, and the man's whole nature is so filled with it that no other thought, no other attitude is possible to him but that of the intense desire to throw himself and all that he has into that mighty plan, and to become, as far as in him lies, a fellow-worker together with the Deity who conceived it.

924.   So this becomes the background of his mind - the dominating thought from which he has to turn away in order to attend to the details of outer life - to which he gladly and instantly returns when his duty to those details is done. When he can attain to this condition he is in a position of far greater safety from evil thought, and he need have no fear that this constant preoccupation with higher things will in any way mar his efficiency down here. He will do his daily work better, not worse, because he is constantly going behind it to something far greater and more permanent; for it is precisely the men with this higher stimulus for a background who have been the most efficient workers of the world.

925.   As Keble puts it

926.   *There are, in this loud stunning tide*

927.   *Of human care and crime,*

928.   *With whom the melodies abide*

929.   *Of the everlasting chime.*

930.   *And then he speaks of them as*

931.   *Plying their daily task with busier feet*

932.   *Because their secret souls a holy strain repeat.*

179

935.   HOUSES

936.   It is the fashion, and not unreasonably, to attach great importance to the influence of environment. When that expression is used people generally mean an environment into which they are born, or one which is imposed upon them from without and is in no way dependent upon their own will. There is, however, another environment which is often forgotten: that which we create for ourselves - the great influence produced upon us in daily life by the place in which we choose to live and the objects with which we voluntarily surround ourselves. One may often judge from the outside of a house something of the disposition of those who inhabit it, and a man's room is to a certain extent an expression of him, for it shows his taste in books, pictures, statues, furniture, wall-paper and flowers; and every one of all these things is constantly reacting upon him, even though he never thinks of it.

937.   One who is a student of occultism will be guided in choosing a house for himself by a number of considerations which would not be likely to occur to the ordinary man, who probably bases his decision principally on such facts as the size and the rent of the house, whether its drains are in order, and how far it is from the tramway or railway station. Such points as these naturally define the area of his choice; the study of the hidden side of things, while not interfering with these, suggests some additional considerations. From our point of view it is material to have as much room as possible about the house - to have it as far removed as possible from its neighbours. Once more, this means no reflection upon the neighbours. They may be all that can possibly be desired, yet it is always better to avoid the mixture of varying vibrations. One may earnestly wish sometimes for the society of one's neighbour, and when that happens it is always possible to visit him or to invite him to call. But to be always in such close proximity to him as to feel every change in his aura - that is a condition of affairs which ought never to exist, although unfortunately it too often does.

938.   In all those long lines of houses which are so common in our great towns, it is impossible, from the occult point of view, to escape from one's neighbour. Whenever he walks up to the dividing wall, his aura must project through it, and it will be seen that, with a neighbour in close contact on each side, we are practically in the room with two families, whose tastes and interests may be absolutely different from our own, who may have all sorts of thoughts and aspirations which clash entirely with those to which we wish to devote ourselves. Even a semi-detached house is better than these, for at least in that we share our quarters with only one family, but the truth is that there ought to be no houses but detached houses, however valuable the ground may be. Certainly no one who understands the power of the unseen influences would take a house which is one of a row, if he could by any possibility avoid it. The same difficulty occurs with our modern flats and apartment houses. They may have many advantages

and their fittings may be all that can be desired, but they are always open to this most serious objection. If, however, a man's circumstances are such that he *must* thus live in common with others, he will at least do all that lies in his power to secure that these others shall be reasonably harmonious.

939.   Another weighty matter from the occult point of view is the aspect of the house. Considerations of physical health prescribe that a sunny rather than a dark house should be chosen, and these are emphatically reinforced when we think of the higher worlds. I have already said something as to the imperious necessity of sunshine and of all that it brings with it. Not only physical disease, but irritability and depression fly before the direct rays of the sun; so plenty of sunlight and fresh air are the first and most prominent desiderata.

940.   The influences of the immediate neighbourhood must also be taken into account. Under no circumstances whatever ought a man to take a house which is near to a public-house, a slaughter-house, a prison, or a butcher's shop. It is also eminently undesirable to be in close proximity to the office of a pawnbroker or a moneylender, or to any place where violent and acrimonious debates and arguments are frequently held - in the latter case because of the wearing effect of constant jarring and angry vibrations, and in the case of the usurer because radiations of sorrow and despair are always connected with his business, and often there is bitter hatred as well. A club, too, should be avoided, if it permits gambling.

941.   The type of the previous tenants may make a great difference in the comfort of a house. If they have been spendthrifts, if they have been quarrelsome, or if they have suffered deeply from long-continued depression, the place may be so impregnated with thought-forms of those varied types as to be a dwelling quite unsuitable for any sensitive family. This difficulty, however, can be overcome by an elaborate demagnetisation, if the student knows how to do it.

942.   Not only the aspect of the house, as regards the points of the compass, but its aspect in the other sense of the word, is also worth noticing. No one should take a house which is ugly, gloomy-looking, or depressing in appearance - not only because of its effect upon himself when he looks at it, but because it is constantly surrounded by a cloud of thought-forms made by neighbours or passing strangers who are disgusted with its appearance. Even though the house outside be pretty, if there is squalid ugliness in the immediate neighbourhood, it is unsuitable. Above all things to be avoided are those long and monotonous lines of mean and sordid-looking houses which one may see in some London suburbs. A garden of some sort is a most valuable asset. In fact, a little cottage in the midst of a large garden is better than the most magnificent house which stands close upon the road in the midst of a row of others.

943.   STREETS NOISE

944.   If the house be in a street, the nature of that street is a matter of great importance. If the road be paved with granite blocks or in any other way conducive to noise, it should be avoided at all costs; whereas a quieter form of paving, such as asphalt or wood, would count much in its favour. A street infested by yelling fiends

in the shape of hawkers is also unfit for the habitation of anyone possessing the usual allowance of nerves - so long as our government neglects to protect us against so flagrant a nuisance. It goes without saying that one should avoid a street in which there is constant heavy traffic or one in the immediate neighbourhood of a railway or tram line - near enough, I mean, to suffer from the noise; for noise, as I have already explained, is one of the greatest defects of our defective civilisation.

945.   Although after a time a man gets used to the noise, and hardly notices it, nevertheless every fresh outburst is a blow to his astral and mental bodies, and the effect of this is precisely that of constantly repeated blows upon the physical body - each one may be no great matter, but after a time the cumulative effect hurts exceedingly. In the physical body this would mean pain, and we should at once understand it and refer it to its source; in the case of the astral body it means irritability; and in the case of the mental body a feeling of fatigue and inability to think clearly. But when these supervene we do not so readily understand them, nor do we always assign them to their true cause. Consequently the neighbourhood of any building which is either noisy or noisome with smoke or chemicals (as a factory might be) is to be sedulously avoided.

946.   Many of my readers may be so situated that it is impossible for them to take all these recommendations into consideration, and I offer them only as a guide to what is desirable when it can be had. If a man who is entirely unfettered is about to choose a house or a site for a house, I should advise him to be governed in his selection by what I have said above; but I know well that most people are practically limited as to the range of their choice by the question of rent, convenient access to their work, and a number of other personal reasons. In such cases a man must simply balance the advantages and disadvantages, and do the best that he can, taking it as the result of his own actions in the past that he cannot do better.

947.   PICTURES

948.   A matter in which a man has usually much greater liberty is the decoration of his room, and it is one of considerable importance to him. For example, the pictures which we hang on the walls of our homes are exercising all the while an unnoticed influence upon us, not only because they keep the expression of certain ideas constantly before our eyes, but also because the artist puts a great deal of himself, of his inmost thought and feeling, into his work, and the effect of all that thought and feeling inheres in the picture and radiates from it just as surely as scent inheres in and radiates from a rose. There is a hidden side to every picture - the conception which was in the artist's mind and heart. That conception, when he formed it, expressed itself clearly in astral and mental matter, even though he may have succeeded but partially in bringing his idea down to the physical world.

949.   Every true artist will acknowledge that, however excellent his work may be, it invariably falls short of what he intended and expected. Yet the conception, as he thought it out, exists really and vividly in the mental world, and the feelings and emotions which he endeavoured to express exist in the astral realm, and these, which we may call the unseen counterparts of the picture, are always radiating vibrations

of their own character, whatever that may be, and are therefore producing a never-ceasing effect upon those who live within their influence.

950.   Manifestly, therefore, it behoves us to be careful as to the nature of the objects of art which we gather around us. We must avoid all pictures whose subjects are mean, sordid or terrible, however accurately or powerfully those subjects may be delineated. It is well also to avoid even those which, though harmless in themselves, are likely to suggest impure thought to undeveloped minds, because such thought-forms will hang about the picture and act as a constant and baneful influence. The modern craze for inane representations of the female face and figure is from this point of view distinctly to be deprecated. So also is that form of artistic realism which sees only the darkest side of life, and recognises nothing as natural unless it be decadent and depraved.

951.   Pictures of sordid scenes of low life, of peasants drinking in an ale-house, of battle scenes or of huntsmen gathered together to slaughter an unfortunate fox: all these will be avoided by the wise man. He will be careful to surround himself only with such pictures as are ennobling, soothing, helpful, those which shed upon him and his an influence tending ever to happiness and peace. Beautiful landscapes and sea-views are usually best of all; pictures also of grand old cathedrals - magnificent buildings with peaceful associations; sometimes a portrait or imaginary figure, if the face be really a fine one, but never under any circumstances one which suggests sorrow, anger or pain.

952.   In religious pictures, for example, the crucifixion, and the garden of Gethsemane must never appear, but the risen and radiant Christ or a reasonably attractive presentment of the Virgin and Child are admissible. In the same way with statues; only those should find a place which are of exquisite beauty, in connection with which there could never be the least thought of impurity. A man should think not only of himself, but of servants and possible visitors. No decent person could have thoughts other than the purest in connection with any picture or statue whatever; but if such a thing hangs or stands where others may see it, it is useless to ignore the fact that low-class minds will form low-class images, and so an object which to us is noble and beautiful may come to radiate abominable influences.

953.   Care must be exercised with regard to photographs. Private friends are of course admissible, or a public man whom one admires; but on no account should the figures of actresses be introduced, as they always attract the most undesirable thought-forms from hosts of impure-minded people. A praiseworthy custom is to have in a prominent position the best available portrait of the ruler of the country, and to surround it constantly with waves of affectionate and loyal thought, for in this way it will radiate an influence of loyalty and devotion upon all who enter the room.

954.   CURIOSITIES

955.   Many people like to surround themselves with all sorts of curious little objects - figures, pieces of pottery, carvings in ivory and ebony and so on. Most of these things are harmless enough, though it means a great deal of trouble to keep

them scrupulously clean, and unless they are so kept, they become a nuisance of an aggravated type. But with regard to some of these little mementos a certain amount of caution is desirable. Many of such things are old, and some of them have a history attached to them - sometimes a terrible history. It is widely known, for example, that a lady in London had in her house for some time an Egyptian mummy-case, the influences connected with which were of so serious a character that she was speedily forced to get rid of it altogether, because of a series of disasters which overtook all who came into contact with it. That is an extreme case, but other kinds of curiosities also have undesirable or mischievous auras.

956.   Many such objects tell their own story, though the owner is often unaware of it. A sensitive person sometimes finds landscapes which are entirely unknown to him or scenes from some foreign land starting up unbidden in his mind. These may come from various sources. They may be mere pictures formed by the imagination, his own or that of some other person in the neighbourhood, either dead or living; they may be examples of casual clairvoyance at a distance; but they may be, and often are, instances of unintentional psychometry, and can be traced to some object in the room.

957.   For every body, of whatever nature it may be, carries within it the power of showing, to those who can see, pictures of its past history, and sometimes these come to the surface unexpectedly. Some are good and some are bad; some are harmless and others are actively unpleasant. When a man acquires some ancient object of unknown history, he has usually no means of telling immediately whether it will prove helpful, harmful or negative, but if he watches carefully he will soon see. Certain types of curiosities are obviously undesirable from the outset - such things, for example, as spears, swords, daggers, or anything which may have been connected with bloodshed.

958.   BOOKS

959.   To a discerning eye a man shows his nature in his choice of books - a choice which is of great importance to him. A man reads a book; he lays it aside and perhaps forgets it; but nevertheless it lies there on his table or his book-shelf and it continues to pour upon him a steady influence, whether for good or for evil. Many books, it is true, have no pronounced influence, and may therefore be considered as neutral. But if a book has done us good, its influence will usually continue to be for good, unless indeed it happens that we outgrow it altogether, and in that case its influence might possibly be a kind of retardation.

960.   The main thing is to avoid definitely evil books - horrible, neurotic studies of characters which are better left unstudied, tales of unnatural and most unpleasant women who are always hovering as near as they dare to the edge of impropriety of some sort, stories of doubtful morality, of shady transactions, or of blank inanity. All these are things for which a sensible man will spare no room on his book-shelves, because they are not worth reading in the first place, and they certainly radiate an impure and unwholesome influence in the second. The great criterion in the formation of a library is that only sane and healthy books should be admitted, for books are specially strong centres of thought-forms, and their unnoticed influence in a man's life is often a powerful one. They should be not too many, but emphatically good of their kind.

961.   FURNISHING

962.   There is hidden side to even so homely a question as that of furniture and colour decoration, since every colour has its own special rate of vibration, and some of these rates are helpful to man, while others are distinctly a hindrance. Broadly speaking, light and delicate tints are good, while heavy, coarse and dark colours are usually to be avoided. Some consideration should also be given to the purpose for which the room is intended; for example, certain shades of red might be not out of place in a dining-room, but would be far from desirable in a room consecrated to sleep or to meditation.

963.   JEWELLERY

964.   Another adjunct of ordinary life, in which the hidden side is of great importance, is jewellery. On the whole, the wearing of jewellery is to be discouraged, because, though every stone has its own special property and influence, the most prominent effect of nearly all of them is to excite bitter envy and covetousness in the hearts of others. Quite a number of women seem to be unable to contemplate a jewel without becoming filled with an inordinate greed to possess it, so that there is scarcely a stone of any beauty or value which is not the centre for many converging streams of jealous longing.

965.   In the case of the great historical jewels we have the additional complication that all kinds of ghastly crimes have been committed in connection with them, and they are therefore usually objects of horror rather than of beauty to any sensitive person. The jewel represents the highest development of the mineral kingdom, and consequently its power of receiving and retaining impressions is much greater than is the case with almost any other object. The Gnostic gems employed in initiation ceremonies two thousand years ago still remain vigorous centres of magnetic influence, as may be seen and felt by any sensitive person who will take the trouble to examine some of those in the British Museum.

966.   At the spot where any great crime has been committed, or where vivid emotions of fear, anger, hatred or revenge have been in action, an astral impression is made which is immediately obvious in its full horror to the clairvoyant, and is frequently sensed to some extent even by persons in whom the higher senses are entirely undeveloped. This is true to a still greater extent of a jewel which has been the cause of many crimes, has been present at them and has absorbed the effect of all the passions which prompted them. Such a jewel retains these impressions with unimpaired clearness for thousands of years, and continues to radiate out from itself the vibrations appropriate to them; and the psychometer sees around it all these pictures of indescribable horror. The wearer of the jewel frequently does not see them, but nevertheless their pernicious effect is constantly exercised upon her.

967.   It is not only in connection with great historical gems that this unpleasantness exists, for I have come across several instances in which ordinary stones have been the occasion of a terrible crime among the miners who discovered them. I know of one such, in which the finder was murdered by another man, but lived long enough

to attach a fearful curse to the gem for the sake of which he had lost his life. This curse was acting so definitely upon various wearers of the jewel fifty years later, that it seemed the safest and best course to throw the stone into the sea - which was accordingly done.

968.   TALISMANS

969.   In a general way, therefore, the occultist avoids all jewellery, and he certainly never wears it for the sake of show. At the same time the fact that a precious stone will retain magnetism so perfectly for so long a time, and will store so much power in such a small compass, makes it a convenient object when a talisman is required for any purpose. For a talisman is not, as is often supposed, a mere relic of mediaeval superstition; it may be a definite and very effective agent in daily life. It is some small object, strongly charged with magnetism for a particular purpose by someone who knows how to do it, and when properly made, it continues to radiate this magnetism with unimpaired strength for many years. The purposes to which such things can be applied are almost infinite in number.

970.   For example, many a student at the beginning of his career is much troubled by impure thoughts. Naturally he sets himself to struggle against them, and maintains a constant watch against their advance; but nevertheless thought-forms of an objectionable nature are numerous and insidious, and sometimes one of them contrives to obtain a lodgment in his mind and causes him much trouble before be can finally shake it off. He may perhaps have been in the habit of yielding himself to such thoughts in the past without realising the evil of it, and if that is so, his thought has acquired a momentum in that direction which is not easy to overcome. A talisman, strongly charged with the powerful magnetism of thoughts of purity, may be an invaluable help to him in his efforts.

971.   The rationale of its action is not difficult to understand. An impure thought expresses itself as a certain definite set of undulations in the astral and lower mental bodies, and it can find entrance into a man's vehicles only when they are either comparatively at rest or vibrating so feebly that its impact can readily overpower the existing rate of motion, and take its place. The talisman is heavily charged with an exactly contrary rate of oscillation, and the two cannot co-exist. One of them must overpower the other and bring it into harmony with itself. The impure thought has probably been made by some casual person, not usually with any definite intent; it is generally simply a suggestion or reminiscence of lower passions. It is not therefore a thing of great power in itself; but it is likely to produce an effect quite out of proportion to its intrinsic strength, because of the readiness with which the average person accepts it and responds to it.

972.   The talisman, on the other hand, has been intentionally charged for a definite purpose by some one who knows how to think; and this is a matter in which definite training makes so much difference that the lightest thought of a man who has learnt how to think is far more powerful than a whole day's desultory musings on the part of an ordinary man. So, when the two streams of thought come into contact, there

is not the slightest doubt as to which will vanquish the other. If we can suppose that the wearer of the amulet forgot his good resolutions, and actually wished for a time for the impure thought, no doubt he could attract it in spite of the talisman, but he would be conscious all the time of great discomfort arising from the discord between the two sets of vibrations.

973.   In most cases, the man who is really trying to do better falls only because he is taken off his guard. The impure thought creeps in insidiously and has seized upon him before he is aware of it, and then he quickly reaches the condition in which for the moment he does not even wish to resist. The value of the talisman is that it gives him time to recollect himself. The disharmony between its undulations and those of the wandering thought, cannot but attract the man's attention, and thus while he wears it he cannot be taken unawares, so that if he falls he falls deliberately.

974.   Again, some people suffer much from apparently causeless fear. Often they are quite unable to give any reason for their feelings; but at certain times, and especially when alone at night, they are liable to be attacked by extreme nervousness, which may gradually increase to positive terror. There may be various explanations for this. Perhaps the commonest is the presence of some hostile astral entity who is persecuting the victim - sometimes in the hope of obtaining through him some sensations which he desires, sometimes in the endeavour to obtain control over him and obsess him, sometimes for sheer mischief and impish love of demonstrating his power over a human being. Here again is a case in which the mediaeval remedy has a distinct practical value. Naturally, the talisman against impurity would not avail in this case, for quite a different sort of motion is required. What is wanted in this case is a centre strongly charged with vibrations expressive of courage and self-reliance - or, if the wearer is of the devotional type, with thoughts of the protective power of his special deity.

975.   For an amulet has a double action. Not only does it operate directly by means of the waves which it radiates, as we have just described in the case of impurity, but also the knowledge of its presence usually awakens the faith and courage of the wearer. In the case of a talisman against fear, such as we are now considering, the two lines of action will be clearly marked. Courage expresses itself in the mental and astral bodies by the strength and steadiness of their striations, and by the calm, steadfast shining of the colours indicating the various higher qualities. When fear overpowers a person all these colours are dimmed and overwhelmed by a livid grey mist, and the striations are lost in a quivering mass of palpitating jelly; the man has for the time quite lost the power of guiding and controlling his vehicles.

976.   The vibrations of strength and courage steadily radiating from the talisman are quite unaffected by the feelings of the wearer, and when the first tremblings of fear begin to manifest themselves they find a difficulty in their way. If unopposed, they would steadily increase, each augmenting and strengthening the other until their power became irresistible. What the talisman does is to prevent them from reaching this condition of irresistible velocity. It deals with them at the commencement, while they are still weak. The resistance which it opposes to them is precisely the same in kind as that which a gyroscope opposes to any effort to turn it aside from its line.

It is so determinedly set in motion in one direction that it will sooner fly to pieces than allow itself to be turned into any other. Suddenly to bring such a power as this into conflict with unreasoning panic would probably result in the complete shattering of the astral body concerned; but if the gyroscopic force of the talisman is already working before the alarm is felt, its determined persistence along its own lines checks the first beginnings of fear, and so makes it impossible for the person ever to reach the later stages of panic terror.

977.   That is its direct operation; but it works also indirectly upon the mind of the wearer. When he feels the first beginnings of fear stirring within him he probably recollects the amulet and clutches at it, and then there arises within him the feeling: "Why should I fear so long as I have with me this strong centre of magnetism?" And so, instead of yielding to the vibrations and allowing them to lengthen themselves until they become unmanageable, he calls up the reserve strength of his own will and asserts himself as master of his vehicles, which is in truth all that is necessary.

978.   There is a third possibility in connection with a talisman, which is in some cases even more powerful than the other two. The object, whatever it may be, has been strongly magnetised by some individual, by the hypothesis a person of power and development, and therefore also probably highly sensitive. That being so, the talisman is a link with its creator, and through it his attention may be attracted. Under ordinary conditions its connection with its originator is of the slightest, but when the wearer is in desperate circumstances he sometimes actually calls upon the maker, much in the way in which the mediaeval devotee when in difficulties invoked the assistance of his patron saint; and that call will unquestionably reach the maker of the amulet and evoke a response from him. If he is still living in the physical world, he may or may not be conscious of the appeal in his physical brain; but in any case his ego will be conscious, and will respond by reinforcing the vibration of the talisman by a strong wave of his own more powerful thought, bearing with it strength and comfort.

979.   Many ignorant men would scoff at such an idea as relic of mediaeval superstition, yet it is an actual scientific fact which has been demonstrated on hundreds of occasions. So far as its direct action goes, a talisman will work only in the direction in which it is made to work; but its indirect action on the faith of the possessor may sometimes take unexpected forms. I remember once making a charm for a certain noble lady, in order to protect her against spasms of extreme nervousness and even positive fear which occasionally swept over her when alone at night. She told me afterwards that this amulet had been of the greatest assistance to her in an emergency which I certainly did not contemplate when I made it.

980.   It appears that on a certain occasion she was driving an exceptionally spirited horse (I believe that her husband made it a sort of boast that he never used horses which anybody else could drive) in a dog-cart, through a forest. The horse took fright at something or other, got the bit between its teeth and dashed madly off the road, and started at a wild gallop among the tree trunks. The groom on the back seat was so certain that they were all destined to immediate death that he threw himself off as best he could, and was sorely injured by the fall; but the lady declares that her

thought at once flew to the charm which she was then wearing, and she says that she knew absolutely that she could not be killed while, as she expresses it, under its protection. This utter certainty kept her perfectly cool and collected, and she steered that dog-cart through the forest with consummate skill. She declares that on the whole she was certainly in the air more often than on the ground as the wheels bounded over roots and crashed through the bushes. But nevertheless, she held on bravely until the horse became tired, and she was able to regain control of it. She thanked me enthusiastically for saving her life by means of the charm; but the truth is that it was not the direct action of the talisman, but the strength of her faith in it, which enabled her to gain so splendid a victory. That was undoubtedly the main factor; there may have been a certain amount of direct action also, because the stilling effect of the strong vibration of the talisman would catch any dawning feeling of fear and calm it, though I had prepared it to deal rather with first symptoms gradually arising than with so sudden an emergency as that.

981.   There are various articles which are to a large extent natural amulets. All precious stones may be said to belong to this category, for each has a distinct influence which can be utilised in two ways. First, the influence necessarily attracts to it elemental essence of a certain kind, and also all such thoughts and desires as naturally express themselves through that essence; and secondly, the fact that it has these natural peculiarities makes it a fit vehicle for magnetism which is intended to work along the same line as those thoughts or emotions. Suppose, for example, it is desired to drive away impure thought. Impure thought means usually a complex set of vibrations, but set on the whole in a certain definite key. In order to resist them a stone should be chosen whose natural undulations are inharmonious with that key, so that they may offer to the impure impulses the greatest possible obstacle. If it is intended to make a talisman against those impure thoughts, a stone which naturally offers resistance to them is the vehicle which can most easily be loaded with the opposing influence.

982.   The vibrations of the particles of the stone are on the physical level, while those of the emotions are on the astral level, several octaves higher; but a stone, the particles of which move naturally on the physical plane in a key which is identical at this level with the key of purity on higher levels, will itself, even without magnetisation, operate as a check upon impure thought or feeling by virtue of its overtones; and furthermore, it can be readily charged at astral or mental levels with the undulations of pure thought or feeling which are set in the same key.

983.   There are instances of decided magnetism of this kind in the vegetable kingdom also. A good example of this is the rudraksha berry, of which necklaces are so frequently made in India. The oscillations connected with it, especially in its small and undeveloped state, render it specially suitable for magnetisation where sustained holy thought or meditation is required, and where all disturbing influences are to be kept away. The beads made from the tulsi plant are another example, although the influence which they give is of a somewhat different character.

984.   An interesting set of natural talismans are those objects which produce strong scents. It has already been mentioned that incense produces a strong effect

along these lines, the gums of which it is composed being specially chosen because the radiations which they give forth are favourable to spiritual and devotional thought, and do not harmonise with any form of disturbance or worry. It is possible so to combine ingredients as to make an incense which will have the opposite effect; this was sometimes done by the mediaeval witches, and is done to-day in Luciferian ceremonies. On the whole, it is generally desirable to avoid coarse and heavy scents, such as that of musk or of sachet powder, as many of them are closely in tune with sensual feelings of various kinds.

985. An object not intentionally charged for that purpose may sometimes have the force of a talisman. A present received from some loved one, if it be of a nature that can be worn or carried about by the recipient, constantly serves to him as a reminder of the donor, and often so far gives the sense of the donor's presence as to prevent him from doing things that he would not do if that donor were looking on. I have heard of more than one case in which a man, wearing a ring or a chain given to him by his mother, was thereby saved from committing some questionable act, or indulging in some improper pleasure, because, just as he was about to yield to the temptation, his glance fell upon the object, and that brought to him so strongly the thought of his mother and of what she would feel if she could see him, that he at once abandoned his project. A letter carried about in the pocket has been known to serve the same purpose, for a man feels: "How can I do this thing with her very letter in my pocket - how can I take that into surroundings where I should be ashamed that she should see me?" I remember one case in which such a struggle ended in the man tearing up the letter and throwing it away in order that he might be able to indulge himself; but usually the opposite result is produced.

986. THINGS WE CARRY ABOUT

987. Thus it will be seen that the objects which we carry about with us in our pockets may have decided influence upon us. A man's watch, for example which he has always with him, becomes strongly charged with his magnetism, and if after wearing it for some years he gives it or lends it to another, that other person, if he be at all sensitive, will be constantly reminded of his friend, and conscious of a feeling as though he were present. I remember that a prominent member of the Theosophical Society, long since dead, used often to make presents of watches to those disciples in whom he was specially interested, charging them strongly before he gave them with whatever quality he thought that the recipient most needed. As his young friends naturally wore those watches, he succeeded in several cases in effecting in them considerable changes of character.

988. MONEY

989. One unpleasant thing (from one point of view) which we all have to carry about with us is money. It will naturally occur to the humorist to say at this point that he could do with a good deal of that kind of unpleasantness. I quite understand

that point of view, and I recognise that in our present civilisation, it is desirable to possess a certain amount of filthy lucre, and even necessary to carry at least a little of it about with one, so as to be prepared for unexpected emergencies. Nevertheless, the fact remains that while money in the abstract is no doubt a good thing to have, if one knows how to use it wisely, money in the concrete form of coins and notes, is frequently charged with the worst possible magnetism. New notes and new coins are harmless enough, but after they have been in circulation for a little time they acquire not only all sorts of physical dirt, but also many varieties of influences, nearly all of them exceedingly unpleasant.

990.　　The reason for this is not difficult to understand, for the magnetism surrounding the coin is produced by the thoughts and feelings of those who have handled it or carried it. First and as a general principle, without taking any special feeling into consideration, any coin which has been handled and carried by a large number of people must inevitably be charged with a great mixture of different kinds of magnetism. It is, therefore, from the point of view of vibrations, a centre of discord around which all kinds of warring influence are boiling up in the wildest confusion. The influence of such a thing as this is disturbing and irritating, and it has, though to a much stronger degree, exactly the same effect upon the astral and mental bodies as has the continued bombardment of radium emanations upon the physical body.

991.　　Several scientific people have discovered by painful experience that to carry a fragment of radium in one's waistcoat pocket, presently produces a peculiarly obstinate sore upon the skin underneath it; just like that, but larger in proportion, is the effect produced on the higher vehicles by the presence of a much-used coin. Copper and bronze coins are in this respect the worst of all - except perhaps old and dirty bank-notes. Gold and silver coins absorb the influences which surround them, but their qualities make them somewhat less receptive to the worst characteristics. From all this, it emerges that it is better not perpetually to have in one's pocket more money than is actually necessary. I have known students who partially met the difficulty by carrying copper or bronze coins only in a purse so strongly magnetised as to be practically impervious to the unpleasant vibrations. Many countries have realised the unsuitability of those metals for daily use, and are adopting nickel as a substitute; and nickel, while not so ` noble' a metal as gold or silver, is much less receptive to evil influence than copper. A noble metal, in alchemical parlance, is one which answers readily to the wave-lengths of the higher thought, but is resistant towards the lower kinds.

992.　　CLOTHING

993.　　We come now to a subject upon which all the considerations dictated by the sight of the higher worlds, and the additional knowledge which occultism gives, are in direct contradiction in nearly every way to the fashions at present prevailing in the West. In a course of researches, extending over many years, it has happened to me to see clairvoyantly a large number of the civilisations of the world, in all parts of it and at widely diverging periods, and it has also come within my duty to examine the inhabitants of at least two other planets. The various races have differed widely in customs and costumes, but never in any of them at any time have I seen anything approaching in hideousness the dress which is at present the fashion in Europe for males.

994. It is supremely ugly, ungainly and unhealthy, and the only point (so far as I can see) which can be urged in its favour is a certain measure of practical convenience. It is tight-fitting, whereas all clothing ought to be loose. It is made principally of materials which are from the inner point of view most undesirable, and the only colours (or lack of colours) which custom permits are precisely the worst that could possibly be chosen. Our outer garments are black, or brown, or grey (and one has only to study *Man Visible and Invisible* in order to see what those hues signify), or if a shade of blue is sometimes permitted, it is so dark that one can scarcely distinguish that it is blue at all.

995. There are certain practical reasons for all these unpleasant features. Our clothes are tight-fitting because we wish to be ready at any moment to exhibit activity in running, jumping or riding. They are made of heavy woollen materials in order to keep out the cold; and they are made in these ugly dark colours in order to disguise the dirt which accumulates upon them after even a single day's wear, owing to the facts that we are not yet sufficiently civilised to make all kinds of fires consume their own smoke, and that we have not yet learnt to make a road that shall be free from dust and mud. If anyone desires to know what a load of unspeakable filth he is carrying about with him, let him take any old coat or other outside garment which he has discarded, and wash it thoroughly in a tub of water, as underclothing is washed; the colour of the water will be a revelation to him.

996. From the occult point of view nothing will justify a man for existing in such a condition of filth. Clothing which is not only washable but frequently washed is absolutely the only kind that is permissible from the standpoint of the thinker. I know quite well that, as things stand in Europe or America, it is practically impossible for the most earnest student to do in this respect what he knows he ought to do; for the slavery of custom is so absolute that a man cannot live among his fellows unless he follows it. It is strange that this should be so, and it is most discreditable to those nations; it absolutely disposes of their claim to be considered liberal or free-minded people; but so it is. Information as to what ought to be done in these matters is therefore unfortunately useless to our Western brothers, because they simply cannot do it; but fortunately there are other countries in the world which, though perhaps equally under the slavery of custom along other lines, happen to have a better custom in regard to this particular matter, and so information about it may be of use to their inhabitants.

997. A man dresses primarily for decency and for the sake of his own comfort; but he ought surely also to consider the aspect which he presents to his fellow-creatures, and even for that reason alone the superlative ugliness of our present costume is a positive sin.

998. I am aware then that, for the Westerner at least, I am suggesting counsels of perfection which cannot be followed, when I say what occultism prescribes in the

matter of dress. I am not speaking of the customs of any race or religion, or of what any man or set of men happens to approve. I am simply prescribing what is dictated by a scientific consideration of the higher side of life and the unseen elements which are all the time entering into it. The prescription then is as follows:

999.   All dress should be loose and flowing, never under any circumstances exercising pressure upon any part of the body, and no part of it which touches the skin should ever be composed of wool or leather. How then are we to keep ourselves warm? Well, the Chinese, who at least in the North of their country suffer under a most appalling climate, contrive to solve the difficulty by using garments of padded silk or cotton, something like eiderdown quilts; and it is quite certain that it is within the resources of science to supply us with a number of efficient substitutes for wool, if there were only a demand for them. Old-fashioned doctors in England used to have a craze for recommending the wearing of wool next to the skin - the very last thing that ever ought to be allowed to touch it; for, as has been well said by a doctor: "It is an animal product which can never be properly cleaned; it creates unnatural heat; it becomes felted and chokes the pores; it absorbs moisture very slowly and dries very slowly, therefore retaining the moisture of the body; it enervates and enfeebles the system, encourages chills and colds, and promotes rheumatism; it often causes (and always irritates) rashes and other skin diseases; it cannot be boiled without destroying the fabric, and it always shrinks." From the occult point of view the condemnation of it is even more emphatic, and includes various other reasons.

1000.   Clothes ought to be of brilliant colours, not only for the sake of giving pleasure to the eyes of our neighbours, but also because of the effect of the colours upon ourselves. The present system of dressing entirely in subfusc hues is undoubtedly productive of a vast amount of depression and stagnation of thought, and by it we entirely lose the different effects which may be produced upon the disposition by the wearing of different colours. When we have advanced sufficiently for a reasonable costume to become possible, it will be of interest to discuss the qualities of the colours, and which are most suitable for particular types of people; at present it would be of little use.

1001.   In many oriental countries the customs in these matters are far more rational. In Burma, for example, when lecturing on a festival day at the Great Golden Pagoda in Rangoon, I have seen my audience stretch before me glowing like a splendid flower-bed with variegated colours. The delicately-coloured satins worn by the Chinese there on festive occasions produce in the glowing tropical sunlight an effect not easy to be surpassed, and one cannot but wonder how it is that we, who certainly belong to a later race than these people, and may not unreasonably claim to have advanced distinctly beyond them in many of the departments of civilisation, should yet have fallen so utterly and lamentably behind them in this particular of dress.

1002.   The worst features of it are really quite recent. I myself can remember in my childhood seeing a few survivals of the ordinary costume of a century ago, when brilliant colours were still worn by gentlemen on other occasions than in the hunting-field. It has really taken us only about a century to reach the lowest possible level in these matters; how long will it take us to rise again to beauty and gracefulness and dignity?

1003.   The subject of clothing leads us to bed-clothing; but there is not much to be said upon this, save that from the occult standpoint feather-beds or thick and heavy mattresses are always undesirable, and that if it be necessary that wool should form part of the covering, at any rate precautions should be taken that it does not touch the skin of the sleeper; for if at other times it is inexpedient to bring into close contact with ourselves that which is saturated with animal influences, and is indeed animal in its very essence, it is a thousandfold more serious to do this when the body is asleep and so specially amenable to such influences. A bed made of interlaced webbing, such as is commonly used at Adyar, is one of the best from the occult point of view.

CHAPTER XVI BY MENTAL CONDITIONS

1006.   THOUGHT-FORMS

1007.   Man clothes himself in other worlds than this, though in a somewhat different way. For in the astral world he draws round himself a veritable garment of the feelings which are habitual to him, and in the mental world a similar garment of the thoughts in which he commonly indulges. I should like to make it thoroughly clear that in saying this I am not speaking symbolically, but am describing an objective fact - objective as far as those higher levels are concerned. It has been repeatedly explained that our feelings and thoughts generate definite forms in the matter which they respectively affect, and that these forms follow the thoughts and feelings which made them. When those thoughts and feelings are directed towards another person, the forms actually move through space to that person and impinge upon his aura, and in many cases blend themselves with it. When, however, the thoughts and feelings are self-centred (as I fear we must admit that the majority of many people's are) the forms do not pass away, but remain clustering round the man who has given birth to them.

1008.   Thus we find that every man has built for himself a shell of such thought-forms, a veritable clothing at their level; thus all this thought and feeling is constantly reacting upon the man himself. He gave it birth; he made it out of himself; and now it is external to him and capable of reacting upon him, though he knows nothing of its propinquity and its power. Floating thus around him, the forces which it radiates seem to him to come altogether from without, and he often regards as a temptation from some external source, a thought which is in reality only a reflection of one of his own of yesterday or of yesterweek. "As a man thinketh, so is he." And this is largely because his own thoughts are the nearest to him and are constantly playing upon him, so that they have a better opportunity than any others to act upon him.

1009.   The constant radiations which pour forth from his thought-forms impregnate the inanimate objects round him, so that even the walls and furniture of his room reflect upon him the thoughts and feelings to which he is accustomed. If a man sitting in a certain chair in a certain room devotes himself for many days to some train or type of thought, he fills the surrounding objects, the chair, the desk, the very walls of the room, with vibrations which express that type of thought. He unconsciously magnetises these physical objects, so that they possess the power of suggesting thoughts of the same type to any other person who puts himself in the way of their influence. Many striking instances of this may be found among the collections of stories which refer to such matters. I have already given one of a number of persons committing suicide, one after another, in the same prison-cell, because the place was reeking with that idea, and they felt it acting upon them as a force from without, which they thought themselves compelled to obey.

1010.   From these considerations emerge two main ideas on the subject of our feelings, which at first sight appear absolutely contradictory: first, that we must be most careful about our feelings; secondly, that they do not matter at all. But when we come to seek for the explanation of this apparent contradiction, we see that it lies in the fact that we are not using the word ` feelings' in quite the same sense in the two statements. We must be careful what feelings we allow to arise within us; we need pay no attention to the feelings which press upon us from outside. True; but in the first case we mean original feelings - *thought*-feelings which emanate from our own minds; in the second case we mean moods, which come without any volition on our part. These latter we can afford to disregard utterly. The mood is the result of our thought of yesterday, and we cannot alter that thought or affect it in any way; our business is with the original thought of to-day, for that thought is within our control, and when it suggests itself we can receive it and adopt it, or we can reject it. And the same is true with our feelings. You say you cannot help your feelings; that is what the ordinary uncomprehending person thinks, but it is not in the least true. You *can* help them and control them if you will.

1011.   MOODS

1012.   We have all had the experience of feeling moods of different sorts coming over us. On one occasion we feel joyful without knowing why, and on another occasion depressed and pessimistic. There may be many reasons for this latter feeling; indigestion in some shape or other is the commonest. It comes often, too, from lack of exercise, lack of sunlight, lack of open air; and too much night-work; but also sometimes it is simply the reaction upon us of previous thoughts of our own - and sometimes of the previous thoughts of someone else. It may be due to the presence of an astral entity who is in a condition of depression, and contrives to communicate his vibration to our astral bodies. But whatever may be its cause, the depression must be thrown aside, and we must endeavour to go on with our work precisely as though it did not exist.

1013.   This is largely a matter of feeling, and that makes it difficult to take a coldly scientific view of it; yet it is precisely that which we must endeavour to do. These moods of ours make no difference whatever to the facts of life. Why therefore should we allow them to influence us? Our future destiny lies before us, and is entirely unaffected by the fact that we take at one time an optimistic and at another a pessimistic view of it. Why then should we allow ourselves to be worried to-day merely because we were worried yesterday, or because some astral entity feels worried? The hidden side of all these moods shows them to come from various causes; but it also shows us clearly that, whatever the causes may be, our duty is to go on with our work, and pay absolutely no attention to them.

1014.   RECURRENT THOUGHTS

1015.   In yet another way, too, we must carefully watch the action of recurring thoughts. What at first was merely an unfounded suspicion - perhaps an unworthy suspicion - may presently solidify itself into a prejudice; not because there is any additional evidence for it, but simply by virtue of its own recurrence. We adopt, often without due reason, a certain attitude towards some person or thing, and then, merely because we have taken it up, we persist in it; and even though we may be quite aware that at first it was nothing but the merest suspicion, by virtue of having thought it over and over again we believe it to be well-founded, and proceed to reason from it as though it were a fact. Thus often prejudices are born, and we have already explained that prejudices are fatal to progress.

1016.   Again, this reaction of thought-forms tends to set up in us certain qualities. Many a man has begun by being, quite rightly, careful as to the expenditure of his money; but the anxious thought which he has devoted to the consideration as to how he should economise has reacted upon him again and again until it has become the dominant idea in his mind - until it has generated within him the quality of avarice. It is not only inward upon its maker that the thought-form pours its influence; it is also radiating outwards. And the effect of that outward vibration is to attract other similar thought-forms which strengthen the action of the original. It is therefore necessary for us to be on our guard in these matters, to watch carefully the thoughts and feelings which arise within us, and to distinguish between those which come from above, from the ego, and those which merely flow in at lower levels.

1017.   FALLING IN LOVE

1018.   Another instance of the repeated action of a thought-form is what is commonly called falling in love. Of this there are at least two clearly marked varieties, which are commonly defined by novelists as "gradually growing into love" and as "falling in love at first sight". This latter phenomenon (if it ever really occurs, as I am inclined to think that it does) must mean the recognition by the ego of one who was well known in previous incarnations; but the former and more ordinary variety is usually due to the intensified action of repeated thought.

1019.   To speak with any degree of common sense on this subject is likely to render one unpopular, because each man regards his lady-love as the only woman in the world who is really an epitome of all the virtues, and is prepared to maintain that proposition at the sword-point if necessary. Yet if it were possible for him to take an unimpassioned and reasonable view of the matter (which of course it is not), he would have to admit that, while she is all this to *him*, there are other ladies in the world who appear to occupy the same position in the minds of other people - people who are, in the abstract, just as intelligent and as capable of forming an opinion on such a matter as he himself is.

1020.   Why then, where there is no question of a tie formed in a previous incarnation, should he select a certain young woman out of all the rest of the world, to be for him an embodiment of all that is noble and beautiful? The truth is unromantic; it is largely a question of propinquity. The normal young man, thrown by circumstances into close relations with the normal young woman, is likely to fall in love with her; and though he would never believe it, if he had been thrown into similar intimate relations with any one of a hundred other equally normal young women, he would have fallen in love with that other just as easily!

197

1021.   In the first place a young lady makes upon him an agreeable passing impression; if he did not meet her again, it is probable that after a few days he would cease to think of her; but if he sees her often, his thought-form of her becomes strengthened and he begins, though he does not know it, to see more deeply into her than he did at first. And this process continues until he learns to see in her the divine reality which lies behind us all. It lies behind all equally, but he has learnt to see it only in her, and therefore for him it takes her form; and when once he has seen it through that form, to him at any rate it can take no other. And so he dowers her in his imagination with all sorts of virtues and all splendid qualities - which *are* in her, as they are in us all, yet may not be manifested through her to other eyes than his. They are in her, because her ego, like all others, is a spark of the Divine Fire; and in Him these qualities inhere and exist in perfection. The manifestation of them in this physical world may be no greater in her than in a hundred others, but he sees them in her because it was through her that he first learnt to realise them at all.

1022.   And so in truth, from the occultist's point of view the rhapsodies of thousands of lovers about the respective objects of their adoration are all true, even though they seem mutually exclusive; for the truth is that that which they all love is One, though for each It manifests through a different vehicle, and because they with their partial vision cannot separate the One from Its manifestation, they endow that special manifestation with qualities which belong not to it but to That which shines through. So all are right in the qualities which they see, and wrong only in claiming exclusive manifestation through the form through which they have learnt to see them.

1023.   Often the impartial outsider finds it difficult to understand, looking at it from the point of view of the physical world, what a certain man saw in a certain woman to induce him to desire to make her his wife. The answer is that the husband saw in her something which is not visible on the physical level; something which is to be discerned only by looking much deeper than that, and his attraction to her was that it was through her that that aspect of the Divine was revealed to him.

1024.   People often say that the lover's imagination gives to his prospective bride qualities which in truth she does not possess. The occultist would say that the lover is right; she does possess them, because God, of whom she is a part, possesses them. And for her lover she is a channel through which he can see Him. But others for whom she is not the channel cannot see those qualities through her, but may at the same time be seeing them through someone else.

1025.   One great advantage of this is that, if the woman be a good woman, she tries to live up to the level of her lover's thought-form of her. She is fully conscious that he is idealising her, that he endows her with qualities which she does not believe herself to possess; but in order that he may not be disappointed, in order that she may be worthy of his love and trust, she tries hard to develop these qualities in herself - to be what he thinks her to be. And because in essence she *is* what he thinks her, because in the Monad behind her those qualities *do* exist, she is often successful, at least to some extent, in bringing them down into manifestation, and thus the confidence of the lover is justified, and his faith in her brings forth her higher self and helps her on the path of evolution.

1026.   All this, be it observed, works both ways, and the woman tries to find her ideal through a man just as does a man through a woman. The human being as at present constituted usually finds his ideal most readily through some one of the opposite sex, but this is not invariably so. Sometimes a younger man adores an elder one, and through his admiration and affection for him obtains his glimpse of that true world which we call the ideal; and sometimes the same feeling exists between a younger woman and an experienced matron.

1027.   Since that real ideal is behind us all alike, the mystic who lives wrapped in solitary contemplation may find it just as perfectly within himself. It is the tendency of every man to seek it, whether through his own self or through another, and the feeling which moves him to seek it is the divinely implanted force of evolution, the desire to find and to return to the Divine from whom we came. For the force which at this early stage can only manifest itself in this way is the very same that later on will bring the man to final union. As Saint Augustine beautifully put it: "God, Thou hast made us for Thyself, and our hearts are ever restless till they find their rest in Thee."

1028.   UNSET BLOSSOM

1029.   A beautiful variant of this, which is often misunderstood, is the "falling in love" of children. Unsympathetic adults often ridicule it, because they know that in nine cases out of ten its object is quite unsuitable, it does not last, and it comes to nothing. All that is true, yet in essence it is the same feeling as that which comes in later life, and it is usually a far purer and more unselfish form of it. If you could penetrate the secret heart of a young lover of ten or twelve, you would find that often he does not even dream of marrying his prospective bride and settling down comfortably to be happy for ever after; his idea is rather to sacrifice himself for her, to exhibit splendid heroism in her defence, and die at her feet. Absurdly romantic, no doubt, yet not without its good effect upon that young heart - indeed, upon both the young hearts concerned.

1030.   To pour out such thought-forms as these is indeed well, both for their creator and their recipient, and they are preparing both for the maturer but not more beautiful feeling which comes in later life. Have you ever seen the vast amount of unset blossom on our cherry-trees or plum-trees? One might think of all that as a useless waste of Nature's energy, because it never comes to fruit. Yet the botanist tells us that it is by no means useless - that it has an important purpose to serve in drawing up the sap and thereby strengthening the tree, and so preparing the way for finer fruit in the autumn than could have existed without it. These innocent young love-affairs of childhood have precisely the same effect; they strengthen the nature and prepare it for the fuller development which comes later.

1031.   OCCULTISM AND MARRIAGE

1032.   Yet in spite of all that I have said above - in spite of the beauty and exaltation of the love affair - can we from the point of view of occultism advise our students to marry? I think the best answer is to be found in the words of our great founder, Madame Blavatsky:

1033.   It depends on the kind of man you mean. If you refer to one who intends to live *in* the world - one who, even though a good, earnest Theosophist and an ardent worker for our cause, still has ties and wishes which bind him to the world - who, in short, does not feel that he has done for ever with what men call life, and that he desires one thing and one thing only - to know the truth, and to be able to help others - then for such a one I say there is no reason why he should not marry, if he likes to take the risk of that lottery where there are so many more blanks than prizes.

(The Key to Theosophy, Section xiii, "Theosophy and Marriage").

1034.   But if the man means to be more than this, if he intends to devote his whole life to Theosophical work, and aspires to become a pupil of one of the great Masters of the Wisdom, then we cannot advise him to divide his attention between that world and this. Again Madame Blavatsky tells us:

1035.   Practical occultism is far too serious and dangerous a study for a man to take up, unless he is in the most deadly earnest, and ready to sacrifice *all, himself first of all*, to gain his end. I am only referring to those who are determined to tread the path of discipleship which leads to the highest goal. (*Ibid.*, Section xiii.)

1036.   There is nothing to prevent a man from loving his ideal as much as he will; the mistake is in the desire for sole possession, in the animal passion which prevents him from being satisfied to worship at a distance, in the jealousy which is annoyed that others should love and worship also. The student who wishes to devote himself even to the uttermost must keep himself free from all entanglement - free for the work; and let him not, as has been the case with many, be deceived by the specious reasoning of his passion, and fall under the delusion that he can work better in chains. But, remember once more, this is only for the man who is absolutely determined to go on to the end. Short of such high resolve, there is a vast amount of good work that may be done - and even of progress that may be made - by taking advantage of the troubles and trials of the ordinary worldly life, and endeavouring to live one's highest, even though it be in chains.

1037.   Another excuse which is sometimes put forward is that it is necessary that bodies should be provided for the high-class in-coming egos who will be needed to do the work; it is argued that students can surely provide these better than the good people of the outer world. This is probably so, and therefore in certain rare cases students have been ordered to marry for this very purpose; but it is surely wisest to wait for such an order from a source that cannot be questioned. Meanwhile we have plenty of good married members who are perfectly capable of providing bodies for the occult workers of the future. Truly there can be no greater honour than to be selected by the karmic Deities to provide those, except the still greater honour of training them when they are provided. Let it be the work then of the student who still retains his ties with the world to provide those bodies, and let those who feel themselves capable of the higher life help in their training. For verily no man can serve two masters, and the path of occultism demands the whole energies of body, soul and spirit.

1038.   CHANGES IN CONSCIOUSNESS

1039.   The human consciousness has wonderful possibilities, and what we commonly call by that name is only the fragment of it which we can use for the moment. We may perhaps take an analogy from the action of our physical senses. There is an enormous gamut of possible vibrations. One little group of those at a certain level appeals to us as light; another little group at a much lower level appeals to us as sound. We are conscious in various ways of other intermediate groups. But we are fully aware from our knowledge of science that the gamut extends at both ends far beyond our possibilities of dealing with it.

1040.   We may suppose the human consciousness to be like that gamut, and the part of it now in action in the physical brain to correspond, let us say, to the block of oscillations which we call sound. Following out the same analogy, we might suppose our block of astral consciousness to be equivalent to the wave-lengths which we call light; but here again there are many undulations capable of carrying light which we cannot see - undulations both below and above our limit of vision. In just the same way, below our physical consciousness and above it, and below our astral consciousness and above that, are further sets of vibrations to which our consciousness might be adapted, but is not.

1041.   There are two ways in which it can be adapted: permanently and intentionally, by the development of that consciousness so that it can receive more of those waves which are above and below its normal possibilities; or temporarily, by some disease or abnormality which shifts our octave of consciousness either upwards or downwards. An example of the first way is the development of psychic powers of all sorts. But it is unnecessary for me to take up the consideration of those here, as I have already done it in other books - *Clairvoyance, The Other Side of Death* and *Some Glimpses of Occultism*. Various drugs have the power of temporarily changing or widening the scope of consciousness, and therefore they enable us to see things normally unseen by us, sometimes at the sacrifice of our ordinary power of vision for the time, and sometimes without robbing us of that.

1042.   What we call our physical consciousness is not a fixed and determinate amount which has always been the same. It has gradually grown to be what it is, and many things which were formerly within its purview have now passed below it - or more accurately, it has so developed itself as to rise above them. Its level is gradually rising; our descendants will be able to see colours which at present are invisible to us - higher, purer and more delicate colours. Whether they will at the same time lose the possibility of appreciating some of the coarsest of the colours which we now know, is uncertain.

1043.   Delirium shifts the place of this consciousness, and often altogether shuts out from us the everyday world which we know, giving us sometimes in its place memories of our past - not only of the past of this life but of the longer-forgotten part of the human race. Such sight as delirium gives often includes the power to see the sufferer's own thought-forms, or those of others, and sometimes also to see the astral and etheric creatures which are around him. In the case of delirium-tremens, for example, the snakes and other horrors are almost invariably creatures of low type which are feasting upon the fumes of alcohol exuding from the body of the drunkard.

CHAPTER XVII BY OUR AMUSEMENTS

1046.   CHILDREN's GAMES

1047.   There is a hidden side even to a thing usually considered so unimportant as the games of children. If the parents think of these at all, it is probably chiefly from the physical point of view. They either disapprove of games in a general way as causing destruction of clothes or enticing the boy away from his school work, or they grant them a qualified approval as at any rate keeping the boy out of their way for a certain number of hours, or as affording him physical exercise which they recognise as a necessity for the development of his body. Sometimes also they are particular as to his associations from a social point of view, and occasionally also from a religious or moral standpoint; but it is probable that most parents regard play as a sort of necessary evil.

1048.   They do not in the least realise that a game, if played as all games ought to be, is a lesson whose value can hardly be overestimated, for it inculcates as nothing else can the virtues of honour, unselfishness and chivalry. Honour first, because of the necessity of abiding with uttermost loyalty by the rules of the game, because of the realisation that a seeming success gained by an infringement of them, no matter how slight, would be dishonestly gained, and so would be no success at all, but the deepest disgrace, whether the delinquency were known to others or only seared into the memory of the culprit himself. Unselfishness, because for success in many games it is absolutely necessary that the unit shall be subordinated to the whole, and that each player shall seek not his own glorification, but the benefit of the side upon which he plays. No one who watches the instant, unhesitating obedience so willingly given in any good school to the captain of an eleven at cricket, or to the coach of a boat's crew, can fail to perceive that this is a most valuable discipline, teaching each to accept loyally and to perform thoroughly the duty assigned to him, looking to the good of the club rather than to his personal desires. Chivalry, because of the rule, invariable among all gentlemanly boys, of giving the opponent the benefit of any doubtful point, and of declining to profit by an accidental advantage. Evil indeed is it for a country when such honour, such unselfishness, such chivalry are not to be found among its children, for the child is father to the man, and as the twig is bent so the tree inclines.

1049.   The great thing to impress upon the child is that though he must always do his best for his own side, in reality it does not matter who wins, as the exercise obtained and the pleasure of the game are the same in any case. It should be explained to him that he must act not only fairly, but also graciously and hospitably in his play; that he must always be ready to applaud good play on the other side, that he must never exult over those who are defeated, but must always endeavour to find excuses for them and minimise the disappointment which they will naturally feel.

1050.   True, others will not always do this for *him*, but he need not be in any way disturbed or annoyed by that, since it simply shows that they have not yet reached the level at which they can put themselves mentally in the place of their opponents. It is natural that a boy should take pleasure in the victory of his school or his side, but he must learn not so to show that pleasure as to hurt in any way the feelings of another.

1051.   Never for a moment must he find pleasure or amusement in anything that hurts or annoys another living creature, whether it be a school-fellow or an animal. The tendency which some ill-taught children show to tease an animal or another child is a manifestation of cruelty, and it must be explained to the child that cruelty of any sort is one of the worst of crimes. The child must remember always to put himself in thought in the place of the other, and so to manifest the uttermost brotherhood, kindliness and love, to be willing always to put aside what he wants in order to give pleasure to other children, and to do what they like.

1052.   I noticed an interesting example of chivalry some time ago, when attending the College boat-races at one of our great Universities. A certain College had held unquestioned for some years the chief place in aquatic affairs, but on this occasion another College succeeded in gaining several places and finally attained the coveted position of Head of the River, defeating its previous holders. Naturally there was great rejoicing, and a triumphal procession was formed in which not only the banner of the winning boat, but also its oars and rudder were carried home in exultant ovation. In their jubilant march the crowd of undergraduates of the victorious College had to pass along the river and in front of the long line of boat-houses, and suddenly I observed that the cheering mob fell silent, furled its flag and lowered its oars and obviously endeavoured to efface itself and hastily assume as unobtrusive a demeanour as possible. Asking what was the matter, I was told that they were approaching the boat-house of the College which had so long held supremacy, and that it would of course be in bad taste to seem to glory over them by parading the conquest before them. Therefore our victors for the time tried to look as much as possible like ordinary students going quietly home; but their magnanimous attempt was at least partially defeated, for before they could steal past they were observed by the defeated crew and their fellow-members, who immediately rushed out from their boat-house to cheer them lustily, while the captain of the defeated boat ran to the great flagstaff of the boat-house and hauled down his College flag in token of cheerful submission to fate. As a spontaneous expression of good feeling on the part of these young fellows just fresh from school, this pleased me greatly, and I could not but see that the public opinion among them was a healthy and enviable one.

1053.   SPORT

1054.   Unfortunately the amusements of adults are not always as harmless and wholesome as those of children. There is nothing to be said against cricket or golf; and rowing and swimming are always admirable, as bringing the etheric, astral and mental bodies into closer contact with the nature-spirits of the water and their influences, which make an agreeable contrast with those to be found upon land. Still more is this true if the swimming is done in the sea, for the variety there is greater. Such change of impressions is always good, as it sets in vibration new parts of the various bodies, and so adds greatly to their general health.

1055.   But it is impossible to reprobate too strongly the revolting cruelty that is sometimes misnamed sport. Needless to say, the crime connected with the murder of defenceless animals far outweighs any benefit that may be incidentally derived from fresh air and exercise. The whole thing is horrible beyond words, and it is difficult to understand how it is possible for civilised and otherwise kind-hearted people to take part in such abomination - and not only to take part in them, but even apparently to enjoy the bloodshed and the cruelty, and to vie with one another in the diabolical work of destruction. No country in which such things happen can claim to be really civilised, and we cannot doubt that when our descendants look back on this period they will find it incredible that we actually indulged in such wholesale and gratuitous barbarities.

1056.   All forms of hunting incur similar reprobation. Even apart from the pain, misery and death inflicted upon the fox, the deer, the hare, or the otter, there is the whole question of the wickedness incurred in the training of dogs for such purposes. The dog is one of the domestic animals which are given into man's care in order that he may advance their evolution. He does not help it, but fatally hinders it, when he trains the animal to be more ferocious than the wolf or the tiger - when he teaches it to kill not for food, as do the wild beasts, but for the mere lust and pleasure of killing. This wanton destruction of the wonderful gift of life, "which all can take but none can give," will surely bring a heavy retribution on the individuals who take part in it, and on the country whose public opinion permits it.

1057.   One terrible thing connected with this is that our children imitate our thoughtless cruelty, and so young souls who would naturally be kind and helpful are led into the commission of these crimes. We can hardly wonder that a boy fishes or hunts, or sets his dog to kill some living creature, when he constantly sees his father doing the same thing. We so engrain cruelty into the young that even after their death it persists in the astral world, and we find the same tendency in the dead boy as in the living - to hunt something about, and to cause it pain and terror. True, unless the shameful example set before him has made him thoroughly wicked, it is easier in the astral world to invoke the boy's good feelings than it is on the physical, because there we can show him in a moment exactly what is the real sensation of the hunted creature, for it is apparent in changings and flashings of colour. So we can appeal directly to the boy's better nature by showing him precisely what he has been doing. In the astral world we have also the advantage that we can deflect the cruel hunting instinct and the passion for destruction into the safe and useful channel of breaking up horrible thought-forms, such as those of devils, which are made by the unfortunate people who suffer under the curse of Calvinistic or similarly blasphemous religious teaching. These thought-forms, though not dangerous when understood, are often a source of great terror to the ignorant, and as they have no real evolving life in them, there is no sin involved in destroying them. Such work develops both chivalry and courage in the boy, inducing him to go about as a knight-errant, helping and protecting the weak, and facing for their sake what appear to him the most formidable odds.

1058. FISHING

1059.   Fishing is another manifestation of the lust for slaughter, and many people indulge in this who would recoil from other forms of enjoyment in which the bloodshed is more obvious, for here, instead of killing or crippling a bird by a shot, they only take the creature out of its element and leave it to die slowly by suffocation. Difficult though it is to understand how it can be so, I really believe that most of this atrocious cruelty is simple thoughtlessness, and the baneful effect of the collective thought-forms clustering round a custom which has come down to us from the barbarous times of the Dark Ages.

1060. HORSE-RACING

1061.   Horse-racing, again, is another so-called sport for which there can be nothing but condemnation. The mere running of horses against one another, if they are not struck or otherwise ill-treated, is no more objectionable than a race between boys, or men; but as matters stand now, the whole mass of ideas which cluster round the turf is objectionable to the highest degree, and from the occult point of view the atmosphere of a race-course is a veritable hell. All the cheating and trickery, all the mad anxiety and avarice, all the hatred and deliberate falsehood, make the whole scene an indescribable nightmare of horrors. Yet decent men will show themselves in such a place and, even worse still, will subject their wives and daughters to its appallingly evil magnetism. Ignorance again, of course, and thoughtlessness; in intention nothing worse than that; but the results are serious nevertheless.

1062. GAMBLING

1063.   Everyone who takes part in horse-racing has his share of the responsibility of all the wickedness of the gambling connected with it, and of the ruin to thousands which it brings in its train. Even on the physical level the evils of gambling and of betting are surely obvious enough; but with the added sight of higher worlds they are a hundred times more objectionable. Men plunge into this foolishness presumably for excitement; but this is a form of excitement which arouses all the worst passions of men, and can do nothing but harm to them, for the moral effect on the man who wins is usually at least as evil as upon him who loses.

1064.   Readers of *Thought-Forms* will remember the awful pictures there given of the thought-forms of the winner and of the loser; those who can see such things for themselves will need no one to inform them of the evils of gambling. It can never be anything but evil in any of its forms; but, if one must pronounce between them, the kind which is pursued at the notorious Casino of Monte Carlo is decidedly the less objectionable of the two, for there the gambling is at least fair, and the victim knows his chances beforehand; also, he wins or loses to an impersonal entity - the bank, and, so does not obviously and intentionally ruin his fellow-men.

1065.   From the occult point of view, betting, alcohol-drinking, corpse-eating and the slaughter of living creatures in sport, are the great blots upon the fair fame of the English nation. If those could be removed we should have made several long steps on the way towards civilisation.

1066.   Although occultism has nothing but unequivocal condemnation for all forms of so-called sport, which in any way whatever injure any living creature, it has not a vestige of the puritan point of view that everything which gives pleasure is necessarily wrong. On the contrary, the promotion of pleasure ranks in the mind of the occultist next to the promotion of progress. It is good to give pleasure to anyone; it is far better still to help him on the path of progress; but it is best of all when it is possible to combine the two. So the occultist welcomes harmless amusement; his only proviso is that it shall be harmless - that it shall not involve pain or suffering or even discomfort or ridicule for any living being.

1067.   THE THEATRE

1068.   The hidden side of a performance at the theatre depends entirely upon the nature of the performance. The passions portrayed by the actors, not being in any sense real, produce practically no effect on higher matter, but unfortunately there seems to be not infrequently a great deal of conceit connected with acting, and a great deal of jealousy of other actors. So far as these exist they represent undesirable influences. The principal effect to be seen at a theatre is the result of the feelings excited in the audience, and these again depend upon the character of the play.

1069.   There seems almost always to be an undercurrent of sensuality directed towards the principal actresses, but the people who make-up the majority of the audience usually follow the plot of the play and feel a mild amount of hatred for the villain and a sort of gentle pleasure when the hero succeeds in over-throwing his machinations. There are some ingenuous people who really throw themselves heart and soul into the play - to whom it is for the time exactly like real life. These send out strong emotions of various kinds as the play progresses, but usually their number is not sufficient to count for much in the general aura of the theatre. There are unfortunately many modern plays which are in themselves of a highly objectionable nature, and the thought-forms of those who patronise them are naturally unpleasant in character.

1070.   One may sum up the matter by saying that to many people a visit to the theatre is like the reading of a novel, but it presents the different characters to them in a manner which makes them more real to them. There are others, on the other hand (perhaps more imaginative people), who when they read a story make for themselves thought-forms of all the characters, and these forms seem to them far more vivid and suitable than any representation in the theatre can be. Such people are always disappointed when they go to see a dramatised representation of one of their favourite stories.

1071.   Others who have not the power of imagination to clothe the characters with definite forms for themselves are very glad to have this done for them by the dramatist's art. For these - and they are the majority of theatre-goers - a visit to the theatre is no more harmful than the reading of a novel, except for the necessary unpleasant surroundings - the tinge of sensuality in the audience, and of conceit and jealousy in the actors, to which I have previously referred, and the spending of a couple of hours in a vitiated atmosphere and in the midst of a more or less excited crowd. From the occult point of view these latter considerations usually rather outweigh the advantage of any possible enjoyment that may be obtained from the performance.

FOURTH SECTION HOW WE INFLUENCE OTHERS

CHAPTER XVIII BY WHAT WE ARE

STACY

1076. THE INTERRELATION OF MEN

1077.   We have been examining the influences to which we are liable, and we have also considered how, by reactions which we do not notice, we are constantly influencing ourselves. Now we come to the third great branch of our subject, the question of how we influence others. What has been already said is sufficient to show us that invariably we must influence them, whether we wish to do so or not; for if, as we have already seen, all these varied influences are constantly playing upon and affecting us, it is quite clear that what we do in our turn must be part of the influence which is acting on those near us. We are all so closely interrelated that no man can live his life to himself alone, and every thought or action is producing its result on others - not only because people see our actions in the physical world and imitate them, but because they are affected by the unseen radiation of the vibrations of our thoughts and feelings.

1078.   We influence people in three ways: by what we are; by what we think and desire; by what we say and do.

1079.   First by what we are; because what we are expresses itself in our various vehicles, and they are constantly pouring out waves of influence which tend to reproduce themselves - that is, to infect other people. So whatever we wish other people to be, we ourselves must be first of all. What then is the idea which we should set before ourselves in this matter? Many would say "To be good," and of course that is the first consideration; but surely we may take that for granted. Anyone who has got so far as even to think about the duty of influencing the world, must by the hypothesis be trying his best to live a good life. Let us then assume the good intention and the earnest endeavour, and let us see what we can do to improve the world around us by our example. I think the first point is the duty of happiness and peace.

1080. THE DUTY OF HAPPINESS

1081.   Let us take happiness first. Unquestionably the Deity means man to be happy. Happiness is a duty; I do not mean merely philosophical calm, though assuredly that is a good thing; I mean active happiness. It is a duty, not only to the Divine Power and to ourselves, but also to others, as I shall presently show; and it is a duty not difficult of accomplishment, if we will only exercise the inestimable faculty of common sense. Yet the majority of men and women are obviously often unhappy; why?

1082.   Unhappiness is a mental condition, so the suffering which comes from sickness or accident is not strictly part of our subject, yet there is often a mental side even to that, which may be greatly minimised by the application of reason. Eternal

207

Justice rules the world, and therefore nothing can, by any possibility, happen to us that we have not deserved; and as that eternal Justice is also eternal Love, everything that happens to us is intended to help us forward in our development, and is capable of doing so, if we will only take it in the right way and try to learn the lesson which it is meant to teach. Since this is true - and those who have probed most deeply into the mysteries of life and death know that it is - to grumble or to repine at suffering is manifestly not only to waste much force uselessly, but also to take an entirely inaccurate and foolish view of life, and to lose what is designed as an opportunity.

1083.   Let us consider some of the more frequent causes of this prevalent unhappiness, in order to see how it can be avoided. Man has displayed exceeding ingenuity in inventing reasons for being miserable, but most of them can be classed under one or other of four heads - desire, regret, fear and worry.

1084.   *Desire* - Much unhappiness arises because people are perpetually yearning for what they have not - for riches, for fame, for power, for social position, for success in all sorts of undertakings. I do not forget that contentment may sometimes denote stagnation, and that what has been called "divine discontent" is a prerequisite to progress. That we should unceasingly endeavour to improve ourselves, to better our position, to augment our power of helpfulness to others - all this is good and estimable, and tends to our evolution; but most of our discontent is anything but divine, because it is not a desire for improvement and usefulness, but rather a mere selfish craving for the personal enjoyment that we expect to derive from riches or from the exercise of power; and that is why so much misery results from it. Press forward, indeed, as ardently as you will; but be happy in your pressing, be cheery under failure, and never be too busy to hold out a helping hand to your fellow-pilgrim.

1085.   Among the most poisonous of the manifold forms of this great weed desire, are those called envy and jealousy. If men would only learn to mind their own business and leave other people alone, many fertile sources of unhappiness would disappear. What is it to you that another man has more money or a larger house, that he keeps more servants or owns better horses, or that his wife is able to indulge in more astonishing vagaries of millinery and dressmaking? All these things afford him a certain kind of opportunity - a test of his capacity for using them aright; he may be succeeding or he may be failing, but in any case you are not his judge, and your business is clearly not to waste your time in criticising and envying him, but to be quite sure that you yourself are fulfilling to the uttermost the duties which appertain to your own state of life.

1086.   Perhaps of all the passions which poor human nature cherishes, jealousy is the most ridiculous. It pretends to love fervently, and yet objects that any other should share its devotion; whereas unselfish affection but rejoices the more when it finds the object of its adoration universally appreciated. Jealousy loathes, above all things, to see evidence of the fondness of for its idol, and yet it is always eagerly watching for confirmation of its suspicions, and will take any amount of trouble to prove to itself the existence of what most it hates! See then how much utterly unnecessary unhappiness is escaped by the man who is strong enough and sensible enough to mind his own business, and refuses absolutely to be drawn into the meshes either of envy or jealousy.

1087. Curb desire and cultivate contentment; let your wants be few and simple and your ambitions for progress and usefulness rather than for possessions; and you will find that you have eliminated one of the most fruitful and potent causes of misery.

1088. *Regret* - It is pitiable to think how many thousands every day are suffering needless, hopeless, useless agonies of regret. You had money perhaps, and it is gone; you had a position, and you have lost it. That is no reason why you should squander your strength and your time in unavailing lamentation. Start at once to earn more money, to make for yourself another position. "Let the dead past bury its dead," and turn your thought to the future.

1089. Yes, and this is true even though the loss has been caused by your own fault, even though that which you regret be a sin. You may have failed, as many a man before you has failed, but you have no time to waste in remorse. If you have fallen, do not lie mourning in the mud, but get up at once, and go on your way more circumspectly. Set your face forward, and push resolutely ahead. If you fall a thousand times - well, get up a thousand times and go on again; it is absolutely useless to sink discouraged by the way. There is just as much reason for the thousandth attempt as there was for the first, and if you persevere success is certain, for your strength grows by repeated effort. A Master once said: "The only repentance which is of the slightest value is determination not to commit the same sin again." The wise man is not he who never makes mistakes, but he who never makes the same mistake twice.

1090. The greatest of all regrets, I know full well, is that for "the touch of a vanished hand, and the sound of a voice that is still". Yet even that most sacred of sorrows may be dispelled, if we are willing to take the trouble to understand. When those whom we love pass from the sight of our physical eyes, we are no longer left gazing at a blank wall, clinging with desperate faith to nebulous uncertainty, hoping against hope for some far distant reunion, as were so many of our forefathers.

1091. Science now treads where ignorance once resigned, and anyone who is ready to examine the available evidence may convince himself that death is but the stepping from one room into another, the gate of a higher and fuller life, and that we have not in any sense *lost* our friends, as we so often erroneously say, but have only lost for the time the power to see them. A little patient study of the facts soon enables us to turn from a selfish contemplation of this illusion of our bereavement to the glorious certainty which opens out before those who are so much dearer to us than ourselves; and thus one of the saddest of all forms of unhappiness is at least greatly mitigated, even when not entirely removed.

1092. *Fear* - I suppose that only those who, like some of the clergy, have had special opportunities of knowing the inner side of men's lives, can be aware of the extent to which humanity suffers from the fear of death. Many a man who shows a brave front to the world, and laughs and smiles with the best, is yet groaning inwardly all the while under the oppression of a secret horror, knowing that death must come, dreading lest the sword should fall. Yet all this is quite unnecessary, and comes only from ignorance, as indeed does all fear; for those who comprehend death feel no dismay at its approach. They know that man does not die, but simply lays aside his body as one lays aside a worn-out suit of clothes; and to them one process is no more terrible than the other. The man who in this twentieth century does not yet know the facts about death, is merely the man who has not taken the pains to look into the matter, and if he suffers from fear of that which does not exist, he has only himself to blame.

1093.   Many are haunted by the apprehension of loss of property, of lapsing into poverty. There are thousands who just manage to live upon such income as they can earn, but they feel that if through sickness or from any other cause supplies should fail them, they would at once be plunged into direct distress. Even when this danger is real, nothing is gained by brooding over it; this ever-present anxiety in no way helps them; they are no whit the safer because this terror hovers over them and darkens all their day.

1094.   These poor souls also should try to understand life, to grasp the purport of this great scheme of evolution of which they find themselves a part; for when once they comprehend a little of its plan they will realise that nothing comes by chance, but that truly all things work together for good, and so pain and trouble and sorrow cannot come unless they are needed, unless they have their part to play in the development that is to be. So they will look forward with hope instead of with fear, knowing that if they loyally do the best they can with each day as it passes, they will have nothing wherewith to reproach themselves, whatever the future may bring forth.

1095.   *Worry* - The same considerations show us the futility of worry and grumbling. If the world be in God's hands, and if we are all working under His immutable laws, manifestly our business is to do our duty in our corner, and to try to move intelligently along with the mighty stream of advancement; but to grumble at the way in which it is working, or to worry as to how matters will turn out, is obviously the height of folly. How often we hear men say: "If it were not for the unfortunate circumstances which surround me, I should be a very fine fellow indeed; I would soon show you what I could do along this line or along that; but, cramped as I am, how can you expect anything from me?"

1096.   Now the man who talks in that way has no conception of the meaning of life. What each man would like best, no doubt, would be a set of circumstances which would give him a chance of using such powers as he already possesses, of showing what he can do. But we must remember that Nature wants to develop us in all directions, not in one only; and to that end we often find ourselves thrown into conditions where we *must* do the very thing that we would say we cannot do, in order that we may learn that lesson and unfold that power, which at present lies latent within us.

1097.   So instead of sitting down and grumbling that we are under the control of adverse circumstances, our business is to get up and control the circumstances for ourselves. The weak man is the slave of his environment; the strong man learns how to dominate it, which is precisely what he is intended to do.

1098.   Then again, see how we worry ourselves about what others think of us, forgetting that what we do is no affair of theirs, so long as it does not interfere with them, and that their opinion is, after all, not of the slightest consequence. Our endeavour must be to do our duty as we see it, and to try to help our fellows whenever occasion presents itself; if your conscience approves your action, no other criticism need trouble you. It is to your Father in Heaven that you are responsible for your deeds, not to Mrs. So-and-so, who is peeping through the blind next door.

1099.   Perhaps the same worthy lady says something spiteful about you, and half-a-dozen kind friends take care to repeat and exaggerate it. If you are foolish you are mightily offended, and a feud is set on foot which may last for months and involve a host of innocent people; and then you actually try to throw the responsibility for all this silly unpleasantness on the shoulders of the neighbour at whose remark you chose to take offence! Use plain common sense for a moment, and just think how ridiculous that is.

1100.   In the first place, in nine cases out of ten, your neighbour didn't say it at all, or didn't mean it in the sense in which you take it, so that you are probably doing her a gross injustice. Even in the tenth case, when she really did say it and meant it, there was most likely some exasperating cause of which you know nothing; she may have been kept awake all night by a toothache or a restless baby! Surely it is neither kind nor dignified to take notice of a hasty word uttered under the influence of irritation. Of course it was quite wrong of her, and she ought to have exhibited the same angelic charity that you yourself always show; I am not defending her in the least; I am only suggesting that because she has done one foolish thing there is no real reason why you should do another.

1101.   After all, what harm has she done you? It is *not* she who is responsible for your annoyance, but your own want of thought. What are her words but a mere vibration of the air? If you had not heard of them you would not have felt offended, and yet *her* part of the action would have been just the same. Therefore, the feeling of anger is *your* fault and not hers; you have unnecessarily allowed yourself to be violently excited by something which in reality is powerless to affect you. It is your own pride which has stirred up your passion, not her idle words. Think, and you will see that this is so. Simple, plain common sense, and nothing more; and yet how few people see clearly enough to take it in that way! And how much unhappiness might be avoided if we only used our brains more and our tongues less!

1102.   These considerations show us that the clouds of unhappiness can be dispelled by knowledge and reason; and it is unquestionably both our interest and our duty instantly and vigorously to set about that dispersion. It is our interest, since when that is done our lives will be longer and more fruitful; "a merry heart goes all the day; a sad one tires in a mile." Make the best of everything, not the worst; watch for the good in the world, and not for the evil. Let your criticism be of that happy kind which pounces upon a pearl as eagerly as the average atrabilious critic flies at a flaw; and you have no idea how much easier and pleasanter your life will become. There is a beauty everywhere in Nature, if we will only look for it; there is always plenty of reason for gladness, if we will but search for it instead of trying to hunt out causes for grumbling.

1103.   It is our duty, for it is thoroughly well established that both happiness and misery are infectious. All who have studied these matters know that these waves of matter, finer than we can see, which are continually radiating from us in every direction, carry with them to those around us our feelings of joy or of sorrow. So if you allow yourself to give way to sadness and despondency, you are actually radiating gloom - darkening God's sunlight for your neighbours, and making your brother's burden heavier for him to bear; and you have no right to do this.

1104.   On the other hand, if you are yourself full of happiness, that radiant joy is poured upon all who come near you, and you become a veritable sun, showering life and light and love in your small circle on the earth, even as the Deity Himself floods them forth through all the universe; and so in your tiny way you are a fellow-worker together with Him.

1105.   PEACE

1106.   Behind the active happiness there must be an abiding peace, and this also we must try to radiate. The lack of peace is one of the most lamentable characteristics of our age. There never was a time when man needed more sorely the sage advice of S. Peter: "Seek peace and ensue it," but the majority know not even in what direction to begin the search, and so they decide that peace is unattainable on earth, and resign themselves to discomfort.

1107.   Man is living simultaneously in three worlds, the physical, the astral or emotional, and the mental, and he has in each of these a body or vehicle through which he expresses himself. At all these levels, in all these vehicles, there should be peace; yet with most of us that is very far from being the case.

1108.   On the physical earth, there is hardly a person who is not complaining of something, who is not frequently ill in some way. One man's digestion is out of order, another has constant headaches, a third finds his nerves breaking down, and so on. In the world of emotion matters are no better, for people are constantly allowing themselves to be shaken and torn by violent feelings, sorrow, anger, jealousy, envy; and so they are quite unnecessarily miserable. Nor are they at peace mentally, for they are perpetually rushing from one line of thought to another, full of worry and hurry, always desiring new things before they have understood or utilised the old. (*good*)

1109.   The causes of this universal unrest are three - ignorance, desire, and selfishness. Therefore, the path to peace consists in conquering these hindrances, and replacing them by their opposites - in gaining knowledge, self-control and unselfishness. Men often think that the causes of their disquiet are exterior to themselves, that sorrow and trouble press upon them from without, not realising that nothing outside can affect them unless they themselves permit it to do so. None but ourselves can ever hurt us or hinder us, just as no one else can make our progress for us. As has been beautifully said in the East, the path lies within us. If we take the trouble to consider it, we shall see that this is so.

1110.   To gain peace we must first gain knowledge - knowledge of the laws under which evolution is working. When we are ignorant of these laws, we are constantly breaking them, constantly pushing aside from the path of the progress of the race in pursuit of some fancied private and personal advantage or pleasure. The steady pressure of the law of evolution forces us back, for our own good, into the path which we have left, we are restless; we struggle against it; we complain of the pain and the trouble as though they had come upon us by mere chance, when all the time it is our own resistance to the guidance of the law that causes us to feel its constraining power.

1111. Our health suffers because we so often live unhealthily; we eat the wrong food, we wear unsuitable clothing, we ignore ventilation and exercise, we pass our lives amidst unsanitary conditions, and then we wonder why our heads ache or why our nerves and digestion fail us. The man who knows the laws of hygiene and takes the trouble to obey them avoids these evils.

1112. Precisely the same is true with regard to the worlds of thought and emotion; these have their natural laws, and to break those laws means suffering. Unfortunately, many people have the idea that all rules relating to these realms of thought and emotion are arbitrary; religious teachers have made the disastrous mistake of talking about the imposition of *punishment* for the breach of them, and so have obscured the plain fact that they are just as much laws of nature as those with which we are familiar in physical life, and that what follows upon any infraction of them is *not* punishment, but merely the natural *result*. If a man seizes a red-hot bar of iron with the naked hand, he will be burnt; but it would not occur to us to describe the burn as a punishment for taking hold of the bar. Yet we often do so describe results which are just as natural and just as inevitable.

1113. Knowledge of the great scheme of evolution and its laws not only shows us how to live so as to earn peace in the future; it also gives us peace here and now in the present, because it enables us to understand the object of life, to see the unity through all its diversity, the glorious final triumph through the mist of apparently hopeless misery and confusion. For when once the scheme is comprehended, its end is no longer a matter of blind faith, but of mathematical certainty; and from that certainty comes peace.

1114. To our knowledge we must add self-control control, not merely of actions and words, but of desires, emotions and thoughts.

1115. For all thoughts and emotions show themselves as waves in the matter of the mental and astral bodies respectively; and in both cases the evil or selfish thoughts are always comparatively slow vibrations of the coarser matter, while the good unselfish thoughts are the more rapid undulations which play only in the finer matter. But a sudden rush of anger or envy or fear overwhelms for a moment the whole of the astral body, and forces it all to swing for that moment at a special rate. This soon calms down, and the body returns to its normal rates of oscillation. But ever after it is a little more ready to respond to the particular rate which expresses that evil passion.

1116. Long ago the great Lord Buddha taught His followers that the life of the ordinary man is full of sorrow, because he attaches himself to earthly things that decay and pass away. He desires wealth and power or position, and he is discontented because he does not gain them, or because, having gained them, he finds them slipping from him. Even to his friends he attaches himself wrongly, for he loves the physical body which must change and fade, instead of the real man who lives on through the ages, and so when his friend lays aside the outer vehicle he mourns him as ` dead' and thinks that he has lost him.

1117.   The whole tendency of our civilisation is to increase desire, to multiply our requirements. Things which were regarded as luxuries by one generation are considered necessities of life by the next, and our desire is ever reaching out in new directions. If we wish for peace; we must learn to limit these desires, to live a simpler life, to be satisfied with comfort without longing for luxury, we must distinguish necessities from superfluities. It is better to decrease our wants and leave ourselves time to rest, rather than to work ourselves to death in the desperate effort to satisfy constantly increasing wants. If we are to have peace, we must certainly control desire.

1118.   Another fertile source of disquiet is the habit that we have of interfering with other people - of perpetually trying to make them see and do things as we see and do them. Many of us seem quite unable to hold a conviction on any subject, social, political or religious, without immediately quarrelling with every one whose convictions happen to be different, and getting up a heated argument about the matter. When we learn ungrudgingly to allow others the same freedom of opinion on every subject that we so unhesitatingly claim for ourselves, when we learn to refrain from criticising them because they differ from us, we shall have advanced far along the path which leads to peace.

1119.   Most of all is it necessary for peace that we should cast aside the personality and acquire unselfishness. So long as we are self-centred, so long as the 'I' is the pivot round which all our universe turns, we insensibly but inevitably expect that it shall be the centre for others as well, and when we find that they are acting without reference to us - without recognising our paramount claims to consideration - we become irritable and self assertive, and peace flies far from us.

1120.   We must realise that we are souls and not bodies; if we identify ourselves (as men usually do) with the physical vehicle, we cannot avoid giving altogether undue importance to what happens to it, and we become, to a large extent, slaves to it and its perpetually changing feelings. It is to avoid such bondage that the Oriental adopts the habit of thought which leads him to substitute for our ordinary phrases: "I am hungry, I am tired," the more exact statement: "My body is hungry, my body is tired."

1121.   It is only one step farther to see that we are equally in error when we say: "I am angry, I am jealous." The true 'I' is the self behind or within all these vehicles, and that self cannot be angry or jealous, though its astral body may; but it is just as much a mistake for a man to identify himself with the astral vehicle as with the physical. He must not be the slave of any of his bodies mental, astral or physical; these three together make up his personality, the temporary and partial expression of him, but they are not he, any more than the clothes are the man.

1122.   These four steps, then, must be taken. We must acquire knowledge by study, and having acquired it, we must put it into practice; we must learn to limit our desires and control our emotions, and we must eliminate the lower personality, and identify ourselves as the self behind. We must substitute altruism for egoism; we must realise the God within us before we can attain "the peace of God which passeth all understanding".

1123.   That is the path to peace. May that peace rest upon us all.

CHAPTER XIX BY WHAT WE THINK

1126. THE REALM OF THOUGHT

1127. A student of occultism trains himself in the art of thinking, and consequently his thought is much more powerful than that of the untrained man, and is likely to influence a wider circle and to produce a much greater effect. This happens quite outside of his own consciousness, without his making any effort in the matter. But precisely because he has learnt the mighty power of thought it becomes his duty to use it for the helping of others. In order to do this effectively he must understand exactly how it acts.

1128. One of the most striking characteristics of the unseen world which lies all about us is the ready response of the finer type of matter of which it is constructed to the influences of human thought and emotion. It is difficult for those who have not studied the subject to grasp the absolute reality of these forces - to understand that their action is in every respect as definite upon the finer type of matter as is that of steam or electricity upon physical matter.

1129. Every one knows that a man who has at his disposal a large amount of steam-power or electrical power can do useful work and produce definite results; but few people know that every man has at his disposal a certain amount of this other and higher power, and that with that he can produce results just as definite and just as real.

1130. As matters stand at present in the physical world, only a few men can have at their disposal any large amount of its forces, and so only a few can become rich by their means; but it is a prominent feature of the vivid interest of the unseen side of life that every human being, rich or poor, old or young, has already at his disposal no inconsiderable proportion of its forces, and therefore the riches of these higher worlds, which are obtained by the right use of these powers, are within the reach of all.

1131. Here, then, is a power possessed by all, but intelligently used as yet by few; it is surely well worth our while to take up the matter, to enquire into it and try to comprehend it. Indeed, there is even more reason for so doing than has yet been mentioned, for the truth is that to some extent we are all already unconsciously making use of this power, and because of our ignorance we are employing it wrongly, and doing harm with it instead of good. The possession of power always means responsibility, so in order to avoid doing harm unintentionally, and in order to utilise thoroughly these magnificent possibilities, it will clearly be well for us to learn all that we can on this subject.

1132. THE EFFECTS OF THOUGHT

1133. What then is thought, and how does it show itself? It is in the mental body that it first manifests itself to the sight of the clairvoyant, and it appears as a vibration of its matter - a vibration which is found to produce various effects, all of them quite in line with what scientific experience in the physical world would lead us to expect.

1134.   There is the effect produced upon the mental body itself, and we find that to be of the nature of setting up a habit. There are many different types of matter in the mental body, and each of them appears to have its own special rate of undulation, to which it seems most accustomed, so that it readily responds to it and tends to return to it as soon as possible when it has been forced away from it by some strong rush of thought or feeling. A sufficiently strong thought may for the moment set all the particles of one division of the mental body swinging at the same rate; and every time that that happens it is a little easier for it to happen again. A habit of moving at that rate is being set up in these particles of the mental body, so that the man will readily repeat that particular thought.

1135.   There is the effect produced upon the other vehicles of the man, which are above and below the mental body in degree of density. We know that physical disturbances in one type of matter are readily communicated to another type - that, for example, an earthquake (which is a movement in solid matter) will produce a mighty wave in the sea (which is liquid matter), and again from the other side that the disturbance of the air (which is gaseous matter) by a storm will immediately produce ripples, and shortly great waves in the ocean beneath it.

1136.   In just the same way, a disturbance in a man's astral body (which we commonly call an emotion) will set up vibrations in the mental body, and cause thoughts which correspond to the emotion. Conversely, the waves in the mental body affect the astral body, if they be of a type which can affect it, which means that certain types of thought readily provoke emotion. Just as the wave in mental matter acts upon the astral substance, which is denser than it is, so also does it inevitably act upon the matter of the casual body, which is finer than it; and thus the habitual thought of the man builds up qualities in the ego himself.

1137.   So far, we have been dealing with the effect of the man's thought upon himself; and we see that in the first place it tends to repeat itself, and that in the second it acts not only upon his emotions, but also permanently upon the man himself. Now let us turn to the effects which it produces outside of himself - that is, upon the sea of mental matter which surrounds us all just as does the atmosphere.

1138.   Every thought produces a radiating undulation, which may be either simple or complex according to the nature of the thought which gives it birth. These vibrations may, under certain conditions, be confined to the mental world, but more frequently they produce an effect in worlds above and below. If the thought be purely intellectual and impersonal - if, for example, the thinker is considering a philosophical system, or attempting to solve a problem in algebra or geometry - the thought-wave will affect merely the mental matter. If the thought be of a spiritual nature, if it be tinged with love or aspiration or with deep unselfish feeling, it will rise upwards into the realm of the higher mental, and may even borrow some of the splendour and glory of the intuitional level - a combination which renders it exceedingly powerful. If on the other hand the thought is tinged with something of self or of personal desire, its oscillations at once draw downwards and expend most of their force in the astral world.

1139.   All these thought-waves act upon their respective levels just as does a wave of light or sound here on the physical. They radiate out in all directions, becoming less powerful in proportion to their distance from their source. The radiation not only affects the sea of mental matter which surrounds us, but also acts upon other mental bodies moving within that sea. We are all familiar with the experiment in which a note struck on a piano or a string sounded on a violin will set the corresponding note sounding upon another instrument of the same kind which has been tuned exactly to the same pitch. Just as the vibration set up in one instrument is conveyed through the air and acts upon the other instrument, so is the thought-vibration set up in one mental body conveyed by the surrounding mental matter and reproduced in another mental body - which, stated from another point of view, means that thought is infectious. We will return to this consideration later.

1140.   Every thought produces not only a wave but a form - a definite, separate object which is endowed with force and vitality of a certain kind, and in many cases behaves not at all unlike a temporary living creature. This form, like the wave, may be in the mental realm only; but much more frequently it descends to the astral level and produces its principal effect in the world of emotions. The study of these thought-forms is of exceeding interest; a detailed account of many of them, with coloured illustrations of their appearance, will be found in the book *Thought-Forms*. At the moment we are concerned less with their appearance than with their effects and with the way in which they can be utilised.

1141.   Let us consider separately the action of these two manifestations of thought-power. The wave may be simple or it may be complex, according to the character of the thought; but its strength is poured out chiefly upon some one of the four levels of mental matter - the four subdivisions which constitute the lower part of the mental world. Most of the thoughts of the ordinary man centre round himself, his desires and his emotions, and they therefore produce waves in the lowest subdivision of the mental matter; indeed, the part of the mental body built of that kind of matter is the only one which is as yet fully evolved and active in the great majority of mankind.

1142.   In this respect the condition of the mental body is quite different from that of the astral vehicle. In the ordinary cultured man of our race the astral body is as fully developed as the physical, and the man is perfectly capable of using it as a vehicle of consciousness. He is not yet much in the habit of so using it, and is consequently shy about it and distrustful of his powers; but the astral powers are there, and it is only a question of becoming accustomed to their use. When he finds himself functioning in the astral world, either during sleep or after death, he is fully capable of sight and hearing, and can move about whithersoever he will.

1143.   In the heaven-world, however, he finds himself under very different conditions, for the mental body is as yet by no means fully developed, that being the part of its evolution upon which the human race is at the present moment engaged. The mental body can be employed as a vehicle only by those who have been specially trained in its use under teachers belonging to the Great Brotherhood of Initiates; in the average man its powers are only partially unfolded, and it cannot be employed as a separate vehicle of consciousness. In the majority of men the higher portions of the mental body are as yet quite dormant, even when the lower portions are in vigorous activity. This necessarily implies that while the whole mental atmosphere is surging with thought-waves belonging to the lowest subdivision, there is as yet comparatively little activity on the higher sub-divisions - a fact which we shall need to have clearly in mind when we come to consider presently the practical possibility of the use of thought-power. It has also an important bearing upon the distance to which a thought-wave may penetrate.

1144.   To help us to understand this, we may take an analogy from the action of the voice of a public speaker. He can make himself heard to a certain distance - a distance which depends upon the power of his voice. In the case of a thought-form that power corresponds to the strength of the vibrations. But the distance to which a speaker can be *understood* is quite another matter, and depends often more upon the clearness of his enunciation than the strength of his voice. That clearness of enunciation is represented in the case of a thought-form by definiteness, clearness of outline.

1145.   Many a man who is not trained in the art of public speaking might send forth a shout which would penetrate to a considerable distance, but would be quite unintelligible. Just in the same way, a man who feels strongly, but is not trained in the art of thinking, may send forth a powerful thought-form which conveys strongly enough the feeling which inspires it - a feeling of joy, of terror or of surprise; and yet it may be so vaguely outlined as to impart no idea of the nature or the cause of the emotion. Evidently, therefore, clearness of thought is at least as necessary as strength of thought.

1146.   Again, the speaker's voice may be clear and strong, and his words may be perfectly audible at the place where an auditor is standing; yet the words convey no meaning to that auditor if he is so preoccupied with some other matter that he is not paying attention. This also has its exact correspondence in the world of thought. One may send out a clear, strong thought, and even aim it definitely at another person, but if that man's mind is entirely preoccupied with his own affairs, the thought-form can produce no impression upon his mental body. Often men in a wild panic do not even hear the advice or orders shouted to them; under the same influence they are equally impervious to thought-forms.

1147.   The majority of mankind do not know how to think at all, and even those who are a little more advanced than that, rarely think definitely and strongly, except during the moments in which they are actually engaged in some piece of business which demands their whole attention. Consequently, large numbers of minds are always lying fallow all about us, ready to receive whatever seed we may sow in them.

1148.   THE THOUGHT-WAVE

1149.   The action of the thought-vibration is eminently adaptable. It may exactly reproduce itself, if it finds a mental body which readily responds to it in every particular; but when this is not the case, it may nevertheless produce a marked effect along lines broadly similar to its own. Suppose, for example, that a Catholic kneels in devotion before an image of the Blessed Virgin. He sends rippling out from him in all directions strong, devotional thought-waves; if they strike upon the mental of astral body of another Catholic, they arouse in him a thought and feeling identical with the original; but if they strike upon a Christian of some other sect, to whom the image of the Blessed Virgin is unfamiliar, they still awaken in him the sentiment of devotion, but that will follow along its accustomed channel, and be directed towards the Christ.

1150.   If they touch a Muhammadan they arouse in him devotion to Allah, while in the case of a Hindu the object may be Krishna, and in the case of a Parsi Ahuramazda. They excite devotion of some sort wherever there is a possibility of response to that idea. If this thought-wave touches the mental body of a materialist, to whom the very idea of devotion in any form is unknown, even there it produces an elevating effect; it cannot at once create a type of undulation to which the man is wholly unaccustomed, but its tendency is to stir a higher part of his mental body into some sort of activity, and the effect, though less permanent than in the case of the sympathetic recipient, cannot fail to be good.

1151.   The action of an evil or impure thought is governed by the same laws. A man who is so foolish as to allow himself to think of another with hatred or envy, radiates a thought-wave tending to provoke similar passions in others, and though his feeling of hatred is for some one quite unknown to these others, and so it is impossible that they should share his feeling, yet the wave will stir in them an emotion of the same nature towards a totally different person.

1152.   THE THOUGHT-FORM

1153.   The work of the thought-form is more limited, but much more precise than that of the wave. It cannot reach so many persons - indeed, it cannot act upon a person at all unless he has in him something which is harmonious with the vibrant energy which ensouls it. The powers and possibilities of these thought-forms will perhaps be clearer to us if we attempt to classify them. Let us consider first the thought which is definitely directed towards another person.

1154.   When a man sends forth from himself a thought of affection or of gratitude (or unfortunately it may be sometimes of envy or jealousy) towards some one else such a thought produces radiating waves precisely as would any other, and therefore tends to reproduce its general character in the minds of those within the sphere of its influence. But the thought-form which it creates is imbued with definite intention, and as soon as it breaks away from the mental and astral bodies of the thinker, it goes straight towards the person to whom it is directed and fastens itself upon him.

1155.   If he happens at the moment to be thinking of nothing in particular, and is consequently in a passive condition, it at once penetrates his mental and astral bodies and is lost in them, just as a comet might fall into the sun. It tends to arouse in them vibrations similar to its own - which means that the man will begin to think upon that particular subject, whatever it may be. If he is in a condition of mental activity, and any part of that activity is of the same nature as the arriving thought-form, it enters his mental body through that part of it which is expressing the sympathetic thought, and adds its strength to that thought. If the recipient's mind is so preoccupied that

219

the thought-form cannot find entrance, it will hover about him until he is sufficiently disengaged to give it an opportunity to gain its object.

1156. In the case of a thought which is not directed to some other person, but is connected chiefly with the thinker himself (as indeed are the majority of men's thoughts) the wave spreads in all directions as usual, but the thought-form floats in the immediate neighbourhood of its creator, and its tendency is constantly to react upon him. As long as his mind is fully occupied with business, or with a thought of some other type, the floating form waits, biding its time; but when his train of thought is exhausted, or his mind for a moment lies fallow, it has an opportunity to react upon him, and it immediately begins to repeat itself - to stir up in him a repetition of the thought to which he has previously yielded himself. Many a man is surrounded by a shell of such thought-forms, and he frequently feels their pressure upon him - a constant suggestion from without of certain thoughts; and if the thought be evil he may believe himself to be tempted by the devil, whereas the truth is that he is his own tempter and that the evil thoughts are entirely his own creation.

1157. There is the class of thought which is neither centred round the thinker nor specially aimed at any person. The thought-form generated in this case does not hang about the thinker, nor has it any special attraction towards another man, so it remains idly floating at the place where it was called into existence. Each man, as he moves through life, is thus producing three classes of thought-forms:

1158. Those which shoot straight out away from him, aiming at a definite objective.

1159. Those which hover round him and follow him wherever he goes.

1160. Those which he leaves behind him as a sort of trail which marks his route.

1161. The whole atmosphere is filled with thoughts of this third type, vague and indeterminate; as we walk along we are picking our way through vast masses of them, and if our minds are not already definitely occupied, these vague, wandering fragments of other people's thoughts often seriously affect us. They sweep through the mind which is lying idle, and probably most of them do not arouse in it any especial interest; but now and then comes one which attracts attention, and the mind fastens upon it, entertains it for a moment or two, and dismisses it a little stronger than it was on arrival.

1162. Naturally this mixture of thoughts from many sources has no definite coherence; though any one of them may start a line of associate ideas, and so set the mind thinking on its own account. If a man pulls himself up suddenly as he walks along the street, and asks himself:

1163. "What am I thinking about, and why? how did I reach this particular point in my train of thought?" and if he tries to follow back the line of his thoughts for the last ten minutes, he will probably be quite surprised to discover how many idle and useless fancies have passed through his mind in that space of time. Not one-fourth of them are his own thoughts; they are simply fragments which he has picked up as he passed along. In most cases they are quite useless, and their general tendency is more likely to be evil than good.

Veronica: what you did earlier + earlier

①

220

1164.   WHAT WE CAN DO BY THOUGHT

1165.   Now that we understand to some extent the action of thought, let us see what use it is possible to make of this knowledge, and what practical considerations emerge from it. Knowing these things, what can we do to forward our own evolution, and what can we do to help others? Obviously, a scientific consideration of the way in which thought works, exhibits it as a matter of far greater importance, not only for our own evolution but also for that of others, than is ordinarily supposed.

1166.   When we look at this question of thought with regard to its effects upon others, we find ourselves brought back again from this different point of view to every one of the considerations which we have already emphasised when speaking of the reaction of this force upon ourselves. This is natural, for what tends to our progress must tend also to that of others. So we must touch these subjects again, though but in passing.

1167.   Since every thought or emotion produces a permanent effect by strengthening or weakening a tendency, and since furthermore every thought-wave and thought-form must not only react upon the thinker, but also influence many other people, the greatest care must be exercised as to the thought or emotion which a man permits within himself. The ordinary man rarely thinks of attempting to check an emotion; when he feels it surging within him he yields himself to it and considers it merely natural. One who studies scientifically the action of these forces realises that it is his interest as well as his duty to check every such upwelling, and consider, before he allows it to sway him, whether it is or is not prejudicial to his evolution and to that of his neighbours.

1168.   Instead of allowing his emotions to run away with him he must have them absolutely under control; and since the stage of evolution at which we have arrived is the development of the mental body, he must take this matter seriously in hand and see what can be done to assist that development. Instead of allowing the mind to indulge in its vagaries he should endeavour to assert control over it, recognising that the mind is not the man, but is an instrument which the man must learn to use. It must not be left to lie fallow; it must not be allowed to remain idle, so that any passing thought-form can drift in upon it and impress it. The first step towards control of the mind is to keep it usefully occupied - to have (as has already been said) some definite, good and useful set of thoughts as a background to the mind's operation - something upon which it shall always fall back when there is no immediate need for its activity in connection with duty to be done.

1169.   Another necessary point in its training is that it shall be taught to do thoroughly that which it has to do - in other words, that the power of concentration shall be acquired. This is no light task, as any unpractised person will find who endeavours to keep his mind absolutely upon one point even for five minutes, He will find that there is an active tendency to wander - that all kinds of other thoughts thrust themselves in; the first effort to fix the mind on one subject for five minutes is likely to resolve itself into spending five minutes in bringing the mind back again and again from various side-issues which it has followed.

1170.   Fortunately, though concentration itself is no easy thing, there are plenty of opportunities for attempting it, and its acquisition is of great use in our daily life. We should learn then, whatever we are doing, to focus our attention upon it and to do it with all our might and as well as it can be done: if we write a letter, let that letter be well and accurately written, and let no carelessness in detail delay it or mar its effect; if we are reading a book, even though it be only a novel, let us read it with attention, trying to grasp the author's meaning, and to gain from it all that there is to be gained. The endeavour to be constantly learning something, to let no day pass without some definite exercise of the mind, is a most salutary one; for it is only by exercise that strength comes, and disuse means always weakness and eventual atrophy.

1171.   It is also of great importance that we should learn to husband our energy. Each man possesses only a certain amount of energy, and he is responsible for its utilisation to the best advantage. The ordinary man wastes his force in the most foolish manner. He is always frittering it away without a shadow of necessity or justification. Sometimes he is full of eager desire for something which is quite unnecessary; or he is full of worry about some fancied evil which he imagines may be impending. At another time he is deeply depressed, but does not know exactly why; but whatever he alleges as the ostensible cause, the fact remains that he is more or less in a condition of excitement and agitation, because he will not take things philosophically, and lay to heart the wise old maxim that, as regards what comes upon us from the outer world, "nothing matters much, and most things don' t matter at all." The thoughts and emotions of an average crowd are like the inhabitants of a disturbed ant-hill, all rushing wildly and aimlessly about in different directions, but causing a vast amount of disorder and tumult; which is precisely why the occultist invariably avoids a crowd, unless duty takes him into it. It is especially necessary for the student of occultism to learn to avoid this dissipation of his energies.

1172.   One way in which the average man wastes a great deal of force is by unnecessary argument. It appears to be impossible for him to hold any opinion, whether it be religious or political, or relating to some matter in ordinary life, without becoming a prey to an overmastering desire to force this opinion upon every one else, He seems quite incapable of grasping the rudimentary fact that what another man chooses to believe is no business of his, and that he is not commissioned by the authorities in charge of the world to go round and secure uniformity in thought and practice.

1173.   The wise man realises that truth is a many-sided thing, not commonly held in its entirely by any one man, or by any one set of men; he knows that there is room for diversity of opinion upon almost any conceivable subject, and that therefore a man whose point of view is opposite to his own may nevertheless have something of reason and truth in his belief. He knows that most of the subjects over which men argue are not in the least worth the trouble of discussion, and that those who speak most loudly and most confidently about them are usually those who know least. The student of occultism will therefore decline to waste his time in argument; if he is asked for information he is willing to give it, but not to waste his time and strength in unprofitable wrangling.

1174.   Another painfully common method of wasting strength is that worry of which I have already written as so serious an obstacle in the path of peace. Many men are constantly forecasting evil for themselves and for those whom they love - troubling themselves with the fear of death and of what comes after it, with the fear of financial ruin or loss of social position. A vast amount of strength is frittered away along these unprofitable and unpleasant lines; but all such foolishness is swept aside for the man who realises that the world is governed by a law of absolute justice, that progress towards the highest is the Divine Will for him, that he cannot escape from that progress, that whatever comes in his way and whatever happens to him is meant to help him along that line, and that he himself is the only person who can delay that advance. He no longer troubles and fears about himself and about others; he simply goes on and does the duty that comes nearest in the best way that he can, confident that if he does that, all will be well for him. He knows that worry never yet helped any one, nor has it ever been of the slightest use, but that it has been responsible for an immense amount of evil and waste of force; and the wise man declines to spend his strength in ill-directed emotion.

1175.   So we see that if it is necessary for his own evolution that man should keep mind and emotion under control, and not foolishly waste his force, it is still more necessary from another point of view, because it is only by such care that he can enable himself to be of use to his fellow men, that he can avoid doing harm to them and can learn how to do good. If, for example, he lets himself feel angry, he naturally produces a grave effect upon himself, because he sets up an evil habit and makes it more difficult to resist the evil impulse next time it assails him. But he also acts seriously upon others around him, for inevitably the vibrations which radiate from him must affect them also.

1176.   If he is making an effort to control his irritability, so perhaps are they, and his action will help or hinder them, even though he is not in the least thinking of them. Every time that he allows himself to send out a wave of anger, that tends to arouse a similar vibration in the mind or astral body of another - to arouse it if it has not previously existed and to intensify it if it is already present; and thus he makes his brother's work of self-development harder for him, and places a heavier burden upon his shoulders. On the other hand, if he controls and represses the wave of anger, he radiates instead, calming and soothing influences which are distinctly helpful to all those near him who are engaged in the same struggle.

1177.   Few people realise their responsibilities in this matter. It is bad enough surely that any evil thought of ours should communicate itself to the minds of any persons within range of us who may happen to be idle and unoccupied. But the truth is much worse than that. In every man there lie germs or possibilities of evil which have come over from a previous life, but have not as yet been called into activity in this incarnation. If we send out an evil or impure thought, it may easily happen that it arouses into activity one of these germs, and so through our lack of self-control there comes into that man's life an evil of which otherwise he might have got rid. We revive in him the dormant tendency which was in the act of dying out, and thereby we delay him in his upward progress.

1178.   So long as that germ is dormant the quality is dying out, but when it is aroused again it may increase to any extent. It is like breaking a hole through a dyke and letting out the water. In fact, a man who sends out an evil thought cannot tell for what amount of evil he may make himself responsible; for a man who becomes wicked, in consequence of that thought, may in turn affect other people, and those yet others in turn; so it is actually true that because of one evil thought generations yet to come may suffer. Happily all this is true of good thoughts as well as of evil, and the man who understands this fact uses wisely the power which it gives him, and may have an influence for good which is beyond all calculation.

1179.   THE RESPONSIBILITY OF THOUGHT

1180.   Possessing this tremendous power, we must be careful how we exercise it. We must remember to think of a person as we wish him to be, for the image that we thus make of him will naturally act powerfully upon him, and tend to draw him gradually into harmony with itself. Let us fix our thoughts upon the good qualities of our friends, because in thinking of any quality we tend to strengthen its vibrations, and therefore to intensify it.

1181.   From this consideration it follows that the habit of gossip and scandal, in which many people thoughtlessly indulge themselves; is in reality heinous wickedness, in condemning which no expression can be too strong. When people are guilty of the impertinence of discussing others, it is not usually upon the good qualities that they most insist. We have therefore a number of people fixing their thought upon some alleged evil in another, and calling to that evil the attention of others who might perhaps not have observed it; and in this way, if that bad quality really exists in the person whom they are so improperly criticising, they distinctly increase it by strengthening the undulation which is its expression. If, as is usually the case, the depravity exists only in their own prurient imagination, and is not present in the person about whom they are gossiping, then they are doing the utmost in their power to create that evil quality in that person, and if there be any latent germ of it existing in their victim, their nefarious effect is only too likely to be successful.

1182.   We may think helpfully of those whom we love; we may hold before them in thought a high ideal of themselves, and wish strongly that they may presently be enabled to attain it; but if we know of certain defects or vices in a man's character, we should never under any circumstances let our thoughts dwell upon them and intensify them; our plan should be to formulate a strong thought of the contrary virtues, and then send out waves of that thought to the man who needs our help. The ordinary method is for one to say to another.

1183.   "O my dear, what a terrible thing it is that Mrs. So-and-So is so ill-tempered! Why, do you know, only yesterday she did this and that, and I have heard that she constantly, etc., etc. Isn't it a terrible thing?"

1184.   And this is repeated by each person to her thirty or forty dearest friends, and in a few hours several hundred people are pouring converging streams of thought, all about anger and irritability, upon the unfortunate victim. Is it any wonder that she presently justifies their expectations, and gives them yet another example of ill-temper over which they can gloat?

1185.   A person wishing to help in such a case will be especially careful to avoid thinking about anger at all, but instead will think with force:

1186.   "I wish Mrs. So-and-So were calm and serene; she has the possibility of such self-control within her; let me try frequently to send her strong, calm, soothing thought-waves, such as will help her to realise the Divine possibility within her."

1187.   In the one case the thought is of anger; in the other it is of serenity; in both alike it will inevitably find its goal, and tend to reproduce itself in the mental and astral bodies of the recipient of the thought. By all means let us think frequently and lovingly of our friends, but let us think of their good points only, and try, by concentrating our attention upon those, to strengthen them and to help our friends by their means.

1188.   A man often says that he cannot control his thoughts or his passions - that he has often tried to do so, but has consistently failed, and has therefore come to the conclusion that such effort is useless. This idea is wholly unscientific. If an evil quality or habit possesses a certain amount of strength within us, it is because in previous lives we have allowed that strength to accumulate - because we have not resisted it in the beginning when it could easily have been repressed, but have permitted it to gather the momentum which makes it difficult now to deal with it.

1189.   We have, in fact, made it easy for ourselves to move along a certain line, and correspondingly difficult to move along another line - difficult, but not impossible. The amount of momentum or energy accumulated is necessarily a finite amount; even if we have devoted several lives entirely to storing up such energy (an unlikely supposition), still the time so occupied has been a limited time, and the results are necessarily finite.

1190.   If we have now realised the mistake we made, and are setting ourselves to control that habit and to neutralise that impetus, we shall find it necessary to put forth exactly as much strength in the opposite direction as we originally spent in setting up that momentum. Naturally we cannot instantly produce sufficient force entirely to counteract the work of many years, but every effort which we make will reduce the amount of force stored up. We ourselves as living souls can go on generating force indefinitely; we have an infinite store of strength on which to draw, and therefore it is absolutely certain that if we persevere we must eventually succeed. However often we may fail, each time something is withdrawn from that finite store of force, and it will be exhausted before we shall, so that our eventual success is simply a matter of mechanics.

1191.   The knowledge of the use of these thought-currents makes it possible for us always to give assistance when we know of some case of sorrow or suffering. It often happens that we are unable to do anything for the sufferer physically; our bodily presence may not be helpful to him; his physical brain may be closed to our suggestions by prejudice or by religious bigotry. But his astral and mental bodies are far more easily impressible than the physical, and it is always open to us to approach these by a wave of helpful thought or of affection and soothing feeling.

1192.   The law of cause and effect holds good just as certainly in finer matter as in denser, and consequently the energy which we pour forth must reach its goal and must produce it effect. There can be no question that the image or the idea which we wish to put before the man for his comfort or his help will reach him; whether it will present itself clearly to his mind when it arrives depends, first upon the definiteness of outline which we have been able to give to it, and secondly upon his mental condition at the time. He may be so fully occupied with thoughts of his own trials and sufferings that there is little room for our idea to insert itself; but in that case our thought-form simply bides its time, and when at last his attention is diverted, or exhaustion forces him to suspend the activity of his own train of thought, ours will at once slip in and do its errand of mercy. There are so many cases where the best will in the world can do nothing physically; but there is no conceivable case in which either in the mental or the astral world some relief cannot be given by steady, concentrated, loving thought.

1193.   The phenomena of mind-cure show how powerful thought may be even in the physical world, and since it acts so much more easily in astral and mental matter we may realise vividly how tremendous the power really is, if we will but exercise it. We should watch for every opportunity of being thus helpful; there is little doubt that plenty of cases will offer themselves. As we walk along the street, as we ride in a tram-car or railway train, we often see some one who is obviously suffering from depression or sadness; there is our opportunity, and we may immediately take advantage of it by trying to arouse and to help him.

1194.   Let us try to send him strongly the feeling that, in spite of his personal sorrows and troubles, the sun still shines above all, and there is still much for which to be thankful, much that is good and beautiful in the world. Sometimes we may see the instant effect of our effort - we may actually watch the man brighten up under the influence of the thought which we have sent to him. We cannot always expect such immediate physical result; but if we understand the laws of nature we shall in every case be equally sure that some result is being produced.

1195.   It is often difficult for the man who is unaccustomed to these studies to believe that he is really affecting those at whom his thought is aimed; but experience in a great number of cases has shown us that anyone who makes a practice of such efforts will in time find evidence of his success accumulating until it is no longer possible for him to doubt. The man should make it part of his life thus to try to help all whom he knows and loves, whether they be living or what is commonly called dead; for naturally the possession or the absence of the physical body makes no difference whatever to the action of forces which are levelled at the mental and astral bodies. By steady, regular practice of this sort great good will be done, for we gain strength by practice, and so, while we are developing our own powers and insuring our progress, the world will be helped by our kindly efforts.

1196.   Thus whatever is truly for our own interest is also for the interest of the world, and what is not good for the world can never in reality be for our interest either.

For all true gain is gained for all. To many a man this may appear a strange statement, because we are accustomed to think that what one man gains another loses; yet it enshrines a great truth. Elsewhere I have shown that if one party to a transaction is unfairly treated, and therefore loses, there is no true gain for the other.

1197.   A straightforward, honest piece of business means gain for both parties. A tradesman, let us suppose, buys his goods wholesale, and then, taking care to say of them only what is strictly true, disposes of them by retail at a reasonable profit. Here all parties gain, for the wholesale merchant and the tradesman make their living, while the purchasers are willing to pay the retail price in order to have the convenience of buying in small quantities. Each person gains what he wishes; no one loses; all are satisfied.

1198.   This is merely a superficial example from the physical world; it is in the higher realms of thought that we may see most clearly how beautifully this rule works. Suppose that a man gains knowledge. He may impart his gain to a hundred others, yet he himself will have lost nothing. Not only so, but even others, to whom he does not impart it, will gain indirectly from his possession of it. Because he has this added knowledge, he is by so much a wiser and more useful man; his words should be the more weighty, his actions the more sagacious, and so others around him should be the better for his learning.

1199.   We may go deeper still. Since the man knows more, not only his words and action but his thoughts will be wiser than before. His thought-forms will be better, the waves flowing from his mental body higher and richer; and these must inevitably produce their result upon the mental bodies of others around him. Like all other waves in nature they tend to reproduce themselves, to provoke a similar rate of undulation in anything with which they come into contact. The same natural law, by the action of which in the physical world you are able to boil the water for your tea or to toast your bread at the fire, makes it absolutely certain that the good effects of additional wisdom will influence others, even though the possessor speaks never a word.

1200.   That is why in all religions so much importance is attached to the company of the good, the wise, the pure. Human qualities are infectious, and it is of the greatest moment that we should be careful to which of them we subject ourselves.

1201.   Take another instance. Suppose that you gain the valuable power of self-control. Perhaps you were formerly a passionate man, and now you have learnt to check that outpouring of force, and to hold it in subjection. Let us see how that affects others about you. In the physical world it is unquestionably pleasanter for them, but them, but let us consider the effect on their finer vehicles. VLADILA

1202.   When in earlier days you allowed yourself to get into a rage, great waves of strong wrath poured out from you in all directions. No one who has seen the illustration of such an outrush as that which appears in *Man Visible and Invisible* , will need to be told what disastrous effects such waves must have produced upon the astral bodies of those who were so unfortunate as to be near you. Perhaps one of those men was himself struggling the same evil habit. If so, the emanations of your fury stirred up similar activity in his astral body, and so you strengthened that evil, you made your brother's task harder, and his burden heavier to bear than it otherwise would have been. And once more I must insist that you have no right to do that.

1203.   But now that you have gained self-control, all this is most happily changed. Still you radiate vibrations, for that is Nature's law, but now they are no longer the lurid flashes of anger, but the calm, measured sweep of the strong waves of love and peace. And these also impinge upon the astral body of your fellow man, and tend to reproduce themselves in him; and if he is fighting a battle against passion, their stately rhythm helps him and steadies him. Your force is being exerted on his side instead of against him, and so you lighten his burden, you aid him on his upward path. Is it not true then that in your gain he has gained also?

1204.   Men are so inextricably linked together, humanity is so truly a unity amidst all its marvellous diversity, that no one can advance or recede without helping or hindering the progress of others. Wherefore it behoves us to take heed that we are among the helpers and not among the hinderers, and that no living being, whether man or animal, shall ever be the worse for any thought or word or deed of ours.

CHAPTER XX BY WHAT WE DO

1207. WORK FOR THE POOR

1208.   The question of what we can do, is one which it is impossible to treat fully, for the reason that each person has his own opportunities, and no two sets of opportunities are alike. We are often asked whether a Theosophist should undertake any of the ordinary charitable lines of work, which are not specially connected with the Theosophical Society. This is a question which each must answer for himself, because the answer to it depends on his special circumstances. I think that it may be laid down as a general rule that when there is specially Theosophical work that he can do, he should devote his time to that, because that is a kind of business that only he can do, whereas many other people can do the ordinary charitable labour as well as he.

1209.   Take for example a case of what is called slum work, the direct help of the poor by visiting them and carrying to them various small comforts. None can deny that this is a most excellent thing to do, and that it sadly needs doing; but if one is to choose between spending a certain time in this distinctly physical occupation and doing something in a higher world which will tend to bring nearer the time when slums shall no longer exist, then I say that the latter is the greater work to do and the better way of employing the time, for only one who has studied Theosophy can help to spread the Theosophical teaching, whereas any good and kind-hearted person, of whatever class, can undertake the task of carrying food and blankets to the poor.

1210.   It is good work, surely, to help to make a road, but we should not put to that task of road-making a man who has qualified himself as an engineer or a doctor. Any man who has a talent in a certain direction or has the knowledge necessary to enable him to work in a particular way, should be employed along his special line, for there are only a few who can do that, whereas anyone can do the unskilled labour of the world, and there are vast numbers who can do only that. Therefore it seems to me that when a Theosophist can employ his time in spreading and teaching Theosophy, he should not put this aside in order to take up a more ordinary kind of work for the world. But if he is so situated that he cannot do anything for the Theosophical propaganda which is his speciality, he ought certainly then to employ his spare time in the highest type of charitable labour within his reach.

1211.   What is required is that he should cultivate a spirit of benevolence, that he should be eagerly watching all day long for opportunities of being helpful. Best of course if he can be useful in the highest way, is guiding people towards Theosophy, but when that is not for the moment possible, he should be helpful in a more ordinary manner. He should employ himself in sending out benevolent thoughts, or in making people happy in the physical world. He should import the idea of helpfulness into every little daily action. Each man must decide for himself how he can best do this, and his study of the hidden side of things will offer him many suggestions; for it makes daily life much more interesting, and enables us much more useful than we could be without it.

1212.   It shows us that many apparently trivial actions reach further than we think, and therefore impresses strongly upon us the necessity for living carefully and recollectedly. It shows a man that every action has its effect upon those around him, even when it seems on the surface to concern himself alone; that for this effect on others he is responsible, and that it offers him a welcome opportunity for doing good. When this is once grasped, he realises that he must order his life from this new point of view - that it must be spent, even in small things, not for himself, but for others. Many a man lives for others in the sense that he regulates his life on what he imagines others are thinking about him; but our student's altruism will be of another sort. He will put before himself for his guidance two stringent rules:

1213.   That everything shall be done unselfishly.

1214.   That everything shall be done with definite purpose, and as perfectly as he can do it.

1215.   THE FORCE OF THE MASTER

1216.   If he does this, if he lives in this way, the Powers who rule the world will soon recognise him and use him, for by living thus he makes himself a ready channel for the power of the Master, a valuable instrument in His hands. Truly, the help of the Holy Ones is given chiefly upon higher planes; but it is not confined to them; it acts in the physical world as well, if we give it the opportunity. The Master will not waste His strength in *forcing* a stream of His energy down into the dense matter of this lower world, because to do that would not be good spiritual economics; it would not be utilising that amount of energy to the best advantage. But if a man already living in our lower world so arranges his life as to make himself a fit channel for that energy, the position is altered, and it becomes worth the Master's while to make an effort which would not otherwise have been remunerative.

1217.   We have to remember that a channel must be open at both ends, not at one end only. The higher end of our channel consists in the devotion and unselfishness of the man, in the very fact that he is anxious to be used, and is ordering his life for that purpose. The lower end is the man's physical body, through which the influence must pass out, and this also needs careful attention, in order that it may not befoul the stream which the Master sends.

1218.   Remember that we are dealing with no vague abstraction, but with a physical though invisible fluid, which permeates the matter of the body and exudes through the pores of the skin, or is projected from the hands or feet. Therefore that body must be pure inside, uncontaminated by flesh-foods, alcohol or tobacco; and it must also be kept scrupulously clean outside by frequent and thorough ablutions, especial attention being paid to the hands and feet. Otherwise the fluid, transmuted with so much care from higher planes, will be polluted as it passes through man, and will fail to achieve the object for which it was sent.

1219.   Although this force radiates from the worthy student at all times, he can also gather it up and pour it out with definite intention upon a particular object. In a previous chapter it was explained how the ordinary man can protect himself from evil influence when shaking hands, or when surrounded by a crowd; but the student, instead of protecting himself, will make out of these unpleasing occurrences opportunities to act upon others. When he shakes hands with a man, he will send the Master's power rushing through his extended arm. The beginner may ask: "How can I do that? And even if I try, how can I be certain that I have succeeded ?"

1220.   All that is needed here is a firm conviction and an intense resolve - a conviction, based upon his study, that this is a thing that can be done, and the intense resolve to do it, which comes from his deep devotion to the Master and his earnest desire to do His will. Success in all magical efforts depends upon the absolute confidence of the operator; a man who doubts his own capacity has already failed. So that all that is necessary is that he should mingle with the hearty welcome which he extends to his visitor the strong thought: "I give you herewith the love of the Master." In the same way, when he finds himself in a crowd, he will spread among the people that same influence of the Master's love; and that outpouring will be for him a far better protection than any shell.

1221.   THE MANUFACTURE OF TALISMANS

1222.   Another use which can be made of this force is to charge certain objects with it, thereby converting them into talismans. I have written before of the effects producible by such charms; I speak now of the process of their manufacture. The more advanced branches of this art require definite knowledge, obtainable only by an extended course of study; but any earnest man can make a temporary talisman which will be of great use to one who needs help.

1223.   One who is accustomed to the work can perform any ordinary process of magnetisation or demagnetisation practically instantaneously by the mere exertion of his will; but the beginner usually finds it necessary to help himself in the concentration of his will by thinking carefully of the various stages of the process and using the appropriate gestures. Suppose, for example, that it is desirable to magnetise some small body (such as a ring, a locket, a penholder) in order to make it an amulet against fear; what is the easiest method of procedure?

1224.   Realise first exactly what is wanted. We wish to load that body with etheric, astral and mental matter heavily charged with a particular set of undulations - those of courage and confidence. The trained occultist would gather together each of those levels such types of matter as will most easily receive and retain vibrations of just that character; the beginner, knowing nothing, of that, must use whatever material comes to hand and so will have to expend a greater amount of force than would be exerted by his more experienced brother.

1225.   The making of an amulet may be likened to the writing of an inscription, and the acquisition of the right kind of matter corresponds to obtaining a perfect surface on which to write. The beginner, who cannot do this must write with greater labour and less perfection of result upon the surface that happens to be available. The first difficulty that confronts him is that his sheet is not even a blank one; his paper already bears an inscription, which must be removed before he can use it. If, the ring or locket has been worn by anyone, it is already full of the magnetism of that person - magnetism which may be better or may be worse than that of the student, but is at any rate different from it, and so is an obstacle - just as any kind of writing, however good, which already fills a sheet of paper, stands in the way of its use for further writing. Even if the ring or pen-holder be quite new, it is likely to contain something of the special magnetism either of the maker or of the seller; so in any case the first thing is to remove whatever may be there - to obtain a clear sheet for our inscription. There are various methods by which this may be done; let me describe a simple one.

1226.　Rest the tip of the forefinger of the right hand against the end of the thumb, so as to make a ring, and imagine a film of ether stretched across that ring like the head of a drum. *Will* strongly that such a film should be made, and remember that that very effort of the will *does* make it, although you cannot see it. Remember also that it is essential to the success of the experiment that you should be quite certain of this fact - that your previous study should have convinced you that the human will has the power to arrange subtle matter in this or any other way.

1227.　Then, keeping your attention firmly fixed upon that film, so as to hold it quite rigid, pass slowly through it the object to be demagnetised, and by so doing you will cleanse it entirely of the etheric part of its previous magnetism. I do not mean that you will leave it without etheric matter, but that every particle of such matter will be swept out and replaced; just as, if a tube is filled with gas and one blows strongly into one end of it, all the gas is driven out; but the tube is not therefore empty, as the pressure of the surrounding air immediately refills it. So the specially charged ether is dredged out of the locket or pen-holder, and its place is taken by the ordinary ether which interpenetrates the surrounding atmosphere.

1228.　The next step is to let the etheric film dissolve, and replace it by one of astral matter, through which the object is again passed. The process may be repeated with a film of mental matter, and we shall then have the object entirely free on all three planes from any sort of specialised magnetism - a clean sheet, in fact, upon which we can write what we will. After a certain amount of practice the student can make a combined film containing etheric, astral and mental matter, so as to perform the whole operation by passing the object once through the ring.

1229.　The operator must then exercise all his strength to fill himself with the qualities which he wishes the amulet to convey (in this case fearlessness and self-reliance), excluding for the moment all thought of other attributes and becoming the living incarnation of these. Then, when he has thus wound himself up to his highest level of enthusiasm, let him take the object in his left hand, or lay it on the table in front of him, and pour magnetism on it through the fingers of his right hand, all the time willing with his utmost strength that it shall be filled with the very essence of valour, calmness and intrepidity.

1230.　It will probably help him in concentration if, while doing this, he repeats to himself firmly again and again such words as: "Courage, confidence, in the Name of the Master," "Where this object is, may no fear enter," or any others expressing a similar idea. Let him do this for a few minutes, never allowing his attention to swerve for a

+ Hoffmann

moment, and he need have no shade of doubt that he has made a really effective talisman.

1231. This process will probably occupy the tyro for some time, but a man who is accustomed to it does it quickly and easily. The trained occultist makes constant use of this power as a means of helping those with whom he comes into contact; he never despatches a letter, or even a postcard, without thinking what good gift of refreshing, consoling or strengthening magnetism he can send with it. He has at his command many other ways of making a talisman besides that which I have described; perhaps it may help towards a fuller comprehension of the subject if I enumerate some of them, even though they are quite beyond the reach of the ordinary student.

1232. VARIETIES OF TALISMANS

1233. Amulets are of all sorts and kinds - literally many thousands of kinds - but they may be arranged for our purposes into four classes, which we will call respectively general, adapted, ensouled and linked.

1234. 1. *General.* The method which I have suggested above produces a talisman of this description. The trained man naturally obtains with less labour a better result, not only because he knows how to use his will effectively, but because he has learnt to select the most suitable materials; consequently the influence of his amulet is stronger, and lasts for many years instead of perhaps for a few months. This form of talisman is quite simple; its business is to pour out a steady stream of undulations expressing the quality with which it is charged, and it will continue to do this with undiminished vigour for a period the length of which depends upon the force originally put into it.

1235. 2. *Adapted.* The adapted amulet is one that has been carefully prepared to fit a particular person. Its maker studies the man for whom it is intended, and notes carefully the deficiencies in his mental, astral and etheric bodies. Then he culls from the matter of the various planes the ingredients of his talisman, just as a physician selects the drugs to compound into a prescription, choosing a certain type of essence in order to repress an undesirable astral tendency, another in order to stimulate the sluggish action of some defective department of mental activity, and so on. Thus he produces an amulet accurately adapted to the needs of a particular person, and capable of doing for that person enormously more than a general talisman can do; but it would be of little use to anyone else but the man for whom it is intended. It is like a skillfully-made key with many wards, which exactly fits its lock, but will not open any other; while a general talisman may be compared to a skeleton key, which will open many inferior locks, but does not perfectly suit any.

1236. 3. *Ensouled.* Sometimes it is desired to establish a centre of radiation which, instead of acting for a few score years at most, shall continue its outpouring through the centuries. In this case it is not enough to charge the selected object with a dose of magnetic force - for, however large that dose may be, it must some time be exhausted; to produce this more permanent result we must bring into play some form of life; and for this purpose one of two methods is usually adopted.

1237. The first is to include in the physical charm a minute fragment of one of those higher minerals which are sufficiently alive to throw out a ceaseless stream of

233

particles. When that is done, the store of force poured into the amulet will last almost indefinitely longer, for instead of radiating steadily in all directions on its own account, it remains self-contained, and charges only the particles which pass through it. The work of distribution is thus done by the mineral, and a vast economy of energy is thereby secured.

1238.   The second plan is so to arrange the ingredients of the talisman as to make it a means of manifestation for any one of certain comparatively undeveloped orders of nature-spirits. There are tribes of these creatures which, though full of energy and strongly desirous to do something with it, cannot express themselves unless they can find some sort of outlet. It is possible so to magnetise an amulet as to make it precisely the kind of outlet required, and thus to ensure the steady outflow through it of a stream of energy at high pressure, which may last for thousands of years, to the intense delight of the nature-spirits and the great benefit of all who approach the magnetised centre.

1239.   4. *Linked.* The linked talisman differs completely from the other kinds in one important particular. All those previously described are made and set going by their creators, and then left to run their course and live their life, just as a clockmaker constructs a timepiece and then sells it to a customer and knows no more about it. But the clockmaker sometimes chooses to remain in touch with his masterpiece, and undertakes to keep it wound and in order; and this corresponds to the arrangement made in the case of a linked talisman. Instead of merely loading the object with influence of a certain type, the operator when he magnetises it brings it into close *rapport* with himself, so that it may become a kind of outpost of his consciousness, a sort of telephone-receiver always connected with him, through which he can reach the holder or be reached by him.

1240.   An amulet of this type does not work mechanically upon the gyroscope principle, as the others do; or perhaps I should rather say it has a slight action of that sort, because it so strongly suggests the presence of it creator that it often acts as a deterrent, preventing the wearer from doing what he would not like the maker to see him do; but its principal action is of quite another kind. It makes a link through which the wearer can at a critical moment send a cry for help to its builder, who will instantly feel the appeal and respond by an outpouring of strength of whatever type may be required.

1241.   Its manufacturer can also use it as a channel through which he can send periodic waves of influence, and so administer a course of treatment - a kind of emotional or mental massage. Such a method of handling a case (I believe our Christian Science friends call it "absent treatment") may be undertaken without an amulet, merely by projecting astral and mental currents; but a talisman makes the work easier, and enables the operator to deal more readily with the etheric double of the subject.

1242.   Usually the link is made only in the physical, astral and lower mental worlds, and is therefore confined to the personality of its constructor; but there are instances when a Great One has chosen to link a physical talisman to Himself in His causal body, and then its influence lasts through the ages. This was done in the case of the physical objects buried at various points of future importance by Apollonius of Tyana.

1243.   DEMAGNETISATION

1244.   It not infrequently occurs that it is desirable to demagnetise objects which are larger than those instanced above. In such cases one may hold the two hands at the requisite distance apart, and imagine a broad band of etheric matter extending between them, with which the previous magnetism can be dredged out as before. Another plan is to hold the two hands one on each side of the object, and send a strong stream of etheric matter through it from one hand to the other, thus washing away the undesired influence. The same force can often be employed in the same way to relieve pain. A headache, for example, is usually either caused or accompanied by a congestion of etheric matter in the brain, and it can often be cured by that same plan of putting the hands one on each side of the sufferer's temples and washing away the congested matter by an effort of the will.

1245.   Another use to which the power of demagnetisation can be put is to clear objectionable influences out of a room. One may have a visitor who leaves an unpleasant atmosphere behind him; or one may find uncomfortable astral conditions prevailing in one's apartment at a hotel; and if such an emergency arises, it is useful to know how to deal with it. One practised in these mild forms of magic would manage the business in a few moments by the exercise of his trained will; but the younger student will probably find it better to employ intermediate means, precisely as the Catholic Church does.

1246.   The cubic content of even a small room is too great for the employment of the dredging tactics previously recommended, so we must invoke the great principle of sympathy and antipathy, and set up within the room a series of vibrations so hostile to the evil influence that the latter is dominated or driven forth. To create such an undulation is not difficult; but means must be found for spreading it rapidly all over the room. One ready method is the burning of incense or pastilles; another is sprinkling of water; but both incense and water must first be passed through the process recommended for the making of a talisman. Their original magnetism must be removed, and they must be loaded with the thought of purity and peace. If that be thoroughly done, when the incense is burned, its particles (each bearing the desired influence) will quickly be disseminated through every cubic inch of air in the room; or if water be used and sprinkled about the chamber, each drop of it will at once become a centre of active radiation. A vaporiser is an even more effective method of distribution; and if rose-water be used instead of ordinary water, the work of the student will be considerably facilitated.

1247.   The method of action of these etheric or astral disinfectants is obvious. The disturbing influence of which we desire to rid ourselves expresses itself in etheric and astral waves of a certain length. Our magnetic efforts fill the room with another set of waves, different in length and more powerful, because they have been intentionally set swinging, which probably the others were not. The two sets of inharmonious vibrations cannot co-exist, and so the stronger overpowers and extinguishes the weaker.

1248.   These are some of the ways in which the force that dwells within man, the

235

force that flows through man, may be used. In this case, as in every other, knowledge is power, in this case, as in every other, additional power means additional responsibility and additional opportunity. If you can readily develop this power, if you can do these things quickly and easily, so much the better for you, so long as you use this advantage unselfishly, and make the world by its means a little happier, a little better, a little cleaner as the result of your efforts.

1249. DO LITTLE THINGS WELL

1250. Remember the second maxim - that everything shall be done as perfectly as we can do it. Charge your letter with magnetism and make a talisman of it, by all means; you will do great good thereby; but do not forget that the mere physical handwriting must be perfect also - first, out of courtesy to the recipient, and secondly, because all work done for the Master must be done with the utmost care, even to the minutest detail. And as *all* our work is work for Him, executed in His name and to His glory, that means that nothing must ever be done carelessly. In this, too, unselfishness may be applied; no one has the right to cause trouble to another by illegible handwriting - to save a few moments of his own time by wasting many minutes of another's.

1251. We must not think that because we know more of the hidden side of things than others, and so are able to add unexpected blessings to daily acts, we are thereby absolved from doing the ordinary part of those acts to the very best of our ability. Not worse but better than that of others must our work be, in every respect and from every point of view, for the honour of the Master whom we serve. *What* the work is that He gives us, matters little; that it should be nobly done matters supremely. And the man who, all his life through, does the small, daily details well and carefully, will not be found wanting when some day he suddenly finds himself face to face with a great opportunity.

1252. The little things in life weigh more than the big things; there are so many of them, and it is so much more difficult to go on steadily doing them. Saint Augustine remarked: "Many there be who will die for Christ, but few there be who will live for Him." Many of us would instantly and gladly do some great thing for the Master; but He does not commonly ask for that. He asks us to live our daily life nobly, not for ourselves but for others; to forget ourselves, only to remember the good of mankind. Let us then form the habit of helpfulness - for it soon becomes a habit, like everything else. It certainly makes life more interesting; and, above all, it brings us every day nearer to Him.

1253. WRITING A LETTER

1254. I mentioned some pages back that an occultist never despatches a letter without putting into it something of strength and encouragement; but it does not need person of a great advancement to perform so elementary an act of magic as this. Anyone may do it with a little trouble, when be understands how these forces work.

1255. We all know that when a psychometrist takes a letter into his hand he can describe the personal appearance of the writer, the condition of his mind at the time of writing, the room in which he was sitting, any other people who happened to be present, and even the surrounding scenery.

1256.   It is manifest, therefore, that a letter brings with it much more than the message written in it, and though only one who is developed as a psychometrist may be able to sense this with sufficient clearness to reduce it to actual vision, yet an effect of some sort must obviously be produced even upon those who do not fully see. The vibrations upon which the psychometrist's observations are founded are there, whether there is or is not anyone present who can see by their means, and they must affect to some extent anyone with whom they come directly into contact. This being so, we see that here is an opportunity for the person who understands. The student can learn the operation of these forces, and can then direct them intelligently as he will.

1257.   Suppose, for example, he wishes to write a letter of condolence and consolation to some friend who has, as we mistakenly phrase it, ` lost'some one near and dear to him. We all know the difficulty of writing such a letter. In attempting it we put upon the paper whatever of solace comes into our minds, and we try to express it as forcefully and sympathetically as we can, yet we are conscious all the while that words are impotent in such a case, and that they can bring but poor comfort to the bereaved one. We feel the futility and inefficiency of our communication, though we send it because we wish to express our commiseration, and we know that we ought to do something.

1258.   Such a letter need not be fruitless and unavailing. On the contrary it may produce the most beneficent effect, and may lead to great alleviation of suffering. Words often fail us, but our thoughts do not; and in the writing of such a letter a man's heart may be filled with the strong wish to bring encouragement and help, however poorly the written lines may express it. If he exercises his will he may make that letter bear with it his thought and feeling, so that they shall react upon the mind and emotions of the recipient, while his eyes are perusing the manuscript.

1259.   We know that currents of thought and feeling can be sent to the mourner immediately and without the physical agency of a letter, and one who has no other pressing work could undoubtedly console and strengthen the sufferer by pouring upon him a steady stream of such thought and feeling. The writing of the letter by no means precludes the student from offering efficient help in that other way as well; but it usefully supplements such work, and carries it on while the student is otherwise engaged.

1260.   Those who are trying on their small scale to help the world soon find that they have a multitude of cases upon their hands, and that they can work best by dividing their time between them. The more advanced student will leave with each such case a puissant thought-form, which will radiate invigoration and cheerfulness until he can again turn his attention to that case. But one who has not yet developed his powers to that extent may readily produce an effect almost equivalent, if he has a physical basis upon which to found the thought-form. A letter furnishes him with exactly such a basis, and into it he can pour healing and strengthening forces until it becomes a veritable talisman. If the writer thinks strongly of his sympathy and affection, and wills earnestly to charge the letter with this thought and feeling, it will assuredly bear this message for him. When it reaches its destination the friend who opens it will naturally recognise the kindly intention of the sender, and by that very recognition will open himself towards the influence, and adopt unconsciously a recipient attitude. As he reads the written message, the helpful thoughts and feelings are playing all the while upon his mind and emotions, and the effect produced upon him will be out of all proportion to the mere physical words.

1261.   The action of the letter does not cease here. The recipient reads it, lays it aside and perhaps forgets it, but its vibrations are nevertheless steadily radiating, and they continue to influence him long after the letter itself has passed from his mind. If he happens to put the letter in his pocket and carry it about with him, its influence upon him will naturally be closer and stronger; but in any case such a letter of helpfulness and good intention will fill the whole room with peace and comfort, so that the mourner will feel its effect whenever he enters his chamber, however unconscious he may be as to its source.

1262.   Obviously it is not only for consolation that this power can be employed. A mother, who feels uneasy as to the temptations which may surround an absent son, may send him letters which will encompass him with a halo of purity and peace, and bear him unconscious and uncontaminated through many a scene of peril. A multitude of words is not necessary; even a humble postcard may bear its message of love and strength, and may be a real shield against evil thought, or an impulse in the direction of good.

1263.   It may occur to some readers that a letter is handled by so many persons before it reaches its destination that any magnetism that it might bring with it would necessarily be of mixed character. There is much truth in this; but the postmen, the sorters and the servants who handle it have no special interest in it, and consequently such influence as their thoughts may exercise upon it is of the most superficial character; whereas the writer has intentionally thrown into it a wealth of feeling which has thoroughly permeated it and is strong enough to overpower all casual connections of this sort.

1264.   Incidentally this helps us to understand that there is always a responsibility attached to this action of writing a letter. We may charge our writing voluntarily with a great force for good, and that needs a special effort of the will; but even without any special effort, our mood when writing undoubtedly impresses itself upon the paper, though naturally not so strongly. If therefore a man be in a condition of irritation or depression when inditing a letter, these emotions of his will be faithfully mirrored in his work, and the letter will bear these vibrations with it and radiate them to the recipient, even though they are not at all intended for him, and the original annoyance or depression was in no way connected with him. If on the other hand the writer is serene and happy, a letter for him, even though it be nothing but a curt business communication, will contain within itself something of these qualities, and will spread a good influence around it.

1265.   It is therefore exceedingly necessary that a person among whose duties it comes to write many letters should cultivate serenity and kindliness, and should endeavour to hold himself in a sympathetic and helpful frame of mind, in order that his letters should carry with them this good influence. One who is captious and critical, dictatorial and ill-tempered, is entirely unfit to hold any secretarial position, as he will inevitably distribute discomfort and dissension to all those who are so unfortunate as to have to correspond with him.

1266.   The preference which many sentimental people feel for a letter written in manuscript, rather than for one produced by means of a typewriter, is due to the fact that in passing the hand again and again over the paper a much greater amount of personal magnetism is stored in the letter than when the hand does not come directly into contact with it; though a student of occultism who writes a letter in type charges it with magnetism by a single effort of his will far more effectually than it is unconsciously charged when written by the hand of one who has not learnt these truths.

1267.   The occultist extends this idea in many other directions. Every present which he gives to a friend, is made to produce a far more permanent result than the mere pleasure that is caused by its arrival. If he gives or lends a book to some one, he does not forget to add to the arguments of the author his own earnest desire that the reader's thoughts may be widened and liberalised. Let us all try to spread help and blessing in this way; assuredly our efforts will not fail to bring about their due effect. Every object about us must be a centre of influence, and we may make its action strong or weak, useful or detrimental. It is for us therefore to see that whenever we make a present to a friend its influence shall be powerful and definite, and always for good. These matters are little studied yet in the outer world, but they represent great truths for all that. Wise men will pay attention to them and govern their lives accordingly, and thereby make themselves both far happier and far more useful than those who are content to remain ignorant of the higher science.

1268.   WORK DURING SLEEP

1269.   One of the most pleasing of the subsidiary points revealed to us by Theosophical study is that of the possibility of usefully employing the hours during which the body is sleeping. I well remember in my younger days how fiercely I resented the necessity of spending time in sleep when there was such an overwhelming amount of work to be done, and how I consequently tried to minimise the time devoted to this. Being healthy and hardy, for some years I managed to exist on only four hours of sleep each night, and thought that I was thereby gaining time for the work which I had to do. Now that I know more about it, I realise that I was in error, how that I could actually have increased my usefulness if I had allowed myself to take an ordinary amount of rest, besides providing myself with a still stronger body for the work of my later years. But it was indeed a comfort to me when I found from the Theosophical literature that only the body is insensible during sleep, and that the real man can continue his work and indeed do all the more of it, and do it better, because he is untrammelled by his physical vehicle.

1270.　Yet even Theosophical students, who are quite accustomed to think about the higher worlds and the possibility of activity in them, often do not realise how entirely *that* is the real life, and this in the physical world only an interlude in it. In our waking consciousness most of us always consider the diurnal life as real, and the nocturnal or dream life as unreal; but in truth the very reverse is the case, as may easily be seen if we remember that in *this* life most of us know nothing whatever of *that*, whereas in *that* life we remember the whole of this. *This* life, therefore, has long daily breaks in its continuity; *that* is continuous from the cradle to the grave and beyond it. Furthermore, because during that life the physical body is for the time laid aside, the ego can manifest much more of himself. The man in his astral body is much more nearly himself than this fettered representation of him which is all that we can see down here. When, later on in our evolution, further development takes place and the man can function in his mental body, we are another whole stage nearer to the reality; indeed, beyond that it is only one stage to the manifestation of the ego in his causal body, having a unified consciousness which extends through all the ages, from the time when long ago he rose from the animal kingdom to the infinity which lies before him.

1271.　Let us see then what we can do with this life at night, while we leave our physical body to its rest. Many forms of activity open before us, and as I have written fully about them in the book called *Invisible Helpers* I will not repeat myself here. I may summarise by saying that during our waking hours we can help anyone whom we know to be in sorrow or suffering, by sitting down and forming a clear strong thought-image of the sufferer, and then pouring out a stream of compassion, affection and strength; but during the night we can do more than this - we can carry this treatment further, because we can ourselves go in the astral body and stand by the bedside of the sufferer, so as to see exactly what is needed, and give whatever may be specially required by the particular case, instead of offering merely general comfort and consolation.

1272.　Help and encouragement, can be given not only to the living but also to the vast host of the dead, and they often seriously need it, owing partly to the false and wicked religious teaching which is so often given, and partly to the blank ignorance of other-world conditions which obtains among the general public on this side of the veil. In such work as this there is infinite variety, yet even this by no means exhausts the possibilities which open before us. In the astral world we can both give and receive instruction. From the anonymity of the astral world we can assist, inspire and advise all sorts of people who would be unlikely to listen to us physically. We can suggest good and liberal ideas to ministers and statesmen, to poets and preachers, and to all the many varieties of writers in books, magazines and newspapers. We can suggest alike plots to novelists and good ideas to philanthropists. We are free to range wherever we will and to do whatever work presents itself to us. Incidentally we can visit all the interesting spots of the world, and see all its most magnificent buildings and its most lovely scenery; its finest art and its grandest music are entirely at our disposal, without money and without price, to say nothing, of the far grander music and the far more splendid colouring of the astral world itself.

1273. What can a man do down here to prepare himself to take part in that higher work? Well, the life is a continuous life, and whatever characteristics a man shows here in his physical body he will assuredly also show in his astral body. If here he is full of cheerfulness and always anxious for an opportunity to do service - then, even though he may remember nothing of it, he may be quite confident that he is employing himself usefully to the utmost of his capacity in the astral realm also. Any limitations of character which show themselves down here, such as irritability, for example, are certainly contracting the sphere of his usefulness in the astral world. And so, if a man who does not bring through any recollection from that life wishes to make quite sure that he is well employed there and is doing his full duty, he can easily be certain of it by carefully making his life here such as he knows to be necessary for that purpose. There is no mystery as to the requirements. Single-mindedness, calmness, courage, knowledge and love will make a thoroughly useful astral worker, and all these qualifications are within reach of any man who will take the trouble to develop them in himself.

1274. It is not difficult to see why all these are necessary. A man cannot throw all his energy into such work as this unless the higher life is for him the one object. Knowledge of the astral world, its habitants and its characteristics he must have; otherwise he will constantly blunder, and will find himself helpless before every emergency which arises. Courage he obviously needs, just as does the man who plunges into unexplored jungles or trusts himself on the surface of the mighty deep. Calmness also he must have, for though it is a sufficiently serious matter for a man to loose his temper in the physical world, it is something infinitely more serious when there is no physical matter to prevent the full swing of the vibrations of anger. Any manifestations of irritability, excitement or impatience in the astral world at once make him a fearsome object, so that those whom he wishes to help fly from him in terror. Love of humanity, and the consequent earnest desire to help, he must possess in the fullest degree, for without that he can never have the patience to deal gently with the panic fear and the unreasoning stupidity which we so often find among the dead. For many of the cases with which we have to deal such exceeding gentleness and long-suffering are required that no man, however energetic and earnest he may be, is of use in dealing with them unless he is full of real affection and has his vehicles perfectly under control.

1275. Much work is done in the astral world besides that in which we are most specially interested. Many physicians visit, during the sleep of the body, cases in which they are keenly interested or about which they feel anxious. In most cases the man in the physical body is not conscious of this, but any new information that he gains from his astral investigations, often comes through as a kind of intuition into the waking consciousness. I have known doctors who are able to do this intentionally and in full consciousness, and naturally this capacity gives them a great advantage over their colleagues. A doctor who dies, often continues after death to take an interest in his patients, and sometimes endeavours to cure them from the other side, or to suggest (to his successor in charge of the case) treatment which, with his newly acquired astral faculty, he sees would be useful. I knew one doctor (a member of our Society) who immediately after his death went round to collect all his patients who had passed over before him, and regularly preached Theosophy to them, so that he now goes about in the astral world with a large band of attendant disciples.

1276.   I have known many cases also of friendships formed in the astral world. It often happens, for example, that members of our Society who live at opposite sides of the world and have no opportunity of meeting physically, yet know one another well in their astral life. When they are actually on opposite sides of the world the day of one is the night of the other, but there is generally sufficient overlapping to make acquaintance possible. Those who are ready and effective lecturers in the physical world, usually continue their activities in that line during sleep. Groups of students continue their meetings and, with the additional facilities which the astral world gives to them, are frequently able to solve problems which have presented difficulties down here.

1277.   Not only dead friends but living friends from the other side of the world are round us all day long, although with our physical eyes we do not see them. We are never alone, and as in the astral world most thoughts are visible, it behoves us to bear that fact in mind, lest we should carelessly send out astral or mental vibrations which would cause pain to those whom we love.

CHAPTER XXI BY COLLECTIVE THOUGHT

1280.   CHURCH HYMNS AND RITUALS

1281.   In an earlier chapter I have explained how the congregation and the parishioners are affected by the ceremonies of the Church, and from what was then said it is not difficult to see how the priest from his side can influence those about him. He has chosen a position the responsibilities of which are great, and in order to discharge them properly it is important that he should know something of the hidden side of things, that he may understand the real meaning of the services of the Church to which he belongs, and how to order them aright.

1282.   Much exception has been taken by the ignorant to the statement always made by the Church that the celebration of the Eucharist is a daily repetition of the sacrifice of the Christ. But when we understand from the occult point of view that that sacrifice of the Christ means the descent into matter of the outpouring of the Second Aspect of Deity, we see that the symbolism is an accurate one, since the outflow of force evoked by the consecration has a special and intimate connection with that department of nature which is the expression of that divine Aspect.

1283.   The priest who comprehends this will not fail to assign to that service its due position, and will take care to surround its culminating point with whatever in the way of ritual and music will add to its effect and prepare the people to take part in it more receptively. Realising also of how tremendous a mystery he is here the custodian, he will approach its celebration with the utmost reverence and awe, for though his attitude towards it makes no difference to the central fact and to its effects, there is no doubt that his deep devotion, his comprehension and co-operation can bring down an additional influence which will be of the greatest help to his congregation and his parish. A priest who has the advantage of being also an occultist has a magnificent opportunity of widespread usefulness.

1284.   As a student of magic, he appreciates to the full, the effect produced by music, and knows how to utilise it so as to produce harmonious and powerful forms. A great deal may be done by inducing the congregation as far as possible to join in the music of the church. It is impossible that they should do so in the production of the more elaborate and magnificent forms, which produce far-reaching effects at higher levels, but they themselves may be helped to an almost incalculable extent if they can be induced to join heartily in stirring and well-chosen hymns and chants.

1285.   This has been more fully recognised by the English branch of the Catholic Church than by the Roman, and a corresponding advantage has been reaped. The powerful influence of the corresponding advantage has been reaped. The powerful influence of the processional hymn must not be neglected, for this operates usefully in all directions; first, by bringing the choir down among the congregation and moving them slowly through the different sections of it, the people are greatly encouraged and helped to throw themselves with vigour into the singing. Secondly, the splendid appearance of a well-organised procession, the colour and light, the rich banners and splendid vestments, all combine to fire the imagination, to raise the people's thoughts above the prosaic level of ordinary life, and to help their devotion and enthusiasm.

1286. CONGREGATIONS

1287. Many of these considerations apply also to ministers of other denominations. Though they have not the power of the priest which brings them into touch with the reservoir of force arranged by the Christ for his Church, they may do a great deal for their congregations, first by their own devotion and secondly by evoking that of their people. The resources of congregational music are at their disposal, and if they can work their followers up to the required level, they also may produce the wonderful results which flow from the combined devotion of a large number of people.

1288. A grand outpouring of force, and a magnificent and effective collective thought-form can thus be made by a gathering of men who join heartily in a service; but there is generally great difficulty in obtaining this result, because the members of the average congregation are entirely untrained in concentration, and consequently the collective thought-form is usually a broken and chaotic mass, instead of a splendid and organised whole. When it happens that a number of occult students belong to such an assembly, they can be of great use to their fellow-worshippers by consciously gathering together the scattered streams of devotion and welding them into one harmonious and mighty current. It is evident at once that every member of congregation has here a definite duty.

1289. MONASTERIES

1290. Better results than those produced by an ordinary congregation are frequently obtained from the united devotions of a body of monks, because they have gradually trained themselves into something approaching to concentration, and are also well used to working together. The influence flowing from a monastery or nunnery of the contemplative order is often beautiful and most helpful to the whole country-side - a fact which shows clearly how foolish and short-sighted is the objection sometimes made by the Protestant that, while the active orders of monks are at least doing good work among the poor and the sick, those who adopt a contemplative line are merely dreaming away their lives in selfish isolation from the rest of the world.

1291. In most of such monasteries the hours of prayer are strictly observed, and the effect of this is a regular out-flow of force over the neighbourhood many times each day. There are some such institutions in which the scheme of perpetual adoration is carried out before the consecrated Host in the chapel of the monastery, and in such a case there is a steady and powerful stream always pouring out, both night and day, bringing to the surrounding country a benefit which can hardly be overestimated.

1292. EFFECT UPON THE DEAD

1293. The effect produced in all these cases is far wider than the ordinary thinker realises. The young student of occultism, if he does not happen to be clairvoyant, sometimes finds it difficult to remember that the host of the unseen is so much greater than the number of the seen, and that therefore the people who benefit by church services or by outpourings of collective thought and feeling are not only the living but also the dead - not only human beings even, but great hosts of nature-spirits and of the lower orders of the angels. Naturally, whatever feeling may be aroused in them reacts upon us in turn, so that many different factors combine to strengthen us when we make any effort for good.

1294.   The Christian Church directs some of her efforts intentionally towards her departed members, and prayers and masses for the dead are a great feature of the life in Catholic countries. A most useful feature certainly; for not only do the good wishes and the outpourings of force reach and help those at whom they are aimed, but also the formation of such prayers and wishes is a good and charitable undertaking for the living, besides providing them with a satisfactory and consolatory outlet for their feelings in the shape of doing something to help the departed instead of merely mourning for them.

1295.   SAVING SOULS

1296.   Hundreds of good and earnest people are putting a great deal of strength and devotion into efforts (as they put it) to "save souls" - which to them generally means imprisoning people within the limits of some particularly narrow and uncharitable sect. Fortunately, their endeavours in this particular direction are not often successful. But we must not suppose that all their energy and thought for others is therefore necessarily wasted. It does not do half the good that it would if it were intelligently directed; but such as it is, it is unselfish and kindly meant, and so it brings down a certain amount of response from higher levels, which is poured upon both the petitioner and the object of his prayers. If the suppliant be earnest and free from conceit, Nature answers the spirit rather than the letter of such a request, and brings general good and advancement to its object without also inflicting upon him the curse of a narrow theology.

1297.   PEOPLE WHO DISLIKE CEREMONIES

1298.   There are in the world many people so constituted that ceremonies of any sort do not appeal to them. It may be asked what kind of provision Nature makes for them, and how they are compensated for their inability to appreciate or to share in the benefits of these various lines of ecclesiastical influence of which I have written. First to a considerable extent they do share in the benefit of them, though they would probably be the last people to admit it. Perhaps they never enter churches; but I have already described how these influences radiate far beyond the mere buildings, and how the vibrations are sent out on all levels, and consequently have something which affects all varieties of people.

1299.   Still, it is clear that such men miss a good deal which the others may gain if they will; what sources then are open to them from which they may obtain corresponding advance? They cannot well gain the same uplifting - nor, I suppose, would they desire it; but they may gain a mental stimulus. Just as the thought of the great saint, radiating out all round him, arouses devotion in those who are capable of feeling it, so does the thought of the great man of science, or of anyone who is highly developed intellectually, radiate out upon the mental level and affect the minds of others, so far as they are capable of responding to it. Its action stimulates mental development, though it does not necessarily act so directly upon the character and disposition of the man as does the other influence.

1300.   Perfect knowledge must make for goodness of life as much as perfect devotion; but we are as yet so far from perfection that in practical life we have to deal rather with the intermediate or even elementary stages, and it seems clear that elementary knowledge is less likely on the whole to affect the character than elementary devotion. Both are necessary, and before Adeptship is reached both must be acquired in their entirety; but at present we are so partially developed that the vast majority of men are aiming at one and to some extent neglecting the other - I mean, of course, the majority of those men who are trying at all, for the greater part of the world has not arrived as yet at recognising the necessity for either knowledge or devotion. The only organisation, in western countries at least, which fully meets and satisfies man's requirements along both these lines appears to me to be the Theosophical Society, and its meetings, small and unimportant though they may seem to an outsider, are capable when properly managed of radiating a powerful influence which will be exceedingly useful to the community.

1301.   THEOSOPHICAL MEETINGS
1302.   A meeting may produce most important results, not only for those who take part in it, but for their unconscious neighbours. But in order that it may do this, the members must understand the hidden side of their meeting, and must work with a view to produce the highest possible effects. Many members utterly overlook this most important part of their work, and have in consequence quite an unworthy idea of what the work of a Lodge is.

1303.   I have sometimes heard a member frankly confess that the Lodge meetings are often rather dull, and so he does not always attend them. A member who makes such a remark has not grasped the most rudimentary facts about the work of the Lodge; he evidently supposes that it exists for the purpose of amusing him, and if its meetings are not interesting to him he thinks that he is better off at home. The excuse for such an attitude (if there is an excuse) is that through many lives, and probably through the earlier part of this life, such a man has been looking at everything entirely from the outside and from the selfish point of view, and he is only now gradually accustoming himself to the true and higher standpoint - the common-sense attitude which takes account of all the factors, the higher as well as the lower and less important.

1304.   The person who attends a meeting for the sake of what he can get, or to be entertained there, is thinking of himself only and not of his Lodge or of the Society. We should join the Society not for anything that we get from it, but because, having satisfied ourselves of the truth of what it proclaims, we are anxious to spread that truth to others as far as possible. If we are merely selfish in regard to this matter, we can buy the Theosophical books and study them without belonging to the Society at all. We join it for the sake of spreading the teaching, and for the sake of understanding it better by discussing it with those who have spent years in trying to live it. We who belong to it do get a good deal from it, in the way of instruction and of help in understanding difficult points, of brotherly feeling and of kindly thought.

1305.   I know that I have received much of all these things during my thirty years of membership, but I am quite sure that if I had joined the Society with the idea of getting something out of it, I should not have gained half of what I have. In my experience of the Society, I have seen over and over again that the person who comes in with the idea "What shall I get?" gains little, because so far as the flowing of higher forces goes he is a *cul-de-sac* ; he is what plumbers call a "dead end," out of which nothing is running. What can there be in the dead end of a pipe but a little stagnant water? But if the pipe be open and the water flows freely, then a vast amount may pass through.

1306.   In the same way, if members come to a meeting, thinking all the time about themselves, and how they like what is said or done, they assuredly gain but little good from it, compared to what they might gain if their attitude were more rational. No doubt such people have spasms of unselfishness; but that is insufficient. The whole life of a member ought to be devoted to trying to fill his place well, and to do his duty to the utmost of his power. Therefore, being a member of the Society and of a Lodge, he has his duty to do from that point of view also. If a member says that Lodge meetings are dull, one always feels inclined to begin by asking him: "What are you doing to allow them to be dull? You are there also and it is your business to see that things are kept going as far as may be." If each individual member feels resting upon him the duty of trying to make each meeting a success, it will be much more likely to succeed than if he goes there just to be amused or even merely to be instructed.

1307.   Let us consider then the hidden side of the meeting of a Theosophical Lodge.

1308.   For the purposes of our illustration, I will take the ordinary weekly meetings, at which the Lodge is prosecuting its definite line of study. I am referring to the meetings of members of the Lodge only, for the occult effect which I wish to describe is impossible in connection with any meetings to which non-members are admitted.

1309.   Naturally, the work of every Lodge has its public side. There are lectures given to the public, and opportunities offered for their questions; all this is good and necessary. But every Lodge which is worthy of the name is also doing something far higher than any work in the physical world, and this higher work can only be done by virtue of its own private meetings. Furthermore, it can be done only if these private meetings are properly conducted and entirely harmonious. If the members are thinking of themselves in any way - if they have personal vanity, such as might show itself in the desire to shine or to take a prominent part in the proceeding; if they have other personal feelings, so that they would be capable of taking offence or of being affected by envy or jealousy - no useful occult effect can possibly be produced. But if they have forgotten themselves in the earnest endeavour to comprehend the subject appointed for study, a considerable and beneficial result, of which they usually have no conception, may readily be produced. Let me explain the reason of this.

1310. We will assume a series of meetings at which a certain book is being used for study. Every member knows beforehand what paragraph or page will be taken at the approaching meeting, and it is expected that he shall take the trouble to prepare himself to bear his part in it intelligently. He must not be in the attitude of the young nestling, waiting with open mouth and expecting that someone else will feed him; on the contrary, every member should have an intelligent comprehension of the subject which is to be considered, and should be prepared to contribute his share of information with regard to it.

1311. A good plan is for each member of the circle to make himself responsible for the examination of certain of our Theosophical books - one taking the first volume of *The Secret Doctrine*, let us say, another the second, another the third, another *The Ancient Wisdom*, another *Esoteric Buddhism*, and so on. Some of the members could easily take two or three of the smaller books, and on the other hand, if the Lodge be large enough, a volume of *The Secret Doctrine* might very well be divided among several members, each taking up a hundred or a hundred and fifty pages. The exact subject to be considered at the next meeting is announced at the previous one, and each member makes himself responsible for looking carefully through the book or books committed to his charge for any reference to it, so that when he comes to the meeting he is already possessed of any information about it which is contained in that particular book, and is prepared to contribute this when called upon. In this way every member has his work to do, and each is greatly helped to a full and clear comprehension of the matter under consideration, because all present are thus earnestly fixing their thought upon it. When the meeting opens, the chairman will first appoint some one to read the passage chosen for study, and will then ask each member in turn what, if anything, his book has to say which bears upon it. After all have thus borne their part, questions may be asked and any points which are not quite clear may be discussed. If any question arises which the older members present do not feel themselves fully competent to answer, it should be written out and sent to the Headquarters of the Society.

1312. If some such plan as that be adopted, no one will have reason to complain of the dullness of the meetings, for every member will exert himself to bear his own part in each of them. Each must go to the meeting in a spirit of helpfulness, thinking of what he can contribute and in what way he can be useful, for upon the attitude of mind much depends. /START/

1313. Let us consider what effect such a meeting will produce upon the neighbourhood in which it is held. We have already noted that a Church service is a powerful centre of influence; how does a Theosophical meeting act in this respect?

1314. To understand that, recall for a moment what has been said as to the action of thought. The thought-wave may be generated at various levels of the mental body. A selfish thought uses the lowest kind of mental matter, while an unselfish thought, or an attempt to comprehend some elevated idea, uses the higher kinds only. An intense effort at the realisation of the abstract - an attempt to comprehend what is meant by the fourth dimension or by the tabularity of a table - means, if successful, a dawning activity of the causal body; while if the thought is mingled with unselfish affection, with high aspiration or devotion, it is even possible that a vibration of the intuitional world may enter into it and multiply its power a hundredfold.

1315.   The distance to which a thought-wave can radiate effectively, depends partly upon its nature and partly upon the opposition with which it meets. Waves in the lower types of astral matter are usually soon deflected or overwhelmed by a multitude of other vibrations at the same level, just as in the midst of the roar of a great city a soft sound is entirely drowned.

1316.   For this reason the ordinary self-centred thought of the average man, which begins on the lowest of the mental levels, and instantly plunges down to correspondingly low levels of the astral, is comparatively ineffective. Its power in both the worlds is limited, because, however violent it may be, there is such an immense and turbulent sea of similar thought surging all around that its waves are inevitably soon lost and overpowered in that confusion. A thought generated at a higher level, however, has a much clearer field for its action, because at present the number of thoughts producing such waves is very small - indeed, Theosophical thought is almost a class by itself from this point of view. There are religious people whose thought is quite as elevated as ours, but never so precise and definite; there are large numbers of people whose thoughts on matters of business and money-making are as precise as could be desired, but they are not elevated or altruistic. Even scientific thought is scarcely ever in the same class as that of the true Theosophist, so that our students have practically a field to themselves in the mental world.

1317.   The result of this is that when a man thinks on Theosophical subjects, he is sending out all round him a wave which is powerful because it is practically unopposed, like a sound in the midst of a vast silence, or a light shining forth on the darkest night. It sets in motion a level of mental matter which is as yet but rarely used, and the radiations which are caused by it impinge upon the mental body of the average man at a point where it is quite dormant. This gives to such thought its peculiar value, not only to the thinker but to others round him; for its tendency is to awaken and to bring into use an entirely new part of the thinking apparatus. Such a wave does not necessarily convey Theosophical thought to those who are ignorant of it; but in awakening this higher portion of the mental body, it tends to elevate and liberalise the man's thought as a whole, along whatever lines it may be in the habit of moving, and in this way produces an incalculable benefit.

1318.   If the thought of a single man produces these results, the thought of twenty or thirty people directed to the same subject will achieve an effect enormously greater. The power of the united thought of a number of men is always far more than the sum of their separate thoughts; it would be much more nearly represented by their product. So it will be seen that, even from this point of view alone, it is an exceedingly good thing for any city or community that a Theosophical Lodge should be constantly meeting in its midst, for its proceedings, if they are conducted in a proper spirit, cannot but have a distinctly elevating and ennobling effect upon the thought of the surrounding population. Naturally there are many people whose minds cannot yet be awakened at all upon those higher levels; but even for them the constant beating of the waves of this more advanced thought at least brings nearer the time of their awakening.

1319.   Nor must we forget the result produced by the formation of definite thought-forms. These also are radiated from the centre of activity, but they can affect only such minds as are already to some extent responsive to ideas of this nature. In these days, however, there are many such minds, and our members can attest the fact that after they have been discussing such a question as reincarnation it not infrequently happens that they are themselves asked for information upon that subject by persons whom they had not previously supposed to be interested in it. The thought-form is capable of conveying the exact nature of the thought to those who are somewhat prepared to receive it, whereas the thought-vibration, though it reaches a far wider circle, is much less definite in its action.

1320.   Here is already a momentous effect upon the mental level, produced quite unintentionally by our members in the ordinary course of their study - something far greater in reality than their intentional efforts in the way of propaganda are ever likely to produce. But this is not all, for by far the most important part is yet to come. Every Lodge of this Society is a centre of interest to the Great Masters of the Wisdom, and when it works well and loyally Their thoughts and those of Their pupils are frequently turned towards it. In this way a force more exalted than our own may often shine out from our gatherings, and an influence of inestimable value may be focused where, so far as we know, it would not otherwise specially rest. This may indeed seem the ultimate limit which our work can attain; yet there is something beyond even this.

1321.   All students of the occult are aware that the Life and Light of the Deity flood the whole of His system - that in every world, at every level, is outpoured from Him that especial manifestation of His strength which is appropriate to it. Naturally, the higher the world, the less veiled is His glory, because as we ascend we are drawing nearer to its Source. Normally the force outpoured in each world is strictly limited to it; but it can descend into and illuminate a lower level if a special channel be prepared for it.

1322.   Such a channel is always provided whenever any thought or feeling has an entirely unselfish aspect. The selfish emotion moves in a closed curve, and so brings its own response on its own level; the utterly unselfish emotion is an outrush of energy which does not return, but in its upward movement provides a channel for a downpouring of divine Power from the level next above, which is the reality lying at the back of the old idea of the answer to prayer.

1323.   To a clairvoyant this channel is visible as a great vortex, a kind of gigantic cylinder or funnel. This is the nearest we can come to explaining it in the physical world, but it does not really give at all an adequate idea of its appearance, for as the force flows down through the channel it somehow makes itself one with the vortex, and issues from it coloured by it, and bearing with it distinctive characteristics which show through what channel it has come.

1324.   Such a channel can be made only if all the thought is earnest and harmonious. I do not mean that there must be no discussion at the meetings, but that all such discussion must invariably be of the most friendly character, and conducted with the fullest brotherly feeling. We must never suppose that a man differs from us is necessarily weak in thought or uncomprehending. There are always at least two sides to every question, so that the man who disagrees may often simply be seeing another side. If that is so, we may gather something from him and he something from us, and in that way we may do each other good; but if we become angry over a discussion we do each other harm and the harmony of the thought-waves is lost. One such thought as that so often spoils a beautiful effect. I have seen that happen many times - a number of people working along quite happily and building up a beautiful channel; suddenly some one of them will say something unkind or personal, and then in a moment the thing breaks up, and the opportunity to help is lost.

1325.   Whenever anyone is speaking, or reading a paragraph, or trying to do anything helpful, try for the time to help him, and do not be everlastingly thinking how much better you could do it yourself. Do not criticise, but give him the aid of your thought. You may afterwards enquire as to any points that are not clear, but do not at the time send a hostile or critical thought against him, because if you do you may interfere with the sequence of his thought and spoil his lecture. Make a mental note of any point about which you wish to ask, but for the time try to see what good there is in what he says, as in that way you will strengthen him.

1326.   A clairvoyant sees the current of thought flowing out from the lecturer, and other currents of comprehension and appreciation rising from the audience and joining with it; but critical thought meets it with an opposing rate of vibration, breaks up the stream, and throws it all into confusion. One who sees this influence in action will find these considerations so forcibly impressed upon him that he is little likely to forget them and act contrary to them. The helpful thoughts of members of his audience tend to make a lecturer's presentation clearer, and to impress it upon those to whom it is not familiar. For this reason, members should be present even at public lectures upon the most elementary subjects delivered by their fellows, in order that they, who understand thoroughly, may help the lecturer by making clear thought-forms connected with his subject, which will impress themselves upon the minds of the public who are trying to understand.

1327.   The man who is occupied in the earnest study of higher things is for the time lifted entirely out of himself, and generates a powerful thought-form in the mental world, which is immediately employed as a channel by the force hovering in the world next above. When a body of men join together in a thought of this nature, the channel which they make is out of all proportion larger in its capacity than the sum of their separate channels; and such a body of men is therefore an inestimable blessing to the community amidst which it works, for through them (even in their most ordinary meetings for study, when they are considering such subjects as rounds and races and planetary chains) there may come an outpouring into the lower mental world of that force which is normally peculiar to the higher mental; while if they turn their attention to the higher side of the Theosophical teaching, and study such questions of ethics and of soul-development as we find in *At the Feet of the Master, Light on the Path,*

The Voice of the Silence and our other devotional books, they may make a channel of more elevated thought through which the force of the intuitional world itself may descend into the mental, and thus radiate out an influence for good upon many a soul who would not be in the least open to the action of that force if it had remained on its original level.

1328.   This is the real and the greatest function of a Lodge of the Theosophical Society - to furnish a channel for the distribution of the Divine Life; and thus we have another illustration to show us how far greater is the unseen than the seen. To the dim physical eye all that is visible is a small band of humble students meeting weekly in the earnest endeavour to learn and to qualify themselves to be of use to their fellow-men; but to those who can see more of the world, from this tiny root there springs a glorious flower, for no less than four mighty streams of influence are radiating from that seemingly insignificant centre - the stream of thought-waves, the cluster of thought-forms, the magnetism of the Masters of the Wisdom, and the mighty torrent of the Divine Energy.

1329.   Here also is an instance of the eminently practical importance of a knowledge of the unseen side of life. For lack of such knowledge many a member has been lax in the performance of his duty, careless as to his attendance at Lodge meetings; and thus he has lost the inestimable privilege of being part of a channel for the Divine Life. Such a man has not yet grasped the elementary fact that he joined not to receive but to give, not to be interested and amused, but to take his share in a mighty work for the good of mankind.

CHAPTER XXII BY OUR RELATION TO CHILDREN

1332.   From the Theosophic standpoint the subject of our relation to children is an exceedingly important and practical one. If we realise the purpose for which the ego descends into incarnation, and if we know to how great an extent its attainment of that purpose depends upon the training given to its various vehicles during their childhood and growth, we cannot but feel that a tremendous responsibility attaches to all who are in any way connected with children, whether as parents, elder relatives, or teachers. It is well, therefore, that we should consider what hints Theosophy can give us as to the way in which we can best discharge this responsibility.

1333.   What is the present condition of our relation to children - to boys, at any rate - here in the midst of our European civilisation? The practical result of nineteen centuries of ostensibly Christian teaching, is that our boys live among us as an alien race, with laws and rules of life of their own, entirely different from ours, and with a code of morals of their own, also entirely different from that by which we consider ourselves bound. They regard grown-up people (in the mass) with scarcely veiled hostility, or, at the best, with a kind of armed neutrality, and always with deep distrust, as foreigners whose motives are incomprehensible to them, and whose actions are perpetually interfering in the most unwarrantable and apparently malicious manner with their right to enjoy themselves in their own way.

1334.   This may sound rather a startling statement to those who have never considered the matter, but any parent who has boys at one of our large schools will appreciate the truth of it; and if he can look back to his own school-days, and in thought realise once more the feelings and conditions of that period (which most of us have so entirely forgotten), he will recognise, perhaps with a start of surprise, that it is not an inaccurate description of what his own attitude once was.

1335.   Whenever the laws and customs of this race (living among us, yet not us) differ from ours, they are invariably a reversion to an earlier type, and tend in the direction of primitive savagery - a fact which might be cited in support of the Theosophical theory that in each incarnation, before the ego has acquired control of his vehicles, the earlier stages of our evolution are hurriedly run through once more. The only right recognised among them is the right of the strongest; the boy who rules their little State is not the best boy, nor the cleverest boy, but the one who can fight best; and their leadership is usually decided by combat, just as it is to this day among many a savage tribe.

1336.   Their code of morals is distinctly their own, and though it cannot be so directly paralleled among primitive races as some of their other customs, it is decidedly on a lower level than even our own. To oppress and ill-treat the weak, and even torture them to the utmost limit of endurance, seems to be thought a comparatively innocent form of recreation, and it would be only an unusually severe case which would arouse even a passing manifestation of public opinion against the offender. The theft of money is, happily, regarded as contemptible, but the theft of fruit or jam is not;

nor, indeed, would the stealing of anything eatable be considered criminal. Falsehood of the most outrageous kind is considered as not only allowable but amusing, when practised upon some too-credulous youngster; if restored to in order to conceal from an adult the misdeeds of a fellow-criminal, it is often looked upon as heroic and noble. But the most heinous crime of all - the very lowest abyss of turpitude - is to call in the intervention of a grown-up person to right even the most flagrant wrongs; and many a weak and nervous child endures agonies both physically and mentally from the barbarity of bullies without breathing a word of his sufferings either to parent or teacher - so deep is the distrust with which public opinion amongst boys regards the hostile race of adults.

1337.   In spite of the terrible suffering which it frequently entails upon the weak and sensitive boy, I am in no way blind to the good side of public-school life - to the courage and self-reliance which it gives to the strong and hardy lad, and the training in the command of the others with which it provides the members of its higher forms. I suppose that England is the only country on earth where the maintenance of order in the small world of school life can be (and is) left practically in the hands of the boys themselves, and there is much in this to be highly commended; but I am at present concerned with the relations between boys as a class and adults as a class, and it can hardly be denied that on the whole these are somewhat strained, the distrust of which I have spoken on the one side being frequently met by dislike and entire want of comprehension on the other.

1338.   Many a man (or woman) thinks of boys only as noisy, dirty, greedy, clumsy, selfish and generally objectionable; and he never realises that there may be a good deal of selfishness in this point of view of his, and that if any part of his indictment is true, the fault is not so much in the boys themselves as in the unreasonable way in which they have been brought up; furthermore, that in any case his duty is not to widen the chasm between them and himself by adopting an attitude of dislike and distrust, but rather to endeavour to improve the position of affairs by judicious kindness and hearty, patient friendliness and sympathy.

1339.   Surely there is something wrong about such unsatisfactory relations; surely some improvement might be brought about in this unfortunate condition of mutual hostility and mistrust. There are honourable exceptions; there are boys who trust their masters, and masters who trust their boys, and I myself have never found any difficulty in winning the confidence of the juveniles by treating them properly; but in a sadly large number of instances the case is as I have described it.

1340.   That it need not be so is shown, not only by the exceptions mentioned above, but by the condition of affairs which we find existing in some Oriental lands. I have not yet had the pleasure of visiting the Empire of Japan, but I hear from those who have been there and have made some study of this question, that there is no country in the world where children are so well and so sensibly treated - where their relations with their elders are so completely satisfactory. Harshness, it is said, is entirely unknown, yet the children in no way presume upon the gentleness of the older people.

1341.   Indeed, no properly treated child ever does or ever would so presume in any country. If he could do so, it would be a clear indication that the adult had failed in his management. All harshness in the treatment of children is a relic of savagery; it may be that when we were at the level of the stone-age we knew no better, but in these days of supposed enlightenment it is simply criminal. The intentional infliction of pain upon any living creature is one of the most serious of sins, and the karma which follows upon it is of the most appalling character. The suggestion that it is intended to produce a good result is no excuse whatever; in this case, as in all others, it can never be right to do evil that good may come. And that quite apart from the fact that good never does come. Nothing but the most horrible evil results from the common delusion on this subject.

1342.　　The whole thing is an abomination which cries to heaven for a remedy, just as is the ghastly, ceaseless slaughter of animals in order that men may degrade themselves by putting into their bodies a peculiarly unsuitable and objectionable form of food. In both these case - the ill-treatment of children and the slaughter of animals - we, in England, are in a condition of absolute barbarism; and the men of the future, looking back upon this time, will find it impossible to understand how such utterly horrible practices could co-exist with the knowledge of philosophy, ethics and religion which we possess. Our eyes are blinded to the wickedness of these things by the glamour of custom; but anyone who studies the hidden side of things soon learns that custom is an entirely unreliable guide and that he must face the facts of nature as they are, and not as ignorant people suppose them to be.

1343.　　This almost universal cruelty to children is the reason for the lack of confidence between them and adults; if we treat them as savages we are doing our best to induce them to act as savages. The incompetent parent or teacher pretends that he intentionally injures a child with a view to correcting his faults; if he knew anything of the real facts of life he would be aware that the effect of such injury is in every case far worse than that of the fault which he imagines himself to be trying to correct. His method is so entirely irrational that it seems to the occultist like the crazy inconsequence of a nightmare - all the more so when we think of the vast mass of hatred, hostility and misunderstanding for which it is responsible.

1344.　　But how, it may be asked, is it proposed that this position of mutual mistrust and misunderstanding should be improved ? Well, it is evident that in cases where this breach already exists, it can only be bridged over by unwearying kindness, and by gradual, patient, but constant efforts to promote a better understanding by steadily showing unselfish affection and sympathy; in fact, by habitually putting ourselves in the child's place and trying to realise exactly how all these matters appear to him. If we, who are adults, had not so entirely forgotten our own childish days, we should make far greater allowances for the children of to-day, and should understand and get on with them much better.

1345.　　This is, however, emphatically one of the cases in which the old proverb holds good, which tells us that prevention is better than cure. If we will but take a little trouble to begin in the right way with our children from the first, we shall easily be able to avoid the undesirable state of affairs which we have been describing. And this is exactly where Theosophy has many a valuable hint to offer to those who are in earnest in wishing to do their duty by the young ones committed to their charge.

1346. THE DUTY OF PARENTS

1347.　The absolute nature of this duty of parents and teachers towards children must first be recognised. It cannot be too strongly or too repeatedly insisted upon that parentage is an exceedingly heavy responsibility of a religious nature, however lightly and thoughtlessly it may often be undertaken. Those who bring a child into the world make themselves directly responsible to the law of karma for the opportunities of evolution which they ought to give to that ego, and heavy indeed will be their penalty if by their carelessness or selfishness they put hindrances in his path, or fail to render him all the help and guidance which he has a right to expect from them. Yet how often the modern parent entirely ignores this obvious responsibility; how often a child is to him nothing but a cause of fatuous vanity or an object of thoughtless neglect!

1348.　If we want to understand our duty towards the child we must first consider how he came to be what he is; we must trace him back in thought to his previous incarnation. Whatever may have been his outward circumstances at that time, he had a definite disposition of his own - a character containing various more or less developed qualities, some good and some bad.

1349.　In due course of time that life of his came to an end; but whether that end came slowly by disease or old age, or swiftly by some accident or violence, its advent made no sudden change of any sort in his character. A curious delusion seems to prevail in many quarters that the mere fact of death at once turns a demon into a saint - that, whatever a man's life may have been, the moment he dies he becomes practically an angel of goodness. No idea could possibly be further from the truth, as those whose work lies in trying to help the departed know full well. The casting off of a man's physical body no more alters his disposition than does the casting off of his overcoat; he is precisely the same man the day after his death as he was the day before, with the same vices and the same virtues.

1350.　True, now that he is functioning only in the astral world he has not the same opportunities of displaying them; but though they may manifest themselves in the astral life in a different manner, they are none the less still there, and the conditions and duration of that life are their result. In that world he must stay until the energy poured forth by his lower desires and emotions during physical life has worn itself out - until the astral body which he has made for himself, disintegrates; for only then can he leave it for the higher and more peaceful realm of the heaven-world. But though those particular passions are the time worn out and done with for him, the germs of the qualities in him, which made it possible for them to exist in his nature, are still there. They are latent and ineffective, certainly, because desire of that type requires astral matter for its manifestation; they are what Madame Blavatsky once called "privations of matter," but they are quite ready to come into renewed activity, if stimulated, when the man again finds himself under conditions where they can act.

1351.　An analogy may perhaps, if not pushed too far, be of use in helping us to grasp this idea. If a small bell be made to ring continuously in an air-tight vessel, and the air be then gradually withdrawn, the sound will grow fainter and fainter, until it becomes inaudible. The bell is still ringing as vigorously as ever, yet its vibration is no longer manifest to our ears, because the medium by means of which alone it can produce any effect upon them is absent. Admit the air to the vessel, and immediately you hear the sound of the bell once more just as before.

1352. Similarly, there are certain qualities in man's nature which need astral matter for their manifestation, just as sound needs either air or some denser matter for its vehicle; and when, in the process of his withdrawal into himself after what we call death, he leaves the astral world for the mental, those qualities can no longer find expression, and must therefore perforce remain latent. But when, centuries later, on his downward course into reincarnation he re-enters the astral realm, these qualities which have remained latent for so long manifest themselves once more, and become the tendencies of the next personality.

1353. In the same way there are qualities of the mind which need for their expression the matter of the lower mental levels; and when, after his long rest in the heaven-world, the consciousness of the man withdraws into the true ego upon the higher mental levels, these qualities also pass into latency.

1354. But when the ego is about to reincarnate, he has to reverse this process of withdrawal - to pass downward through the very same worlds through which he came on his upward journey. When the time of his outflow comes, he puts himself down first on to the lower levels of his own world, and seeks to express himself there, as far as is possible in that less perfect and less plastic matter. In order that he may so express himself and function in that world, he must clothe himself in its matter.

1355. Thus the ego aggregates around himself matter of the lower mental levels - the matter which will afterwards become his mind-body. But this matter is not selected at random; out of all the varied and inexhaustible store around him he attracts to himself just such a combination as is perfectly fitted to give expression to his latent mental qualities. In precisely the same way, when he makes the further descent to the astral world, the matter of that world which is by natural law attracted to him to serve as his vehicle is exactly that which will give expression to the desires which were his at the conclusion of his astral life. In point of fact, he resumes his life in each world just where he left it last time.

1356. His qualities are not as yet in any way in action; they are simply the germs of qualities, and for the moment their only influence is to secure for themselves a possible field of manifestation by providing suitable matter for their expression in the various vehicles of the child. Whether they develop once more in this life into the same definite tendencies as in the last one, will depend largely upon the encouragement or otherwise given to them by the surroundings of the child during his early years. Any one of them, good or bad, may be readily stimulated into activity by encouragement, or, on the other hand, may be starved out for lack of that encouragement. If stimulated, it becomes a more powerful factor in the man's life this time than it was in his previous existence; if starved out, it remains merely as an unfructified germ, which presently atrophies and dies out, and does not make its appearance in the succeeding incarnation at all.

1357.   This, then, is the condition of the child when first he comes under his parents' care. He cannot be said to have as yet a definite mind-body or a definite astral body, but he has around and within him the matter out of which these are to be builded.

1358.   He possesses tendencies of all sorts, some of them good and some of them evil, and it is in accordance with the development of these tendencies that this building will be regulated. And this development in turn depends almost entirely upon the influences brought to bear upon him from outside during the first few years of his existence. During these years the ego has as yet but little hold over his vehicles, and he looks to the parents to help him to obtain a firmer grasp, and to provide him with suitable conditions; hence their responsibility.

1359.   THE PLASTICITY OF CHILDHOOD

1360.   It is impossible to exaggerate the plasticity of these unformed vehicles. We know that the physical body of a child, if only its training be begun at a sufficiently early age, may be modified to a considerable extent. An acrobat, for example, will take a boy of five or six years old, whose bones and muscles are not yet as hardened and firmly set as ours are, and will gradually accustom his limbs and body to take readily and with comfort all sorts of positions which would be absolutely impossible for most of us now, even with any amount of training. Yet our own bodies at the same age differed in no essential respect from that boy's, and if they had been put through the same exercises they would have become as supple and elastic as his.

1361.   If the physical body of a child is thus plastic and readily impressible, his astral and mental vehicles are far more so. They thrill in response to every vibration which they encounter, and are eagerly receptive with regard to all influences, whether good or evil, which emanate from those around them. They resemble the physical body also in this other characteristic - that though in early youth they are so susceptible and so easily moulded, they soon set and stiffen and acquire definite habits which, when once firmly established, can be altered only with great difficulty.

1362.   When we realise this, we see at once the extreme importance of the surroundings in which a child passes his earliest years, and the heavy responsibility which rests upon every parent to see that the conditions of the child's development are as good as they can be made. The little creature is as clay in our hands to mould almost as we will; moment by moment the germs of good or evil quality brought over from the last birth are awakening into activity; moment by moment are being built up those vehicles which will condition the whole of his after-life; and it rests with us to awaken the germ of good, to starve out the germ of evil. To a far larger extent than is ever realised by even the fondest parents, the child's future is under their control.

1363.   Think of all the friends whom you know so well, and try to imagine what splendid specimens of humanity they would be if all their good qualities were enormously intensified, and all the less estimable features absolutely weeded out of their characters.

1364.   *That* is the result which it is in your power to produce in your child, if you do your full duty by him; such a specimen of humanity you may make him if you will but take the trouble.

1365. THE INFLUENCE OF PARENTS

1366. But how? you will say; by precept? by education? Yes, truly, much may be done in that way when the time comes; but another and far greater power than that is in your hands - a power which you may begin to wield from the very moment of the child's birth, and even before that; and that is the power of the influence of your own life.

1367. To some extent this is recognised, for most civilised people are careful of their words and actions in the presence of a child, and it would be an unusually depraved parent who would allow his children to hear him use violent language, or to see him give away to a fit of passion; but what a man does not realise is that if he wishes to avoid doing the most serious harm to his little ones, he must learn to control not only his words and deeds, but also his *thoughts*. It is true that you cannot immediately see the pernicious effect of your evil thought or desire upon the mind of your child, but none the less it is there, and it is more real and more terrible, more insidious and more far-reaching than the harm which is obvious to the physical eye.

1368. If a parent allows himself to cherish feelings of anger or jealousy, of envy or avarice, of selfishness or pride, even though he may never give them outward expression, the waves of emotion which he thereby causes in his own desire-body are assuredly acting all the while upon the plastic astral body of his child, tuning its undulations to the same key, awakening into activity any germs of those sins that may have been brought over from his past life, and setting up in him also the same set of evil habits, which when they have once become definitely formed will be exceedingly difficult to correct. And this is exactly what is being done in the case of most of the children whom we see around us.

1369. THE AURA OF A CHILD

1370. As it presents itself to a clairvoyant, the subtle body of a child is often a most beautiful object - pure and bright in its colour, free, as yet, from the stains of sensuality and avarice, and from the dull cloud of ill-will and selfishness which so frequently darkens all the life of the adult. In it are to be seen lying latent all the germs and tendencies of which we have spoken - some of them evil, some of them good; and thus the possibilities of the child's future life lie plain before the eye of the watcher.

1371. But how sad it is to see the change which almost invariably comes over that lovely child-aura as the years pass on - to note how persistently the evil tendencies are fostered and strengthened by his environment, and how entirely the good ones are neglected! And so incarnation after incarnation is almost wasted, and a life which, with just a little more care and self-restraint on the part of parents and teachers, might have borne rich fruit of spiritual development, comes practically to nothing, and at its close leaves scarce any harvest to be garnered into the ego of which it has been so one-sided an expression.

1372.   CARELESSNESS OF PARENTS

1373.   When one watches the criminal carelessness with which those who are responsible for the bringing-up of children allow them to be perpetually surrounded by all kinds of evil and worldly thoughts, one ceases to marvel at the extraordinary slowness of human evolution, and the almost imperceptible progress which is all that the ego has to show for life after life spent in the toil and struggle of this lower world. Yet with so little more trouble so vast an improvement might be introduced!

1374.   It needs no astral vision to see what a change would come over this weary old world if the majority, or even any large proportion of the next generation, were subjected to the process suggested above - if all their evil qualities were steadily repressed and atrophied for lack of nourishment, while all the good in them was assiduously cultivated and developed to the fullest possible extent. One has only to think what they in turn would do for *their* children, to realise that in two or three generations all the conditions of life would be different, and a true golden age would have begun. For the world at large age may still be distant, but surely we who are members of the Theosophical Society ought to be doing our best to hasten its advent: and though the influence of our example may not extend far, it is at least within our power to see that our own children have for their development every advantage which we can give them.

1375.   The greatest care, then, ought to be taken as to the surroundings of children, and people who will persist in thinking coarse and unloving thoughts should at least learn that while they are doing so, they are unfit to come near the young, lest they infect them with a contagion more virulent than fever.

1376.   Much care is needed, for example, in the selection of the nurses to whom children must sometimes be committed; though it is surely obvious that the less they are left in the hands of servants the better. Nurses often develop the strongest affection for their charges, and treat them as though they were of their own flesh and blood; yet this is not invariably the case, and, even if it be, the servants are almost inevitably less educated and less refined than their mistresses. A child who is left too much to their companionship is therefore constantly subjected to the impact of thought which is likely to be of a less elevated order than even the average level of that of his parents. So that the mother who wishes her child to grow up into a refined and delicate-minded man should entrust him to the care of others as little as possible, and should, above all things, take good heed to her own thoughts while watching over him.

1377.   Her great and cardinal rule should be to allow herself to harbour no thought and no desire which she does not wish to see reproduced in her son. Nor is this merely negative conquest over herself sufficient, for, happily, all that has been said about the influence and power of thought is true of good thoughts just as much as of evil ones, and so the parents' duty has a positive as well as a negative side. Not only must they abstain most carefully from fostering, by unworthy or selfish thoughts of their own, any evil tendency which may exist in their child, but it is also their duty to cultivate in themselves strong, unselfish affection, pure thoughts, high and noble aspirations, in order that all these may react upon their charge, quicken whatever of good is already latent in him, and create a tendency towards any good quality which is as yet unrepresented in his character.

1378.   Nor need they have any fear that such effort on their part will fail in its effect, because they are unable to follow its action for lack of astral vision. To the sight of a clairvoyant the whole transaction is obvious; he distinguishes the waves set up in the mind-body of the parent by the inception of the thought, sees it radiating forth, and notes the sympathetic undulations created by its impingement upon the mind-body of the child; and if he renews his observation at intervals during some considerable period, he discerns the gradual but permanent change produced in that mind-body by the constant repetition of the same stimulus to progress. If the parents themselves possess astral sight, it will, no doubt, be of great assistance to them in showing exactly what are the capabilities of their child, and in what directions he most needs development; but if they have not yet that advantage, there need not therefore be the slightest doubt or question about the result, for that must with mathematical certainty follow sustained effort, whether the process of its working be visible to them or not.

1379.   With whatever care the parents may surround the child, it cannot but be (if he lives in the world at all) that he will some day encounter influences which will stimulate the germs of evil in his composition. But it makes all the difference in the world which germs are stimulated *first*. Usually the evil is thoroughly awakened into activity before the ego has any hold upon the vehicles, and so when he does grasp them he finds that he has to combat a strong predisposition to various evils. When the germs of good are tardily aroused they have to struggle to assert themselves against a set of inharmonious thought-wave which are already firmly established; and often they do not succeed. If, however, by exceeding care before birth and for several years after it the parents are fortunate enough to be able to excite only the good undulations, as the ego gains control he finds it naturally easy to express himself along those lines, and a decided habit is set up in that direction. Then when the evil excitation comes, as come it surely will some time or other, it finds a strong momentum in the direction of good, which it strives in vain to overcome.

1380.   The command of the ego over this lower vehicles is often but small, unless he is unusually advanced; but his will is always for good, because his desire in connection with these vehicles is to evolve himself by their means, and such power as he is able to throw into the balance is therefore always on the right side. But with his at present somewhat uncertain grasp upon his astral and mental bodies, he is frequently unable to overcome a strong tendency in the direction of evil when that has been already established. If, however, he finds the strong tendency set up in the opposite direction, he is enable thereby to get hold of his vehicles more effectually; and after he has done that, the evil suggestion which comes later can only with difficulty succeed in obtaining an entrance. In the one case there is in the personality a taste for evil, a readiness to receive it and indulge in it; in the other there is a strong natural distaste for evil which makes the work of the ego much easier.

1381.   Not only should a parent watch his thoughts, but his moods also. A child is quick to notice and to resent injustice; and if he finds himself scolded at one time for an action which on another occasion caused only amusement, what wonder that his sense of the invariability of Nature's laws is outraged! Again, when trouble or sorrow comes upon the parent, as in this world it sometimes must, it is surely his duty to try, as far as possible, to prevent his load of grief from weighing upon his children as well as upon himself; at least when in their presence he should make a special effort to be cheerful and resigned, lest the dull, leaden hue of depression should extend itself from his astral body to theirs.

1382.   Many a well-meaning parent has an anxious and fussy nature - is always fidgeting about trifles, and worrying his children and himself about matters which are really quite unimportant. If he could but observe clairvoyantly the utter unrest and disquiet which he thus produces in his own higher bodies, and could further see how these disturbed waves introduce quite unnecessary agitation and irritation into the susceptible vehicles of his children, he would no longer be surprised at their occasional outbursts of petulance or nervous excitability, and would realise that in such a case he is often far more to blame than they. What he should contemplate and set before him as his object, is a restful, unruffled spirit - the peace which passeth all understanding - the perfect calm which comes from the confidence that all will at last be well.

1383.   Above all things must he strive to become an embodiment of the Divine Love, so that he may fully realise it in his own life, in order that he may flood with it the life of his child. The body must live in an atmosphere of love; he ought never to meet with a jarring vibration, never even to know in his young days that there is anything but love in this world. And when the time comes, as come it unhappily must, when he learns that in the outside world love is often sadly lacking - all the more let him feel that his home will never fail him, that there, at least, he may always count upon the uttermost love, the fullest comprehension.

1384.   It is obvious that the training of the parents' character which is necessitated by these considerations is in every respect a splendid one, and that in thus helping on the evolution of their children they also benefit themselves to an extent which is absolutely incalculable, for the thoughts which at first have been summoned by conscious effort for the sake of the child will soon become natural and habitual, and will, in time, form the background of the parents' entire life.

1385.   It must not be supposed that these precautions may be relaxed as the child grows older, for though this extraordinary sensitiveness to the influence of his surroundings commences as soon as the ego descends upon the embryo, long before birth takes place, it continues, in most cases, up to about the period of maturity. If such influences as are above suggested have been brought to bear upon him during infancy and childhood, the body of twelve or fourteen will be far better equipped for the efforts which lie before him than his less fortunate companions, with whom no special trouble has been taken. But he is still far more impressionable than an adult; he still needs to be surrounded by the same boundless sea of never-failing love; the same strong help and guidance upon the mental level must still be continued, in order that the good habits both of thought and of action may not yield before the newer temptations which are likely to assail him.

1386. Although in his earlier years it was naturally chiefly to his parents that he had to look for such assistance, all that has been said of their duties applies equally to anyone who comes into contact with children in any capacity, and most especially to those who undertake the tremendous responsibilities of the teacher. This influence of a master for good or for evil over his pupils is one that cannot readily be measured, and (exactly as before) it depends not only upon what he says or what he does, but even more upon what he thinks. Many a master repeatedly reproves in his boys the exhibition of tendencies for the creation of which he is himself directly responsible; if his thought is selfish or impure, then he will find selfishness and impurity reflected all around him, nor does the evil caused by such a thought end with those whom it immediately affects.

1387. The young minds upon which it is reflected take it up and magnify and strengthen it, and thus it reacts upon others in turn and becomes an unholy tradition handed down from one generation of boys to another, and so stamps its peculiar character upon a particular school or a particular class. Happily, a good tradition may be set up almost as easily as a bad one - not quite as easily, because there are always undesirable external influences to be taken into account; but still a teacher who realises his responsibilities and manages his school upon the principles that have been suggested will soon find that his self-control and self-devotion have not been fruitless.

1388. THE NECESSITY FOR LOVE

1389. There is only one way in which either parent or teacher can really obtain effective influence over a child and draw out all the best that is in him - and that is by enfolding him in the pure fire of a warm, constant, personal love, and thereby winning his love and confidence in return. More than any other qualification is this insisted upon in Alcyone's wonderful book *Education as Service* - a book which every parent and teacher should read, for the sake of the sweet spirit which it breathes, and the valuable hints which it contains.

1390. It is true that obedience may be extorted and discipline preserved by inspiring fear, but rules enforced by such a method are kept only so long as he who imposes them (or some one representing him) is present, and are invariably broken when there is no fear of detection; the child keeps them because he must, and not because he wishes to do so; and meantime the effect upon his character is of the most disastrous description.

1391. If, on the other hand, his affection has been invoked, his will at once ranges itself on the side of the rule; he wishes to keep it, because he knows that in breaking it he would cause sorrow to one whom he loves; and if only this feeling be strong enough, it will enable him to rise superior to all temptation, and the rule will be binding, no matter who may be present or absent. Thus the object is attained not only much more thoroughly, but also much more easily and pleasantly both for teacher and pupil, and all the best side of the child's nature is called into activity, instead of all the worst. Instead of rousing the child's will into sullen and persistent opposition, the teacher arrays it on his own side in the contest against distractions or temptations; the danger of deceit and secretiveness is avoided, and thus results are achieved which could never be approached on the other system.

1392. It is of the utmost importance always to try to understand the child, and to make him feel certain that he has one's friendliness and sympathy. All appearance of harshness must be carefully avoided, and the reason of all instructions given to him should always be fully explained. It must indeed be made clear to him that sometimes sudden emergencies arise in which the older person has no time to explain his instructions, and he should understand that in such a case he should obey, even though he may not fully comprehend; but even then the explanation should be always given afterwards.

1393. Unwise parents or teachers often make the mistake of habitually exacting obedience without understanding - a most unreasonable demand; indeed, they expect from the child at all times and under all conditions an angelic patience and saintliness which they are far indeed from possessing themselves. They have not yet realised that harshness towards a child is always not only wicked, but absolutely unreasonable and foolish as well, since it can never be the most effective way of obtaining from him what is desired.

1394. A child's faults are often the direct results of the unnatural way in which he is treated. Sensitive and nervous to a degree, he constantly finds himself misunderstood and scolded or ill-treated for offences whose turpitude he does not in the least comprehend; is it wonderful that, when the whole atmosphere about him reeks with the deceit and falsehood of his elders, his fears should sometimes drive him into untruthfulness also? In such a case the karma of the sin will fall most heavily upon those who by their criminal harshness have placed a weak and undeveloped being in a position where it was almost impossible for him to avoid it.

1395. If we expect truth from our children, we must first of all practise it ourselves; we must think truth as well as speak truth and act truth, before we can hope to be strong enough to save them from the sea of falsehood and deceit which surrounds us on every side. But if we treat them as reasonable beings - if we explain fully and patiently what we want from them, and show them that they have nothing to fear from us, because "perfect love casteth out fear" - then we shall find no difficulty about truthfulness.

1396. A curious but not uncommon delusion - a relic, perhaps, of the terrible days when, for its sins, this unhappy country of England groaned under the ghastly tyranny of puritanism - is, that children can never be good unless they are unhappy, that they must be thwarted at every turn, and never by any chance allowed to have their own way in anything, because when they are enjoying themselves they must necessarily be in a condition of desperate wickedness! Absurd and atrocious as this doctrine is, various modifications of it are still widely prevalent, and it is responsible for a vast amount of cruelty and unnecessary misery, wantonly inflicted upon little creatures whose only crime is that they are natural and happy. Undoubtedly Nature intends that childhood shall be a happy time, and we ought to spare no efforts to make it so, for in that respect, as in all others, if we thwart Nature we do so at our peril. A hymn tells us:

1397.   *God would have us happy, happy all the day,*

1398.   and in this case as in all others it is our duty and our privilege to be fellow-workers together with Him.

1399.   It will help us much in our dealings with children if we remember that they also are egos, that their small and feeble physical bodies are but the accident of the moment, and that in reality we are all about the same age; so that we owe them respect as well as affection, and we must not expect to impose our will or individuality upon theirs. Our business in training them is to develop only that in their lower vehicles which will co-operate with the ego - which will make them better channels for the ego to work through. Long ago, in the golden age of the old Atlantean civilisation, the importance of the office of the teacher of the children was so fully recognised that none was permitted to hold it except a trained clairvoyant, who could see all the latent qualities and capabilities of his charges, and could, therefore, work intelligently with each, so as to develop what was good in him and to amend what was evil.

1400.   In the distant future of the sixth root-race that will be so once more; but that time is, as yet, far away, and we have to do our best under less favourable conditions. Yet unselfish affection is a wonderful quickener of the intuition, and those who really love their children will rarely be at a loss to comprehend their needs; and keen and persistent observation will give them, though at the cost of much more trouble, some approach to the clearer insight of their Atlantean predecessors. At any rate, it is well worth the trying, for when once we realise our true responsibility in relation to children we shall assuredly think no labour too great which enables us to discharge it better. Love is not always wise, we know; but at least it is wiser than carelessness, and parents and teachers who truly love will be thereby spurred on to gain wisdom for the sake of the children.

1401.   RELIGIOUS TRAINING

1402.   Many members of our Society, while feeling that their children need something to take the place filled in ordinary education by the religious training, have yet found it almost impossible so to put Theosophy before them as to make it in any way intelligible to them. Some have even permitted their children to go through the ordinary routine of bible lessons, saying that they did not know what else to do, and that though much of the teaching was obviously untrue it could be corrected afterwards. This course is entirely indefensible; no child should ever waste his time in learning what he will have to unlearn afterwards. If the true inner meaning of Christianity can be taught to our children, that indeed is well, because that is pure Theosophy; but unfortunately that is not the form which religious instruction takes in ordinary schools.

1403.   There is no real difficulty in putting the grand truths of Theosophy intelligibly before the minds of our children. It is useless to trouble them with rounds and races, with mulaprakriti and planetary chains; but then, however interesting and valuable all this information may be, it is of little importance in the practical regulation of conduct, whereas the great ethical truths upon which the whole system rests can, happily, be made clear even to the childish understanding. What could be simpler in essence than the three great truths which are given to Sensa in *The Idyll of the White Lotus*?

1404.   The soul of man is immortal, and its future is the future of a thing whose growth and splendour have no limit.

1405.   The principle which gives life dwells in us and without us, is undying and eternally beneficent, is not heard, nor seen, nor smelt, but is perceived by the man who desires perception.

1406.   Each man is his own absolute lawgiver, the dispenser of glory or gloom to himself - the decreer of his life, his reward, his punishment.

1407.   These truths, which are as great as is life, itself, are as simple as the simplest mind of man. Feed the hungry with them.

1408.   We might express these more tersely by saying: "Man is immortal; God is good; as we sow, so shall we reap." Surely none of our children can fail to grasp these simple ideas in their broad outline, though as they grow older they may spend many a year in learning more and more of the immensity of their full meaning.

1409.   Teach them the grand old formula that "death is the gate of life" - not a terrible fate to be feared, but simply a stage of progress to be welcomed with interest. Teach them to live, not for themselves, but for others - to go through the world as friends and helpers, earnest in loving reverence and care for all living things. Teach them to delight in seeing and in causing happiness in others, in animals and birds as well as in human beings; teach them that to cause pain to any living thing is always a wicked action, and can never have aught of interest or amusement for any right-thinking or civilised man. A child's sympathies are so easily roused, and his delight in doing something is so great, that he responds at once to the idea that he should try to help, and should never harm, all the creatures around him. He should be taught to be observant, that he may see where help is needed, whether by man or by animal, and promptly to supply the want so far as lies in his power.

1410.   A child likes to be loved, and he likes to protect, and both these feelings may be utilised in training him to be a friend of all creatures. He will readily learn to admire flowers as they grow, and not wish to pluck them heedlessly, casting them aside a few minutes later to wither on the roadside; those which he plucks he will pick carefully, avoiding injury to the plant; he will preserve and tend them, and his way through wood and field will never be traceable by fading blossoms and uprooted plants.

1411.   PHYSICAL TRAINING

1412.   The physical training of the child is a matter of the greatest importance, for a strong, pure, healthy body is necessary for the full expression of the developing soul within. Teach him from the first the exceeding importance of physical purity, so that he may regard his daily bath as just as much an integral part of his life as his daily food. See to it that his body is never befouled with such filthy abominations of modern savagery as meat, alcohol or tobacco; see to it that he has always plenty of sunlight, of fresh air and of exercise.

1413.   We have seen in an earlier chapter how horrible are the surroundings in a great town; and if these are evil in their influence on adults, they are ten times worse for the more sensitive children. The truth is that no children ought ever to be brought up in a town at all; and those whose evil karma compels them to work in such places should at least try if possible to live a little way outside of them for the sake of their children. It is far better for the children to be brought up in the country, even though it be in comparative poverty, than that, in order to amass money for them, the parents should allow them to grow up amidst all the noxious influences of a large town. Where the urban life is unfortunately unavoidable, they should at least be taken out of the city as often as possible, and kept out as long as possible.

1414.   So shall your child grow up pure, healthy and happy; so shall you provide, for the soul entrusted to your care, a casket of which it need not be ashamed, a vehicle through which it shall receive only the highest and best that the physical world can give - which it can use as a fitting instrument for the noblest and the holiest work.

1415.   As the parent teaches the child, he will also be obliged to set the example in this as in other things, and so the child will thus again civilise his elders as well as improve himself. Birds and butterflies, cats and dogs, all will be his friends, and he will delight in their beauty instead of longing to chase or destroy them. Children thus trained will grow up into men and women who recognise their place in evolution and their work in the world, and each will serve as a fresh centre of humanising force, gradually changing the direction of human influence on all lower things.

1416.   If thus we train our children, if we are thus careful in our relations with them, we shall bear nobly our great responsibility, and in so doing we shall help on the grand work of evolution; we shall be doing our duty, not only to our children, but to the human race - not only to these particular egos, but to the many millions yet to come.

CHAPTER XXIII BY OUR RELATION TO LOWER KINGDOMS

1419. DOMESTIC ANIMALS

1420.   We have a responsibility which must not be forgotten towards the animals which we draw around us. This may be of two kinds, or rather of two degrees. A farmer in the course of his business has to deal with a large number of animals which may be described as semi-domesticated. His duty towards them is clearly to feed them well and to take all possible care to keep them in perfect health. He may sometimes attach to himself some one of these, but on the whole his relation towards them is in the mass only, and as they are yet far from the possibility of individualisation, it is not likely that his influence over them can go far, or be more than a general one. His relation with them is, in fact, a business relation, though he should look after them as carefully as though they were human.

1421.   The case is quite different with the really domestic animals which live in the house with us, and come into intimate personal relations with us. No one is obliged to keep a dog or a cat, but if he does so he incurs a much greater responsibility towards that animal than the farmer has towards any member of his flock. It would be unpardonable selfishness for anyone who keeps such an animal to think only of his own pleasure in connection with it, and not of the animal's development.

1422.   The domestic animal is in fact a kind of younger child - with this difference, that whereas the child is already an ego and has to be helped to control his new vehicles, the animal is not yet a separate ego and has to be helped to become one. The process of the individualisation of an animal has been often described; notes upon it may be found in *A Text-book of Theosophy, The Inner Life, Man Visible and Invisible* and *The Christian Creed*. A perusal of what is there written will show at once along what line our duties to the animals lie. We must endeavour to develop their affection and their intellect, and the principal factor in both those developments is the affection which we feel for them.

1423.   I have written at considerable length, in *The Inner Life*, Vol. ii, upon mistakes which are frequently made by men in their relation to domestic animals. All those mistakes are due to a selfish attitude with regard to the animal, an endeavour to employ him for the gratification of our own evil passions - as, for example, when a dog is trained to hunt, and made in that way to do vastly more harm than his forefathers ever did as wild beasts in the jungle. For the wild beast kills only for food, when impelled to do so by hunger; but the dog is trained to kill for the pleasure of killing, and is thereby degraded in the scale of evolution instead of being raised.

1424.   Between the two categories, of really domestic animals and farm animals, we may place the horse, for it comes into more individual relation with the rider than does the farm animal, and yet at the same time it is far from possessing the intelligence of the dog or the cat. It also must be treated intelligently, and above all with unvarying kindness. The rider should remember always that the horse does not exist solely to serve him, but has an evolution of its own which it is his duty to forward. There is no wrong in his utilising it to help him, because the association with him may develop its affection and intelligence; but he must treat it always as he would treat a human servant, and never forget its interest while he is making it serve his own.

1425.   BIRDS

1426.   A student of the hidden side of life cannot but deprecate the practice of keeping birds in cages. Perfect liberty and the sense of great open spaces are of the very essence of the life of a bird, and his misery at being imprisoned is often intense and most pathetic. This is always especially marked in the case of those birds which are natives of the country, and all such ought certainly at once to be set free.

1427.   Foreign birds, which can live happily only in other climates, come under a different category. They also spend most of the time in memories of splendid tropical scenes, and in longing for the home from which they have been taken - to which they ought to be sent back at the earliest possible moment. The sin there lies with those who originally caught them; and those who keep them now share in it only so far as that their action makes it profitable. A student who has already thoughtlessly acquired such birds as these, can hardly do other than keep them, unless he is in a position to return them to their native country; but he should provide them with the largest cages, and let them out of them to fly about the room as often as possible, while he certainly should not encourage a nefarious traffic by buying any more of such creatures.

1428.   The only rational and useful relation that we can establish with birds is that which occasionally exists in country places - that food is regularly put out for the birds in a certain place and they come and take it, while remaining otherwise perfectly free. If a man wants to keep a bird, he should keep it precisely as he would keep a cat - provide it with plenty of food and an abiding place whenever it chooses to accept it, but leave it otherwise free to go where it will. The difficulty in the way is that the bird's intelligence is so much less developed than the cat's that it would be more difficult to get it to understand the conditions of the arrangement. By far the best plan is to have nothing to do with foreign birds, but to try to make friends of the wild birds of the neighbourhood.

1429.   Individualisation is not a possibility, as the bird is not developing along our line; when it transcends the bird evolution is passes directly into one of the higher orders of nature-spirits. Nevertheless, kindness shown to birds arouses gratitude and affection in them, and helps them forward in their evolution.

1430.   PLANTS

1431.   Another direction in which we may exercise a good deal of influence if we will, is upon the plants in our gardens. Plants, like animals, are quick to respond to wise and loving care, and are distinctly affected not only by what we do for them physically, but also by our feelings towards them. Anyone who possesses astral sight will be aware that flowers delight in and respond to a feeling of admiration. The feelings of the vegetable differ rather in degree than in kind from those of the animal or of the human being, and they bear somewhat the same relation to those of the animal as do those of the animal to those of the human being.

1432.   The animal is less complex in his emotions than the human being, but he is capable of affection and hatred, of fear and pride, of jealousy or of shame. Some animals, too, seem to have a sense of humour; at any rate, they keenly enjoy playing tricks on one another, and they object greatly to being made to appear ridiculous or to being laughed at. There is nothing to show that these emotions are less in proportion in the animal than they are in us; but we may say that the animal has fewer emotions and that they are less complex, and his methods of expressing them are more limited.

1433.   If we descend to the vegetable kingdom, we find that the vegetable has scarcely any power of expression; but we shall be making a grave mistake if we therefore assume that there are no feelings to express. Emotion in the vegetable kingdom is again far less complex even than that of the animal, and it is altogether vaguer - a sort of blind instinctual feeling. The chief physical manifestation of it is the well-known fact that some people are always fortunate with plants, while others are always unfortunate, even when the physical measures adopted are precisely the same. This difference exists everywhere, but in India it has been specially noted, and certain people are described as having the lucky hand, and it is recognised that almost anything which those people plant will grow; even under quite unfavourable conditions, and that anything which they cultivate is sure to turn out well. When this influence is universal over the vegetable kingdom it is not a question of individual liking, but of certain characteristics in the person, and certain qualities in his astral and etheric vehicles which prove generally attractive, just as there are some people with whom all dogs will at once make friends, and others who without effort can manage the most recalcitrant horses.

1434.   But plants are also capable of individual attachment, and when they get to know people well, they are pleased to see (or rather to feel) them near. A person who pours upon his flowers a stream of admiration and affection evokes in them a feeling of pleasure - first of a general pleasure in receiving admiration, which might be thought of as a sort of germ of pride, and then, secondly, a feeling of pleasure at the presence of the person who admires, which in the same way is the germ of love and gratitude. Plants are also capable of anger and dislike, though outwardly they have hardly any means of showing them.

1435.   An occultist who has a garden will make a point of seeing that it is in every way perfectly and carefully looked after, and more than this, he will himself make friends with the flowers and trees and shrubs, and will go sometimes to visit them and give each its due meed of admiration, and so in giving pleasure to these lowly organisms he will himself be surrounded by a vague feeling of affection.

1436.   It may be said that the feeling of a vegetable can hardly be strong enough to be worth taking into account. It is true that the influence exerted by it upon a human being is less than would be produced by the feeling of an animal; but these influences do exist, and though the feeling of one plant may not seem important, the feeling of hundreds begins to be a recognisable factor, and if we wish to make the best possible conditions, we must not ignore our less developed brethren of the lower kingdoms. That much even from the purely selfish point of view; but the occultist naturally thinks first of the effect upon the plant.

1437.   When we form a garden we are drawing round us a number of members of the vegetable kingdom for our own pleasure; but at the same time this affords us an opportunity of helping them in their evolution, an opportunity which should not be neglected. Plants differ much in their power to receive and respond to human influences. A large tree, for example, with its slow growth and its long life, is capable of forming a far stronger a attachment than anything which is merely annual. Such a tree comes to have a decided personality of its own, and is even sometimes able temporarily to externalise that personality, so that it can be seen by the clairvoyant. In such a case it usually takes upon itself human form for the time, as I have mentioned in *The Inner Life*, Vol. ii. Those who wish to understand how much more intelligence there is in the vegetable kingdom than we usually think, should read a delightful book called *The Sagacity and Morality of Plants* by J.E. Taylor.

1438.   NATURE-SPIRITS

1439.   This wonderful evolution has been described in an earlier chapter, but from the point of view of its effect upon us, rather than of ours upon it. Here we must consider the outer side of that relation - the influence which we may exercise upon the nature-spirits of our neighbourhood, and the friendship which we may make with them. Many of their tribes are so beautiful and so interesting that their acquaintance would repay cultivation, and we may help to develop their intellect and affection, and so do them much good. Those of them who possess etheric bodies have the power to make themselves physically visible if they choose, so men who are happy enough to gain their friendship may occasionally be rewarded by a view of them even with ordinary sight. There is also a probability that such friends may be helped by these elves to attain flashes of temporary clairvoyance, in order that in that way they may see them.

1440.   A fairy has many points of resemblance to a wild animal, and the method of making friends with him is much what we should have to adopt if we were trying to tame birds or deer. He is shy and distrustful towards man; how is this distrust to be overcome? One who wishes to study at first-hand the habits of a bird usually goes to the haunt of the creature, conceals himself, and remains perfectly quiet, in the hope that the bird will not see him, or if it does, will be reassured by his absolute stillness. The etheric sight of a nature-spirit pierces through walls or bushes, so it is hopeless to attempt to evade his observation; and for him the stillness which is important is not that of the physical body, but of the astral. He objects to the filthy physical emanations of the average man - of meat, of tobacco, of alcohol, and of general uncleanliness; obviously one who wishes to make friends with him must be free from all these. He objects, too, to storms of passion and impurity; so the man who seeks him must also be free from all low and selfish feelings, such as lust, anger, envy, jealousy, avarice or depression.

1441.   These negative qualifications being in order, can anything positive be done to invite the approach of so coy a visitor? Animals can often be attracted by the offer of food, but as a fairy does not eat, that particular allurement is not available in his case. The student can provide for him conditions which he is known to enjoy. Strong unselfish affection or devotion, or indeed any high feeling which burns steadily and without wild surgings, creates an atmosphere in which the nature-spirit delights to bathe.

1442.   The man - the right sort of man - who rests for a while in some lovely, lonely spot - in a wood perhaps, or by a stream or a waterfall - and revels in such thoughts as have been suggested, is quite likely to become aware of an unfamiliar presence, of something fascinating, yet strange and non-human; and perchance, if fortune greatly favours him, he may even see as well as feel, when the shy, wild creature becomes a little more accustomed to him, and gradually learns to trust and like him. But if the student remembers that to the nature-spirit this is an adventure such as it would be for a mouse to make friends with a cat, or for a man to endeavour to establish fraternal relations with a tiger in the jungle, he will learn to exercise unlimited patience, and not to expect immediate results.

1443.   Almost all nature-spirits delight in music, and some are specially attracted by certain melodies; so if the experimenter happens to be a performer upon some portable instrument, such as the flute, it may increase his chances of success if he plays upon it. I knew an elf in Italy who was so fascinated by a particular piece of music that when it was played on the piano, he would actually leave the wood in which he dwelt and come into the drawing-room to enjoy it and dance to it - or rather to bathe in its sound-waves, to pulsate and sway in harmony with them. But I never knew him to do this if there were more than two or three people in the room - and even those must be friends whom he had learned to trust.

1444.   More than once I have seen a shepherd-boy in Sicily, sitting in some lonely spot on the hillside, playing on his home-made double Pan-pipe like an ancient Greek, with an appreciative audience of fairies frisking round him of which he was probably blissfully unconscious, though no doubt their delight reacted upon him and added zest to his playing. Sometimes the peasants *do* see the nature-spirits, however; plenty of instances may be found in Mr. Wentz' *Fairy Faith in Celtic Countries*.

1445.   INANIMATE SURROUNDINGS

1446.   We are all the while exerting an influence even on what we commonly consider our inanimate surroundings. Some of these, by the way, are not quite so inanimate as we are apt to think. We all know that the Divine Life exists in the mineral kingdom as well as in those which are higher, and in that sense rocks, stones, and minerals may rightly be thought of as alive. But certain objects have a more vivid and special kind of life, the study of which is of great interest.

1447.   To explain it, we must revert for a moment to a familiar analogy. We know how the life of the elemental essence of the astral body gathers itself up into a kind of personality (which we call the desire elemental) and exists for the time as a separate being with definite desires and dislikes of its own, and with sufficient power to exercise a great effect in the course of its life on the man whose vehicle it informs. We know that the similar consciousness animating the cells of the physical body (including of course its etheric part) manifests itself in certain instinctive movements. In a way analogous to this, the consciousness which animates the molecules of certain minerals will combine into a temporary whole when those molecules are welded together into a definite form; and especially is this the case when that form demands the presence and attention of man, as machinery does.

1448.   A SHIP

1449.   The most perfect example of what I mean is to be found in a ship, for there we have a structure built of an enormous number of component parts, and usually of different substances. Kipling's story of *The Ship that Found Herself* is not mere fiction, but has a real and important truth behind it. When a ship is first built she is not thus conscious of herself as a unit, but is a mere aggregation of a number of separate sentiences. But the whole fabric *does* become in time a unit of consciousness or awareness - being to a certain extent aware of itself as a whole - however dim and vague its percipience may be as compared with our own.

1450.   And that consciousness has what we can hardly describe as otherwise than feelings, indistinct though they are as compared with anything to which we usually give that name. Such an obscure semi-entity certainly may (and often does) like one person better than another, so that one person can do with it what another cannot. This in no way modifies the other fact that some men are better seaman than others, and with a little practice can get out of any ship the best that is to be got. Just so, some men are splendid riders, and can almost immediately establish a friendly understanding with any horse; but quite apart from that, a horse may become attached to a certain man, and learn to understand his wishes far more readily than a stranger's. The same thing is true of the vaguer consciousness of the ship. I do not wish to be understood as suggesting by this term anything comparable, in definiteness or responsiveness, to the consciousness in man; but there certainly is a something, however loose and uncertain, which we cannot define by any other word.

1451.   MACHINES

1452.   The same thing is true of a railway engine, of a motor-car or a bicycle. Just as the driver or rider becomes accustomed to his machine and learns to know exactly what it will do, and to humour its various little tricks, so the machine in its turn becomes used to the driver and will do more for him in various ways than for a stranger. The same must be true of many other sorts of machinery, though for that I have not had the benefit of personal observation.

1453.   Apart from the influence acquired by an individual over the blended consciousness of a machine, the mere blending itself produces an effect upon the molecules of the substance of which it is made. Iron which has formed part of a machine, and so has experienced what is for it this exaltation of consciousness, may be thought of as somewhat more developed than iron which has not been used in the building of a self-contained system. It has become capable of responding to additional and more complicated vibrations, and that for a mineral is evolution. It is more awake than other iron. This condition of greater vitality would be easily visible to a clairvoyant who had learnt its indications, but I do not know of any method by which it could be observed physically.

1454.   The additional power of response is not always of the same kind, and variants of it may be aroused in different ways. Wrought iron, for example, is much more alive than cast iron, and this result is produced by the frequent blows which it receives in the process of its working. The same thing may be observed to a greater degree with a horse-shoe, for not only has that been wrought in the first place, but it has been subjected to constant striking upon the road when it was worn by the horse. This long-continued process has awakened it in a certain way which makes it exceedingly repulsive to some of the lowest and most malignant types of the astral and etheric entities; and that is the reason for the old superstition, that when hung over the door it kept away evil and brought good fortune to its possessor.

1455.   Another interesting point with regard to this curious composite consciousness is that after a certain time it gets tired - a fact which has frequently been observed by those who have much to do with machinery. After a certain time a machine, though perfectly in order, gets into a condition in which it will not work properly, but becomes slack in its action. It often seems impossible to do anything to cure it, but if it is left alone for a time it presently recovers its tone and will go on working as before.

1456.   Metals show plainly that they are subject to fatigue. A steel pen will sometimes scratch and write badly when it has been used continually for several hours, but the clerk who understands nature so far, will put the pen aside, instead of throwing it away, and maybe the next day will find it even better than it was at first. A barber often finds his razor refusing to take a keen edge, and it is quite customary for him to say that it is "getting tired" and to put it aside to rest. Some days later that same razor will be in perfect order, keen and sharp as ever.

1457.   Railway engines are known to want regular rest, and after a certain amount of work are put into the shed, and allowed to cool; and so the engine has its rest just as regularly a human being. So we see that fatigue is one of the conditions possible to the mineral kingdom and may be felt by metals as well as by men in their physical bodies. (See *Response in the Living and Non-living*, by Professor J.C. Bose.) As a matter of fact fatigue is not felt anywhere except in the physical world.

1458.   There are men, but so far I know only few, who are unusually charged with electricity, and thus produce a special effect upon any metal with which they habitually come into contact. It is said, for example, that such people cause quite considerable deflections of a ship's compass when they come near it; but this is physical, and hardly occult.

1459.   UNLUCKY SHIPS
1460.   A curious instance of the intervention of the hidden side in the ordinary affairs of life is furnished by the experience of practical men connected with such matters, that certain ships or engines are what is called unlucky - that accident after

274

accident occurs in connection with them, without any obvious negligence to account for it. Naturally some machines are better made than others; some men are more careful than others; but I am not referring to cases into which either of these factors enters. In some cases where two ships or two engines are precisely similar, and the men who manage them are of equal capacity, one proves always fortunate, or meets with only an average proportion of accidents, while the other is perpetually in trouble for no obvious reason.

1461. There is no question at all that this is so, and it offers an interesting problem to the occult student. I am inclined to think that various reasons may sometimes comes into play in producing the results. In one such case at least it appeared to be due to feelings of intense hatred nourished by all the men against the first captain of the vessel, who seems to have been a petty tyrant of the most objectionable description. A large number of men continually cursed the captain, the ship, and all that belonged to her, with all the will-power at their command; and the state of their feeling produced this evil result, that disaster after disaster overtook her. By the time that that captain was removed, the ship had acquired a definite reputation of being unlucky, and so her successive crews have surrounded her with thought-forms to that effect, which naturally enough justify themselves by continuing the series of misfortunes.

1462. In other cases I think that ill-feeling directed towards the builder of the vessel has produced similar results. I doubt whether any such directions of evil force would in themselves be sufficient actually to cause serious misfortune. But in the life of every ship there are a great many occasions on which an accident is only just averted by vigilance and promptitude - in which a single moment's delay or slackness would be sufficient to precipitate a catastrophe. Such a mass of thought-forms as I have described would be amply sufficient to cause that momentary lack of vigilance or that momentary hesitation; and that would be the easiest line along which its malignity could work.

1463. STONE USED IN BUILDING

1464. In speaking of our houses, I have already mentioned the effect which we are constantly producing upon the walls which surround us and the articles of furniture in our rooms. It obviously follows that stone which has been used for a building is never afterwards in the same condition as the stone which is as yet unquarried. It has been permeated, probably for many years in succession, with influences of a certain kind, and that means that for ever after it is capable of responding to such influences more readily than is the unused stone.

1465. We are therefore actually assisting in the evolution of the mineral kingdom when we use these various materials for our buildings. I have already explained how the different influences which we put into them react upon us; so that just as a church radiates devotion, and a prison radiates gloom, so each house in the business part of a city radiates anxiety and effort, too often coupled also with weariness and despair. There are instances in which a knowledge of these facts may prove useful in the prosaic matters of physical life.

1466. SEA-SICKNESS

1467.   We know, for example, that many sensitive ladies are often seized with the pangs of sickness as soon as they go on board a vessel, even though the sea may be perfectly smooth and there may be no physical excuse for the sensation. No doubt this is partially auto-suggestion, but most of it comes from outside. Many a cabin is so thoroughly loaded with this suggestion that it requires considerable mental force for a newcomer to resist it; so it is not only the physical consideration of fresh air which makes it desirable for anyone who is likely to suffer in this way to be on deck as much as possible.

FIFTH SECTION CONCLUSION

CHAPTER XXIV THE RESULTS OF THE KNOWLEDGE

1472.   A SUMMARY

1473.   To know something of the hidden side of nature makes life far more interesting for us; interesting most of all, naturally, to the clairvoyant who can see it, or to the sensitive who can feel it, but interesting in a less degree even to those who cannot directly see or feel, and equally important to all, because all are influencing and being influenced, even though it be unconsciously to themselves so far as their physical brain is concerned.

1474.   In each case, as we have considered it, I have tried to indicate the lesson to be learnt from it, but I will summarise the results here. First and foremost we learn the duty of happiness, the necessity of casting away from us depression and sorrow, even under the circumstances which most readily produce it in those who do not know. Yet at the same time we learn that life must be taken seriously, and must be lived not for selfish enjoyment but for the helping of our fellow-men. We see that we must be on our guard against unsuspected influences, such, for example, as the prejudices connected with race, religion, or class, and the weight of public opinion, never allowing these to bias our judgment, but trying always to arrive at the truth and to weigh the facts for ourselves; that we must not yield ourselves unquestioningly even to presumed spiritual inspiration, but in that case also must "try the spirits" and use our common sense.

1475.   We learn desirability of systematic work or training; the futility of taking offence, of becoming angry, or of allowing our serenity to be disturbed in any way whatever, and the necessity of maintaining a ceaseless watch over our thoughts as well as our words and actions, lest they should draw round us unpleasant influences and act as temptations to our neighbours. And we see that from those influences which we have mentioned above and from all others which are undesirable, we can readily protect ourselves by the formation of shells, though a better protection still is to be so full of the divine Love, that it is always pouring itself out from us in the shape of love to our fellow-men.

1476.   We learn the danger of becoming slaves to the alcohol, corpse-eating or tobacco habits; we learn to keep ourselves free from participation in the cruelties so-called sport; we realise that we must be careful of the situation and the decoration of our houses or rooms, avoiding harmful influences and taking care always to flood them with sunlight and fresh air; that our clothing should be dictated by considerations of health and common sense, and not merely by fashion; that those who have the good fortune to be specially in contact with children, should treat them with the uttermost love, gentleness and patience; that we should recognise the brotherhood of all forms of the Divine Life in our treatment of animals and plants; that we should never work unnecessary destruction upon anything, whether it be what we call animate or inanimate, since the occultist knows the Divine Life in everything, and respects it; that what we are, what we think and what we do are even more important in relation to their action upon others than upon ourselves; that we must preserve the uttermost truth in thought and speech, and utter no word that is not true, kind, pleasant and helpful; that every man possesses a certain amount of force and is responsible for making the best use of it. We learn that ignorance of the law is not accepted by Nature as an excuse, because it does not alter the effect of what we do; that evil is but the dark shadow of good, and is always temporary, while good is eternal; and that while, in everything human, good and evil are mixed, yet the powers behind always use to the utmost the good in everything and everybody.

1477.   These points on which I have written are but specimens of a vast host, for to everything there is an unseen side, and to live the life of the occultist is to study this higher, hidden side of Nature, and then intelligently to adapt oneself to it. The occultist looks at the whole of each subject which is brought before him, instead of only at the lowest and least important part of it, and then orders his action according to what he sees, in obedience to the dictates of plain common sense, and to the Law of Love which guides the Universe. Those therefore who would study and practise occultism must develop within themselves these three priceless possessions - knowledge, common sense and love.

1478.   Such if the course of action suggested to us by a study of the hidden side of things. But remember that this hidden side will not always remain hidden, for every day more and more of our fellow-men learning to understand, because one by one, scattered here and there, more and more are learning to see it. Since it is obvious that this is the line of evolution and that the few who see now are only precursors of the many who will see hereafter, what in the light of these considerations may be predicted as the probable future of humanity?

1479.   THE FUTURE

1480.   Ingenious speculation upon this subject is a prominent feature of our modern fiction. It was attempted by Edward Bellamy in *Looking Backward,* and more recently by Mr. H. G. Wells in a number of quaintly interesting works. The line most usually taken is to pursue to a logical conclusion some of the many socialistic theories which are at present in the air, and to endeavour to calculate how these will work in practice among men as we know them. In one of the pleasantest of these books, *In the Days of the Comet,* Mr. Wells boldly introduces an entirely new factor - a change in the constitution of our atmosphere which suddenly inoculates mankind with common sense and fraternal feeling. When that is achieved, naturally many other obvious changes immediately follow: war becomes a ridiculous impossibility, our present social system is regarded with horror and amazement, our business methods are thrown aside as unworthy of human beings, and so on. For this much of common sense we may surely presently hope in real life, though it will probably come much more slowly than in Mr. Wells' story.

1481. It may be of interest to see what light is thrown upon the problem of the future by the higher extensions of human consciousness of which we have spoken elsewhere. We find that from this point of view the future divides itself into three parts - the immediate, the remote, and the ultimate; and, oddly enough, it is of that which is furthest from us that we are able to speak with the greatest certainty, because the plan of evolution is visible to the higher sight, and its goal is clear. Nothing can interfere with the attainment of that goal, but the stages that lead up to it may be largely modified by the free-will of the individuals concerned, and can, therefore, be foreseen only in their general outline.

1482. The end, so far as this cycle is concerned, is the accomplishment of the perfection of man. Each individual is to become something much more than what we now mean by a great and good man, for he is to be perfect in intellect and capacity as well as spirituality. All the intellect of the greatest philosopher or man of science, and far more; all the devotion and spirituality of the greatest of saints, and far more; these are to be the possessions of every unit of humanity before our cycle ends.

1483. To understand how such a stupendous result can be possible, we must grasp the plan by which evolution works. Obviously, on the ordinary theory of one poor little life of seventy years, followed by an eternity of purposeless joy or suffering, nothing of this sort could ever be achieved; but when once we realise that what we commonly call our life is only one day in the real life, and that we may have just as many of such days as are necessary for our development, we see that the command of Christ: "Be ye perfect even as your Father in heaven is perfect," is no vain hyperbole, but a plain direction which we may reasonably expect to be able in due time to obey.

1484. The ultimate future, then, is perfection for every human being, no matter how low or undeveloped he may now be. Man will become more than man. This is what was meant in the early Church by the doctrine of ' deification' to which many of the Fathers refer. It is a matter not of pious opinion but of utter certainty to those who see the working of the scheme.

1485. Obviously, however, we are yet very far from this attainment; a long upward path lies before us before we can reach that far-distant summit, and though on the whole it rises steadily, there must necessarily be many minor ups and downs in the future as there have been in the past. History shows us that hitherto the advancement mankind has been cyclic in its character.

1486. Each unit lives his long series of progressive lives, not in one race but in many successive races, in order that he may learn the special lessons which each has to teach. One can image a soul incarnating in ancient India to develop religious fervour, in classical Greece to gain artistic capacity, in the Rome of the Caesars to learn the immense power of discipline and order, among ourselves at the present day to acquire the scientific habit of mind, and so on.

1487. The same great host of souls sweeps on through all ages, animating all the these races in turn, and learning from all; but the races themselves arise, grow, decay and fall as they are needed. So when a nation loses its former glory and falls behind in the race (as, for example, modern Greece seems to have done in comparison with ancient Greece), it does not mean that a certain group of men is decadent, but that there are at the moment no souls who need precisely the type of training which that race at its best used to give, or that that training is now being given elsewhere.

1488. Consequently, the physical bodies of the descendants of those great men of old are now animated by souls of a lower type, while the great men themselves are now (as ever) in the forefront of evolution, but incarnated in some other race, in order to grow still greater by developing in new directions. A race dies precisely as a class at a university might die, if there were no longer any students taking up that particular subject.

1489. Clairvoyance enables us to examine a much larger section of the earth's past history than can be reached along ordinary lines; and this fuller study of the past makes it possible, to some extent, to forecast by analogy some of the steps in the more immediate future. From such a study of the records it appears fairly certain that we are at the moment passing through a transition period, and that instead of representing, as we often fondly imagine, the highest development yet seen on earth, we are in reality in the trough between two waves of progress. The democratic tendency of which some of us are so proud, does not represent, as is generally supposed, the ultimate achievement of human wisdom, but is an experiment which was tried thoroughly and carried out to its logical conclusion thousands of years ago, and then abandoned in universal disgust as irrational, unworkable, and leading to endless confusion. If we are to repeat the course of that experiment, it seems unpleasantly certain that we shall have to pass through a good deal of this confusion and suffering once again, before we arrive at the stage of common sense which Mr. Wells so happily describes in the story previously mentioned.

1490. But when that madness is over and reason begins to reassert itself, it is manifest that there will be before us a period of far more rapid progress, in which we shall be able to avail ourselves of many aids which are not now at our disposal. The mere fact that the use of the higher faculties is slowly spreading among humanity, will presently make an almost incalculable difference in many directions.

1491. Imagine a condition in which all deception or fraud will be impossible, in which misunderstandings can no longer occur, because each man can read the thought of the other - in which no one will ever again be set to do work for which he is unfitted, because from the first, parents and tutors will be able to see exactly the capacities of those committed to their care - in which a doctor cannot make mistakes, because he will see for himself exactly what is the matter with his patient, and can watch in detail the action of his remedies. Think what a difference it will make in our lives when death no longer separates us from those whom we love, because the astral world lies open to us just as does the physical; when it will be impossible for men any longer to doubt the reality of the Divine scheme, because its lower stages are visibly before their eyes. Art and music will be far grander then, for astral colours and harmonies will be at our command as well as those which we now know.

1492.   The problems of science will be solved, for the vast additions to human knowledge will blend all its branches into one perfect scheme. Geometry and mathematics will be far more satisfactory, because we shall then see what they really mean and what part they play in the splendid system of the worlds.

1493.   Geometry as we have it now is but a fragment; it is an exoteric preparation for the esoteric reality. Because we have lost the true sense of space, the first step towards that knowledge is the cognition of the fourth dimension. For example, there are five, and only five, possible regular solids - those which are sometimes called the Platonic Solids; to us, that is an interesting fact and no more, but the student who has been initiated into the Mysteries knows that, with a point at one end of the series and a sphere at the other, they make a set of seven which bears a mystic meaning, explaining the relations one to the other of the different types of matter in the seven planes of our Solar System, and the power of the forces that play through them. Treated only from the physical plane, studied as ends in themselves, instead of as means to an end, geometry and mathematics must always remain incomplete, like beautiful avenues that lead nowhere.

1494.   Every feature of life will be wider and fuller, because we shall see much more than we do now of the beautiful and wonderful world in which our lot is cast; understanding more, we cannot but admire and love more, so we shall be infinitely happier, as we draw steadily nearer to that ultimate perfection which is absolute happiness, because it is union with the Eternal Love.

CHAPTER XXV THE WAY TO SEERSHIP

1497.   I have no doubt that many people will find it difficult to believe much of what I have written. I sympathise with them, because I realise quite well how fantastic much of it would have appeared to *me* before I had studied these matters or was able to see them for myself. I know also that, without throwing the slightest imputation upon my good faith, many people will inevitably doubt whether I have seen all these things clearly and reported them exactly. One quaint criticism was offered by a friend, who said:

1498.   "It seems as though you had written this to justify your own peculiarities, for the things that you recommend here are just those in which you differ from many others."

1499.   The friend was confusing cause and effect; if I do, or try to do, these various things which I have prescribed, it is just because I have seen with regard to them what I have described in the book. If, however, there are those, as there well may be, who find these things hard to believe, I can only say to them that the best way to get corroboration of any of the Theosophical ideas is to take them for granted and work with them, for then it will soon be found that they prove themselves.

1500.   It is within the power of every man to develop the faculties by which all this has been seen, nor is there any mystery as to the method by which such development is achieved. These faculties will inevitably come to every one in the course of his evolution, but most men still stand a long way from the point at which they are likely to unfold, though sporadic flashes of clairvoyance are by no means uncommon, and many people have at least a certain amount of sensitiveness.

1501.   Let me not be misunderstood when I say that the ordinary man is still far from the probability of possessing these senses. I do not mean because he is not good enough, for it is not a question of goodness at all - although it is certainly true that if a man of impure or cruel tendency should acquire such faculties he would do far more harm than good with them, to himself and to every one else. I mean that the whole trend of modern life and thought is unfavourable to such unfolding, and that the man who wishes to undertake it must to a great extent abstract himself from the life of the world and get himself into an entirely different atmosphere.

1502.   Such a life as I have prescribed on this book is precisely that which would put a man into a favourable position for the growth of these faculties; and it is not difficult to see how far from this is the ordinary life of the present day. That is why it seems unhopeful to suggest to the average person that he should undertake the task of opening out these powers. They are unquestionably within his reach; but to get himself into a position from which he could begin a real effort towards them means already much radical alteration in the life which he has been accustomed to live. And then, even when he has gradually eradicated from his body all the poisonous products of flesh, alcohol and tobacco, when he has raised his aspirations from the lower to the higher, when he has cast out from himself all traces of self-consciousness or impurity - even then the effort required is greater then many men could make.

1503. The eventual result is as certain as the working out of a problem in Euclid, but the time occupied may be long, and iron determination and an indomitable will are required for the work; and these are faculties which at present are the possession of but few. Nevertheless "what man has done man can do" if he will; I who write have succeeded in this thing, and I have known others who have succeeded; and all who have gained that prize feel it to be far more than worth all the efforts put forth in the course of its attainment. Let me then conclude my book by a plain statement, made as simply as possible, of what these powers are, by means of which it has been written, why they are desirable, and how they may be acquired.

1504. A fish is a denizen of our world, just as a man is; but it is obvious that his conception of that world must be exceedingly imperfect. Confined as he is to his one element, what can he know of the beauty of landscapes, of the glory of sunsets, of the far-reaching interests of our varied and complex human life? He lives on a globe of which he knows almost nothing; yet no doubt he is perfectly satisfied, and thinks that what he knows is all there is to know.

1505. It is not flattering to our self-conceit, yet it is an absolute fact, that the majority of mankind are precisely in the position of the fish. They are living in a world, only one small department of which is within their ken; yet they are quite content with that, and are usually blankly ignorant or fiercely incredulous as to the wider and grander life which surrounds them on every side.

1506. How do we know of this wider life? Not only by religious revelation, but because there are men who have learnt how to see, not indeed the whole of our world, but at least much more of it than is seen by most people. These are the men whom we call seers, or clairvoyants.

1507. How do they see more than others? By the opening of latent faculties - faculties which every one possesses, but which few as yet know how to use. Every man has other vehicles of matter finer than the physical - what St. Paul calls a "spiritual body" as well as a "natural body". Just as through the senses of the physical body we become aware of physical things, so through what may be called the senses of these finer bodies do we become aware of higher things.

1508. The advantages of such sight are manifold. For its possessor most of the problems of life are solved; for him it is not a matter of belief but of knowledge that man survives what is called death, that eternal Justice rules the world, that there is no possibility of final failure for anyone, and that, however deceptive appearances may be, in reality all things are working together for good. The man who is a seer can not only learn much more than others; he can also be much more helpful to his fellows than others.

1509. Since this seership is so desirable, since it lies latent in every one of us, is it possible for us to develop it ? Certainly it is possible, if we are willing to take the trouble; but for most men it is no light task, for it means self-control and self-denial, perseverance and single-mindedness. Other men have done it, so you can do it; but you cannot do it unless you are prepared to throw all your strength into the effort, with an iron determination to succeed.

1510.   The motive too, must be pure and good. The man whose enquiry is prompted merely by curiosity, or by an ignoble desire to obtain advantage or wealth for himself, will do well to take warning in time, and leave any sort of occult training severely alone until mental and moral growth are further advanced. For added power and knowledge mean added responsibility, and the higher sight may be a curse instead of a blessing to a man who is not ready for it.

1511.   There are many ways by which the inner sight may be opened, and most of them are full of danger, and decidedly to be avoided. It may be done by the use of certain drugs, by self-hypnotisation, or by mesmerism; but all these methods may bring with them evil results which far outweigh the gain. There is, however, one process which can by no possibility do harm, and that is the way of thought-control and meditation. I do not say that the undertaking is easy; on the contrary, it is excessively difficult; but I do say that it can be done by determined effort, because it *has* been done.

1512.   The man who wishes to attempt this must begin by acquiring control over his mind - a herculean task in itself. He must learn to concentrate himself upon whatever he may be doing, so that it shall be as well done as is possible for him to do it. He must learn to wield his mind as a skilful fencer wields his weapon, turning it at will in this direction or that, and able to hold it as firmly as he wishes. Try to keep your mind fixed on one definite subject for five minutes; before half the time has passed you will find that wandering thoughts have slipped in unawares, and that the mind has soared far away beyond the limits which you set for it. That means that it is not perfectly under your control, and to remedy this condition of affairs is our first step - by no means an easy one.

1513.   Nothing but steady practice will give you this power; but fortunately that practice can be had all day long, in business as well as during hours of leisure. If you are writing a letter, keep your mind on that letter, so that it may be written perfectly, clearly, quickly. If you are reading a book, keep your mind on that book, so that you may fully grasp the author's meaning, and gain from it all that he intended you to gain.

1514.   In addition to thus practising concentration in the ordinary course of life, it will help you greatly if you set apart a certain time each day for special effort along these lines. Early morning is the most suitable; but, at any rate, it should be at time when you can be sure of being undisturbed, and it should always be at the same hour, for regularity is of the essence of the prescription. Sit down quietly and get your mind perfectly calm; agitation or worry of any sort is absolutely fatal to success. Then turn the mind upon some subject selected beforehand, and consider it attentively and exhaustively, never allowing your thoughts to stray aside from it in the slightest degree, even for a moment. Of course at first they *will* stray; but each time you must drag them back again and start afresh. You will find it best to take concrete subjects at first; it is only after much practice that the more abstract can profitably be considered.

1515.   When through long habitude all this has become thoroughly familiar to you, when you have attained the power of concentration, and when the mind is well under your control, another step may be taken. Begin now to choose for the subject of your morning meditation the highest ideal that you know. What the ideal is does not matter in the least, for we are dealing now with basic facts and not with outer forms. The Hindu may take Shri Krishna, the Muhammadan, Allah, the Parsi, Zoroaster, the Buddhist, the Lord BUDDHA, and the Christian, the Lord Christ, or if he be a Catholic, perhaps the Blessed Virgin or one of the Saints. It matters not at all, so long as the contemplation of that ideal arouses within the man all the ardour, devotion and reverence of which he is capable. Let him contemplate it with ecstasy, till his soul is filled with its glory and its beauty; and then, putting forth all the strength which his long practice of concentration had given him, let him make a determined effort to raise his consciousness to that ideal, to merge himself in it, to become one with it.

1516. He may make that endeavour many times, and yet fail; but if he perseveres, and if his attempt is made in all truth and unselfishness, there will come a time when suddenly he knows that he has succeeded, when the blinding light of the higher life bursts upon him, and he realises that ideal a thousandfold more than ever before. Then he sinks back again into the light of common day; yet that one momentary glimpse can never be forgotten, and even if he goes no further, life will never look the same to him as it did before he saw.

1517. But if he persists in his endeavour, that splendid flash of glory will come to him again and yet again, each time staying with him longer and longer, until at last he will find himself able to raise his consciousness to that higher level whenever he wishes - to observe, to examine and explore that phase of life just as he now does this; and thus he joins the ranks of those who *know*, instead of guessing or vaguely hoping, and he becomes a power for good in the world.

finis

Parchment Books is committed to publishing high quality
Esoteric/Occult classic texts at a reasonable price.

With the premium on space in modern dwellings, we also strive - within the
limits of good book design - to make our products as slender as possible,
allowing more books to be fitted into a given bookshelf area.

Parchment Books is an imprint of Aziloth Books, which has established itself as
a publisher boasting a diverse list of powerful, quality titles, including novels of
flair and originality, and factual publications on controversial issues that have
not found a home in the rather staid and politically-correct atmosphere of many
publishing houses.

Titles Include:

Secret Doctrines of the Rosicrucians	Magus Incognito
Corpus Hermeticum	(trans. GRS Mead)
The Virgin of the World	Hermes Trismegistus
Raja Yoga	Yogi Ramacharaka
Theosophy	Rudolf Steiner
The Interior Castle	St Teresa of Avila
The Gospel of Thomas	Anonymous
Pistis Sophia	(trans. GRS Mead)
The Signature of All Things	Jacob Boehme
The Secret Destiny of America	Manly P Hall
Practical Mysticism	Evelyn Underhill
The Rosicrucian Mysteries	Max Heindel
The Conference of Birds	Farid ud-Din Attar
Meetings With Remarkable Men	G I Gurdjieff
The Voice of the Silence	H P Blavatsky
Psychic Self-Defence	Dion Fortune
The Masters and the Path	C W Leadbeater
The Voice of the Silence	H P Blavatsky

Obtainable at all good online and local bookstores.

View Parchment Books' full list at:

www.azilothbooks.com

We are a small, approachable company and would love to hear any of your
comments and suggestions on our plans, products, or indeed on absolutely
anything.   Aziloth is also interested in hearing from aspiring authors whom we
might publish. We look forward to meeting you. Contact us at:

info@azilothbooks.com

CATHEDRAL CLASSICS

Parchment Book's sister imprint, Cathedral Classics, hosts an array of classic literature, from ancient tomes to twentieth-century masterpieces, all of which deserve a place in your home. A small selection is detailed below:

Mary Shelley	*Frankenstein*
H G Wells	*The Time Machine; The Invisible Man*
Niccolo Machiavelli	*The Prince*
Omar Khayyam	*The Rubaiyat of Omar Khayyam*
Joseph Conrad	*Heart of Darkness; The Secret Agent*
Jane Austen	*Persuasion; Northanger Abbey*
Oscar Wilde	*The Picture of Dorian Gray*
Voltaire	*Candide*
Bulwer Lytton	*The Coming Race*
Arthur Conan Doyle	*The Adventures of Sherlock Holmes*
John Buchan	*The Thirty-Nine Steps*
Friedrich Nietzsche	*Beyond Good and Evil*
Henry James	*Washington Square*
Stephen Crane	*The Red Badge of Courage*
Ralph Waldo Emmerson	*Self-Reliance, and Other Essays, (series 1&2)*
Sun Tzu	*The Art of War*
Charles Dickens	*A Christmas Carol*
Fyodor Dostoyevsky	*The Gambler; The Double*
Virginia Wolf	*To the Lighthouse; Mrs Dalloway.*
Johann W Goethe	*The Sorrows of Young Werther*
Walt Whitman	*Leaves of Grass - 1855 edition*
Confucius	*Analects*
Anonymous	*Beowulf*
Anne Bronte	*Agnes Grey*
More	*Utopia*
Farid ud-Din Attar	*The Conference of Birds*

full list at: www.azilothbooks.com

Obtainable at all good online and local bookstores.

CPSIA information can be obtained at www.ICGtesting.com
Printed in the USA
BVOW03s0037050216

435334BV00010B/166/P